Ecological Design Handbook

Ecological Design Handbook

Sustainable Strategies for Architecture, Landscape Architecture, Interior Design, and Planning

Fred A. Stitt, Editor
Director, San Francisco Institute of Architecture

McGraw-Hill

New York San Francisco Washington, D.C. Auckland Bogotá
Caracas Lisbon London Madrid Mexico City Milan
Montreal New Delhi San Juan Singapore
Sydney Tokyo Toronto

McGraw-Hill

A Division of The McGraw·Hill Companies

2 3 4 5 6 7 8 9 0   DOC/DOC   0 4 3 2 1 0

ISBN 0-07-061499-7

The sponsoring editor for this book was Wendy Lochner and the production supervisor was Sherri Souffrance.

Printed and bound by R. R. Donnelley & Sons Company.

 This book was reprinted on recycled, acid-free paper containing a minimum of 50% recycled de-inked fiber.

McGraw-Hill books are available at special quantity discounts to use as premiums and sales promotions, or for use in corporate training programs. For more information, please write to the Director of Special Sales, McGraw-Hill, Two Penn Plaza, New York, NY 10120-2298. Or contact your local bookstore.

126.95
8/05

Dedicated to Dr. Phil Hawes, architect of the Biosphere 2.

For his freely giving of his every waking hour
to the cause of a better world through ecological design.

ACKNOWLEDGMENTS

Thanks to you all for making it happen:

Penny Burbank, Chief Editorial Assistant
Charles Sholten, Architectural Graphics and Consulting

Matt Fulvio, editorial consulting
Robert Hickling, technical consulting
Chandler Vienneau, editorial consulting
Sarah Gannon, editorial consulting
Beia Spiller, editorial assistant

The dedicated and always supportive work of
Wendy Lochner, Senior Editor, Architecture, McGraw-Hill
and her always on-top-of-it assistant, Robin D. Gardner.

And special thanks to Skip Wenz,
founder of the Ecological Design Program
at the San Francisco Institute of Architecture.

TABLE OF CONTENTS

Part Eight
ARCHITECTS AND THEIR WORK

Introduction

The most important architectural news at the beginning of the 21st century isn't about CADD or the latest design fashion. It's the fact that Ecological Design and Ecological Architecture are coming into their own as professional design disciplines.

Although many architects have long used alternative materials, energy-saving systems, and solar energy, we haven't seen a all-out profession-wide commitment to ecological design.

This is rapidly changing. Design competitions, requests for design proposals, and published architectural projects increasingly emphasize the ecological component. Firms that prepared themselves for this work over the years are reaping the rewards of high demand and appropriate fees to repay their investments in their expertise.

Meanwhile, architectural and engineering firms are seeking graduates who can provide the ecological design skills that most offices still lack. Some are investing in eco-design continuing education for their employees.

The design schools are responding. It was hard to find *any* college-level eco design program when we introduced ours at the San Francisco Institute of Architecture in the mid-'90's.

Now dozens of schools (for whom this book was created) are beginning to offer substantial programs and detailed technical classes in the disciplines presented in this book. Student enthusiasm for the subject and public/business/government demand are merging to push more schools to provide comprehensive education in these life-sustaining subjects.

The Ecological Design Handbook is a total review of the subject: history, theory, how-to applications, and futurist visions through all eco-design related disciplines. It's a road map for design professionals, educators, and students who want to understand and apply this broad discipline in its totality.

We'll welcome your suggestions for content of future editions: SFIA@aol.com.

Fred A. Stitt, Architect
Director, San Francisco Institute of Architecture
Director, Ecological Design Consortium

Part One

ARCHITECTURE AND BUILDING

THE GREATEST OPPORTUNITY

Chapter 1

Why Go Green?

by Dianna Lopez Barnett with William D. Browning.

From A PRIMER ON SUSTAINABLE BUILDING
Rocky Mountain Institute

> "It's not easy being green."
>
> -KERMIT THE FROG, 1972

Why go green? The reasons are numerous. Although green buildings cost about the same as conventional ones, their improved aesthetics, comfort, and performance translate into higher initial sales prices and rents, and then into lower operating costs. Green buildings are much cheaper to heat, cool, and light. Because they consume so much less energy, they produce correspondingly less pollution. Lower utility bills make them more affordable. Last but not least, they are healthier spaces in which to work or live—important now that typical Americans spend 80% of their time indoors.

MARKET PERFORMANCE AND ECONOMICS

The economic argument for sustainable buildings is compelling. In a housing market dominated by tract homes, consumers find distinctive green buildings eminently desirable. For example, home prices in the nation's oldest green neighborhood—Village Homes in Davis, California— now command $11 more per square foot than homes nearby.[1] Homes in a green development in Sacramento sell for $15,000 more than homes in adjoining subdivisions built by the same developer and builders.[2] This is not merely a California phenomenon: the Green Builder Program in Austin, Texas, has demonstrated that consumers there are willing to pay a premium for green homes. The advantages of going green are not limited to home builders and buyers. Many business owners have discovered that shoppers patronize stores built with them and the earth in mind. Consider, for example, Wal-Mart's experimental "Eco-Mart" in Lawrence, Kansas.[3] In its first few months, the store's daylit half has shown a substantially higher sales rate than the conventionally lit side. A green building can even help a company increase its market share. The once-stodgy image of NMB, a Netherlands bank, was transformed after it constructed a widely acclaimed headquarters, complete with indoor waterfalls. This one-half-million-square-foot building uses one-tenth the energy per square foot of the bank's former building. Since moving in, NMB has become the second-largest bank in the country—in large part due to the change in public perception created by the building's architecture.

Green buildings also offer advantages to landlords. Reduced water and energy costs allow for a larger profit margin or more competitive leasing arrangements. Typical savings in annual operating costs of $ 1 per square foot can be used for rent concessions or for improvements to attract and retain tenants. Since leasing brokers often compete over 5 or 10 cents per square foot, efficiency is a remarkable leveraging tool.[4]

Because of such benefits, dozens of businesses have discovered the advantages of green buildings, including The Body Shop, Compaq Computer, the National Audubon Society, Natural Resources Defense Council, Sony, West Bend Mutual Insurance, and Verifone.

REDUCED RESOURCE CONSUMPTION

A green building or development will be much more resource-efficient than a conventional building or development of similar size. A 50% reduction in energy use is relatively easy to achieve, and 80 to 90% reductions are possible with good design.[5]

Making buildings efficient saves money and the environment. For example, saving one unit of electricity inside a building saves having to burn three or four units of fuel, often coal, at the power plant. Reducing the average house's energy use by 80% will reduce its CO_2 emissions by almost 90,000 pounds over its 30-year lifetime. Reducing water use by 30% would avoid the creation of over 4 million gallons of waste water during the same period.

Green developments also make wise use of other natural resources. Poorly designed or sited buildings scar the landscape, take valuable agricultural lands out of production, and diminish wildlife habitat. Green projects, on the other hand, can restore and enhance natural habitats, preserving valuable landscapes while adding to the marketable amenities of the project. The elegant design of new buildings, in concert with the imaginative reuse of old ones, can significantly lower the consumption of building materials, thus protecting forests and endangered species.

If a house is cheaper to operate, it is more affordable. The reduced costs may make ownership possible for some individuals who might not otherwise be able to qualify for a mortgage. Many lenders are now required to consider projected utility bills as a factor in mortgage qualification. Energy Rated Homes of America, for example, provides ratings that banks and mortgage insurers, including the FHA and VA, can use to write "energy-efficient mortgages."[6] From the homeowner's perspective, it certainly makes more sense to spend hard-won income on a tax-deductible, equity-building mortgage than on perpetual utility bills.[7]

These same issues hold true for commercial buildings. The less money a business must spend on mortgages and utility bills, the more is available to pay off business loans, invest in capital improvements, increase inventories, or hire new employees.

PRODUCTIVITY

From an employer's standpoint, the strongest reason to build green has to do with worker productivity. This single benefit of green buildings is so dramatic that it alone is a compelling argument for their construction, as the chart on the following page shows.

The idea that human beings will be more productive in pleasing surroundings has an intuitive logic that has now been demonstrated scientifically. Several recent studies have shown that making a building environmentally responsive can increase worker productivity by 6% to 15% or more. Since a typical commercial employer spends about 70 times as much money on salaries as on energy, any increase in productivity can dramatically shorten a green building's payback period, while making a business much more profitable. Saving $1 per square foot in energy costs can have a significant effect on a building's financial performance, but that saving is absolutely swamped by the benefit of keeping workers-employed at an average annual cost of at least $130 per square foot-happy and productive.

HUMAN HEALTH

If it's hard to work smart in a dumb building, it's also hard to stay healthy in a sick one. Although no one really knows what percentage of health problems are related to building ecology, there is little doubt that many work-related illnesses, headaches, and eyestrain are directly related to poor lighting, inadequate fresh air, harsh acoustics, and the gloomy surroundings that prevail in many office spaces. In several studies, when a company moved into a green building, absenteeism dropped by 15% to 25%, and sick-leave use was significantly reduced. This suggests that such buildings are not just nicer; they are also healthier.

Workers like the combination of daylighting and efficient electric lighting that green buildings provide. They like the pleasing views. They like the fresh air. They like the calm—the absence of harsh noises produced by mechanical devices laboring to heat or cool a poorly designed structure. In short, they like being in a space designed with human beings in mind. Workers at NMB, the Netherlands bank, like their new offices so much that many spend more time in the building. Together, all these enhancements serve to increase worker morale, improve the quality of work performed, reduce mistakes, and raise productivity.

While this information is especially relevant for employers, it is also important for home-owners and home builders. Families also benefit from the natural lighting, better ventilation, air quality, and comfort found in sustainable homes. The fact that such buildings are easier to heat and cool contributes to this sense of well-being, as lower utility bills free up money for other uses.

NOTES

1. Kim Hamilton and William D. Browning, "Village Homes: A Model Solar Community Proves its Worth," *In Context*, No. 35, p. 35. In 1991 dollars. Discussions with the developer in August 1994 reveal a 30% premium for Village Homes.

2. William D. Browning, *Green Development: Determining the Cost of Environmentally Responsive Development*, Master's thesis, Real Estate Development, Massachusetts Institute of Technology, July 1991, p. 64.

3. Green Development Services is currently conducting research on more than 80 examples of green buildings and developments in this country and around the world.

4. Evidence from leasing buildings rated by Britain's Building Research Establishment Environmental Assessment Method indicates that tenants are willing to pay more for a green building.

5. William Browning, *Negawatts for Ahmanson Ranch*, Consulting Report, Rocky Mountain Institute, 1992, p. 1. California Title 24 energy standards were used as the baseline for energy consumption of a single-family home. Efficiency measures were then modeled to enhance the building's energy performance. Projected energy savings of between 10% and 82% were possible using different packages of proven "off-the-shelf" efficiency technologies.

6. Fannie Mae and Freddie Mac allow higher mortgage-to-income ratios for energy-efficient homes. This allows people to buy several thousand dollars more worth of home than they otherwise could.

7. President William J. Clinton and Vice President Albert Gore, Jr., *The Climate Change Action Plan*, October 1993, outlines a specific initiative to promote energy-efficient mortgages and make them more widely available across the country.

Chapter 2

Green Building Design

From A PRIMER ON SUSTAINABLE BUILDING
by Dianna Lopez Barnett with William D. Browning.
Rocky Mountain Institute

"When you build a thing you cannot merely build that thing in
isolation, but must also repair the world about it,
and within it...and the thing which you make
takes its place in the web of nature."

-CHRISTOPHER ALEXANDER, ARCHITECT, 1977

The overall goal of green building design is quite simple: you want to design a wonderful build-ing—a building that is bright and well-lit, that is warm in winter and cool in summer, that is as comfortable as it is healthy, that is energy- and resource- efficient, that is functional and long-lived, and that promotes the well-being of its occupants and the earth.

Before beginning the design work, consider these five principles: First, remember the im-portance of thorough planning. Sustainable design is front-loaded—the work comes at the begin-ning, the rewards later. Early decisions are in many ways the most important, so allow enough time for conceptual thinking. Do not "design in haste and repent at leisure."

Second, sustainable design is more a philosophy of building than a building style. Most energy efficiency and other green technologies are essentially "invisible"; that is, they can be blended into any architectural style. While green features can be highlighted to demonstrate a building's connection to the environment, they do not have to dominate the design.

Third, green buildings don't need to be inordinately expensive or complicated. Although environmental awareness or rapid paybacks from reduced operating expenses could justify spending more money for a sustainable building, that's usually not necessary. Indeed, there is no intrinsic reason why a $40,000 home should not be as green as an $800,000 mansion.

Fourth, an integrated approach is critically important. If you design a conventional building, then throw a laundry list of technologies at it, you're liable to end up with a piecemeal or "50 stupid things" approach—one that may cost more and perform slightly better than a conventional building. On the other hand, adopting this Primer's recommendations in a systematic manner will result in a more livable, economical building. An integrated approach may incur higher prices for some pieces in order to achieve larger savings for the whole. For example, you may spend more on better windows which will allow you to spend less on a smaller furnace. This will always result in lower operating costs; in many cases, it will lower capital costs too.

Finally, although a green building will be more than just energy-efficient, minimizing energy consumption is so central a goal that it should serve as an organizing principle. Thus, the various design elements of a green building fall into three broad categories: energy-saving architectural features; an energy-conserving building shell; and energy-efficient furnaces, air conditioners, water heaters, lights, and other appliances.

AN ANCIENT ART

"The true basis for the more serious study of the art of architecture lies with those indigenous humble buildings that are to architecture what folklore is to literature, or folksong to music..."

-FRANK LLOYD WRIGHT, ARCHITECT, 1930

In discussing green design, a bit of historical perspective is useful. It's important to understand that the idea is not new For millennia, most buildings were of necessity sustainable. It is only in the past century or so, as cheap energy, large sheets of glass, and air conditioning appeared, that architecture lost its moorings and forgot the ancient truth that the most important building covenants are dictated by the earth. A building designed to heed its surroundings will naturally be more energy efficient and will make elegant and frugal use of local materials.

If we modern Americans, who spend an average of 80% of our time indoors, wish to exist in harmony with our environment, we must do by choice what our ancestors did out of necessity-design with the climate and with a sense of place.

"The bottom line of green is black."

-TEDD SAUNDERS, BUSINESSMAN, 1994

What does a green building cost to build? Sometimes a bit more, sometimes less, but in general it should cost about the same as a conventional one of the same size. However, a look at the bottom-line cost will not always reveal differences and cost-shifting within the green building's budget. Take windows, for example.

Efficient superwindows are more expensive than standard windows. However, installing superwindows can reduce heat gain in hot climates, net a higher heat gain in cold climates, and reduce lifetime energy costs. The reduction in unwanted heat flows allows you to downsize (or even eliminate) the heating and/or cooling system. A smaller heating, ventilating, and air conditioning (HVAC) system will cost less to buy, often enough less to immediately offset the additional price of the superwindows. Of course, the building will be far cheaper to run. In addition, superwindows cut noise, improve radiant comfort, and even eliminate perimeter zone heating in commercial buildings, saving floor space. Altogether, they yield ten kinds of significant benefits, of which saved energy is only one.

Similarly, important indirect savings can result from using water-efficient toilets, showerheads, and faucets. Efficient hardware costs little, if any-thing, extra to buy, yet can save money on tap fees and septic-system sizing as well as giving you lower monthly water bills.

Note, however, that the full financial benefits will only accrue if you take an integrated approach. Installing superwindows without downsizing the HVAC, or high-performance toilets without reducing the leach-field size, will lower your operating costs, but will not allow savings on capital costs. It's far better to come out ahead in both the short and the long run.

Bottom line? In designing a green building, vigilantly root out waste and redundancies. Continually ask, "By doing this, what can be eliminated?" The art of green design is not just what is put into a building, but what is left out. The nicest systems are the ones you no longer need.

Each region of the country has a traditional building form or "vernacular architecture." Since these styles embody a great deal of experience, wisdom, and cleverness, it's worth studying the layout, basic design, and orientation of older buildings in some detail for valuable clues and ideas. In particular, vernacular architecture is almost always climactically appropriate.

> "… we must at the outset take note of the countries
> and climates in which buildings are built."
>
> -VITRUVIUS, ARCHITECT, 110 BC

For example, the "dogtrot"-style homes found in the South are an ideal response to a hot, humid climate. But where the climate is hot and dry, the "courtyard" adobe found in New Mexico makes more sense. In cloudy, cold New England, a compact "saltbox" design works well.

Incorporating suitable elements of vernacular design into a building will improve its energy efficiency and comfort. For example, adding adobe or other thermal mass to houses in the deserts of the Southwest can make them much easier to keep cool.

Depending on the climate, other features such as wide overhangs, airlock entries, arcades or porches, atria, and natural ventilation may boost the building's efficiency.

One aspect of vernacular architecture that is frequently overlooked is building color. Roof color, especially, may substantially affect a building's energy use. In a hot climate, a white or light-colored roof in combination with well-placed shade trees can lower the building's cooling load by 30%.[1] Another important aspect is the absorption of the infrared half of solar energy: some pastel finishes reflect infrared well, while some visually "white"-looking asphalt shingles absorb it.

SOLVING FOR PATTERN

> "…you are on the right track when your solution for
> one problem accidentally solves several others. You decide to
> minimize automobile use to conserve fossil fuels, for example,
> and realize that this will reduce noise, conserve land by mini-
> mizing streets and parking, multiply opportunities for
> social contact, safer for children."
>
> -MICHAEL CORBETT, DEVELOPER, 1984

Vernacular architecture works so well in large part because it "solves for pattern"—a key concept in sustainable design. The term, if not the concept, may be unfamiliar: it comes from an essay in which Wendell Berry—a Kentucky farmer, poet, and author—examines the nature of solutions, good and bad, found in American agriculture. Although Berry's focus is farming, many of his points are relevant to architecture. In his words, "They will serve the making of sewer systems or households as readily as they will serve the making of farms." According to Berry, a good solution will:

- solve more than one problem, while not making new problems.
- satisfy a whole range of criteria; be good in all respects.
- accept given limits using, so far as possible, what is at hand.
- improve the balances, symmetries, or harmonies within a pattern.

If Berry's list seems ambitious, that's because it is. He is not looking for solutions "that solve problems by ignoring them, accepting them as trade-offs, or bequeathing them to posterity." But it should be noted that, although their criteria may not be as sweeping as Berry's, many architects and builders already solve for pattern, or attempt to, on every job. Examples of existing building materials, construction techniques, and design strategies that solve for pattern are numerous. Using low-e windows in conjunction with passive solar design cuts utility bills, makes rooms more comfortable at night, and reduces furniture fading.

Here's another example. Most housing developments deal with storm run-off by channeling it into concrete storm drains and then to a municipal sewage system. In big storms, the run-off overloads the treatment plant; the rainwater, now mixed with sewage, overflows into streams. A better alternative is a natural drainage system with surface swales, tiny check dams, and depressions that can serve as temporary retention ponds and percolation beds. By mimicking nature, this system produces beautiful landscaping, reduces off-site water flow, eliminates sewage-treatment concerns, and costs substantially less to build and maintain than conventional storm drainage. It solves for pattern.

A busy contractor trying to finish a building on time and within budget might not think she has time to solve for pattern. In order for your building or development to solve for pattern, the bulk of the work must be done up front, in the process of making fundamental decisions about the building's shape, size, orientation, and layout. Sometimes an ingenious solution can be jury-rigged at the last minute by a clever builder, but it's not wise to count on that. If you can't afford to do it right the first time, how can you afford to do it twice?

If green buildings and green developments have so many advantages, why aren't more being built? It's not because they are more expensive; typically they aren't. And it's not because builders don't care about the environment; many do. But there are good reasons why green buildings still command just a sliver, albeit a steadily expanding one, of the building market. First and foremost, the field is still very new; word is just getting around. To talk of a "green" building five years ago, when many developments now coming on line were being planned, was to discuss which paint to use.

GETTING STARTED

> "Whatever you can do, or dream you can, begin it.
> Boldness has genius, power, and magic in it."
>
> -GOETHE, 1820

A second hurdle is posed by the logistical and time constraints that architects and builders face. All building projects are complicated due to permits, scheduling, weather, interest rates, lumber costs, and so on. With so many variables to consider and so many pitfalls to avoid, builders like to keep things as simple as they can. There's little room in the construction industry for anything suggestive of "experimentation."

A third concern is marketability. In the intensely competitive housing market, the safest path is the tried-and-true. In typical "Catch 22" fashion, some use the excuse that the "marketplace" is not interested in green buildings and we know that because no one is building them. However, if no one is offering such buildings, how can the marketplace respond? Those builders who take the risk are well rewarded, but if no one in a given area has tried it, few have the leverage or boldness to be the first. There is also a problem of incentives: many, although not all, of the financial and other benefits of green buildings accrue to the ultimate owner, rather than the builder or contractor. The bottom line is that building green is a new challenge for an industry that often feels challenged enough as it is.

We recognize that the green agenda is an ambitious one and that making the commitment to follow it can be intimidating. For now at least, sustainable buildings require more thought and planning than conventional construction. Additional lead time is needed to master the wealth of new information, design tools, ecological understanding, and building products that have recently become available.

How can you cost-effectively incorporate this new information? Perhaps the best way is to tackle the process incrementally. Before beginning a project, ask yourself how big a bite you can take. Can you tackle the issue of energy efficiency? Habitat protection? Selection of healthy building materials? Take on only as much as you are comfortable with. Learn from each project, then bite off a little bit more, do it better the next time, and steadily expand the scope and depth of your design integration.

Greenness isn't all or nothing, black or white. There's a spectrum: some buildings are better, some worse. A tract home being built today with its better insulation, windows, and appliances is much greener in some respects than one built twenty years ago. The industry is headed in the right direction.

The priorities you place on different aspects of green design will vary from job to job and client to client. The first step is simply making a commitment to minimize a project's overall environmental impact. A key issue for any building, and one of the easiest to address, is energy efficiency. Saving energy has a powerful multiplier effect. The aspect of green design that currently requires the most effort is probably the selection of green building materials. Right now, they are sometimes difficult to find and often cost more than conventional materials. The market, however, is changing rapidly and this will become easier.

To repeat, a building that is partly green is far better than one that's not. So, go as green as your time, skills, client, and project permit. If your decisions save some lumber, some energy, or some water, you're definitely doing the right thing. Next time, try even more.

NOTES

1. From Southern California Edison Consumer Information sheets, referring to a study by Lawrence Berkeley Laboratory. The color of a building material must be considered in conjunction with the absorptivity and emissivity of the material. For example, a white asphalt-shingle roof will absorb more heat that a white aluminum roof. Light colors are generally better than dark colors for reducing heat gain, but whiteness to the eye is not a reliable indicator of infrared absorptance.

Chapter 3

Why is Architecture Oblivious to the Environment?

An Interview with Ian McHarg
From DESIGN OUTLAWS ON THE ECOLOGICAL FRONTIER
by Chris Zelov & Phil Cousineau

IAN MCHARG
Ian McHarg founded the department of Landscape Architecture at the University of Pennsylvania in 1954 and has become identified as the founder of ecological planning and design. He has written numerous articles and professional reports, but is best known for the classic Design with Nature, a finalist for the National Book Award in 1969. He was awarded the National Medal of Art from President Bush in 1992.

Question:

Why is Architecture Oblivious to the Environment?

Modern architecture is not even remotely modern. It doesn't partake of any significant body of knowledge which has been developed in modern times.

Question:

You wrote the book, Design with Nature. What does this title mean?

I'm very pleased with the title of my book DESIGN WITH NATURE because it really has so many shades of meaning. The first important one is the preposition "with." By and large, almost all architecture since the industrial revolution has been designed without reference to nature. As if the environment, either natural or social was not consequential. The egos of the artists were the crucial thing, and the signature of the artist was really the most important thing. Reference to the environment as a basis for finding form was not ever involved. It was absolutely categorically rejected in the International Style, where the assumption was that there was a generic architectural solution which was appropriate to all people, in all places, at all time, which of course, has been demonstrated to be inappropriate for all places, and all people, and all times! DESIGN WITH NATURE is our protestation. If you're going to design, design with nature. Nature's been designing so much longer than man. The idea that we can invent it is a kind of maniacal delusion.

I suppose we've got to consider the subject of architecture. I've been teaching at this university for thirty-seven years. I am a—what's the word—well, I speak loudly, and with a good deal of conviction! I will say, of all my failures, my greatest failure has been at the University of Pennsylvania where, after thirty-seven years of very noisy and assertive teaching, I have had absolutely no effect on architecture whatsoever. I've spoken at most architecture schools in the United States with, I would say, virtually no effect. Moreover, my book which was described by the American Collegiate Schools of Architecture as one of the most widely read textbooks in architecture sure, has, to the best of my knowledge, had no effect whatsoever. So there's a sadness about this.

Now why is architecture so oblivious to the environment? Why do no architecture schools require any students, ever, to learn anything about the environment, either natural or social? I think that an architect, really, fundamentally, is a prima donna, and that intelligence is not really thought to be an important attribute in creating buildings. This is thought to occur by drawing interminably, preferably late at night, in an advanced state of exhaustion, on yellow paper. It's believed that this will produce some creative experience. I've often said that perhaps architecture could be most effective by a frontal lobotomy. If the brain is not really used, then it should be removed as an impediment.

Formal intelligence about the natural environment, the social environment, is not a part of the curriculum of architecture. Of course it's not a part of the practice of architecture. Architecture has devolved into an exercise which is in supreme competition with millinery and confectionery. At best it's simply, obviously, a cosmetic addition. A sort of wallpaper on the surface which is subject only to style. But at worst, I think it's probably more properly described as fixing a smile on a cadaver. Anyway, it's certainly not serious. The word "modern," which is used for modern physics, modern chemistry, modern biology, is erroneously used in modern architecture. Modern architecture is not even remotely modern. It doesn't partake of any significant body of knowledge which has been developed in modern times.

I think the remedy is very, very simple. People should be required to know what they're doing before they do it. They should know the implications of their contemplated acts. If you go into work in the physical world, you should well know about physical processes, in terms of the environment, geology, hydrology, meteorology, and so on. You're living in the biological world, so somebody's got to know about the plants, and the animals, and the microorganisms, because they're a very, very complex interacting system, and you can disturb them to a great detriment (not only to them, but to yourself).

I'd require students to be able to understand something about physics physical processes physical environment. Along with biological processes, the biological environment. Something about social processes, the social environment. Then the next step is far and away the most difficult one. It's not enough simply to know what the environment says. It's more important to understand what the implications are of building in some environments. Some environments are very tolerant. Some environments are incredibly intolerant. One should be able to distinguish this. Some environments are suitable for one purpose, but not suitable for other purposes. The discrimination to know which, that's an important skill.

By far and away, the most important task is to have an appropriate expression of adaptations. We mentioned this before. I mean, if you go to a pueblo you know perfectly well you're in an arid environment. You know something about the culture, too. The building expresses this. It would seem to me there should be an expression which is appropriate to the place, both in terms of materials and in terms of forms.

The quest for modern architecture, it seems to me, should have two parts. People have been engaged in architecture for thousands and thousands of years, and a very large number of very intelligent and very passionate people have engaged in this thing, so there must be a lesson to be learned. When I went to Harvard, Walter Gropius insisted that modern architects do not study historic architecture until their last year, lest they become corrupted. Can you believe this? In every other science you observe all the insights of previous years, right? Of generations, of centuries, which are continuously corrected and so on. That body of knowledge—there's something learned and time passes and if it still holds true today—by all means, learn it today.

That's not true in architecture. It would seem to me there are two great realms, or three, perhaps. One is to understand physical and biological systems. The other is to identify the appropriateness of adaptations which have been accomplished in historic times, and so on. Then the third is to identify from these historic times that there were many problems not solved and many technologies of our improving on all of these.

The beginning of a modern architecture, and appropriate architecture, and landscape architecture, and planning, I think, should have to engage people who know about the land: how it came to be, how it works, what the implications upon that land are of making any adaptation, being able to discriminate about where are appropriate places, and most of all, being able to find appropriate locations and appropriate form.

The next one, of course, is the invocation of a grand design: God's Grand Design, which evolution represents. Of course, the final part of it is imperative: Design with nature. I am a censorious Presbyterian. I like this imperative thing: You bastards! Design with nature, or else I'll grind you up for dog food!

RESPONDING TO THE ENVIRONMENT

The question is, did man historically design with nature? Of course the answer is yes! They had to understand nature for their survival. Ethnographers who study primitive societies today realize they've got to understand the environment to understand the culture, its language, its religion, its ethics, its art. All the stuff that ethnographers and anthropologists have done around the world is very, very clear testimony these peoples are, in fact, specific adaptations of specific environments. Which is visible, again, in their religions, and their art, and their economy, and their language, and their foodstuff. The whole damned thing. This immediacy of the environment and the person has been lost in the Western culture. It's been lost not only physically, it's also been lost intellectually. Yet if one wants to be serious about it, the problem has not changed. The problem of design really does require that we do understand the environment. What it is. What it can permit. Which areas are suitable for what. Which areas are unsuitable.

There should be a response of adaptation, a response of design. Of course this was true in the whole world until the advent of the Industrial Revolution. People didn't know any other way of doing it. A simple little boy like me, with a book called THE BOOK OF THE BRITISH EMPIRE, which I got on my fourteenth birthday, could turn the pages, and I didn't have to look at the captions to realize I was in China, or Malaysia, or seeing Australian Aboriginals, or

Eskimos. It was not only people. It was a conjunction of the people, the buildings, the forms of plants, and the animals, the whole. All of these things spoke about adaptation to specific environment. The environments were characteristic, and they were absolutely different.

Then along comes the bloody International Style and says the same stupid stencil is co-equally suitable for everyone, everywhere. So that everywhere, whether Reykjavik, or Glasgow, or Hong Kong, or Singapore, or New York, they have the same stupid, bloody buildings made, obviously, for termites or lobotomized human beings. Why? Because of their abstractions. They've got nothing to do with human physiology, human psychology, and certainly nothing to do with geology, hydrology, rocks, salts, plants, or animals!

How can a tradition which has lasted for the whole history of man be so quickly abandoned? Well, it has been! The question is, can we retrieve it? I don't know whether we can or cannot. Should we retrieve it? Of course.

All the plants and all the animals are specific to their environment, so when you invoke an environment, the plants and animals spring to mind. I say prairie. You see the short and the long grasses—that's right—and you see the buffalo, and so on. I say desert, right? And I suddenly see all the sand, and you see the scrubby thing, and you see the nocturnal animals. I say tundra, and we've got reindeer, and we've got mosses, and lichen, and so on. In every single case, you identify Arctic, tundra, taiga, burrow, forest, savannah, short grass prairie, long grass prairie, tropical rain forest, every single one of these. When you make a statement about the environment, you already see, in your mind's eye, the plants, the animals that comprise it, right? They're exquisitely fit. They're appropriate.

So should the works of man be. Why shouldn't the work of men be as appropriate? If I were dropped from a plane by night (and I was a parachutist, once upon a time) then, as the dawn lifted and I had to find out where the hell I was and identify it, there's only one place in the United States where I could do it infallibly. That's the pueblo. If I found myself somewhere in New Mexico, in Zuni [pueblo], or Acoma, and saw these thick walls, and small apertures, and flat roofs, I would know that I'm in a desert environment.

Chapter 4

Design Theory

by Malcom Wells

From: GENTLE ARCHITECTURE
McGraw-Hill

Why is it that almost every architect can recognize and appreciate beauty in the natural world and yet so often fail to endow his own work with it? Most modern buildings are something less than inspiring, sometimes far less. But when architects bring photographs back from trips they often exhibit great sensitivity to composition, color, and proportion. What's wrong?

Why is it that so much of the new, less destructive architecture is even uglier, more poorly proportioned, than that of conventional design? Some say it's because architects who are interested in, say, solar heating and waterless toilets tend to be technicians at heart rather than designers. Others put the blame on the profession's lack of design experience under the new priorities. But those reasons aren't convincing: many new movements generate their purest and freshest expressions right at the start.

The fault probably lies with our education. How do you turn someone into an artist? It's doubtful that schools can ever be expected to do it. They can offer a wide exposure to great ideas, to great buildings, but the art seed seems to be planted in only a gifted few at birth, and germinates in ways we cannot understand. Perhaps the best that schools of architecture can do is present the widest range of experience to the potential designer, teach him the environmental consequences of his craft, and then hope for the best. As a result we might at least have *harmless* ugly buildings instead of all these harmful ones, and the artists among us could put more solid foundations under their works.

Before the modern movement came along, architects were drilled, endlessly, in classical forms, which, of course, once had natural, organic bases. Until well into the twentieth century architects were taught the old rules of proportion, balance, and symmetry as well as the classical orders.

"For the first two hundred years or so, American architects and builders were guided by a fairly effective body of theoretical postulates, however unsophisticated or unformulated they may have often been. These principles derived in about equal parts...from folk experience and formal scholarly knowledge....At any time prior to the death of Thomas Jefferson in 1826, both the architect and his building would have been disciplined, structured, 'held in shape,' by a clear and comprehensible reference frame of needs and means.

Crisis in architectural aesthetics did not appear till around the last century. Because of industrialization specialized designers sprang up. The architect then worked for the wealthy businessman, entrepreneur—gave him what he wanted but began to lose touch with the common man, factory worker, his needs. And the result of the architect's isolation from his real client is the increasing prevalence of the abstract, the formal, and the platitudinous in architectural and urban design.

...the fundamental tensions (between the formal and the functional) remained; in fact, they grew steadily sharper with the rise of industrialism, and they are accurately reflected in the curriculums of our schools today. The effort of the schools to resolve this contradiction has been, generally academic, always at the expense of the craft elements of the field. From one point of view this has been both inevitable and desirable. Modern architectural problems can no more be solved by carpentry than can spacecraft be built by village blacksmiths. However, the shift in training away from craftsmanship has been more toward mere technology than a truly scientific investigation of architecture as a whole. . . less and less able to encompass the complexity of modern technology, the architect's function is truncated. His designing becomes more and more a process of assemblage, more removed from functional necessity and therefore more susceptible to the pressures of fad and fashion."[1]

Classical study must have been maddening to the creative few, but to all the rest, the great majority, it must have been a comfort to be still learning the old rules while the world was changing. But classical principles could no longer be applied when the modern movement expanded. There were no precedents, no classical forms, no long history of what worked and what didn't, and there were all those new materials and mechanical systems to accommodate, so the teachers of architects had to develop ad hoc rules, roofless theories of proportion and scale, of composition and form, with you-know-what-kind of results. Students of architecture today are often pushed toward a deliberate unrelatedness to the earth, to an instability, toward making materials perform against their better natures in spite of a desperate need to get back onto better terms with our own planet.

The trouble is that mediocre design is teachable: it can be reduced to a system of rules. Good design can't. Frank Lloyd Wright, who at his best produced hundreds of poetically beautiful buildings, is virtually ignored by schools of architecture in this country. His eye and hand were so sure that in some of his buildings it's impossible to tell where the land influence ended and the man influence began. The title "organic" which he gave his work was not bestowed lightly. He knew what he was doing.

Wright never went to an architectural school. He studied engineering. And yet such was his artistic gift that his works were far more than the mere assembling of mechanical parts.

But how in the world do you produce the Wrights-to-be? There is no way. The man's architecture simply can't be packaged and labeled. Nothing is worse, either, than half-baked versions of Wright's buildings. Perhaps they should never be attempted, and the schools of architecture are probably right in refusing to encourage anything that's too obviously rehashed Taliesin.

We're in a period of great change, and it's hard to see, from inside that period, what will be quite obvious to those who manage to outlive it. Certainly there are rules we must follow. There are life values to express. There are codes and site restrictions and historic precedent to guide us, and we know that simplicity, unity of theme, and design restraint will never let us down. We even have a few stunning examples of the new architecture to inspire us. But the design spark-the divine spark-continues to move in mysterious ways.

> "The architect works with form and mass just as the sculptor does, and like the painter he works with color. But alone of the three, his is a functional art. It solves practical problems. It creates tools or implements for human beings and utility plays a decisive role in judging it."[2]

THE AVERAGE ARCHITECT

The work of America's best-known architects is seen with some frequency in the pages of popular magazines and newspapers. We're all to some degree conscious of what it is the stars of the profession are doing. But what about the average U.S. architect, in Memphis, say, or Tacoma? Is he responding at all to the horrors of our increasingly poisonous environment?

It's hard to say. His current response, as measured by what we see of his architectural efforts along the street, is sometimes enough to ruin your day. But awareness has come late to our profession, and the new buildings being thrown up now are, after all, the products of design processes that went on two, three, or even four years ago. You have to visit a drafting room to see what's being designed today. There, overdue changes are beginning to appear. Nothing is focused yet however, and you see a lot of tokenism-solar panels, special glazings, those sort of things. You hear a lot of energy talk, too, much of it straight out of the environmental information in the ads the architects are reading. A lot of familiar old products are now being palmed off as being energy-saving, or good for the land, when it's pretty obvious they are nothing of the kind. It wouldn't matter if we weren't chewing up the countryside.

When my son Sam saw this drawing, the directness of his response surprised me. "All you have to do is run it backwards." Of course! It's just like the bombs in *Slaughterhouse Five* that rose out of inward-shrinking explosions that made buildings whole again, up into the bomb bays of airplanes that flew backward to their bases, where the bombs were removed, disassembled, reduced to their raw materials, put back into the earth, and covered with beautiful forests. Maybe such ideas are only pleasant dreams—fantasies of a world that could never be. Given our present state of laziness, that's all they seem. If anything is to change for the better, however, we've got to produce a society that can run it all backwards, making rich, green cities out of urban deserts.

Architects have got to be among the leaders of that turnaround. It's not that we deserve such leadership. There just doesn't happen to be another group, ready with its T-squares and drawing boards, in sight.

THE STARS OF THE PROFESSION

In 1978, architect Philip Johnson made headlines when he suddenly forsook the slick steel and glass boxes he had helped make popular in America. According to his partner, John Burgee,

> "We started to get into this direction because of the restrictions on the use of glass boxes brought on by the energy crisis-it seemed wrong to us to continue to do the International Style here. . . . We wanted to express this different time more fully, to try to get away from that flat surface and into carved and molded ones. . . We are searching; we are looking for a way into the language of stone ."[3]

Architect Robert Geddes sees architecture's possibilities in "the proper connections between social form and physical form" and believes that an understanding of the nature of social institutions, their values, their norms of behavior, their rituals, is the most helpful way for an architect to get started.

Nathan Silver, writing about the Corbusier revival in America and the five architects best known for its popularity—Peter Eisenman, Michael Graves, Charles Gwathmey, John Hejduk, and Richard Meier—sees their work as "temporary, minor, local and harmless; the product of mildly talented men," and defends their right to do such work in this way:

"If people want maintenance problems and high heating bills in their houses, there is as yet no law against that in America, and criticism of the ethics of a life conspicuously consumed in the privacy of one's home would surely be unlibertarian—what else could 'the pursuit of happiness' mean?"5

He rightly sees the buildings themselves as no problem. Their problems will be corrected by later occupants or by the natural forces already a work upon them.

Here we see some of the most talented and influential architects in America apparently unaware of, or at least unmoved by, the biological foundations of all life and art. Here is Philip Johnson, the great taste-maker of modern architecture, the AIA gold medalist, suddenly doing what some critics call "Chippendale skyscrapers" and rooftop falseworks, while he searches for "the language of stone." Here is Geddes prescribing a comprehension of social form as the first step for an architect, and here are the Big Five, their misplaced Corbusian adventures admittedly too insignificant to have any physical effect on the world, but their every move monitored and admired by America's most sophisticated architects. And here is the vast army of American architects-all the professionals, all the students, and all the teachers—quietly trying to reproduce the stuff they see in the architectural press.

If ever we needed great designers, it is now. The environmental architecture of America is almost without exception depressingly ugly. Many people on first sight rightly decide they want no part of it. The great tastemakers and designers of our time flounder through stylistic revivals while the potential for really appropriate architecture goes unrecognized. This is perhaps the first time, in the hundred years since, we began our stampede away from being an agrarian society, that we've had knowledge of, and at least some concern about, the physical and ecological consequences of architecture. We have a chance to turn the whole built environment—houses, buildings, highways, cities—off its suicidal course, and the brightest, most respected architects of our time refuse to have anything to do with it.

Ah, if only Frank Lloyd Wright were alive! Too bad he wasn't born 20 or 40 or even 60 years later. It's hard to believe he was brought into the world just after the Civil War, that he was a grown man before McKinley was president. Wright's buildings are still so stunningly modern they seem to be waiting in the future, somehow, for us to catch up with them. Wright, who lived his long life in an age when the world's supply of low-cost fuel and natural resources seemed endless, nevertheless experimented with passive solar heating, earth cover, berming, and task lighting. Just think what he might have given us if he'd been alive today!

In the largest sense, it doesn't matter at all. The great issues of our time go far beyond architecture. Listen to what Lewis Mumford had to say on that subject when he was asked why he no longer writes about architecture:

"Because the real problems of civilization aren't soluble by the architect or by any one group of people. The real problems are much more profound and will require much more thorough study. That's why my work during the last 15 years has turned away from the specific problems of building and of architectural form. I interpret what's been done and see the danger of the sterile life as an acceptable mode of living, but our problems are the problems of controlling nuclear energy, the problems of lessening the amount of industrial pollution, the problems of making the environment itself relatively stable and self-renewing and favorable to life of every kind, not just to man's life. We have to look after the bacteria and the insects as well as man if we're to have a really balanced environment. This is the profound meaning of the whole ecological process which is now gradually seeping into people."[6]

Seen in that light, architecture is, of course, nothing more than the thinnest of cosmetics.

GENTLE ARCHITECTURE

I've been having second thoughts about "watersaving" shower heads. Do they save more water than conventional spray nozzles? They seem certain only to save more than a fool. A waster with a gadget is still a waster; a shower taken by a saver is efficient regardless of nozzle type. The only water-saving shower head worth having is the one between the ears. That's where all real savings begin.

Architecture used to have boundaries. It started at the front wall and ended at the rear. A building was conceived, planned, financed, built, and occupied by a succession of specialists each of whom stuck to his appointed role. How the building affected, or was affected by, the condition of timberland in Oregon, or wildlife a mile down its watershed, or by Middle Eastern politics, had no part in the decisions that produced it. Not until recently were we even asked to think about such things. Now, all of a sudden, we see that they may be at the very heart of architecture.

It's beginning to dawn on us that our responsibilities reach beyond drawings and specifications, beyond the immediacy of Project 326. No longer can we simply walk away from it on dedication day, without a backward glance, already thinking of Project 327.

The materials with which we build are torn from the earth in ways so brutal they stun the first-time visitor. A logging site, a cement mine, or a gravel pit, especially when stumbled upon in an area of great natural beauty, can shock and repel. But we no longer trust first impressions. After an hour's tour of the place, calluses form. A week's exposure brings indifference. And a lifetime's? Who can say? The architect picks materials from his brightly colored catalogs, and the Caterpillars roll. From mine to mill to shop, the beautiful and the natural lose more and more of their identity as immense amounts of energy turn them bright and plastic. Assembled as "completed" buildings, they have barely begun their decades of waste.

Each day, huge tractor-trailers enter the city. Coal, oil, gas, water, paper, nuclear power, gasoline, chemicals, food- all head straight for buildings, there to be turned into wastes and carted away by trucks and pipes, and by the winds, lost forever. Is this part of what architecture is all about? Of course it is. Architecture is involved all the way.

In a better world, architects would not only launch their buildings, they'd train the crews to sail them. What good is R-40 insulation if doors are left open? Or underground architecture if you drain a marsh to get it? Backward and forward, out of the land and into the future, buildings move through time at a cost no one can count. It's more a matter of earth-in-tuneness, anyway, than of accounting, this gentler way of building toward which we grope.

Right now, fuel prices are showing us the way. House fuel, car fuel, stomach fuel-each new shortage nudges us closer to world vision. Given enough scarcity and enough time we might produce an architecture to succeed Rudofsky's.[*] But the cost! And every minute lost sees 10 million water-saving shower heads left turned on too long.

Not until the day when the architect takes his client by the hand and talks to him about the real costs of construction will we be on our way. Not until the Client walks in, having already counted these costs, will we be almost there.

But architecture must be more than just a balanced budget. It must, in every sense, be art as well. The appropriate almost always is.

[*] Bernard Rudofsky's *Architecture without Architects* (Doubleday, New York, 1969) and *The Prodigious Builders* (Harcourt, New York, 1979) are essential for all who would design or build.

1. James Marston Fitch, *American Building 2: The Environmental Forces That Shape It,* Houghton Mifflin, Boston, 1975.

2. S. E. Rasmussen, *Experiencing Architecture*, MIT. Press, Cambridge, Mass., 1959.

3. *The New York Times,* May, 1978.

4. *Architectural Record,* November ,1977.

5. Nathan Silver, *"The House That Modernism Built,"* *Harper's,* August, 1977, p. 77.

6. Reprinted from an interview in *Tract*, No. 22, a quarterly issue by the Gryphon Press of Lewes, Sussex, England.

Part Two

SITE

Chapter 5

Nature and Architecture

by Frank Lloyd Wright
From Frank Lloyd Wright: His Living Voice
selected and edited by Bruce Brooks Pfeiffer
The Press at California State University

"The place for an architect to study construction first of all,
. . . is the study of nature."

-FRANK LLOYD WRIGHT, JUNE 28, 1958

The place for an architect to study construction first of all, before he gets into the theory of the various formulas that exist in connection with steel beams, girders, and reinforced concrete, is the study of nature. In nature you will find everything exemplified, from the blade of grass to the tree, from the tree to the geological formations to the procession of eras beginning with the first from the sea downwards. And when you get a sense in your mind of that continuity and that elemental sense of process according to the nature of materials, you've got the basis for an architect's conceptions, for his practice, even.

When we are in Arizona there is no more profitable study in the world than to go out into the desert and see where, by necessity of the economy of materials, a marvelous scientific structure arises from God knows where -- but you can see how, as in the saguaro cactus, for instance, or in any of the tubular forms that require a strong stalk against the wind and against attack. Everything in the desert has to be armed, because it has to preserve its existence by opposition to all other forms of life in the desert.. So the saguaro grows these thorns and spikes not for fun, not just because it likes them, but because it has to have them in order to live.

You'll notice too the principle of nature that never shows any regard for anything in the way of economy. That's what makes the study of economy so artificial, so difficult, so fruitless, and in most cases so useless. When nature made these spikes, for instance, on the cactus, she didn't stop with just what was enough. She began to like the idea of the spike, and a spike became spikes to such an extent that everything bristled all over and the bristles became very beautiful. And the more bristles there were, the more beautiful the thing became.

So nature has no regard for economy except, now here's a contradiction in terms, in order to get exuberance. She did economize on material in the stalk by using the lattice instead of the solid wall. But when it comes to these other expressions, even to the bloom which is way beyond anything you can conceive in these circumstances, the desert blossoms and takes on this prolific quality. And the spines, the spikes, the fences seem to be an inconsistency.

It is the study of nature in that sense that makes the ground work for wisdom of the architectural mind. It is not formed from books. It is not formed from theories. It is formed by keen observance of the processes, characteristics, and forms that take place around you, before you, everywhere. And as the conditions change, you will find all the forms changing. As the materials are called upon by nature to do certain things, and the results become evident, you'll see how form really does follow function. But that is the very least of the act. That's only the platform upon which these natural forces seem to operate and rest, because you will see this marvelous exuberance that is beauty. I remember William Blake said, "Exuberance is beauty." And I never understood what he meant. I thought that it was rather demoralizing and misleading until I began to see that what he meant was that everything as far as it can go in excess, according to nature, is good. Like the profusion of leaves on the tree, like the branch that puts out blossoms on a blossoming tree.

The more, the more richly, they are put forth, the more that is given, the more delight we take in the thing. All through nature you will find these propositions confronting you, and in their solution and study, and appreciation, and the love with which you take them in you will build up within yourselves a certain power, which is capable of judging quantities, effects, and proportions. I think perhaps from the study of nature in true sense, the most valuable thing you will get out of it is this sense of proportion. And you will not be afraid of exuberance, so long as that exuberance is in proportion and in character to the purpose of its origin.

So when you are told to study nature, that doesn't mean you are to go out and just look at the hills and the way the animals conduct themselves and what is visible on the surface. The study of nature means Nature with a capital N, Nature, inner nature, nature of the hand, of this apparatus, of this glass. The truth concerning all those things is architectural study, and the more you pursue it, the more that pursuit becomes you, the more your vision will become attuned to elemental things. And the more productive man you'll be in this field we call architectural design.

Chapter 6

How to Uncover the Secrets of the Land

by David Deppen

From a lecture given on February 14, 1998
ECOLOGICAL DESIGN EDUCATION CONFERENCE
San Francisco Institute of Architecture

When I was a child, I was a "Lewis and Clark" of my corner of Pennsylvania. No vacant lot, creek, woods, or byway was safe from my explorations. I drank in a constant stream of stories from the land. In college I embraced more sophisticated ways. Diagrams full of arrows became a new picture of the land to me. While these abstractions of site analysis are sometimes helpful, they have always seemed a bit too abstract.

I am going to describe some methods which I have been rediscovering for understanding the land where I build. These methods are quick and powerful—and fun. They are applicable to city lots as well as acreage. These approaches apply to all scales, from a room addition to a regional plan and are flexible in adapting to the time available. If only one fast trip to a site is possible, these methods are just as applicable as they would be over many months of visits.

I constantly hear a debate regarding the real purpose for building in harmony with the land. One camp says the purpose is for better human accommodation. Respect for the trees, topography, and the sun path are essentials for creating wonderful places for people. Another camp insists that the natural world has values above human greed. This view asserts that the purpose of ecological building is to do the least amount of harm to the natural world.

At heart, I am not a partisan in this debate. The important and immediate lesson to me is this: *Both views require an uncompromising new attentiveness to studying sites.* It's been said that all politics is local. I believe that all architecture is local. Architecture is fundamentally different from other forms of culture. Unlike books, cars, clothes, music, or ideas, it stays put. Architecture is culture integrated into a unique piece of land. Our first task is to understand the living nature of that piece of land.

LAND IS LIVING

I'm amazed that some architects think their sites are canvases—and that they are painters. I am also amazed that the entire construction industry—that multi-billion dollar keystone of our culture—has no clue that our land is living. We have to start educating ourselves. Let's begin with a nearby piece of land. Is it forlorn? No! It's bursting with life!

Let's start with the soil itself. *It's alive!* Picture a thimble full of soil. You are looking at several billion living organisms. Some soil scientists think of the soil and vegetation in it as a vast super-organism. They see a web of relationships so complex that we have barely begun to understand them. Think about the words we use. How often have you heard soil referred to as "dirt," not by the uneducated but by our society's gifted designers. "Dirt" is "matter out of place." Every piece of land is the center of a network of connections, from the soil community, to the individuality of every plant and animal, to the drama of the human lives there.

Several years ago in *Dead Poet's Society*, Robin Williams' character (portraying a charismatic literature teacher) introduced millions of people to Walt Whitman. Whitman made the "land is living" idea clear to me in his poem, *This Compost*. In that tale, he can't figure out where all the eons of plant and animal corpses are. He fears that the surface of the earth is a thin veneer covering a vast corruption. After mustering up the resolve to cut open the sod, he marvels at the working of the soil. We creatures give it our leavings. And, Whitman reminds us, it gives us such sweet things in return.

Building on the land is part of the great process of creation and change. What's missing from our current ways is acknowledging and respecting the living nature of the land.

OPENNESS

The most important aspect of learning about a site, I've found, is my frame of mind. It boils down to this: be open and listen. I try to totally empty myself. This is very hard to do, but I am at the site to absorb!

In our design culture the overwhelming activity when first setting foot on a site is to expound brilliant design ideas. A typical site analysis "discussion:"

"We could span the canyon."

"We could build a tower here."

"We could replant the whole area in native plants."

All of these may be good ideas. But despite the enormous pressure to instantly come up with brilliant designs, it is simply inappropriate to design be
fore knowing the site.

Whenever I'm at a site with others, the entire focus seems to revolve around saying "We could do this, and we could do that." It seems to be human nature to leave our mark on the space around us. There is another pitfall—looking at a site as a place to plug in a past favorite design. This guarantees zero learning. I've found that the only way I can do the crucial core site study is to be alone. The silence is important. The openness is important. Sometimes it will work with two respectful people (teacher and student), but with several people, it is a social scene. The attention is focused on the interaction between the people. Don't get me wrong, this interaction is fine—later! It is invaluable in the give- and-take of design, but first we must be open to the land. I find these words helpful in reminding myself of this state of mind:

Listening

Non-judgment

Emptiness

Awareness

Humility

Patience

The heart of the approach I am advocating is in the next three sections. Each section describes a mindset which is a powerful personal skill for learning about the land: the tracker, the interviewer, and the scholar. I've found through daily experience that each of these diverse skills is complimentary to the others. And I have found that doing one naturally flows into doing the others.

My inspiration here is an Apache called Stalking Wolf. In *The Tracker*, his apprentice, Tom Brown, has written gripping accounts of Stalking Wolf's methods. A track is the evidence of activity on the land—a story written on the earth itself. The physical evidence people leave of their activities in their neighborhood could be considered tracks, as much as the footprints of a fox. To track, Stalking Wolf taught *intermittent attention*. It is a constant refocusing between minute detail and the whole pattern around it. When I taught myself to do this, I began to experience a vividness around me which I had never felt before.

On one occasion, Tom asked Stalking Wolf why he was spending a long time gazing at a robin. Stalking Wolf replied by asking Tom about the patterns on the robin's feet, the structure of its breast feathers, the color of its eyes. This reply astonished me as much as it did Tom. I realized how little I was seeing. I found that I was leaping from object to object, thinking, "Oh, I know what that is—now let's go on to something new." I wondered if I really could look at a familiar tree or wall and learn more about it every time. The more I do this, the more I realize how worthwhile it is.

Whenever I think these tracker skills are hard to learn, I remind myself that they are already a part of us. For thousands of generations, we were all hunter-gatherers, and everything about us was shaped for success in tracking. For less than a few hundred generations (and often much less), we have been farmers. For only a few generations (if any, in some cases), we have been workers. The patient, observant, respectful taking in of the world is in our very nature.

A few years ago I wanted to grow yerba buena, the "good herb" of Spanish California (also, the namesake of the village which preceded San Francisco). As a "rare plant," I sought it through many specialty nurseries. Finally, I located it at a university botanical garden. Then one day, in the frame of mind of the tracker, quiet and observant, I laughed as I saw it growing right next to me quite near my house. It was hidden from one point of view and obvious to another. As a tracker, I also began to see animals—mammals—that were never visible before. And I will tell you the most astonishing part of it: they are not afraid! I think that because I feel empty and open, they can sense my respect for the world.

Before we leave the subject of tracking, I would like to mention the importance of what we wear on the site. I am often dismayed when I witness designers on a "site visit." Dressed to the nines, they hover at the edge of the site, or stick to predictable paths. Sleeves may be rolled up(!), but every action says "Don't get dirty!" To know the site you must first get dirty!

I always have a set of old clothes ready to go: loose-fitting knockabouts whose fate I don't have to worry about. I must have no thought of keeping them clean and unrumpled. Here is a simple test for deciding whether or not clothes are suitable: would you be happy rolling around on the ground in them? Well-worn sneakers or running shoes are perhaps the most crucial part of this wardrobe. With every step, I literally feel more of the land.

INTERVIEWER

Talking to people often reveals some of the most valuable things I learn about a site. I think there are two reasons for this: each of our lives is a vast Library of Congress of memories, and we all want to tell about what we know. Recently, a survey of business leaders produced a list of the ten most important books of recent decades. Number one was Steven Covey's *Seven Habits of Highly Effective People*. Habit No. 5 is "Seek first to understand, then to be understood." Covey says this is the single most important principle in personal communication. I've found it also works wonders in learning about the land. I don't find it easy, but it is worth the constant effort! I've studied dozens of successful interviewers. My impression is that the best are listeners who are fully open to the moment, even when they don't know where the conversation may lead. They are supportive and sympathetic to the other person. Preparation is also very important. I carry some insightful questions in one pocket, and in the other I'll have interesting research to contribute.

At any site, interviewing neighbors is a must. As a birthright, we Americans have a passion for obstructing anything new which might be built next to us. When I look around at the mess we've created, I find this quite understandable. But new healing means new building. The old obstructionist ways must become more selective! I've found that if handled properly, neighbors who are knee-jerk reactors can also become allies.

In Oregon, I once started work on a site overlooked by a beautiful old house. The new house would change forever the isolated feeling of the original residents. Here was fertile ground for endless skirmishes between old-timers and interlopers. Since I couldn't sit on the site through a year's weather cycle, I arranged an interview with the old-timers to talk about the local micro-climate. Throughout the course of the morning, my questions convinced the potential adversaries that the project design would be sensitive beyond what they had dreamed. I learned more than I had imagined, including the whereabouts of tongues of fog and quirky winds. The potential obstructionists became watchdogs for us, and advocates of what we were doing.

Many specialists also possess invaluable site knowledge at this informational level. Notice I have not used the word "consultant." Among soils engineers, civil engineers, planners and the like, I've only known a few consultants who could rise beyond the narrow liability-conscious confines of their professional world. I like to seek out local people and buy some of their time to walk the site. A while back, I found a local city arborist who moonlighted in just this way. He saw the remnants of the original orchard which were invisible to me. He spotted a rare local tree that was a favorite of the local Native Americans. And he demonstrated how to prune and save many trees which looked hopeless to me. A number of other very knowledgeable local specialists are sometimes surprised when I want to hire them to walk a site. They are self-employed back hoe operators, naturalists (often teaching at a local community college), local artists, and of course, local old-timers.

Government agency people are very valuable for interviewing, and they are often the most difficult. They are generally very hard to contact, particularly as local government tightens its belt. The best time is first thing in the morning. They are usually caught in a bureaucratic web of procedures and non-commitment. They are crucial, however, since they can guide us through the regulatory maze when cultivated as allies. This maze is usually harder on ecologically-sound projects than on the disasters! The eco-projects tend to be more conscientious about following the rules, and they often lack the sophisticated legal war machines of the typical development interests.

The telephone is my best friend in agency interviews. I can move quickly with a lot of people. To keep the momentum going, I suggest getting a personal reference from the person you're speaking to for the person to call. "Sue suggested I call you. She mentioned that you are the most knowledgeable person regarding (whatever topic)." A benefit of creating alliances with agency people is that they will begin to talk about how the other agencies could be obstructive to "our" project. Getting them involved in an informational capacity at an early point in the game will make them far more helpful about doing their jobs later on.

SCHOLAR

For any site, mountains of knowledge exist on paper. In fact, one of the best parts of scholarship is getting to use maps. Maps! Those beautiful pictures of the land! But first off a word of caution—not only are maps selective, sometimes they are simply wrong. For over a century and a half, the most learned cartographers of the world mapped California as an island. When expeditions reported to the authorities in Spain that there were no island straits, they were told to return to look harder.

Not only do I treat maps with skepticism, I look at them in new ways. My favorite way is both simple and powerful—*turn the map upside-down*! Start doing this to every map you encounter. Suddenly, preconceived notions vanish. New patterns emerge. I hadn't understood the geography of the Great Basin of the American West until doing this. I look at a map upside-down, sideways, obliquely, and from underneath (place against a window). Do it—you'll be amazed.

For a particular site, I like to review many different kinds of maps. In addition to the site topographical survey, the single most valuable map is the U.S. Geological Survey's "71/2 Minute Quadrangle" of your area. It usually covers an area of about 6 x 8 miles (Scale: 1 inch = 2000 feet). What is so important is that you can both precisely locate your site and see detailed relationships and context all around it. Get this map for every project you work on. To cover virtually all of the continental United States, the U.S. Geological Survey has published about 57,000 different maps. The easiest way to get one for your area is generally at your sporting goods store.

Other valuable maps are:

• Local zoning map and its related requirements.

• Soil Conservation Service Surveys.

These books are published county by county. They are soil-type overlays on aerial photo sheets, plus much more. Look in your local phone book under "U.S. Department of Agriculture."

• County Assessor's Tax Roll Maps.

These show perhaps our culture's most enduring patterns on the land. Look under "County Government" in the phone book.

• Aerial Photographs.

Check with your local planning department and aerial survey services. (Confirm timeliness of photos.)

• Historic maps.

These will show hidden patterns—especially water and transportation features. Railroad lines and footpath systems sometimes emerge that are guides for the future. Lost streams and water edges usually pop up. Start at the history section of the local library.

• International Climate Maps.

Find the climates around the world which are similar to yours. The California coast is classified as the Mediterranean climate. There are five areas around the world with this climate. Studying local climactic-responsive building patterns in the other areas with the same climate can be very useful.

For a wealth of easily accessible information, chect the environmental impact report for nearby past projects. These will be on file at the local library. Explorers' journals and accounts of local Native American life are often invaluable. Malcolm Margonin's *Ohlone Way* is a panorama of life in the San Francisco Bay Area before the Europeans settled here. Until reading this account, I had no idea that the skies were once black with migrating waterfowl. I was even more amazed to learn that my region was a "tended landscape." There was not a wilderness here hundreds of years ago, but rather, the area was benignly cultivated by the local peoples. And here's another favorite source: historic landscape paintings. I constantly learn from 19th century artist William Keith, who roamed my area.

When I think of scholars of the land, one person stands out. He is Matt Downey, History professor at the University of Colorado. On a July afternoon at the Wright-Ingraham Institute's high plains field station, he described a different way to see the history of the American West. Instead of moving around choosing events, we stood at that one place. There, next to the tiny canyon on Running Creek, we watched and listened to him bring to life every chapter in the history of the West, describing what we would have seen from that spot over the years. We met trapper-mailman Dick Wooten and the Cherokee from back East who first discovered gold in the area. We heard the racket of the first railroad that caused a local population explosion. And we heard the creaking wheels of the "floating schoolhouse" which Board members would steal from each other. History pulsated in front of us. Matt Downey shared this with me over 25 years ago, but it is as fresh to me as if he said it yesterday. His purpose was to show that every piece of land has a story to tell. Whenever I'm at a site, I think of its continuing story.

The best place to begin to practice the technique I have described is where you live right now. I can guarantee you that if you begin to practice these methods at home, you will be shocked at how little you know about the place. Even if you've lived there for years, this will be true. It certainly happened to me.

Try these exercises . . .

Track these from their sources to their destination:

     1. Domestic Water.

     2. Sewage.

     3. Runoff.

     4. Electricity.

     5. Natural Gas.

Find out what Rock and Soil the building is resting on.

Observe your relationship to these:

     6. Views.

     7. Sky.

     8. Trees.

     9. Animals.

Where you are most:

     10. Uncomfortable.

     11. At Peace.

Why is this so important? Simply because once you possess a knowledge and respect about your home's connection to the world, your work at other sites will be more alive. By similarities and contrasts, you can more quickly and profoundly absorb the characteristics of other places.

*   *   *

A final note: think of all these methods as an opportunity for lifelong learning. I'm sure you'll have a great time along the way. And the land will be healthier for your efforts.

Chapter 7

Selecting a Site for Your Passive Solar Home

by Lib Reid-McGowan

From A SIMPLIFIED GUIDE
North Carolina Solar Center

A good passive solar house requires more than just a good design and quality construction. It also requires that the plan and the site be considered together during the design phase to assure that they work together to optimize solar performance. The best-designed solar house plan will not work unless it is placed properly on a building site which allows solar access. Similarly, a lot with clear solar access provides little advantage to the building placed upon it unless the building is designed and oriented to take advantage of the site's solar potential. Some people decide first upon the house plan they want, and then search for a lot which accommodates it; others start with a lot with solar potential and then look for a plan which would use it to advantage. The order here does not really matter; the important thing is to realize that good solar house plans or good solar lots do not exist as separate entities; they meet their potential only when plan and lot are properly integrated to create the successful solar house.

A passive solar house is one which is designed and oriented to take maximum advantage of the sun. Since the sun's path in the northern hemisphere passes through the southern sky, passive solar homes are designed to maximize southern exposure. The house can be of any shape, but it is usually laid out so that the major living areas of the house are either located on the south side or have direct access to a room which is. For a rectangular house, maximizing solar access can be achieved by orienting the house so that its long axis runs from east to west.

The majority of the solar house's windows are located on the south side so that they can receive the maximum amount of heat from the sun in winter when it is low in the southern sky. In the summer, when the sun follows a longer and higher path, overhangs located over south-facing windows and walls will help shade these areas from direct sunlight to reduce overheating. Overhangs located on the east and west do not shade effectively because the sun is much lower in the sky when it shines from the east or west.

As far as solar performance is concerned, it makes no difference whether the solar portion of the house is the front, the back, or the side; what matters is that the house must be placed on the lot so that the solar portion can be faced as close as possible to true south with a minimal amount of shading in the solar access zone. To avoid overheating in summer, the solar portion's orientation should not deviate by more than 15 degrees from true south. A southeastern deviation is less harmful than a southwestern deviation.

WHAT IS THE SOLAR ACCESS ZONE?

Facing solar surfaces to the south is not enough to ensure their performance; you must also make sure that the area to the south is clear of obstructions which would block the sun from reaching them. There should be no significant blockage between 9 AM and 3 PM, solar time, in the winter. At North Carolina's latitudes, this means that the area extending from 45 degrees east of south to 45 degrees west of south should be kept clear of obstructions which would block the sun.

THE SUN'S PATH

How far back does this solar access zone extend? Obstructions directly to the south of the building need to be located at a distance of at least 1.7 times their height away from the surface to avoid shading the building in winter. Obstructions located along the 45 degrees lines east or west of south need to be at least 3.5 times their height away from the building to avoid shading. Remember that the sun is lower in the sky and casts longer shadows in winter, so don't automatically assume that just because your site appears to be out of the shade in summer that it will also be unshaded in winter.

WHAT MAKES A GOOD SOLAR SITE?

A good solar site is one that will allow placement of the house so that its solar surfaces face true south with a minimal amount of shading in the solar access zone. It is helpful to have control over as much area as possible in the solar access zone since tall trees or multi-story buildings added later to the south of your house have the potential to reduce its solar performance by shading.

Lots which are deep from north to south offer the homeowner more control over the solar access zone, as does siting the house toward the north end of the lot. For lots located on the north side of the street (suitable for houses with solar "fronts"), the street can act as part of the buffer against development in the solar access zone. Locating the houses's septic drainage field within the solar access zone (assuming soil type and slope are suitable there) is another strategy for maintaining solar access, since that area will need to be cleared of vegetation.

WHAT ABOUT EASEMENTS AND RESTRICTIVE COVENANTS?

Developers may include easements or covenants with the deeds of lots which can affect the ability of those lots to be used for solar houses in either a positive or a negative way. If lots are deeded with a solar easement, it removes from the homeowner the burden of negotiating an easement with neighbors and protects the investment in a solar home. On the other hand, the development may include restrictive covenants that would preclude placing solar collectors or photovoltaic arrays on the roof, or might restrict the homeowner from removing trees within the solar access zone. The developer might also retain the right of way for an integrated landscaping plan, such as planting a row of trees lining the street (which would block solar access on the lots north of the street). Be sure to ask about zoning laws and covenants attached to a deed before purchasing a lot for your solar home.

TIPS FOR SOLAR LOT HUNTING

Look for roads that run from east to west. Since standard subdivision practice calls for lot lines perpendicular to the street and houses fronting parallel to the street, this is the easiest way to find lots suitable for siting houses with the long axis running east to west.

If your plan has a solar front, look at lots on the north side of the street; if it has a solar back, look on the south side.

If possible, visit the site in late December to observe how heavily the site will be shaded in winter. Look for lots that are deep from north to south to allow a maximum amount of control over the solar access zone. Look for flat or south-sloping lots which allow maximum solar access. Avoid north-sloping areas, since they cast longer shadows and make obtaining solar access more difficult. Find out about zoning regulations and restrictive covenants in the development.

Chapter 8

The Living Landscape: An Ecological Approach to Landscape Planning

Edited by Doug Aberley

From FUTURES BY DESIGN:
THE PRACTICE OF ECOLOGICAL PLANNING

The New Catalyst Bioregional Series
by Frederick Steiner: New Society Publishers

There is a need for a common language among all those concerned about social equity and eco-logical parity as a common method which can transcend disciplinary territorialism, be applicable to all levels of government, and incorporate both social and environmental concerns. For, as the poet Wendell Berry has observed, "The mentality that destroys a watershed and then panics at the threat of flood is the same mentality that gives institutionalized insult to black people then panics at the prospect of race riots." [3]

An approach is needed that can assist planners to analyze the problems of a region as they relate to each other, to the landscape, and to the national and local political economic structure. This might be called an applied human ecology. Each problem is linked to the community in one or more specific ways. Banking is related to real estate, is related to development pressure, is re-lated to schools, is related to rising tax base, and is related to retirees organizing against increas-ing property taxes. This approach identifies how people are affected by these chain reactions and presents options for the future based on those impacts.

Aldo Leopold, the University of Wisconsin wildlife biologist, was perhaps the first to ad-vocate an "ecological ethic" for planning.[17,18] He was joined by such individuals as Lewis Mumford and Benton MacKaye,[23] who were strongly influenced by the Scottish biologist and town planner, Patrick Geddes and the English garden city advocate Ebenezer Howard. Others who have proposed and/or developed ecological approaches for planning include the Canadian forester, G. Angus Hills;[13] the Israeli architect and town planner, Artur Glikson;[11] the American landscape architects, Philip Lewis,[19] Ian McHarg,[26] Anne Spirn,[39] and John Lyle;[21] the American regional planner, Jon Berger (with John Sinton[2]), and the French geographer and planner, Jean Tarlet.[43]

ECOLOGICAL PLANNING METHOD

What is meant by ecological planning? Planning is a process which, utilizes scientific and technical information for considering and reaching consensus on a range of choices. Ecology is the study of the relationship of all living things, including people, to their biological and physical environments. *Ecological planning* may be defined as the use of biophysical and sociocultural information to suggest opportunities and constraints for consensual decision-making about the use of the landscape. Ian McHarg has summarized a framework for ecological planning in the following way:

> "All systems aspire to survival and success. This state can be described as syntropic-fitness-health. Its antithesis is entropic-misfitness-morbidity. To achieve the first state requires systems to find the fittest environment, adapt it and themselves. Fitness of an environment for a system is defined as that requiring the minimum of work and adaptation. Fitness and fitting are indications of health and the process of fitness is health giving. The quest for fitness is entitled adaptation. Of all the instrumentalities available for man for successful adaptation, cultural adaptation in general and planning in particular, appear to be the most direct and efficacious for maintaining and enhancing human health and well-being."[27]

> Arthur Johnson explained the central principle of this theory:

> "The fittest environment for any organism, artifact, natural and social ecosystem, is that environment which provides the [energy] needed to sustain the health or well-being of the organism/artifact/ecosystem. Such an approach is not limited by scale. It may be applied to locating plants within a garden as well as to the development of a nation."[15]

The ecological planning method is primarily a procedure for studying the biophysical and sociocultural systems of a place to reveal where a specific land use may be best practiced. As Ian McHarg has summarized repeatedly in his writings and many public presentations:

> "The method defines the best areas for a potential land use at the convergence of all or most of the factors deemed propitious for the use in the ab-

sence of all or most detrimental conditions. Areas meeting this standard are deemed intrinsically suitable for the land use under consideration."

As presented in Figure 8-1, there are eleven interacting steps. An issue or group of related issues is identified by a community—that is, some collection of people—in step 1. These issues are problematic or present an opportunity to the people or the environment of an area. Goals are then established in step 2 to address the problem(s). Next, in steps 3 and 4, inventories and analyses of biophysical and sociocultural processes are conducted, first at a larger level, such as a drainage basin or an appropriate regional unit of government, and second at a more specific level, such as a watershed or a local government.

In step 5, detailed studies are made that link the inventory and analysis information to the problem(s) and goal(s). Suitability analyses are one such type of detailed study. Step 6 involves the development of concepts and options. A landscape plan is then derived from these concepts in step 7. Throughout the process, a systematic effort is made to educate and involve citizens. Such involvement is important in each step but especially so in step 8 when the plan is explained to the affected public. In step 9, detailed designs are made that are specific at the individual land-user or site level.

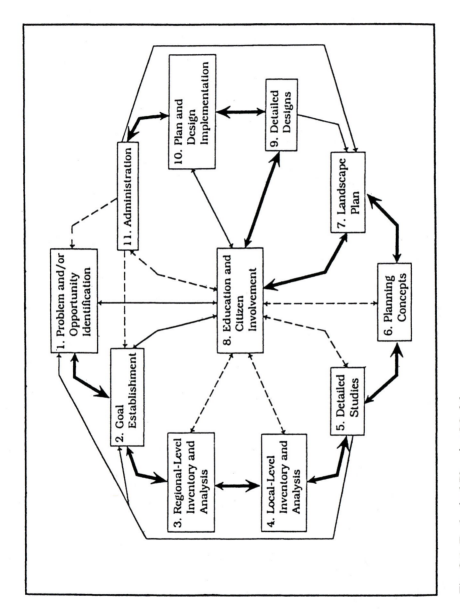

Fig. 8-1 Ecological Planning Model

These designs and the plan are implemented in step 10. In step 11, the plan is administered. The heavier arrows in Figure 8-1 indicate the flow from step 1 to 11. Smaller arrows between each step suggest a feedback system whereby each step can modify the previous step and, in turn, be changed from the subsequent step. Additional arrows indicate other possible modifications through the process. For instance, detailed studies of a planning area (step 5) may lead to the identification of new problems or opportunities or the amendment of goals (steps 1 and 2). Detailed designs (step 9) may change the landscape plan, and so on. Once the process is complete and the plan is being administered and monitored (step 11), the view of the problems and opportunities facing the region and the goals to address these problems and opportunities may be altered, as is indicated by the dashed lines in Figure 8-1.

This process is adapted from the conventional planning process and its many variations (see, for instance Hall;[12] Roberts;[37] McDowell;[25] Moore;[30] and Stokes et al.,[42] as well as those suggested specifically for landscape planning: Lovejoy;[20] Fabos;[8] Zube;[51] Marsh[24] and Duchhare[6]). Unlike some of these other planning processes, design plays an important role in this method. Each step in the process contributes to and is affected by a plan and implementing measures, which may be the official controls of the planning area. The plan and implementing measures may be viewed as the results of the process, although products may be generated from each step. The approach to ecological planning developed by McHarg and his colleagues at the University of Pennsylvania differs slightly from the one presented here. The Pennsylvania, or McHarg, model places a greater emphasis on inventory, analysis, and synthesis. This one places more emphasis on the establishment of goals, implementation, administration, and public participation, yet does attempt to do so in an ecological manner.

STEP 1: IDENTIFICATION OF PLANNING PROBLEMS AND OPPORTUNITIES

Human societies face many social, economic, political, and environmental problems and opportunities. Since a landscape is the interface between social and environmental processes, landscape planning addresses those issues that concern the inter-relationship between people and nature. The planet presents many opportunities for people and there is no shortage of environmental problems.

Problems and opportunities lead to specific planning issues. For instance, suburban development is occurring on prime agricultural land, which local officials consider a problem. A number of issues arise, such as land-use conflicts between new suburban residents and farmers, and division of financial responsibility for public services for the newly developed areas. Another example might be an area with the opportunity for new development because of its scenic beauty and recreational amenities, such as an ocean beach or mountain town: how can the new growth be accommodated while protecting the natural resources that are attracting people to the place?

STEP 2: ESTABLISHMENT OF PLANNING GOALS

In a democracy, the people of a region establish goals through the political process. Elected representatives will identify a particular issue affecting their region—a steel plant is closing, suburban sprawl is threatening agricultural land, or a new power plant is creating a housing boom. After issues have been identified, then goals are established to address the problem. Such goals should provide the basis for the planning process.

Goals articulate an idealized future situation. In the context of this method, it is assumed that once goals have been established there is a commitment by some group to address the problem or opportunity identified in step 1. Problems and opportunities can be identified at various levels. Local people can recognize a problem or opportunity and then set a goal to address it. As well, issues can be national, international or global in scope. Problem solving, of which goal setting is a part, may occur at many levels or combinations of levels. Although goal setting is obviously dependent on the cultural-political system, the people affected by a goal should be involved in its establishment.

Goal-oriented planning has long been advocated by many community planners. Such an approach has been summarized by Herbert Gans:

> "The basic idea behind goal-oriented planning is simple; that planners must begin with the goals of the community—and of its people—and then develop those programs which constitute the best means for achieving the community's goals, taking care that the consequences of these programs do not result in undesirable behavioral or cost consequences."[10]

There are some good examples of goal-oriented planning, such as Oregon's mandatory land-use law.[34,7,16] However, although locally generated goals are the ideal, too often goals are established by a higher level of government. Many federal and state laws have mandated planning goals for local government, often resulting in the creation of new regions to respond to a particular federal program. These regional agencies must respond to wide-ranging issues that generate specific goals for water and air quality, resource management, energy conservation, transportation, and housing. No matter at what level of government goals are established, information must be collected to help elected representatives resolve underlying issues. Many goals, particularly those which are the focus of this essay, require an understanding of biophysical processes.

STEP 3: LANDSCAPE ANALYSIS, REGIONAL LEVEL

After a community has identified the problems and opportunities that it faces and has reached some consensus concerning its goals to address those issues, then the information can be collected to achieve community goals. Information about nature has often been used in an ad hoc manner in planning. Only that information needed to achieve a specific goal is collected—and too often it is disconnected information. For instance, since flooding is recognized by a community as a hazard to human safety, the responsible elected officials adopt a goal to prevent buildings in flood-prone areas. These areas are mapped and building restricted. The goal is one-dimensional.

The basic premise of ecology is that everything is connected to everything else. As a result, the ecological approach differs from more traditional methods. Whereas in conventional planning only the flood-prone areas are identified, in ecological planning, the complex matrix of factors related to flooding would be considered. Flooding is the result of the interaction of several natural phenomena—rainfall, bedrock, terrain, temperature, and vegetation, for instance. Since ecological planning rests on an understanding of relationships, broader-range information about the biophysical processes of an area must be collected and analyzed. Moreover, the sequence of collecting it is important.

Older, larger-scale components of the landscape exert a strong influence on more ephemeral elements. Regional climate and geology help determine soils and water drainage systems of an area that, in turn, affect what vegetation and animals will inhabit a place. As a result, in ecological planning one begins the inventory with the older elements and proceeds to the youngest.

When conducting such an inventory, it is useful to identify boundaries so that the various biophysical elements can be compared with each other over the same spatial area and at the same scale. Often such a planning area is defined by legislative goals, as, for instance, with the New Jersey Pinelands.

Ideally, several levels of inventories from regional to local are undertaken. A hierarchy of levels is identified so that the planning area may be understood as part of a larger system and specific places may be seen as parts of a whole. The drainage basin at the regional level and the watershed more locally are ideal units of analysis for ecological planning. A *watershed* is an area drained by a river or river system, also called a *catchment area* or, at a larger scale, a *drainage basin.* Eugene Odum suggests the watershed as "a practical ecosystem unit for management that combines natural and cultural attributes,"[30] while Peter Quinby[36] notes that watershed boundaries can be used as ecosystem boundaries. The watershed is a handy unit that contains biological, physical, social, and economic processes. Watersheds have discrete boundaries yet can vary in scale, providing flexibility for adaptation to social, economic, and political concerns. Watersheds also offer linkages between the elements of regions, making them an ideal unit of analysis since the flow of water, which provides the linkage throughout the watershed, may be easily visualized.

The use of drainage basins and watersheds for planning is not new. John Wesley Powell, who introduced the term *region* to North America, essentially suggested the use of watersheds in his 1879 plan for the American West. The use of watersheds is also consistent with past efforts of watershed conservancies and river basin commissions, such as the Delaware River Basin Commission, the Columbia River Basin Commission, and the Tennessee Valley Authority; with programs of the U.S. Soil Conservation Service (which may be renamed the Natural Resources Conservation Service), the Army Corps of Engineers, the National Parks Service, and the U. S. Forest Service; and with joint Canadian-American efforts in the Great Lakes region. But more often than not, units other than watersheds—political boundaries, most frequently—are used. Still the principle of hierarchy can apply to political boundaries, with counties or other similar levels of government forming the regional scale, and cities or towns being used as the unit for local landscape analysis.

Conventional approaches to planning have incorporated socioeconomic analyses. Connecting such studies to biophysical information for planning is relatively new. Planners use a variety of types of social information, and these materials fall into three basic categories: existing data, new information from existing data, and original information. These data include quantitative information, such as the number of people living in an area counted by a census, as well as more qualitative data, such as the perceptions of people about the visual impacts of a new roadway or dam.

Planning projects and programs require different types of social information. For example, a growth management plan requires an estimate of future population, and economic and development trends. This quantitative information can be derived from existing sources. Conversely, for the placement of a new electric transmission line, planners need to collect original, qualitative information about perceptions and reactions through interviews with affected residents. Because of the variety of possible planning projects and programs, a blanket prescription cannot be given for the specific social inventories that should be conducted. The issues that have stimulated the planning process as well as the goals that have been identified to resolve those problems and opportunities will determine the types of data to be collected and analyzed.

An understanding of current and possible future population trends and characteristics will probably be essential for a community to achieve many of its goals. In Oregon, for instance, local governments are required to address specific goals concerning agriculture and housing. As a result, planners must inventory and analyze information concerning trends in farm population (such as whether it is growing or declining) and characteristics of the agricultural community (such as the average age of farmers). Planners must also analyze population trends and characteristics and forecast future possibilities to make recommendations about housing needs.

To accomplish this, planners need to understand local economies. For example, it is important to know the percentage that farming contributes to the economic base of a community, as well as the primary commodities and their markets. Through an analysis of the local agricultural economy, planners can determine how healthy it is, whether or not it is worth protecting, and if intervention is necessary to improve local farming systems. The economic base of the community helps planners analyze community needs. If the economic base is comprised of primary industries (such as farming, fishing, mining, and logging) rather than those of the tertiary sector (such as retail, wholesale, and services), then demands for housing, for instance, will be different. Where primary industries are involved, it may be necessary for houses to be relatively close to farmland, the ocean, the mountains, or forests. With tertiary industries, the linkage between home and workplace may be less spatially dependent.

Conventional planning processes have considered and incorporated population and economic studies. But the social characteristics have not been related to the landscape—a major difference between conventional approaches
and ecological planning. Through an ecological approach, social processes are connected to landscape features. For instance, agriculture can be related to specific combinations of biophysical elements that vary with crops. Wheat requires different climate, water, and soil characteristics than do cranberries. Rural housing has different needs than high-rise apartments. Different users of the

land—cranberry farmers or high-rise apartment dwellers—place different demands on the landscape as well.

Each human community must *be* viewed as having unique characteristics. The population growth of a major Texas city—Dallas, Texas, for instance—of 500 people per year may not be dramatic or even the source of concern. But in a rural west Texas country, the same growth may be quite significant and have consequences for several land uses, especially agriculture and housing. Although ranching may have great symbolic value in Dallas, the number of real cowboys may be few, while in a west Texas county, people actively engaged in ranching may constitute the most important economic sector. Certainly, the landscape in Dallas, and the biophysical process that created it, differs from that of west Texas. As a result, each place—whether in Texas, Oregon, or New Jersey, or Wales, North Holland, or Tuscany—must be inventoried and analyzed for its special qualities.

**STEP 4: LANDSCAPE ANALYSIS,
LOCAL LEVEL**

During step 4, processes taking place in the more specific planning area are studied. The major aim of local-level analysis is to obtain insight into natural processes and human plans and activities in the immediate area. Such processes can be viewed as the elements of a system, with the landscape a visual expression of the system.

This step in the ecological planning process, like the previous one, involves the collection of information concerning the appropriate physical, biological, and social elements that constitute the planning area. Since cost and time are important factors, existing published and mapped information is the easiest and fastest to gather. If budget and time allow, however, inventory and analysis may be best accomplished by an interdisciplinary team collecting new information. In either case, this step is an interdisciplinary collection effort that involves search, accumulation, field checking, and mapping of data.

Ian McHarg and his colleagues have developed a layer-cake simulation model that provides a central group of biophysical elements for the inventory. Categories include geology, physiography, groundwater, surface water, soils, climate, vegetation, wildlife, and people. UNESCO, in its Man and the Biosphere Program, has developed a more exhaustive list of possible inventory elements (Table 8-1).

Table 1. UNESCO Total Environmental Checklist: Components and Processes

Natural Environment — Components

Soil	Energy Resources
Water	Fauna
Atmosphere	Flora
Mineral Resources	Micro-organisms

Natural Environment — Processes

Biogeochemical cycles	Fluctuations in animal and plant growth
Irradiation	Changes in soil fertility, salinity,
Climatic processes	alkalinity
Photosynthesis	Host/parasite interactions, and
Animal and plant growth	epidemic processes

Human Population — Demographic Aspects

Population Structure:

• Age	Population size
• Ethnicity	Population density
• Economic	Fertility and mortality rates
• Educational	Health statistics
• Occupational	

Human Activities and the Use of Machines

Migratory movements	Mining
Daily mobility	Industrial activities
Decision making	Commercial activities
Exercise and distribution of	Military activities
authority	Transportation
Administration	Recreation activities
Farming, fishing	Crime rates

Societal Groupings

Governmental groupings	Information media
Industrial groupings	Law-keeping media
Commercial groupings	Health services
Political groupings	Community groupings
Religious groupings	Family groupings
Educational groupings	

Products of Labor

The built-environment:

• Buildings	Food
• Roads	Pharmaceutical products
• Railways	Machines
• Parks	Other commodities

Culture

Values	Technology
Beliefs	Literature
Attitudes	Laws
Knowledge	Economic System
Information	

Source: Boyden, 1979.

Table 2: U.S. Geological Survey Land-Use and Land-Cover Classification System for Use With Remote Sensor Data

Level I	Level II
1. Urban or built-up land	11 Residential
	12 Commercial and services
	13 Industrial
	14 Transportation, communications, and services
	15 Industrial and commercial complexes
	16 Mixed urban or built-up land
	17 Other urban or built-up land
2. Agricultural land	21 Cropland and pasture
	22 Orchards, groves, vineyards, nurseries, and ornamental horticulture
	23 Confined feeding operations
	24 Other agricultural land
3. Rangeland	31 Herbaceous rangeland
	32 Shrub and brush rangeland
	33 Mixed rangeland
4. Forest land	41 Deciduous forest land
	42 Evergreen forest land
	43 Mixed forest land
5. Water	51 Streams and canals
	52 Lakes
	53 Reservoirs
	54 Bays and estuaries
6. Wetlands	61 Forested wetland
	62 Non-forested wetland
7. Barren land	71 Dry salt flats
	72 Beaches
	73 Sandy areas other than beaches
	74 Bare exposed rocks
	75 Strip mines, quarries, and gravel pits
	76 Transitional areas
	77 Mixed barren land
8. Tundra	81 Shrub and brush tundra
	82 Herbaceous tundra
	83 Bare ground
	84 Mixed tundra
9. Perennial snow ice	91 Perennial snowfields
	92 Glaciers

Source: Anderson et al., 1976.

Land classification systems are valuable for analysis at this stage because they may allow the planner to aggregate specific information into general groupings. Such systems are based on inventoried data and on needs for analysis. Many government agencies in the United States and elsewhere have developed land classification systems that are helpful. The Soil Conservation Service, the U.S. Forest Service, the U.S. Fish and Wildlife Service, and the U.S. Geological Survey (USGS) are agencies that have been notably active in land classification systems. However, there is not a consistency of data sources even in North America. In urban areas, a planner may be overwhelmed with data for inventory and analysis. In remote rural areas, on the other hand, even a Soil Conservation Service survey may not exist, or may be old and unusable. An even larger problem is that there is little or no consistency in scale or in the terminology used among agencies. A recommendation of the National Agricultural Lands Study[31] was that a statistical protocol for federal agencies concerning land resource information be developed, led by the Office of Federal Statistical Policy and Standards. One helpful system that has been developed for land classification is the USGS Land Use and Land Cover Classification System (Table 8-2).

Several American agencies are developing integrated mapping programs using geographic information systems (GIS). The U.S. Environmental Protection Agency's environmental monitoring and assessment program (EMAP) is partially based on the ideas of McHarg.[28] EMAP was proposed to be a broadly conceived ecosystem inventory integrating regional and national scales, allowing for monitoring and assessment, and designed to influence decision—making. The U.S. Fish and Wildlife Service has developed a comprehensive, national biological diversity information system, using GIS technology, to organize existing data and improve spatial aspects of environmental assessment. The system is called Gap Analysis and identifies gaps in the representation of biological diversity in protected areas. Gap Analysis uses vegetation types and vertebrate and butterfly species as indicators of biodiversity.[38] The U.S. Fish and Wildlife Service and other federal agencies are collaborating with states in the Gap Analysis Program. In 1993, Secretary of the Interior Bruce Babbitt recommended a National Biological Survey which would provide nation-wide ecological data. These efforts indicate massive environmental data will soon be available, ultimately in digital form, in North America and globally.

The ability of the landscape planner and resource manager to inventory biophysical processes at the regional level may be uneven, but it is far better than their capability to assess human ecosystems. An understanding of human ecology is essential in conducting a sociocultural inventory and analysis. Since humans are living things, *human ecology* may be thought of as an expansion of ecology—how humans interact with each other and their environments. Interaction then is used as both a basic concept and an explanatory device. As Gerald Young,[46,48,49,50] who has illustrated the multidisciplinary scope of human ecology, noted:

> "In human ecology, the way people interact with each other and with the environment is definitive of a number of basic relationships. Interaction provides a measure of belonging, it affects identity versus alienation, including alienation from the environment. The system of obligation, responsibility, and liability is defined through interaction. The process has become definitive of the public interest, as opposed to private interests which prosper in the spirit of independence."[47]

STEP 5: DETAILED STUDIES

Detailed studies link the inventory and analysis information to the problem(s) and goal(s). For example, suitability analyses, as explained by McHarg,[26] can be used to determine the fitness of a specific place for a variety of land uses, based on thorough ecological inventories and on the values of land users. The basic purpose of the detailed studies is to gain an understanding about the complex relationships between human values, environmental opportunities and constraints, and the issues being addressed. To accomplish this, it is crucial to link the studies to the local situation. As a result, a variety of scales-may be used to explore linkages.

A simplified suitability analysis process is provided in Figure 8-2. There are several techniques that may be used to accomplish suitability analysis. Again, it was McHarg who popularized the "overlay technique."[26] This technique involves maps of inventory information superimposed on one another in order to identify areas that provide, first, opportunities for particular land uses, and second, constraints.[14] MacDougall[22] has criticized the accuracy of map overlays and made suggestions on how they may be made more accurate. Steinitz et al.[41] have provided a history of the use of hand overlays of mapped information, and Neckar has written a profile of Warren Manning, who was responsible for the idea of overlaying maps to represent natural systems.

Although there has been a general tendency away from hand-drawn overlays, there are still occasions where they may be useful. For instance, they may be helpful for small study sites within a larger region or for certain scales of project planning. However, the limitations of hand-drawn overlays include, for instance, the fact that after more than three or four overlays they may become opaque. There are the accuracy questions raised by MacDougall[22] and others that are especially acute with hand-drawn maps, and there are limitations for weighting various values represented by map units.

Numerous GIS programs have been developed that overcome these limitations and replace the technique of hand-drawn overlays. Some of these programs are intended to model only positions of environmental processes or phenomena, while others are designed as comprehensive information storage, retrieval, and evaluation systems. These systems are intended to improve efficiency and economy in information handling, especially for large or complex planning projects.

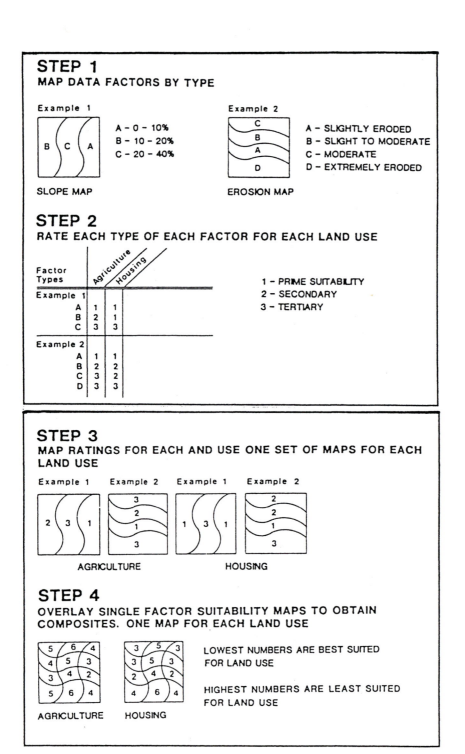

Fig. 8-2 Suitability Analysis Procedure

This step involves the development of concepts for the planning area. These concepts can be viewed as options for the future, based on the suitabilities for the use(s), that give a general conceptual model or scenario of how problems may be solved. This model should be presented in such a way that the goals can be achieved. Often more than one scenario has to be made. These concepts are based on a logical and imaginative combination of the information gathered through the inventory and analysis steps. The conceptual model shows allocations of uses and actions. The scenarios set possible directions for future management of the area and, therefore, should be viewed as a basis for discussion where choices are made by the community about its future.

Choices should be based on the goals of the planning effort. For instance, if it is the goal to protect agricultural land yet allow some low-density housing to develop, different organizations of the environment for those two land uses should be developed. Different schemes for realizing the desired preferences also need to be explored.

The Dutch have devised an interesting approach to developing planning options for their agricultural land re-allocation projects. Four land use options are developed, each with the preferred scheme for a certain point of view. Optional land-use schemes of the area are made for nature and landscape, agriculture, recreation, and urbanization. These schemes are constructed by groups of citizens working with government scientists and planners. For instance, for the nature and landscape scheme, landscape architects and ecologists from the *Staatsbosbeheer* (Dutch Forest Service) work with citizen environmental action groups. For agriculture, local extension agents and soil scientists work with farm commodity organizations and farmer cooperatives. Similar coalitions are formed for recreation and urbanization. What John Friedmann[9] calls a dialogue process begins at the point where each of the individual schemes is constructed. The groups come together for mutual learning so that a consensus of opinion is reached through debate and discussion.

Various options for implementation also need to be explored, which must relate to the goal of the planning effort. If, for instance, the planning is being conducted for a jurisdiction trying to protect its agricultural land resources, then it is necessary not only to identify lands that should be protected but also the implementation options that might be employed to achieve the farmland protection goal.

The preferred concepts and options are brought together in a landscape plan which gives a strategy for development at the local scale. The plan provides flexible guidelines for policy-makers, land managers, and land users about how to conserve, rehabilitate, or develop an area. Enough freedom should be left so that local officials and the land users can adjust their practices to new economic demands or social changes.

This step represents a key decision-making point in the planning process. Responsible officials, such as county commissioners or city council members, are often required by law to adopt a plan. The rules for adoption and the forms that the plans may take vary widely. Commonly in the United States, planning commissions recommend a plan for adoption to the legislative body after a series of public hearings. Such plans are officially called *comprehensive plans* in much of the United States, *general plans* in California and Arizona, and *master plans* in Colorado. In some states, such as Oregon, there are specific, detailed elements that local governments are required to include in such plans. Other states permit much flexibility to local officials for the contents of these plans. On public lands, various federal agencies—including the U.S. Forest Service, the National Park Service, and the U.S. Bureau of Land Management—have specific statutory requirements for land management plans.

The term *landscape plan* is used here to emphasize that such plans should incorporate natural and social considerations. A landscape plan is more than a land-use plan because it addresses the overlap and integration of land uses. It may involve the formal recognition of previous elements in the planning process, such as the adoption of policy goals, and should include both written statements about policies and implementation strategies, as well as a map showing the spatial organization of the landscape.

STEP 8: CONTINUED CITIZEN INVOLVEMENT AND COMMUNITY EDUCATION

In step 8, the plan is explained to the affected public through education and information dissemination. Actually, such interaction occurs throughout the planning process, beginning with the identification of issues. Public involvement is especially crucial as the landscape plan is developed, because it is important to ensure that the goals established by the community will be achieved in the plan.

The success of a plan depends largely on how much people affected by the plan have been involved in its determination. There are numerous examples of both government agencies and private business suddenly announcing a plan for a project that will dramatically impact people without consulting those individuals first. The result is predictable—the people will rise in opposition to the project. The alternative is to involve people in the planning process, soliciting their ideas, and incorporating those ideas into the plan. Doing so may require a longer time to develop a plan, but local citizens will be more likely to support it than to oppose it and will often monitor its execution.

STEP 9: DETAILED DESIGNS

To design is to give form and to arrange elements spatially. By making specific designs based on the landscape plan, planners can help decision makers visualize the consequences of their policies. Carrying policies through to arranging the physical environment gives meaning to the process by actually conceiving change in the spatial organization of a place. Designs represent a synthesis of all the previous planning studies. During the design step, the short-term benefits for the land users or individual citizen have to be combined with the long-term economic and ecological goals for the whole area.

STEP 10: PLAN AND DESIGN IMPLEMENTATION

Implementation is the employment of various strategies, tactics, and procedures to realize the goals and policies adopted in the landscape plan. On the local level, several different mechanisms have been developed to control the use of land and other resources. These techniques include voluntary covenants, easements, land purchase, transfer of development rights, zoning, utility extension policies, and performance standards. The preference selected should be appropriate for the region. For instance, in urban areas like King County, Washington, and Suffolk County, New York, traditional zoning has not been effective in protecting farmland. The citizens of these counties have elected to tax themselves to purchase development easements from farmers. In more rural counties like Whitman County, Washington, and Black Hawk County, Iowa, local leaders have found traditional zoning effective.

One implementation technique especially well suited for ecological planning is performance standards. Like many other planning implementation measures, *performance standards* is a general term that has been defined and applied in several different ways; basically, it means that criteria are established and must be met before a certain use will be permitted. These criteria are usually a combination of economic, environmental, and social factors. This technique lends itself to ecological planning because criteria for specific land uses can be based on suitability analysis.

STEP 11: ADMINISTRATION

In this final step, the plan is administered. *Administration* involves monitoring and evaluating the plan on an ongoing basis. Amendments or adjustments will no doubt be necessary because of changing conditions or new information. To achieve the goals established for the process, planners should pay especial attention to the design of regulation review procedures and to the management of the decision-making process.

Administration may be accomplished by a commission comprised of citizens with or without the support of a professional staff. Citizens may also play an important role in administering local planning through participation via commissions and review boards that oversee local ordinances. To a large degree, the success of citizens' boards and commissions depends on the extent of their involvement in the development of the plans that they manage. Again, Oregon provides an excellent example of the use of citizens to administer a plan. The Land Conservation and Development Commission, comprised of seven members who are appointed by the governor and supported by a professional staff, is responsible for overseeing the implementation of the state land-use planning law. Another group of citizens, 1,000 Friends of Oregon, monitors the administration of the law. Public support of the law is evident from the defeat of several attempts to abolish mandatory state-wide land-use planning in Oregon.

WORKING PLANS

A method is necessary as an organizational framework for landscape planners, and can be used to compare and analyze case studies. To fulfill their responsibilities to protect public health, safety, and welfare, planners should base their actions on a knowledge of what has and what has not worked in other settings and situations. A large body of case-study results can provide an empirical foundation for planners. A common method is helpful both for practicing planners and for scholars who should probe and criticize the nuances of such a method in order to expand and improve its utility.

The approach suggested here should be viewed as a working method. The pioneering forester, Gifford Pinchot, advocated a conservation approach to the planning of the national forests of the United States. His approach was both utilitarian and protectionist, and he believed "wise use and preservation of all forest resources were compatible."[45] To implement this philosophy, Pinchot in his position as chief of the U.S. Forest Service required "working plans." Such plans recognized the dynamic, living nature of forests. In the same vein, the methods used to develop plans should be viewed as a living process. However, this is not meant to imply that there should be no structure to planning methods. Rather, working planning methods should be viewed as something analogous to a jazz composition—not a fixed score but a basis for improvisation.

The method offered here has a landscape ecological—specifically human ecological—bias. As noted by the geographer Donald W. Meinig, "Environment sustains us as creatures; landscape displays us as cultures."[29] As an artifact of culture, landscapes are an appropriate focus for planners faced with land-use and environmental management issues. Ecology provides insight into landscape patterns, processes, and interactions. An understanding of ecology reveals how we interact with each other and our natural and built environments. We still know little of such relationships but our understanding is expanding all the time. As Ilya Prigogine and Isabelle Stengers have observed, "Nature speaks in a thousand voices, and we have only begun to listen."[35]

NOTES

1. Anderson, James R., Ernest E. Hardy, John T. Roach, and Richard E. Witmer, A *Land Use and Land Cover Classification System for Use with Remote Sensor Data* (U.S. Geological Survey Professional Paper 964), USGPO, 1976, 28 pp.

2. Berger, Jonathan, and John W. Sinton, *Water, Earth, and Fire,* Johns Hopkins University Press, 1985, 228 pp.

3. Berry, Wendell, A *Continuous Harmony, Essays Cultural and Agriculture,* Harcourt Brace Jovanovich, 1972, 182 pp.

4. Boyden, Stephen, *An Integrative Ecological Approach to the Study of Human Settlements* (MAB Technical Notes 12), UNESCO, 1979, 87 pp.

5. Davis, Frank W., David M. Stoms, John E. Estes, Joseph Scepan, and J. Michael Scott, "An Information Systems Approach to the Preservation of Biological Diversity," *International Journal of Geographical Information Systems 40(1) 55-78, 1990.*

6. Duchhart, Ingrid, *Manual on Environment and Urban Development,* Ministry of Local Government and Physical Planning, Nairobi, Kenya, 1989, 86 pp.

7. Eber, Ronald, "Oregon's Agricultural Land Protection Program" in *Protecting Farmlands,* Frederick R. Steiner and *John E.* Theilacker (eds.), AVI Publishing Company, 1984, pp. 161-171.

8. Fabos, Julius Gy., *Planning the Total Landscape,* Westview Press, 1979, 181 pp.

9. Friedmann, John, *Retracking America,* Anchor Press/Doubleday, 1973, 289 pp.

10. Gans, Herbert J., *People and Plans,* Basic Books, 1968, 395 pp.

11. Glikson, Artur, *The Ecological Basis of Planning,* Matinus Nijhoff, 1971, 115 pp.

12. Hall, Peter, *Urban and Regional Planning,* Halsted Press/John Wiley & Sons, 1975, 312 pp.

13. Hills, G. *A., The Ecological Basis for Land-Use Planning,* (Research Report No. 46), Ontario Department of Lands and Forests, 1961, 204 pp.

14. Johnson, A. *H.,* Jonathan Berger, and Ian L. McHarg, "A Case Study in Ecological Planning: The Woodlands, Texas" in *Planning the Uses and Management of land,* Marvin T. Beatty, Gary W. Petersen, and Lester D. Swindale (eds.), American Society of Agronomy, Crop Science Society of America, and Soil Science Society of America, 1979, pp. 935-955.

15. Johnson, A. H., "Guest Editorial: Human Ecological Planning Methods and Studies," *Landscape Planning* 8:107- 108, 1981.

16. Knaap, Gerrit and Arthur C. Nelson, *The Regulated Landscape, Lessons on State Land- Use Planning from Oregon,* Lincoln Institute of Land Policy, 1992, 243 pp.

17. Leopold, Aldo, "The Conservation Ethic," *The Journal of Forestry,* 31(6):634-643, 1933.

18. Leopold, Aldo., A *Sand County Almanac and Sketches Here and There,* Oxford, 1949, 295 pp.

19. Lewis, Philip H., "Ecology: The Inland Water Tree," *American Institute of Architects Journal,* 51(8):59-63, 1969.

20. Lovejoy, Derek (ed.), *Land Use and Landscape Planning,* Barnes & Noble, 1973, 308 pp.

21. Lyle, John, *Design for Human Ecosystems,* Van Nostrand Reinhold, 1985, 279 pp.

22. MacDougall, E. Bruce, "The Accuracy of Map Overlays," *Landscape Planning,* 2:23-30, 1975.

23. MacKaye, Benton, "Regional Planning and Ecology," *Ecological Monographs,* 10(3):349-353, 1940.

24. Marsh, William M., *Landscape Planning,* Addison-Wesley, 1983, 356 pp.

25. McDowell, Bruce D., "Approaches to Planning" in *The Practice of State and Regional Planning,* Frank S. So, Irving Hand, and Bruce D. McDowell (eds.), American Planning Association, 1986, pp. 3-22.

26. McHarg Ian L., *Design With Nature,* Doubleday/The Natural History Press, 1969, 197 pp.

27. McHarg Ian L., "Human Ecological Planning at Pennsylvania," *Landscape Planning* *8:109-120, 1981.*

28. McHarg, Ian, John Radke, Jonathan Berger, and Kathleen Wallace, A *Protoypte Database for a National Ecological Inventory, U.S.* Environmental Agency, 1992, 113 pp.

29. Meinig, D. W., "Introduction" in *The Interpretation of Ordinary Land*scapes, D. W. Meinig (ed.)., Oxford University Press, 1979, pp. 1-7.

30. Moore, Terry, "Planning without Preliminaries," *Journal of the American Planning* Association, 54(4):525-528, 1988.

31. National Agricultural Lands Study, *Final Report,* U.S. Department of Agriculture and Council on Environmental Quality, 1981, 94 pp.

32. Neckar, Lance M., "Developing Landscape Architecture for the Twentieth Century: The Career of Warren H. Manning," *Landscape Journal 8(2): 78-91, 1989.*

33. Odum, Eugene P., *Fundamentals of Ecology,* W. B. Saunders, 1971, 574 pp.

34. Pease, James R., "Oregon's Land Conservation and Development Program" in *Planning for the Conservation and Development of Land* Resources, Frederick R. Steiner and Hubert N. van Lier (eds.), Elsevier Scientific Publishing, 1984, pp. 253-271.

35. Prigogine, Ilya and Isabelle Stengers, *Order Out Of Chaos*, Bantam Books, 1984, 349 pp.

36. Quinby, Peter A., "The Contribution of Ecological Sciences to the Development of Landscape Ecology: A Brief History," *Landscape Research, 13(3):9-11, 1988.*

37. Roberts, John C., "Principles of Land-Use Planning" in *Planning the Uses and Management of Land,* Marvin T. Beatty, Gary W. Petersen, and Lester D. Swindale (eds.), American Society of Agronomy, Crop Science Society of America, and Soil Science Society of America, 1979, pp. 47-63.

38. Scott, J. Michael, Frank Davis, Blair Csuti, Reed Noss, Bart Butterfield, Craig Groves, Hal Anderson, Steve Caicco, Frank D'Erchia, Thomas C. Edwards, Jr., Joe Ulliman, and R. Gerald Wright, "Gap Analysis: A Geographic Approach to Protection of Biological Diversity," *Wildlife Monographs,* 123:1-41, 1993.

39. Spirn, Anne Whiston, *The Granite Garden,* Basic Books, 1984,334 pp.

40. Steiner, Frederick, *The Living Landscape,* McGrawHill, 1991, 356 pp.

41. Steinitz, Carl, Paul Parker, and Lawrie Jordan, "Hand-Drawn Overlays, Their History and Prospective Uses," *Landscape Architecture,* 66:444-455, 1976.

42. Stokes, Samuel N., A. Elizabeth Watson, Genevieve P. Keller, and J. Timothy Keller, *Saving America's Countryside,* Johns Hopkins University Press, 1989, 306 pp.

43. Tarlet, Jean, *La Planification Ecologique: Méthodes et Techniques,* Eco-nomica, 1985, 142 pp.

44. Wallace, McHarg, Roberts, and Todd, *Woodlands New Community (4* volumes), 1971-1974, Various pages.

45. Wilkinson, Charles F., and H. Michael Anderson,"Land and Resource Planning in National Forests," Oregon *Law Review,* 64(1&2):1-373, 1985.

46. Young, Gerald L., "Human Ecology as an Interdisciplinary Concept: A Critical Inquiry," *Advances in Ecological Research,* 8:1-105, 1974.

47. Young, Gerald L., "Environmental Law: Perspectives from Human Ecology," *Environmental Law,* 6(2):289- 307, 1976.

48. Young, Gerald L, *Human Ecology as an Interdisciplinary Domain: An Epistemological Bibliography,* Vance Bibliographies, 1978, 62 pp.

49. Young, Gerald L. (ed.), *Origins of Human Ecology,* Hutchinson Ross Publishing, 1983, 415 pp.

50. Young, Gerald L., "A Conceptual Framework for an Interdisciplinary Human Ecology," Acta Oecologiae *Hominis,* 1:1-136, 1989.

51. Zube, Ervin H., *Environmental Education,* Brooks/Cole, 1980, 148 pp.

Part Three

SUN AND WIND

Chapter 9

The Passive Solar Concept

From THE PASSIVE SOLAR HOUSE
by James Kachadorian
Chelsea Green Publishing Company

A French engineer named Felix Trombe is credited with the simple idea of building a solar collector comprised of a south-facing glass wall with an air space between it and a blackened concrete wall (see Figure 9.1). The sun's energy passes through the glass, and is trapped and absorbed by the blackened wall. As the concrete warms, air rises in the space between the glass and the blackened concrete wall. Rectangular openings at the bottom and top of the Trombe wall allow this warm air to flow to and from the living space. This movement of air is called thermosiphoning. At night the blackened concrete wall will radiate, or release, its heat to the interior.

The process can, unfortunately, reverse at night bringing warm air from the living space over to the cold glass. As this warmer air is cooled by the glass, it drops to the floor which, in turn, pulls more warm air from the living space. In the process, thermosiphoning is reversed. The colder it is outside, the more the Trombe wall will reverse thermosiphon. One way to control this heat loss is mechanically to close the rectangular openings at night and to reopen them when the sun comes out.

The Trombe wall is the "Model A" of passive solar design; that is, it is elegant in its simplicity and dependability, but has been largely supplanted by more modern technology. The Trombe wall example, however, illustrates some important principles. The system requires no moving parts, no switches to turn motors on or off, and no control systems; yet when it is functioning properly, it will collect, store, and then radiate heat back into the living space, even after the sun has gone down.

By contrast, an active solar collector is an ancillary system; instead of incorporating heat collection, storage, and release into the structure of the building, active systems are made up of devices attached to the structure. (Active systems also represent "add-on" expenses for a home—features that are additional to those that you would normally purchase.) Active systems will not work without a pump or blower operating. Typically, solar collectors are placed on the roof. Water pipes deliver water heated by the collectors to a storage tank and heated water is pumped out of the storage tank as needed. These systems will not work by themselves, as they need to have sensors "tell" switches to turn on pumps or blowers to mechanically activate the circulation of water.

The "passive" Trombe wall and the active solar collector system represent the technological range of solar heating systems from most basic to most complicated.

KEEP IT SIMPLE AND LET NATURE HELP YOU

Given the challenge of designing and building a naturally solar-heated home, the most widely applicable system is simple, passive, and does not add cost to construction of the home. Let's look at the materials which one has already committed to purchasing. Used properly, these materials become the building blocks of the naturally heated home. We need concrete to build the base of the house, and we all like windows and patio doors. Also, let's take a critical look at the building site, because much can be done to make home orientation and vegetation function as heating and cooling assists.

Let's start by finding a south-facing house site. For the sake of discussion, let's locate this house in Hartford, Connecticut, which is at north latitude 41°5', or "41 degrees 5 minutes." If the home faces true south, you will get the maximum solar benefit, but as you rotate your home off true south the solar benefit is reduced. At solar noon in February in Hartford, Connecticut, the cost of being oriented at an angle other than true south is indicated in Table 9-1 below.

TABLE 9-1

TRUE SOUTH	100% SOLAR BENEFIT
Rotate 22 1/2 degrees off true south to south-southwest or south-southeast	92% solar benefit
Rotate 45 degrees off true south to southwest or southeast	70% solar benefit
Rotate 67 1/2: degrees off true south to west-southwest or east-southeast	36% solar benefit

As you can see, the reduction in solar benefit increases exponentially as you rotate the home's orientation away from true south. Within 20 degrees or so of true south, the cost of variation in lost solar benefit is minimal, which allows some latitude in placing the house on a site that presents obstacles such as slopes and outcroppings (see Figure 9-2).

Ideally, the north side of the site will provide a windbreak, with evergreen trees and a protective hillside. These natural features will protect the home from the harsher northerly winds and weather. Deciduous trees on the east, south, and west will shade the home in summer, yet drop their leaves in winter, allowing sunlight to reach the home. Note in the drawing how the south glass would be shaded in summer, yet the ease with which sunlight will penetrate through the deciduous trees in winter.

The ideal orientation for a solar house is with its long axis perpendicular to true south (or 0° on the diagram). Because of various factors, it's sometimes necessary to shift the orientation somewhat. Within 20 degrees of true south, the cost in solar gain is minimal, but as the orientation shifts more drastically, the house will significantly lose solar benefits.

KNOW YOUR SITE

Spend some time on your proposed home site. Try camping on the site to learn about its sun conditions in different seasons. Make a point of being on the site at sunrise and sunset at different times of the year. Develop a sense for which direction the prevailing wind comes from. Use your imagination in order to picture the view from each room. Mark the footprint of your new home on the ground, and develop a "feel" for what each room will be like after the home is constructed. In addition to solar orientation, consider access, view, wind direction, snow removal, power, septic, and of course, water. Carefully investigate your water source. Sometimes it's advisable to drill the well in advance of building your home just to be sure of the cost, quantity, and quality of your water.

The long axis of a solar home should run east to west, presenting as much surface area to the sun as possible. If your new home measures 24 by 48 feet, maximize the amount of surface that the sun will strike by siting your home with the 48-foot dimension running east-west.

USE WINDOWS AND PATIO DOORS AS SOLAR COLLECTORS

If you locate the majority of the windows and patio doors on the east, south, and west elevations of the home, they can act as solar collectors. One often sees pictures of solar homes with huge expanses of south-facing glass tilted to be perpendicular to the sun rays. Let's remember that you want your home to be comfortable all year-round. Tilted glass, though technically favorable during certain heating months, is very detrimental in summer. One has to design on a 12-month basis, and understand where the sun is at each time of the year, in order to comprehend how the sun may be most beneficial to your home.

Figure 9-3 shows the sun's angles at three different times of the year—January 21, March 21, and June 21, at north latitude 40 degrees. We can see in January that the sun's low altitude almost directly strikes the south-facing vertical glass, which demonstrates again the importance of facing a home true south.

The March 21 and June 21 illustrations show that as the days grow longer, the breath of solar aperture widens, meaning that a home will gain more solar heat and light from its eastern and western windows. The altitude of solar noon rises to 50.0 degrees on March 21 and 73.5 degrees on June 21.

MAKE USE OF THE LOW SUN ANGLE IN WINTER

In Vermont at the winter solstice (December 21), the sunlight shining through a south-facing patio door will penetrate twenty-two feet into the home. On the summer solstice (June 21), the sun will only enter the building a few inches.

A dentist in New Hampshire placed a small round dental mirror flat on the sill of his south-facing patio door, and each day at noon he made a mark on the ceiling where the reflected sunlight hit. In twelve month's time, can you guess what kind of geometrical pattern was on his ceiling? An elongated figure-8. The mark closest to the south wall was made at the summer solstice, and the mark farthest from the wall was made at the winter solstice.

Let's examine south-facing glass at solar noon. If you plant a deciduous tree on the south side of your home, the sun's rays will shine through the canopy in winter when the leaves are gone. Yet in summer, the tree's canopy will absorb almost all of the sun's heat. Plant deciduous trees at a distance from the home, based on the height to which the tree is expected to grow and the size of the anticipated canopy. If deciduous trees exist on your site, cut down only those that directly obstruct the clearing needed to build the home. Thin adjacent trees' branches after you have gained experience with their shading patterns in both winter and summer.

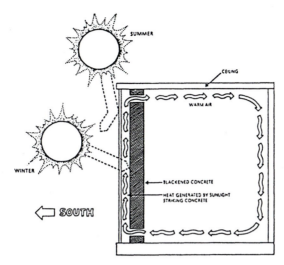

Fig. 9-1 A Trombe wall, a thermally effective but aesthetically poor design for storing and circulating sun-warmed air. At night, the process can reverse, and warm air may be drawn back out of the living space to escape through the cool glazing.

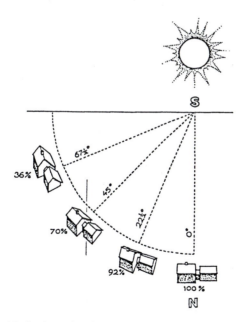

Fig. 9-2 The ideal orientation for a solar house is with its long axis perpendicular to true south (or 0° on the diagram). Because of various factors, it's sometimes necessary to shift the orientation somewhat. Within 20 degrees of true south, the cost in solar gain is minimal, but as the orientation shifts more drastically, the house will significantly lose solar benefits.

79

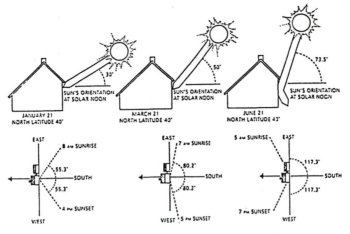

Fig. 9-3 The sun's angles at three representative times of the year.

Because of the high angle of the summer sun, its heat will bounce off vertical south-facing glass, unlike the almost direct horizontal hit your solar collectors will get in winter. This "gadget" called a solar home will "automatically" turn itself on during the coldest months and shut itself off during the summer months, so that solar collection is maximized for heat gain when you need the extra heat, and minimized when heat would be uncomfortable. As you grasp these basic dynamics, you have started to let nature work for you. Table 9-2 shows the amount of energy received by vertical south-facing glass at solar noon at 40 degrees north latitude. As you can see, the amount of energy received by vertical south-facing glass in December or January is almost triple the amount received in June.

TABLE 9-2

DATE	BTUS / SQ. FT.
September 21	200
October 21	234
November 21	250
December 21	253
January 21	254
February 21	241
March 21	206
April 21	154
May 21	113
June 21	95

What about east- and west-facing glass? We frequently hear about south-facing glass, but at the beginning and end of the heating season, as you can see from the illustration, east- and west-facing glass make good solar collectors, as well. In March, sunrise is at 7:00 AM versus 8:00 AM in January and 5:00 AM in June. Due to the angle of the sun being perpendicular to east-facing glass as the sun rises, and perpendicular to west-facing glass as the sun sets, east- and west-facing glass do not "turn off" as solar collectors in summer. We have to be more careful about the amount of east- and west-facing glass we use. We also have to consider location as more of a factor in the distribution of east- and west-facing glass. For example, a solar home located in Pennsylvania, which requires energy for summer cooling, should have less east- and west-facing glass than a home located in northern New England. Now that you understand how effectively windows and patio doors function as solar collectors, you will see why I continue to emphasize that you should use the windows and patio doors that you are already committed to purchase to not only enhance the livability of a new solar home, but also to serve as an automatic solar collection system.

STORE THE SUN'S FREE HEAT
FOR NIGHT TIME USE

The other important material we have already committed to purchase for our new home is concrete and/or concrete building blocks. To store heat we need to have *mass*, or a body of material that can hold heat. Water is the storage medium of choice in active solar systems because it holds 62.4 BTUs per cubic foot per degree Fahrenheit, making it an excellent theoretical storage medium. Concrete holds only about 30 BTUs per cubic foot per degree Fahrenheit, but has an advantage: when building a new home, we have already committed to buy tons of it. Used properly, concrete becomes another integral component in a household solar heating-and-cooling system.

I have described the way in which the Trombe wall utilizes concrete as part of a solar collection system. A solar house uses trees, hills, and the varying angles from which the sun strikes a home during the year to enhance its ability to collect sunlight and store its heat. I have emphasized the importance of facing a home south, and we've begun to think about rearranging materials that we would have purchased anyway, such as windows and concrete. Ideally, your new solar home will not cost you any extra money.

And there are other, non-monetary characteristics of a well-built solar home, including tightness of construction, absence of air leaks, and judicious venting to supply plenty of fresh air without wasting heat. Layering the walls to prevent heat loss and providing proper venting are crucial to energy-efficiency.

Let me quote from another letter from an enthusiastic solar homeowner, this one in South Harpswell, Maine:

"We find it takes a special way... dealing with life and the environment... We have come to feel great pride in our woodpile. It is not a beautiful piece of garden architecture, but you sure feel secure when you look at it. And the house has to be set exactly right to catch the sun's rays in the colder months, and our southern deciduous trees do not cast shadows to interfere with maximum solar energy. Our daily lives and routines have been altered somewhat—keeping woodboxes filled, stove work done regularly, thermal shutters closed at about 4 PM once winter sets in. You develop a whole philosophy of working with nature and you become committed to a life style in which your house is almost a family member that you care for. There's extra work for sure, but the pleasure you get is worth the extra effort, as we seem to watch the world around us as we never did before. It is important to us now to know when the sun will rise and set—and the direction and velocity of the wind—and the temperature of the air."

Chapter 10

Passive Solar:

Sunspaces and Special Design Considerations

by James Kachadorian

From THE PASSIVE SOLAR HOUSE
Chelsea Green Publishing

It is easier to understand a concept if one can point to an example and say, "Aha, that's what makes it work." Sunspaces and greenhouses satisfy conventional expectations about solar design in that they reach high daytime temperatures, and anyone can understand why. Just as a car left with its windows closed in a hot summer parking lot will become an oven, so the sunspace will build up high temperatures, which will allow a positive transfer of heat from areas that are warm to areas that are cooler, for instance from the 90-degree sunspace to the 70-degree interior of the house. Sunspaces are overglazed on purpose, and designed to overheat.

It might seem that a sunspace that is gathering enough heat to become 90 degrees Fahrenheit on a cold, 15-degree but sunny winter day would be beneficial to the home. And yes, it can be beneficial. However, the same overglazed sunspace that accumulated all that heat during the cold but sunny day will need lots of added heat when the sun goes down to prevent it from freezing, which means that the sunspace or greenhouse will tend to draw heat from the rest of the house as its flow of solar heat reverses course, back out through the glazing.

It is not uncommon for a sunspace to soar in temperature to 90-plus degrees during the day, and then "struggle" to maintain 32 degrees at night. The large nighttime loss is due, of course, to the overglazing. Even the most energy-retentive thermal-pane glass has only a fraction of the insulation capacity or R-value of unglazed wall.

In order to analyze any benefits that may come from a feature such as a sunspace, one has to calculate the daytime heat gains and factor these against nighttime losses. For the sunspace to be a net benefit, you will also need to provide for an effective means of transferring the solar heat from the sunspace into the house.

In making these sunspace heat gain and loss calculations, one must also remember that the sunspace is taking up wall space on the south facing elevation. Ideally, it will be located in front of a patio door that can be closed at night. This will isolate the sunspace thermally from the primary living space. A patio door is already an effective solar collector. Adding a sunspace in front of a south-facing patio door amounts to putting a solar collector in front of a solar collector. And yet a sunspace placed in front of a patio door will shade the living space, making the room darker than it would be without the sunspace.

TILTED GLASS—A LIABILITY

Most readers will be able to picture the typical sunspace or greenhouse design, in which south-facing glass is tilted so that the angle of winter sun is more perpendicular to the panes of glass. Tilted glass is a more effective solar collector than vertical glass. In February at 48 degrees north latitude, tilted glass will be approximately 20 to 30 percent more effective than vertical glass. However, in summer, tilted glass will continue to be more perpendicular to the sun's rays than vertical glass, and will continue to take in heat. The common problem of summertime overheating in sunspaces may be easier to explain than solve.

Because of gravity, providing window insulation for tilted glass is a more complicated problem than providing the same kind of covering for vertical glass. Special rails or attachments will be needed to hold the window insulation snugly against the sloping glass. In addition, on tilted glass nighttime condensation will drip on to window coverings, causing stains and possible degradation of the insulating material.

Through our monitoring process of a prototype home with a sunspace in Royalton, Vermont, we found that there was no discernible difference in overall thermal performance of the home with or without the added sunspace. The sunspace, however, did not take heat from the home, or was thermally neutral. That is, any daytime heat derived from the sunspace was "paid" back at night to maintain minimum temperatures.

The illustration shows a representative four-panel sunspace. Assuming that the east and west elevations of the sunspace have 40 square feet of glass per side, this sunspace has the following specifications:

East glass	40 square feet
South glass	200 square feet
West glass	40 square feet
Wall area, unglazed	330 square feet
Roof area	91 square feet
Volume	1,300 cubic feet

The net performance of a sunspace can be improved by thermally isolating it. For example, by placing the sunspace outside of a sliding glass door and closing this door at night and on sunless days, you can minimize the amount of heat that the home needs to "pay back" during times when the sunspace is not collecting solar heat. You will also need to provide supplementary heat to the interior of the sunspace to maintain minimum temperatures at night and on overcast days.

Remember that about two-thirds of the fuel needed for a solar home will be consumed in December, January, and February. As you can see from the table, a sunspace located in Burlington, Vermont, needed additional heat in those months, so it added an energy burden to the house at the time of year when energy loads and expenses are already greatest. In Hartford, Connecticut, a comparable sunspace was close to breaking even in terms of costs and benefits, even in those three months. For the sunspace to yield a significant improvement in the performance of a solar home, it has to contribute positively in those three winter months. The house really doesn't need a boost of solar heat in September, October, November, March, April, or May, since during these transitional months, the solar home probably needs no purchased energy at all, or very little purchased energy. And, as indicated above, in summer months the sunspace may be more likely to be a cooling burden than a heating benefit. A sunspace's performance can be improved if a Solar Slab is used for its base and thermal mass. A small duct fan actuated by a thermostat at 50 degrees will in most cases transfer enough heat back into the sunspace to prevent it from freezing, provided that the sunspace and the Solar Slab are properly sized and constructed.

Whenever glass is placed at an angle, the thermal stresses and temperature variations are substantially increased, and the force of gravity is effectively pulling the glazing panes or panels sideways to the direction they were designed to accommodate, making it difficult to keep seals from leaking. Only quality rooftop windows and rooftop fixed glass made for tilted use should be used. Because of the expense of commercial glazing units and ancillary products, many attempts to reduce costs have been made by do-it-yourself builders who re-use glass panels out of patio doors and set them in wooden frames to reduce costs.

Most warranties from window manufacturers are voided when glass that has been designed and manufactured to be placed vertically is placed at an angle. Glass expands at approximately the same rate as aluminum. Attempts to set tilted glass in wooden frames with wooden mull caps most likely will fail, because the glass and wood have incompatible coefficients of expansion. The glass will expand more rapidly than a wooden mull cap; the sealant used between the glass and the mull cap will crack, which will result in a water leak. In addition, in tilted glass the manufacturer's seal between the two panes of glass is also subjected to extraordinary thermal and gravitational stresses, and is likewise prone to leak. Have you ever driven by a homemade sunspace and noticed that the glass is fogged up? That is due to the failure of the factory seal between the dual panes. Commercially manufactured rooftop units are specifically designed and tested for tilted use, are warranted against water leakage and seal failure, and are made out of tempered safety glass. Glass placed at an angle should always be tempered safety glass to prevent possible injury.

IT'S NOT ALL BAD NEWS — SUNSPACES ARE FUN

Does this mean that homeowners should never add a sunspace or greenhouse? No, not at all. Sunspaces are fun to have; they provide a place to grow flowers year-round and to start spring seedlings. They provide a place to simply luxuriate in 90-degree heat when the outside temperature is in the teens on sunny winter afternoons. They provide an uplift to the spirit, when plants are bathed in sunlight and blooming in the dead of winter. And sunspaces present no special heating or cooling challenges in most regions in the relatively mild months of spring and autumn.

If you understand the possible benefits, and are willing to address the challenges, a sunspace may be "Just what the doctor ordered." But if you believe that adding a sunspace is going to pay for itself by heating your house, you may want to reconsider.

Finally, another popular use for sunspaces is as retrofits on older homes. After hearing me out all through an explanation of the costs and difficulties like the explanation above, a prospective sunspace buyer responded, "I understand completely what you have said, but my husband and I own an ancient 'Four-square' home that is hopelessly inefficient. We have no hope of ever being able to afford a new home, and all I want is to have at least one place in my home that's warm when the sun is out." Pretty hard to say no to that.

IDEAL VERSUS ACTUAL CIRCUMSTANCES

So far we have presumed the existence of ideal conditions under which to build a solar home. We have described a naturally heated and cooled home that takes full advantage of what is available to us, from the vantage point of both macro- and micro-environments.

Approach your home building project in this manner. Try to utilize all of the elements that are there to work with, in the best possible ways, and build the most environmentally sensitive home possible for a given location and set of circumstances. Try to think positively about each aspect of your site, your design, and your energy options. Remember that the sun is everywhere, and with careful planning you can build a home that harmonizes with solar energy.

But let's go over a few examples that demonstrate less than ideal situations. Suppose the garage or other structure has to be placed in such a way that it will obscure all the east-facing glass. The practical remedy is to rotate the home counter-clockwise so that the south facing glass is about 15 to 20 degrees off of true south, with the south elevation now facing south-southeast. This will allow your south-facing glass to begin to collect energy earlier in the day. Conversely, if your west-facing glass for some reason will be obstructed, you can rotate the home 15 to 20 degrees clockwise to allow the south-facing glass to collect compensatory heat from the afternoon's westerly sun.

If you live in a region where it frequently may be necessary to use air conditioning for summer cooling, you can reduce morning and afternoon solar gain by shading the east- and west-facing glass with plantings of deciduous trees, and use of thermo-Shutters or other window insulation. You can also consider reducing the amount of east and west-facing glass.

Probably the biggest "no-no" is to buy north-facing land or sites located in deep, sunless valleys or canyons. Homesites with primarily northern exposures just don't get "bathed" by the sun. One of my former clients bought a lot in Maine, with a view of the ocean, and it wasn't until the builder visited the site with a compass that the man discovered that what he had imagined was a south view of the ocean was a north view. By this time the man was too far committed not to build his retirement home on that site. Given this challenge, we selected a saltbox design, and placed an array of roof windows in the long slope of the side that is normally the unglazed north roof, which in this situation was faced south. The high side of the saltbox that normally faces south was actually facing north, giving the residents full benefit of the ocean view. The amount of glass on what was now the north elevation was drastically reduced from the design specifications, and fitted with thermo-shutters. The home performed reasonably well, though the situation was far from ideal. Our solution was the best that could be managed with existing circumstances, and truth be told, these homeowners would not have ended up better off with a conventional instead of a solar home in that same situation.

The real moral of this story is to always take a compass with you when you are looking at house sites. There really is no substitute for a site with a good southern exposure.

OTHER WAYS TO USE ENERGY WISELY

Certain kinds of commercial or manufacturing processes generate excess "Purchased" energy during the day, which if not vented outside will overheat the building. Why not store this excess purchased energy for nighttime use after the workday is over? For instance, consider the examples of an office building filled with heat producing electronic equipment such as computers, or a dormitory building that is required by code to produce surplus hot water, or a library that has lighting requirements that result in excess lamp-generated heat. Why not circulate such waste or byproduct heat to other parts of the building, and/or store excess heat? A Solar Slab allows the storage of so-called waste heat for later use. The challenge of solar design is to consider every aspect of the planned building's energy situation over the lifetime of the structure.

Sometimes energy goals requirements appear to conflict. The library, for example, needs to provide a high degree of quality lighting to meet standards; but these lights give off excess heat. By circulating the air that has been warmed with already purchased electric-light energy through the Solar Slab, heat can be stored for later use rather than vented to the outside.

Another example: The college dormitory has a high hot water requirement for showering. In order to meet the demand, a large amount of hot water capacity is needed; however, showering usually takes place for a short period of time in the morning or evening, while the rest of the time hot water is stored in water heater tanks and kept up to temperature with periodic applications of electric or fossil-fuel energy. A solution to this problem is to use water-to-air heat exchangers for space heating, utilizing the domestic hot water for more than one "enduse," thereby eliminating the need for a separate furnace. It is also entirely practical, and very cost-effective, to use solar thermal techniques for heating or at least preheating water with sunshine, which in some regions can reduce conventional water heating expenses dramatically.

Examine all available heat sources, and maximize your provisions for benefiting from the specific conditions of your site. Rearrange the materials already committed to the building project in order to efficiently collect and store heat. Whether building a solar home or an office capable of storing excess purchased energy, we should use every technique available to reduce our use of finite and expensive fuels.

SOLAR ELECTRICITY

In most parts of the U.S., the present cost of having a power company provide electricity to a remote homesite is in excess of $24,000 per mile of added powerline. A viable alternative is to live "off-the-grid," producing your own electricity with solar photovoltaic modules. Early solar electric systems used 12-volt technology developed for recreational vehicles and boats. This required major lifestyle adjustments, as all the electrical equipment in the home had to be specially designed to run on 12-volt power.

Recent advances in storage battery technology, high-tech control equipment, and highly reliable DC/AC inverters have now made the off-the-grid home a very attractive option. With the use of a properly sized inverter, direct current generated by sun-tracking solar electric modules is converted to ordinary 115-volt alternating current, allowing the use of ordinary electrical appliances.

It is now entirely practical to live comfortably off-the-grid by producing solar electricity for storage in batteries, and utilizing solar space heating, a domestic solar hot water system, propane gas for refrigeration and cooking, and backing up the whole arrangement with a propane-

or gasoline-powered generator. And with the right wind conditions and access to a year-round stream, an ideal site would even permit residents to harvest wind energy and hydroelectricity with the new micro-turbines, which are perfectly sized for household needs.

While we have concentrated in this book on the challenges and opportunities of solar home heating and cooling, hopefully the examples given here will help readers view the prospect of building energy-efficient and environmentally sensitive buildings with a greater sense of possibility and determination.

Chapter 11

Calculating Solar Energy and Power

by Matthew Buresch

From PHOTOVOLTAIC ENERGY SYSTEMS
McGraw-Hill

Solar power and solar energy can be represented in different ways: peak power, average daily power, and average daily energy. The distinction between power and energy must be fully understood. Energy is a state of matter that represents a "capacity to do work," while power indicates the rate at which an energy transaction is taking place. In other words, energy is an intangible quantity, while power is the rate at which that quantity can be, or is being, delivered or dissipated. Solar power is an instantaneous measurement of the rate at which energy is being received from the sun at any moment, while solar energy is measured over a period of time and is an accumulated capacity to do work.

Solar cells generally are rated in peak power or peak watts. The earth, however, experiences peak power for only about one hour around solar noon of each clear day. At latitudes between 0 degrees and 50 degrees, clear-day peak power on a latitude-tilted south-facing surface is about 950 watts per square meter plus or minus 15% throughout the year, with the power being on the low side in the winter and on the high side in the summer.

Instances of natural concentration can cause this figure to jump briefly to 1300 or 1400 watts per square meter when sunlight is both direct and reflected off clouds. Sunlight reflected off snow can also be significant.

Rating solar cells in peak power or peak watts can be misleading if the distinction between power and energy is not fully understood. As we continuously witness, the sun's power level rises from zero each morning and climbs to its maximum at solar noon, only to drop back to zero at sunset. Rating a solar cell in peak watts clearly puts it in its best light and is no indication of how it will perform over an entire day. A more representative solar-power rating would be the daily average power in clear weather, which is about 8/10 of one sun or 800 watts per square meter. An average power rating, nonetheless, leaves questions unanswered because the length of a day varies throughout the year. A comprehensive solar-cell rating would be the average energy output per day. Since the average daily energy varies in different parts of the country and on different days of the year, this figure would have to be qualified by referring to a particular site and time of year.

The average daily energy per unit area, the power level versus time per unit area, and the daytime temperature and precipitation are vital information needed to design a photovoltaic array. Measured insulation data automatically incorporate most of the variables involved in calculating solar energy. The length of the day, the height of the sun's path, the altitude and latitude of a site, the direct-beam and diffuse components of light, and the weather patterns are all taken into account when insolation data are measured. Determining the solar power versus time of day will indicate when and how long this solar energy is available. The daytime temperature affects the voltage and efficiency of a solar cell, and the precipitation indicates how often the cell will be covered with snow.

The major government agency responsible for collecting solar insulation data for the United States is the Department of Commerce Weather Bureau Climatological Center; for the world it is the World Meteorological Organization (WMO). Various universities and private concerns have established independent weather stations that can also be reliable sources for climatic data. The most common instruments used for measuring insolation utilize either the thermoelectric or the bimetallic expansion technique. Thermoelectricinstruments (normally called pyranometers) can be accurate within 3% to 5% if properly operated, while bimetallic instruments can at best be expected to maintain an accuracy within 10% or more. Pyranometers are widely used in the United States, Europe, and Africa, while bimetallic expansion instruments are generally used in South America and Asia.

When assessing the reliability of insolation data, three issues must be considered. First, how accurate are the insolation-measuring instruments, and have they been maintained properly? The major causes of errors in data has been improper weather-measuring operation. Second, over how long a period have the insolation data been measured? Insolation should be measured at a site for at least 10 to 20 years in order to average out aberrant weather patterns (in the United States, weather measuring began to be widespread and reliable only during the early 1950s).

Long-term changes in weather patterns resulting from astronomical considerations or human impact on the atmosphere will inevitably be overlooked by weather-measuring activities during the recent past. Third, how close is the proposed photovoltaic system site to the weather station? In most cases, a solar electric generator will be installed at a considerable distance from the nearest source of solar insolation data. In such instances, a comparison must be made of the differences in the terrain of the weather station and that of the solar installation. Differences in altitude, latitude, vegetation, and proximity to mountain ranges and bodies of water must be considered and accounted for.

AVERAGE DAILY SOLAR ENERGY

Most daily solar energy data available for the past few decades have been measured on a horizontal surface. The energy-maximizing orientation (tilt and surface azimuth angle) of a surface is not considered in these data. In the Northern Hemisphere, it is fair to assume that a surface will be facing due south (with a surface azimuth angle = 0), since this position optimizes the energy received throughout the day any place north of the Equator. The optimal tilt angle over an entire year, however, depends on the latitude of a site and therefore can vary considerably. The horizontal energy data must be adjusted to energy expected on a tilted surface; a series of equations have been developed to perform this calculation.

The conversion of average daily energy per square meter on a horizontal surface to a tilted surface depends on the declination (time of year), the latitude of a site, and the tilt angle of a south-facing sloped surface. It is also necessary to know the relative proportions of direct, diffuse, and reflected light that a tilted surface would experience. The first stage in the conversion process involves determining the ratio between tilted and horizontal radiation. The final stage is to multiply this ratio by the average daily horizontal energy to provide an accurate value for the energy on a south-facing tilted surface. Let us go through these calculations step by step.

The relative proportion of diffuse to total insolation (assuming light reflection is zero) is calculated from the clarity coefficient Kt, using the empirical formula found in Equation (3-9). The clarity coefficient is the ratio between the insolation experienced at a site and the insolation that would be experienced if the earth had no atmosphere; this coefficient is based on measured data and is given for different sites and months of the year. Since light reflection is assumed to be zero, the ratio of direct-beam to total insolation for a horizontal surface must be 1 minus the ratio of diffuse to total insolation.

The ratio of direct-beam insolation on a tilted surface to direct-beam insolation on the horizontal can be estimated (according to Lui and Jordan) by ignoring the effects of the atmosphere on sunlight and using Equation (3-8). The variables in this equation are the latitude, declination of the sun, surface tilt angle, and sunset hour angle of the horizontal and the tilted surface. The declination for any day can be found by using Equation (3-3) or by reading it off the graph in Figure 11-5. The sunset hour angles for the horizontal and for the tilted surface are computed using Equations (3-6) and (3-7). During the summer months, the sun may set on the tilted surface before it sets on the horizon (at these times the sun also would rise first on the horizon and then on the tilted surface). Consequently, Equation (3-7) requires that we take the minimum of two calculations.

The amount of light that is reflected off the ground is estimated by using a factor that ranges from 0 to 1. Common reflection coefficients for different materials are listed in Table 11-1. By visually comparing the reflections off different materials and using the list in Table 11-1, a reasonably accurate reflection coefficient can be assumed.

TABLE 11-1

Snow	= 0.7 - 0.87
Concrete	= 0.31 - 0.33
Tar and gravel roofs	= 0.12 - 0.15
Asphalt paved roads	= 0.10 - 0.12

The ratio of average daily energy on the tilted surface to that on the horizontal surface is calculated using Equation (3-10). Notice how the equation is the sum of three different factors that indicate the relative proportions of direct-beam, diffuse, and reflected light. Multiplying the daily horizontal energy for the location and month under consideration by the ratio computed above will provide us with the information we are looking for: average daily energy per square meter on a tilted surface for a specific site and time. Figure 11-1 a to c summarize the solar energy available on a south-facing tilted surface at various locations in the United States.

(a)

(b)

Figure 11-1 (a) Average daily availability of total solar radiation on a south-facing 45°
tilted surface for the United States in the fall, in kWh/m^2. (b) Average daily availability
of total solar radiation on a south-facing 45° tilted surface for the United Sates in the
winter, in kWh/m^2.

(c) Average daily availability of total solar radiation on a south-facing 45° tilted surface for the United Sates in the spring, in kWh/m². (d) Average daily availability of total solar radiation on a south-facing 45° tilted surface for the United Sates in the summer, in kWh/m².

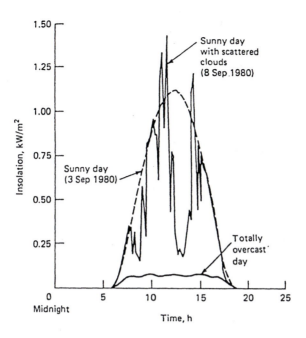

Figure 11-2 Clear-day solar power on a horizontal surface versus time of day for three different days of the year. (M.I.T. Lincoln Labratory, Concord, Mass., weather station.)

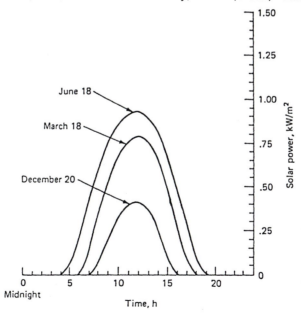

Figure 11-3 Solar power on a latitude-tilted south-facing surface versus time of day for partly cloudy weather with natural sunlight concentration resulting from light being reflected off clouds. (M.I.T. Lincoln Laboratory, Natural Bridges National Monument, Utah, weather station.)

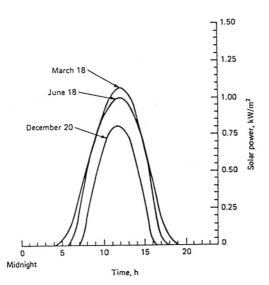

Figure 11-4 Clear-day solar power on a latitude-tilted south-facing surface versus time of day for three different days of the year (M.I.T. Lincoln Laboratory, Concord, Mass., weather station.)

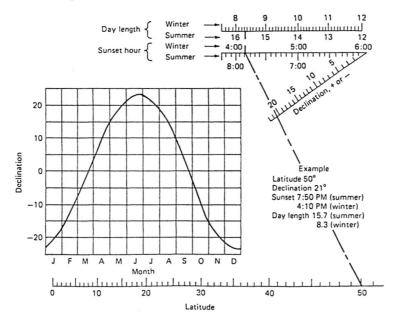

Figure 11-5 Whillier's nomogram for determining the length of day and time of sunset. (Adapted from: John A. Duffie and William A. Beckman, *Solar Engineering of Thermal Processes,* John Wiley & Sons, New York, 1980, p. 14; originally from Whillier, *Solar Energy* 9, Pergamon Press, Elmsford, N.Y., 1965, p. 164).

$$\delta = 23.45 \sin\left(360\,\frac{284 + n}{365}\right) \qquad (3\text{-}3)$$

$$\omega_s = \cos^{-1}(-\tan\phi\tan\delta) \qquad (3\text{-}6)$$

$$\omega_s' = \min\left[\begin{array}{l}\cos^{-1}(-\tan\phi\tan\delta), \\ \cos^{-1}(-\tan(\phi - \beta)\tan\delta)\end{array}\right] \qquad (3\text{-}7)$$

$$\overline{R}_b = \frac{\cos(\phi - \beta)\cos\delta\sin\omega_s' + (\pi/180)\omega'\sin(\phi - \beta)\sin\delta}{\cos\phi\cos\delta\sin\omega_s + (\pi/180)\omega_s\sin\phi\sin\delta} \qquad (3\text{-}8)$$

$$\frac{\overline{H}_D}{\overline{H}} = 1.390 - 4.027\overline{K}_T + 5.531\overline{K}_T^2 - 3.108\overline{K}_T^3 \qquad (3\text{-}9)$$

$$\overline{R} = \frac{\overline{H}_T}{\overline{H}} = \left(1 - \frac{\overline{H}_d}{\overline{H}}\right)\overline{R}_b + \frac{\overline{H}_d}{\overline{H}}\left(\frac{1 + \cos\beta}{2}\right) + \rho\left(\frac{1 - \cos\beta}{2}\right) \qquad (3\text{-}10)$$

where δ = the sun's declination angle ($-23.45°$ to $+23.45°$)

n = day of year (1 to 365)

ω_s = sunset hour angle on a horizontal surface

ω_s' = sunset hour angle on a tilted surface

ϕ = the site's latitude angle (0° to 90°) in the Northern Hemisphere

β = tilt or slope angle of a south-facing surface (0 to 180°; $\beta > 90$ means that the surface is facing downward)

$\overline{R}_b$ = ratio of monthly average daily direct-beam radiation on a tilted south-facing surface to that on a horizontal surface

$\overline{H}_d$ = monthly average daily diffuse radiation on a horizontal surface

$\overline{H}$ = monthly average daily total radiation on a horizontal surface

$\overline{K}_t$ = clarity coefficient: the ratio of insolation on the earth to insolation directly outside the earth's atmosphere

$\overline{R}$ = ratio of monthly average daily total radiation on a tilted south-facing surface to that on a horizontal surface

$\overline{H}_T$ = monthly average daily total radiation on a tilted south-facing surface

ρ = reflection coefficient: the fraction of light reflected by a surface (0 to 1)

DAILY SOLAR POWER

Solar power received on earth varies throughout the day as a result of changes in the incident angle of sunlight on a surface, the amount of obstructing atmosphere sunlight must pierce, and the length of a day. A typical plot of solar power versus time on a clear day is shaped like a half sine wave with its crest at solar noon, as shown in Figure 11-2. On a partly cloudy day, the solar power level jumps up and down as the sun passes in and out behind clouds, so that the power/time-of-day plot becomes erratic, as shown in Figure 11-3. Notice in Figure 11-3 how solar power momentarily can rise above the normal clear-day power level during instances of natural concentration when indirect light is received from reflection off clouds.

The curve of solar power versus time of day varies for different days of the year. The number of sunlight hours and the clear-day peak power on a horizontal surface both reach their maximum on the summer solstice (June 21st) and drop to their minimum on the winter solstice (December 21st), as shown in Figure 11-2. The clear-day peak power on a latitude-tilted, south-facing surface reaches its maximum on the equinoxes (March 21st and September 21st), as portrayed in Figure 11-4, because the sun's rays are most perpendicular to the tilted surface at that time of year.

A solar power/time-of-day curve can be estimated from three pieces of information: the sunrise time, the sunset time, and the peak power at solar noon. An approximate plot of solar power versus time of day will be useful when designing a photovoltaic array to satisfy a load demand.

Knowing the time of sunset and the length of day for a particular site requires knowing the site's latitude and the sun's declination. The nomogram in Figure 11-5, devised by Whillier, is a useful and simple tool for determining a day's length and sunset time, and is valid for sites in both the Northern and Southern Hemispheres. To use this chart, note the latitude and declination points for the place and time in question as they are found on their respective axes of the nomogram, then draw a line through these two points until the line touches the sunset hour axis.

The sunset time and length of day are read off the two charted lines as shown in the example. The sunrise time simply equals the sunset time minus the length of day. The length of day and time of sunrise and sunset can also be found in most newspapers and almanacs.

The average clear-day peak solar power at sea level on a south-facing surface tilted within 10" of the latitude angle is about 950 W/m^2 for latitudes between 0' and 50'. The sun's higher and lower path in the sky during different months and seasons of the year causes this value to fluctuate somewhat. Changes in altitude above sea level result in an increase in average clear-day peak power of about 20 W/m^2 per 1000 ft, or about 300 meters, of elevation, because at higher altitudes there is less atmosphere intercepting the sun's rays. Therefore, at an altitude of 5000 ft., or 150° m, the average clear-day peak power will be about 1050 W/m^2.

The sky is not always clear, for the sun's direct-beam rays often are blocked by clouds. When the sky is cloudy, the amount of sunlight that is readily convertible into electricity by a photovoltaic cell is substantially reduced, by at least 50% during thin cirrus cloud cover and by about 75% or more during denser cumulus cloud cover. The total sunlight hours divided by the total possible sunshine time is called the percentage of possible sunshine. This percentage, measured for different parts of the United States and different times of year, is given in Table 11-2. Multiplying the clear-day peak power for a particular time of year by the percentage of possible sunshine for that month will yield an approximate average peak power for the month that will be sufficiently accurate for our purposes. This estimate will overlook the effects of airborne dust, pollution, or humidity; if any of these conditions becomes excessive, it must be measured and adequately accounted for.

We have three data points on a solar-power/time-of-day curve that can be plotted on a graph. At sunrise and sunset the solar power is zero, while at solar noon the solar power is at its peak, as estimated using the technique outlined above. If these three data points are plotted on a suitably scaled graph, they can be interconnected by drawing a curve that approximates the shape of the clear-day power curves shown in Figure 11-2. Our plot is only a monthly average and does not trace the sudden changes in power level that occur on partly cloudy days. This technique assumes that cloud cover is spread out fairly uniformly throughout the day, which often is not the case.

Table 11-2 Average Percentage of Possible Sunshine: Selected Cities.

State and station		Length of record, years	Jan	Feb	Mar	Apr	May	June	July	Aug	Sept	Oct	Nov	Dec	Annual
AL	Montgomery	25	47	53	58	64	66	65	63	65	63	66	57	50	59
AK	Juneau	30	33	32	37	38	38	34	30	30	25	19	23	20	31
AZ	Phoenix	80	78	80	83	89	93	94	85	85	89	88	83	77	86
AR	Little Rock	32	46	54	57	61	68	73	71	73	68	69	56	48	63
CA	Los Angeles	32	69	72	73	70	66	65	82	83	79	73	74	71	73
	Sacramento	27	45	61	70	80	86	92	97	96	94	84	64	46	79
	San Francisco	38	56	62	69	73	72	73	66	65	72	70	62	53	67
CO	Denver	26	72	71	69	66	64	70	70	72	75	73	65	68	70
CN	Hartford	21	58	57	56	57	58	58	61	63	59	58	46	48	57
DE	Wilmington†	25	50	54	57	57	59	64	63	61	60	60	54	51	53
DC	Washington	27	48	51	55	56	58	64	62	62	62	60	53	47	57
FL	Jacksonville	25	57	61	66	71	69	61	59	58	53	56	61	56	61
	Key West	17	72	76	81	84	80	71	75	76	69	68	72	74	75
GA	Atlanta	41	47	52	57	65	69	67	61	65	63	67	60	50	61
HI	Honolulu	23	63	65	69	67	70	71	74	75	75	67	60	59	68
ID	Boise	35	41	52	63	68	71	75	89	85	82	67	45	39	67
IL	Chicago	33	44	47	51	53	61	67	70	68	63	62	41	38	57
	Peoria	32	45	50	52	55	59	66	68	67	64	63	44	39	57
IN	Indianapolis	32	41	51	51	55	61	68	70	71	66	64	42	39	58
IO	Des Moines	25	51	54	54	55	60	67	71	70	64	64	49	45	59
KS	Wichita	22	59	59	60	62	64	69	74	73	65	66	59	56	65
KY	Louisville	28	41	47	50	55	62	67	66	68	65	63	47	39	57
LA	Shreveport	23	49	54	56	55	64	71	74	72	68	71	62	53	64
ME	Portland	35	55	59	56	56	56	60	64	65	61	58	47	53	58
MD	Baltimore	25	51	55	55	55	57	62	65	62	60	59	51	48	57

Table 11-2 Continued

State and station		Length of record, years	Jan	Feb	Mar	Apr	May	June	July	Aug	Sept	Oct	Nov	Dec	Annual
MA	Boston	40	54	56	57	56	58	63	66	67	63	61	51	52	59
MI	Detroit	32	32	43	49	52	59	65	70	65	61	56	35	32	54
	Sault St. Marie	34	34	46	55	55	56	57	63	58	46	41	23	28	48
MN	Duluth	25	49	54	56	54	55	58	67	61	52	48	34	39	54
	Minneapolis-St. Paul	37	51	57	54	55	58	63	70	67	61	57	39	40	58
MS	Jackson	11	48	55	61	60	63	67	61	62	58	65	54	45	59
MO	Kansas City	3	64	54	61	65	67	72	84	69	51	62	46	54	64
	St. Louis	16	52	51	54	56	62	69	71	66	63	62	49	41	58
MT	Great Falls	33	49	57	67	62	64	65	81	78	68	61	46	46	64
NE	Omaha	40	55	55	55	59	62	68	76	72	67	67	52	48	62
NV	Reno	33	66	68	74	80	81	85	92	93	92	83	70	63	80
NH	Concord	34	52	54	52	53	54	57	62	60	54	54	42	47	54
NJ	Atlantic City	15	49	48	51	53	54	58	60	62	59	57	50	42	54
NM	Albuquerque	36	73	73	74	77	80	83	76	76	80	79	78	72	77
NY	Albany	37	46	51	52	53	55	59	64	61	56	53	36	38	53
	Buffalo	32	34	40	46	52	58	66	69	66	60	53	29	27	53
	New York‡	99	50	55	56	59	61	64	65	64	63	61	52	49	59
NC	Charlotte	25	55	59	63	70	69	71	68	70	68	69	63	58	66
	Raleigh	21	55	58	63	64	60	61	61	61	60	63	63	56	60
ND	Bismarck	36	54	56	60	58	63	64	76	73	65	59	44	47	62
OH	Cincinnati	60	41	45	51	55	61	67	68	67	66	59	44	38	57
	Cleveland	34	32	37	44	53	59	65	68	64	60	55	31	26	52
	Columbus	24	37	41	44	52	58	62	64	63	62	58	38	30	53

State	City														
OK	Oklahoma City	23	59	61	63	63	65	73	75	77	69	68	60	59	67
OR	Portland	26	24	35	42	48	54	51	69	64	60	40	27	20	47
PA	Philadelphia	33	50	53	56	56	57	63	63	63	60	60	53	49	58
	Pittsburgh	23	36	38	45	48	53	60	62	60	60	56	40	30	50
RI	Providence	22	57	56	55	55	57	57	59	59	58	60	49	51	56
SC	Columbia	22	56	59	64	67	66	65	64	65	65	66	64	60	63
SD	Rapid City	33	54	59	61	59	57	60	71	73	67	65	56	54	62
TN	Memphis	25	48	54	57	63	69	73	72	75	69	71	58	49	64
	Nashville	33	40	47	52	59	62	67	64	66	63	64	50	40	57
TX	Amarillo	34	69	68	71	73	73	77	77	78	74	75	73	67	73
	El Paso	33	78	82	85	87	89	89	79	80	82	84	83	78	83
	Houston	6	41	54	48	51	57	63	68	61	57	61	58	69	56
UT	Salt Lake City	38	47	55	64	66	73	78	84	83	84	73	54	44	70
VT	Burlington	32	42	48	52	50	56	60	65	62	55	50	30	33	51
VA	Norfolk	19	57	58	63	66	67	68	65	65	64	60	60	57	63
	Richmond	25	51	54	59	62	64	67	65	64	63	59	56	51	60
WA	Seattle-Tacoma	10	21	42	49	51	58	54	67	65	61	42	27	17	49
	Spokane	27	26	41	53	60	63	65	81	78	71	51	28	20	57
WV	Parkersburg	78	32	36	43	49	56	59	62	60	59	54	37	29	48
WI	Milwaukee	35	44	47	51	54	59	63	70	67	60	57	41	38	56
WY	Cheyenne	40	61	65	64	61	59	65	68	68	69	68	60	59	64
PR	San Juan	20	65	69	74	69	61	57	64	65	59	59	57	56	63

Source: U.S. National Oceanic and Atmospheric Administration; reproduced in *Solar Energy Handbook: Theory and Application* by Power Systems Group, Ametek, Inc., published by Chilton Book Co., 1979, p. 46.

*Average data, except as noted, for period of record through 1975.

†Data not available; figures are for a nearby station.

‡City office data.

104

Chapter 12

Building the Home Energy Machine

by Michael Potts

From THE INDEPENDENT HOME
Living Well with Power from the Sun, Wind, and Water

Chelsea Green Publishing Company

While seeking to build from the outside in, with full awareness of the particularities of region, neighborhood, and site, we should also undertake the planning required to build from the inside out. What functions, precisely, do we require of our home? Each of us will answer differently, and a family's answers will inevitably change as the individuals change, as the children leave, as the builders age. Anyone who builds an innovative, appropriate shelter hopes to be free from preconception but perspicacious about small yet important elements. If we intend to leave behind so much of conventional architecture and still build a successful home, we must carry with us only truly essential luggage. Happiness is a good measure for necessity. For example, it does not make us particularly happy to know that we are expensively hoarding eighty gallons of hot water in our domestic hot water tank.

And what is the widest temperature range within which we can live healthily and happily? The answer to this crucial question, factored together with the meteorological realities of our chosen site, determines for most of us the largest expense in our energy budget: the cost of heating and cooling our space. We must identify and answer these and many other energy questions completely and flexibly before building starts to build a successful independent home.

In the past, houses have been planned by assuming indefinite continuation of present circumstances. Selection of heating and lighting strategies, for example, has invariably been based on current costs. Scarcities and pollution have proved that we must anticipate steeply rising energy costs. We have also seen that we should plan for cost-effectiveness based on original equipment cost *plus* the equipment's energy consumption over its whole life. Consider glass, which easily outlasts most houses; will high-tech glass, undeniably more expensive than single-pane glass but much more efficient, pay for itself over a span of time that will probably be longer than our own lifetimes? If so, then the better glass is the correct choice even if we shall not be around at payback time.

The primary energy consumers in a conventional house are space heating and cooling, refrigeration, hot water, and lighting. By conscientiously examining our largest energy uses, we will find ways to lighten our load and simplify our lives. Some of these ways of lightening the load should be taken into consideration before a final decision is made about the site, while other solutions must be found and incorporated into our house plans as we begin the process of building.

Naturally, a home's energy budget depends on region. In a tropical climate like Hawaii's, a well-designed home on a benign site will require neither heating nor cooling. In northern Alaska, even the best sited and best constructed home will carry a heavy burden in wintertime lighting and heating. Even if energy costs are tolerable at present, there are powerful reasons to seek to reduce energy consumption from the outset by eliminating loads or seeking alternative sources. This logic should be applied to each instance of energy use.

PAYING THE PRICE FOR CLIMATE CONTROL

Formal architecture might manage to create interior space that is visually connected with the outdoors yet completely isolated and regulated atmospherically. As soon as architects got the technology they needed to defy a site's natural climate, they defined a narrow comfort envelope within which, it was decreed, the human organism functions optimally: temperature between 68 and 72 degrees Fahrenheit (20 and 23 degrees Celsius), with between 60 and 70 percent relative humidity. Elaborate devices, strategic materials, and awesome energy are poured into achieving this goal.

Although other cultures abide by temperature extremes quite gracefully, one might almost expect this revision to be offered for inclusion in our U.S. Bill of Rights: "the right to life, liberty, comfortable interior space within a narrow range of parameters, and happiness of pursuit." Curious climatic abuses result from this fetish of ours—I have been too hot in Boston's winter, and too cold in Fort Worth's summer—as do a variety of ills, from Legionnaires' Disease to Sick Building Syndrome, which result from our precipitous willingness to defeat the environment with biologically disruptive technologies. Like willful children, as soon as we found a way to defy nature, we did so, without ever contemplating the repercussions. When the Arabian wake-up call came in 1973, and energy awareness gradually took hold as a result of the oil embargo, the supposedly sacrosanct comfort ranges were redefined, and a be-cardiganed President begged us to comply.

Our reliance on brute force, high-tech heating, ventilation, and air conditioning (HVAC) solutions is largely the result of our abandonment of the homestead for many hours of every working day. When we stay at home, it is easy to open and close windows, feed the fire, and otherwise regulate our home, but on most days, when we return home exhausted from a hard day's work, we expect to be greeted by a welcoming, comfortable, well-regulated environment. There is a sharp irony to the fact that many of us must leave our homes to earn enough to support the machines that keep our homes habitable in our absence. Who, precisely, are we working for? The energy we buy in order to work—fuel for the commute, and the cost of maintaining a comfortable home space even when no one is home—is a hidden tax on our productivity which many independent homesteaders refuse to pay.

Some of my heroes, vigorous old ones who create beauty even as they age beyond my youthful imagining, showed me as I planned my house that a life connected with nature's grittiness is longer and more vivid than one lived within the comfort envelope. Now, a decade or two later, I willingly take part in the spirit of the season by wearing several layers, or as little as possible, as the climate requires, in preference to expensively denying the elements. As already noted, my cat's fur adapts to the season whether the house is within the envelope or not; in matters like this, my cat is seldom wrong. To put it quite simply, I enjoy, as an independent power producer, living in space that buffers me within rather than isolating me from the weather, and invites me to participate in the seasonal responses of my local ecosystem.

Even before widening our tolerance for temperature extremes, we may find that sensible design will enclose space that regulates itself quite readily. Two key factors apply: incident solar radiation (which yields a coined word, *insolation*) and thermal mass. Using glass, we can invite sunlight in to heat our space to a livable temperature. Sufficient thermal mass (material that holds heat well, like masonry, earth, or water) within our space will attain a comfortable temperature, then act as a buffer, radiating heat or coolness to keep the space comfortable. Such self-regulation, with no ongoing expense, is a grand solution, but attaining it is not at all simple. Too much glass, and the temperature varies wildly no matter how much mass is enclosed; too much mass, and the temperature never becomes comfortable. The ideal glass-to-mass ratio is delicate, site- and design-specific, and therefore hard to plan for, but instead must be found through experimentation. In a breakthrough house, one unlike any house built before, this can be complicated, because glass and mass are often costly to include and difficult to adjust. Most architects find it easier to avoid the issue altogether by employing powerful HVAC units. One possible solution is to start with a small, conceptual space, and tune it until the principles are grasped, then enlarge along the same proportions. This is unworkable for architects, who wish to present completed totality, but fits the alternative builder's gradualist mode exactly. Another tactic is to provide a means to isolate exterior glass and mass from the rest of the house, as Wes and Linda have done by interposing operable windows, so that the active thermal components may be opened to the house when they are working, and closed when they are not.

Wood and glass houses, though quickest to build, have almost no thermal mass and are therefore at the mercy of ambient outside temperatures. Concrete, rock, masonry, tile, earth, water, and other dense materials provide thermal mass. If placed where they intercept the sun and are directly heated, the arrangement is said to have *direct gain*. Gain can be improved by making the mass a dark color, so it absorbs the incident sunlight maximally. Where sunlight strikes materials such as wood, cork or vinyl tile, cloth, or other less dense materials that hold heat poorly, and the heat is given up to the air which then heats available thermal mass by convection, the process is less efficient, and is termed *indirect gain*. Floor plans where the southern quarter is dedicated to direct gain thermal mass are most successful; this quarter is the right place for a greenhouse.

POUNDING TIRES:
KEN ANDERSON'S STORY

Ken Anderson is an architect who works for Michael Reynolds. He is building his own earthship at Star, one of two earthship communities near Taos, in northern New Mexico. His enthusiasm and delight in this approach to home-building kept us both smiling as he talked.

I came out here from New Jersey, Philadelphia, and New Haven, and there's a good chance I'll stay here until I die. My goal, when I graduated, was to get as far away, philosophically and geographically, as I could. I had no idea how to build the buildings I was drawing.

When I got here, Mike Reynolds put me to work on an earthship, and I stayed with it from scratch, a year and a half, from the first hellish tires. I really learned architecture on that job.

I learned everything I know about building that way, and right now, I can't say I remember much I learned at Yale. A love for architecture, I suppose, and an open mind about design.

Now I've learned to draw buildings the way I'd build them: first the hole, then the tires, the greenhouse, the plaster fill. When you're involved in building, you understand the whole system. It's unlike basements, which nobody understands; we know they're down there, and have things in them, but they're pretty mysterious, really.

The idea of the first *Earthship* book was to make it possible to build an earthship by yourself. Some of the best earthships are owner-built from the first book. "Who needs to draw it? Let's just go out and build it." That worked for some, but in general we learned from people out there that there was too much bureaucracy, so we made a set of generic plans that give the inspectors, building departments, and engineers everything they need to see that we've thought this idea through. For fifteen hundred dollars you get the generic plan set and enough consulting time to get started; you build the generic structure, and get signed off, then make custom modifications with your finishes. We believe the generic earthship is a very sound and satisfactory home.

There are well over a hundred tire houses scattered around: New Mexico, of course, and Arizona, California, Oregon, Oklahoma, Washington, Colorado, Kentucky, Tennessee, Arkansas. The oldest ones are eighteen or twenty years old, and still look great. Mike is always improving things, seeking new solutions to problems that come up—you saw the hay-bale temporary house? We've completely cleaned Taos of tires, so last year we had a tractor trailer load brought in from Colorado.

Every earthship we've worked on has a building permit. We have made a conscious effort to establish the viability of this building method, and to work with building departments so they would know what we were trying to do.

It takes five or six hundred tires to make a small house; if you start with the house excavated from a hill, you can cut down on the number of tires. There are about three wheelbarrows of earth in each tire, and it takes two people about fifteen minutes to pound a tire. Maybe you can do thirty tires a day, and at the end of a few days, you see the house forming up, and you get a second wind. As the tires fill with tamped earth, they swell and interlock with the row below, so the walls are very strong. The walls are usually U-shaped (and we call each bay a "U") which also adds strength. We usually alternate a full U, sixteen feet wide and eighteen feet deep, used for living space, with a mechanical U, which is shallower and usually houses battery and electrical systems, water pumping, filtering, and other utilities. The simplest earthship is a full U and a mechanical U.

Along the top of a tire wall, you put in a cement and steel or a wood bond-beam, to hold the wall together, and for attaching the roof. The sloping front wall involves some pretty special construction techniques, and the glass isn't cheap, so generally you need a good carpenter to do that part.

The traditional way of adobe roof building, using vegas and latillas, works very well, but we're working with trusses, too, which use much less wood. You can buy vegas at the lumberyard for three or three-and-a half dollars a lineal foot, which is expensive, or harvest them in the national forest, mostly standing dead, with a vega permit which costs about three dollars for each vega, then strip them, which is labor intensive. We use some fairly high-tech sealants, six-mil plastic sheeting to seal over the tires and berm, and then a modified bitumen roof coated with acrylic over the Styrofoam roof insulation.

I have chosen my building plot at Star, and I've been stockpiling tires and cans in a storage bin. The groundbreaking is this weekend! I expect to get the shell walls and roof put up this summer, so the 'ship can start charging up its walls. The tires are like batteries, and they take up to a year to get charged with heat. By winter, it will stay a constant sixty-five to seventy. Next summer, we'll finish the interior and install the electric and water systems, and it will be ready to inhabit.

Mike's idea about the earthship is that it should be self-sufficient. Electricity comes from eight 51-watt modules on the roof and ten golf cart batteries. The electrical center makes the unusual connections, and gives the electrician a standard breaker box that he knows how to work with. We do the same thing with the water system; we want to give the tradesmen systems they understand, with standard fittings and connections for them to tie into. All the lights are 12-Volt DC, compact fluorescent, and all plugs and appliances are 110-volt AC. Water comes from the roof, and is kept in a catchment inside the 'ship. We figure that you can live with eight inches a year of rain if you recycle the gray water into the indoor planters and use a solar or composting toilet. The water system consists of a simple system of filters and a pump, and runs off the electrical system. These two systems cost between sixty-five hundred and eight thousand dollars, depending on what you need, although we've done much more complicated systems.

Star is about forty-five minutes from Taos by four-wheel-drive (although it will take less time once Star is more fully inhabited and the roads are improved). It's near the Rio Grande gorge, and the views are great. You buy the land under your house and membership in Star for two to ten dollars a square foot, depending on whether you choose the high-density or low-density area. High-density means a minimum of fifty feet between houses, and low- means four hundred feet. I really haven't decided which I like better, but the land will be affordable either way. The expensive parts, not counting the labor (and about 85 percent of earthships are owner-built) are backhoe excavation, tire and can procurement, metal lathing, and the glass, cement, and lumber in the bond-beams, roof, and glass wall. My earthship itself won't cost thirty dollars a square foot, so for under fifty thousand, and two years of work, I'll have a nice home that completely takes care of me. Within a few years, we will establish an architecture office at Star. I'll probably cut down to working three or four days a week, providing architectural services and construction management to my future neighbors.

SIMPLE, PASSIVE, AND MASSIVE

In a thermal-mass heated home, it may take a year or two for interior temperatures to "pop" or come to equilibrium, and even then, a certain amount of heating or cooling may be required to deal with seasonal excesses. In northern New Mexico, where adobe houses are the regional norm and where the earthship was invented, adequate ventilation must be provided or interior temperatures will exceed the outside where breezes blow. In winter, a small amount of heat will be required, or the dwelling's temperature will drop into the high 50s during stormy periods when it goes down to -10 degrees outside. In the same area, wood-frame houses without heating and cooling are intolerable most of the year.

Massive stone or brick fireplaces, concrete and masonry furnaces, and other self-heating structures can also provide thermal mass. If the combustion techniques used to heat such a mass are clean and rationally fueled, they work exceedingly well. The Siberian stove, for example, need only be fired once a day even in a harsh climate; its recirculation of exhaust and its high-temperature firebox assures that the smoke that finally escapes has been thoroughly cleaned of noxious combustibles, and the substantial pile, once heated, continues to radiate heat for hours. High-tech schemes for using electricity to actively circulate warm air through rock bins and dimorphic salts play well in popularized science magazines and attract the attention of government boondogglers, but have proved to be too complicated to work well. In space heating and cooling, simple, passive, and massive are best.

Heat rises, and in the absence of active circulation the top eighteen inches of a heated room may have a temperature ten degrees above the eighteen inches just over the floor. Air currents set up when people move about help mix this precious warm air only if the distance above their heads is limited. All this argues in favor of low ceilings. We have been conditioned to believe that anything less than a foot above our heads feels very close (although I have been in experimental homes with very low ceilings and found myself adapting quickly). But how many of us are taller than six-and-a-half feet? Eight-foot ceilings, we are told, feel dignified, and are convenient to build because paneling usually comes eight feet tall, but eight-foot ceilings have nothing other than custom to recommend them. Building codes generally permit ceilings as low as seven feet six inches.

Considering that approximately 10 percent of our heating budget goes into heating an additional six inches, I hope we can agree that seven feet six inches is ample.

While on the subject of heating, firewood management is a worth a bit of attention. When home systems are planned starting with the energy to be used, we will be able to think about ways to make heated air circulate naturally through the home. But we must also plan how firewood gets from bulk storage to the wood stove. We try, in Caspar, to get in a week's supply before a storm breaks; special firewood doors make this an easy operation.

DOORS INDOORS?

Doors inside a small house make sense only when we wish to heat a single room. Doors represent a compromise between conflicting needs: we won't be able to move from room to room, to foster or prevent air exchange, and to interpose a temporary wall across an opening, for privacy. Doors should therefore be light, which means small. Conventional hinged doors always waste the floor space and wall space within and behind their arc, and closed, they interfere with air circulation. Archways work better in almost every way. Privacy can be created by juxtaposing walls, screens, and archways so that rooms have the sense of privacy desired. As with any radical idea, it is best to prepare well in advance for an easy retreat; use standard doorway sizing and framing practices if you have any doubts about adopting my suggestion of eschewing doors.

Thermal mass heating, and any other strategy that relies upon separating indoor and outdoor temperatures, calls for insulation measures in direct proportion to the difference between outdoor seasonal ambiance and the indoor ideal. Considered over the life of a house, it is easy to conclude that the thickest insulation, the highest R-value, the best glass, the most thorough reduction of infiltration, is cost-effective from the vantage point of energy savings. Good siting, excellent design, and superb insulation should make it possible to build a passively heated house in almost every habitable climate. In other words, most energy expended on space heating and cooling is a direct result of bad planning, negligent design, and sloppy insulation. Now, as the energy buzzards come home to roost, we pay the price.

Changing technology may offer a chance to improve on earlier solutions, and new houses will be built to accommodate such changes. Low-emissivity, high-tech glass was not available in California when I put windows in my house, nor was it in my budget based on short-sighted, pre-1973 energy cost-benefit calculations. I was wrong. Two decades later, the cost-effectiveness curves have crossed: energy costs are stubbornly climbing, and the cost of high-tech glass is lower than ever due to its enthusiastic acceptance by the building fraternity. Replacing single pane glass with low-emissivity windows will probably eliminate my need for a wood stove on all but the coldest winter nights.

The standard way to measure the heating and cooling requirements of a house are *degree-days*, the difference in degrees between maximum (for cooling) or minimum (for heating) temperatures and the comfort baselines, totaled over the average year. Taking 80 degrees as the high comfort baseline, for example, if the outside temperature climbs to 100 on a given day, the house requires cooling capacity of twenty degree-days. If this condition persists over a one-hundred-day cooling season, the house will require sufficient cooling for two thousand degree-days a year.

Good insulation and adequate thermal mass should be able to buffer, in all but the most unforgiving climates, nearly all of our heating and cooling needs. Problems result where ambient temperatures remain far above or below the comfort baseline, day and night, for long periods. In the desert example given above, where daytime temperatures climb to 100 degrees, everything depends on nighttime; if outside temperatures drop to 70, then thermal mass maybe recharged by opening windows, and during the daytime, insulation (including shaded, southern glass areas) and thermal mass should keep the house comfortable. If nighttime temperatures remain high, usually due to lack of wind currents and large thermal masses in the environment, we grudgingly grant that a problem exists, which may justify expending energy.

In high degree-day cooling locations, intelligent use of overhangs and seasonal shading are crucial, as is sensitive siting, to take advantage of any shade and to capture any breeze. Indigenous structures built in such unforgiving sites offer a number of ingenious passive measures for surviving the withering heat. Often, not far below the blistering surface, the earth maintains a constant and relatively low temperature, so underground houses work well. Cooling towers, which use convection to circulate cool air from underground or from protected sources or which provide evaporative cooling, and wind scoops positioned to catch cooler breezes a dozen feet above the ground, cost nothing to operate after they are constructed. All else failing, the sun itself may be converted, using photovoltaic panels, into energy to run cooling equipment. The worst solution of all (yet the most applied) is to build a poorly conceived and uninsulated house, and then importing at great expense to occupant and planet the electricity required to run a powerful air conditioner.

Insulation and proper siting are also the best—and practically the only—passive remedies in high degree-day heating locations. In Arctic, mountainous, and far northern lands the sun is too feeble, and too often obscured, to offer much opportunity for collecting the sun's heat. The earth may be deeply frozen and therefore not much use in providing protective buffering. Streams may also be frozen solid, and the only possible source of excess energy may be the wind. The indigenous response is to use the snow itself as an insulator, to dress warmly, and to hope for spring.

In less extreme cold locations, like the Colorado Rockies, where degree-day heating requirements are nevertheless high, the solar/thermal-mass solution often works well because the sun still shines brightly, despite lingering cold from wind and snow. Running water offers hydroelectric potential, which is the only alternative energy source that can be reliably and economically devoted to supplying electricity for heat. And in most such places, forests are abundantly regenerative, and can be counted on to provide a fair quantity of winter fuel from a reasonably modest area of woodland.

Our preference for homes surrounded by sufficient land takes us back to the time before the dependent home, when it was the job of the sun, the woodlot, and the prevailing breezes to condition interior space. Heating and cooling are examples of tasks not well suited to electricity (unless we have a surplus). Before electricity, humans found it difficult to preserve a high quality of life in an urban settlement of a quarter-million people or more, primarily because that many people consuming energy in close quarters were dirty and dangerous. Now that electricity allows us to do the dirty work elsewhere and deliver energy in an apparently clean and extremely concentrated way, our cities are able to support enormous masses of denatured humanity.

BUILDING IN HARMONY WITH SOURCES

By taking our energy needs into account very early in the planning stages of a new, independent house, it should be possible to integrate a variety of sources and vastly improve our homestead's performance.

The solar energy which falls on a south-facing roof can be either a curse (as an undesirable heat source for the space within) or a blessing (as a source of electricity and hot water). We know that low-voltage electricity does not travel long distances efficiently. Moreover, we find that the area required for solar panels—photovoltaic modules plus solar hot water panels—often corresponds nicely to half of the house's roof area, but only if the roof faces south. A very satisfactory and cost-effective accommodation can be reached by dedicating roof space to capturing the sun, thereby incorporating the solar panels into the house's existing profile. One of the more progressive utility companies, Sacramento Municipal Utility District (SMUD), is petitioning their ratepayers to "Give Us Your Roofs" for precisely this purpose.

To take advantage of this design economy, the house's roof must be planned to align with the site's solar aperture, where the sun may be captured most effectively. The sun's path across the sky has two variables, time of day and time of year. At noon on the summer solstice, the sun will ride at its highest point, due south, at an angle above the true horizon of the latitude plus 23 degrees. At noon on the winter solstice, it will appear due south at an angle of the site latitude less 23 degrees. (The earth's axis is angled at 23 degrees to the sun's plane, which causes seasons.) At noon on the equinoxes, spring and autumn, the sun can be found due south at the angle of the site's latitude above the horizon. Through the rest of the year, the sun commutes between these points. The proper angle of exposure for any solar capture device corresponds to the site's latitude plus or minus the seasonal fraction of the sun's semiannual range of 23 degrees. A fair compromise, choosing the site's latitude as the roof's angle to the horizontal, only varies from the optimum by approximately 23 degrees at the solstices. If maximum electrical loads are expected in the dead of winter, as is typical, the savings realized by mounting modules on the roof (as opposed to free-standing racks) can be invested in enough additional modules to compensate for the inefficiency of slightly misaligned modules for part of the year.

Please note that compasses seldom point to true north, but rather to magnetic north. Either get the local correction before using a compass to orient the house, or make careful observations using the time-honored Boy Scout method: with a tall stick and pegs mark the shadow's end over several days; the shortest shadow points due south.

Carpenters express roof pitch as the ratio of rise to run, where run is always twelve. In Caspar, where winter sun is at a premium, I have devoted a section of roof to solar harvesting, and angled it to be perpendicular to the sun about a month before and after the winter solstice, or 18 degrees higher than my latitude, a precipitous pitch of fourteen in twelve. My best solar aperture is slightly west of due south because of trees I do not care to cut and typical wintertime cloud patterns. Solar energy experts have special tools for predicting the solar aperture and its changes over the solar year, and can help get the roof pointed exactly right. Getting it wrong can easily subtract 20 percent efficiency from your array.

Coincidentally, increasing the roof pitch with latitude serves the need to employ steeper roofs in snowier lands. Since snow will cling to a glass surface at or below a 50-degree pitch (particularly if the surface is dirty), some thought must be given, if the homestead relies on PV for snow season power, to convenient ways to clear the snow.

Roofs can be used to capture another precious commodity, water. In much of the world, roof catchment is the primary source of domestic water, but in conventional American home-building, roof run-off is considered more a nuisance than a resource. Roof-captured water requires careful treatment, particularly in a suburban or urban setting, but as our water resources come closer to their limits, we ought to put these pennies from heaven to good use. Thanks to gravity, it takes very little effort to divert roof run-off to a holding tank; it takes even less when this intent is incorporated into your plan early on. If the run-off is to be used for drinking or to water edible plants, care should be taken to select a roof surface that does not spoil the water with leachates or unfilterable impurities. The manufacturers of the roofing material will be able to provide reliable information.

Someday in the near future we will see photovoltaic roofing materials, and the economy of renewables will be complete. What would shed precipitation better than a glass roof? Until then problems with expansion and module maintenance make it necessary to install the panels on top of a roof covering with a life expectancy at least as long as that of the modules, which we know to be approximately thirty years.

Photovoltaic panels are very sensitive to heat: they don't like it, and become less productive as they warm up. This perverse behavior cannot be corrected by the usual means—you do not want to shade your array—so the next best thing you can do is attach them to the roof in a way that keeps them as cool as possible. My modules are firmly affixed to vertical rails that provide a chimney which draws cool air in at the bottom. Without this chimney, the temperature behind my panels will be as much as 30 degrees above the ambient on a sunny day, which decreases module performance by about 10 percent. Panels don't care how they are aligned, but the chimney effect can be enhanced if they are installed with their long dimension oriented vertically.

You may note that I emphasize firm attachment of array to structure. When strong winds blow, modules are expensive, fragile, sharp-edged kites waiting to fly. Aficionados of the electrical code don't worry as much about this as I do; they worry instead about another unlikely but potentially devastating event, lightning. And they want every module and metal part individually grounded.

There is a brisk argument in the solar community about the efficacy of racking and tracking as compared to solid installation. By seasonally tinkering with the horizon angle of the modules, small gains in efficiency can be made; by adjusting module orientation for time of day, relatively greater gains can be made. Racks and trackers are usually rated to withstand 120-mile-per-hour winds; in Caspar, or wherever the weather gets serious, that is inadequate. As a veteran of winter's lusty gusts, and having seen the effects of serious storms and weathering, I hold with those who favor solidity.

To my eye, a tracker full of photovoltaic modules in the yard is just slightly less offensive than a powerline swooping in from the street: it bespeaks a lack of forethought and a hint of impermanence. Many who look to home energy harvesting as a long-term power source are attracted to photovoltaics because of their elegant passivity. If it is impossible to orient the home's roof correctly, it would be better to see panels on an outbuilding with an appropriately sloped roof than a tracker in the yard. Possibly the batteries and power-conditioning equipment could live inside the same shed.

To maximize summertime energy harvesting (for agricultural pumping, for example) trackers make sense in a benign climate. Active trackers which use electronics to follow the sun are accurate to within half a degree, and get on the job first thing in the morning, while passive trackers that use freon (a CFC) but safely encapsulated, we hope, and not prone to escape) are less accurate, and take half an hour to wake up in the morning. Both are beneficent technology, but the active trackers are better, and of course cost twice as much. A tracker might improve summertime energy yields by 40 percent, and wintertime yields by half that, and usually costs about half as much as the panels it carries. In other words, it is more cost-effective to solidly mount 20 percent more modules to maximize the winter energy harvest. Over twenty years, I believe a strategy of buying 20 to 40 percent more panels and mounting them solidly on the roof will prove to be the most trouble-free and economical. New technology arriving in the marketplace in the coming year may change my mind, but presently available panels with optical concentrators must be kept pointed directly (to within a quarter of a degree) at the sun, and existing active trackers are barely capable of pointing this precisely.

The *solar fraction* is the percentage of a household's energy requirements that can reasonably be expected to be generated by harvesting solar energy. In some sites, where cloud cover is rare and the sun beats down unimpeded, the fraction is 100 percent. An old government map of solar resources showed such spots in red, while less gifted sites ranged through the spectrum to blue where, at one time, it was thought that no solar capture was feasible. Vermont was all blue, but this estimate, like the report of Mark Twain's demise, was premature. Richard Gottlieb, perennial candidate for governor of Vermont, has been cheerfully harvesting solar electricity for almost two decades, and reports that in his part of the state (the South) the solar fraction could be as much as 70 percent. Deficits, of course, may be made up with more modules and a bigger battery bank, but it more sensible to develop a second energy harvesting method if possible.

ALTERNATIVE ENERGY GOTCHA!S

Things that spin, sing. Where photovoltaic panels rest in the sun, quietly generating electricity, generators that convert rotational energy into electricity—wind-spinners, hydro-turbines, and motor generators—make noises that may be disconcerting and that certainly intrude on rural peace and quiet. Owners of homes with micro-hydro turbines and wind machines close by told me that they found the sound reassuring in the night, but I wonder if this sentiment is shared by other family members and neighbors. These devices are best at a distance—wind machines, in particular, as far away as possible—and distance creates problems. As noted above, electricity loses energy when it travels. The grid that connects all the plugs in America wastes during transmission up to half the electricity it carries. Distance costs power, and so does conversion. Where possible, we want to generate the same form of electricity that we intend to use. Low-voltage electricity loses more energy, proportionally, and so spinners and turbines at a distance usually spin high-voltage alternators or generators. Furthermore, moving parts, particularly those in contact with hostile forces like water, wind, and heat, inevitably require periodic attention and replacement. The extra maintenance requirements, and the conflict between electricity's preference for proximity and our need to keep spinners at a distance, often mean that PVs, which look to be more expensive when only the price of another kind of generator is considered, are cost-competitive when the whole installation is accounted for. Add the fact that PVs are likely to decrease in cost and increase in efficiency more than competing technologies, and you have a compelling argument in favor of building a good site for PVs even if you don't expect to use that source right away.

When we can, we build our houses out of the wind. Wind strips heat out of a house, and wind-chill makes a place very uncomfortable, so our homesites are seldom good windsites. Only on the flattest of plots will homesite and windsite be the same. On the other hand, since we seldom build houses where the wind resource is best, because it would be too windy there, it is easy to distance ourselves from the *thwocka-thwocka* of these noisy devices. Hydro turbines need less distance, as their high pitched whirr is easily kept inside the massive cement housings they prefer. Just remember: the wind machine is best not attached to the house, and the micro-hydroelectric turbine somewhere other than under the bed.

PLANNING FOR MAINTENANCE AND CHANGE

Plan to install extra electrical outlets. There never seem to be enough, and electricians report this to be their commonest and least favorite electrical job. Install twice as many as required by code (which usually calls for one every twelve feet) with special attention to areas where you expect to work or concentrate electrical equipment. Underwriters Laboratories reports that many electrical fires result from faulty or damaged extension cords. This danger can be circumvented by anticipating where extra outlets will be needed, and wiring accordingly. Trade electricians usually charge by the outlet box, not by the hour, and bid their jobs based on the box count; on my travels I heard prices as high as twenty dollars a box. Naturally, if our eye is on the job cost, we may be tempted to cut costs. As always, remember that you will pay for such false economies the whole time you live in the house. It is much cheaper to install an extra outlet when the walls are open than to add one afterward.

Make maintenance easy. If simple tasks like changing lightbulbs and water filters are inconvenient, we are likely to leave them undone. Proud owners showed me many innovative arrangements for making periodic maintenance easier, from built-in light fixtures with hinged translucent covers held closed by magnets, to built-to-size trays under the sink so that the welter of household chemicals kept there could be easily set aside while changing filters or working on plumbing. Traps and pipes inevitably drip when being serviced. By building cabinetry that easily allows us to slide in a plastic tub or tray before the dribbling begins, and out again without spilling, and by designing the plumbing so that connections are above the places where a tub can be set, we make the chore quite a bit more pleasant.

Placing lights in the dark places where someone must occasionally work is a novel idea that often occurs too late to homebuilders, even if they expect to work on their own systems. The same goes for outlets in places where power will be required only occasionally; by wiring with such foresight, our tool-gathering task is lessened by at least one extension cord.

Chapter 13

Wind Power

Evaluating the Technology–
What Works and What Doesn't

by Paul Gipe

From WIND POWER FOR HOME & BUSINESS:
Renewable Energy for the 1990s and Beyond

Chelsea Green Publishing Company

"Hey, that's a funny lookin' windmill you got there. What is it?"

"A VAWT. "

"Don't get smart with me, son. I asked you a simple question."

"Actually, it's an articulating, straight-bladed VAWT."

"Can't you speak in English? I don't work for the government, you know."

"Some call it a giromill."

"Well, that's better. Why didn't you say so in the first place?
For a moment there I thought you were speaking in tongues."

As wind technology has grown, so has its vocabulary. At times it may seem as if the wind industry does speak in tongues. Nearly every conceivable wind turbine configuration has been tried at least once—most only once. Designs have run the gamut from the familiar farm windmill to contraptions such as the giromill. Despite the plethora of imaginative designs developed during the 1970s, only a few approaches have since proved successful.

During the past decade small wind machines designed for residential or remote uses where simplicity is required, have evolved into highly integrated designs with few moving parts. These advanced small wind turbines typically use a rotor with three blades that spin about a horizontal axis upwind of the tower. Most of these designs drive a permanent-magnet alternator and have demonstrated exceptional reliability with little or no maintenance. Similarly, most of today's medium-sized wind turbines, like those used in California wind plants, share many characteristics. Most use three blades and drive induction generators. And until the early 1990s, nearly all successful designs used simple, fixed-pitch blades.

In this chapter we'll look at where the technology stands today, and why designs such as these have become commonplace. We'll also look at the important difference between wind machines that use drag to drive their rotors and those that use lift, why modern wind machines use only two or three blades, what materials are used to make these blades and the advantages of each, the kinds of controls used to protect the wind turbine, and the types of transmissions and generators now being used.

ORIENTATION

There are two great classes of wind turbines, horizontal and vertical axis machines (see Figure 13-1). Conventional wind turbines, like the Dutch windmill found throughout northern Europe and the American farm wind mill, spin about a horizontal axis. As the name implies, a vertical axis wind turbine (VAWT) spins about a vertical axis much like a top or a toy gyroscope.

HORIZONTAL AXIS

Because the wind changes direction, all horizontal axis wind machines have some means for keeping the rotor into the wind. Consequently, either the entire wind machine and its tower, or the top of the wind machine where the rotor is attached must change its position relative to the wind.

Traditionally the rotors of horizontal axis wind machines have been placed upwind of their towers and there was some device for keeping the rotor into the wind. On the Dutch windmill, for example, the miller had to constantly monitor the wind. When the wind changed direction the miller laboriously pushed a long tail pole or turned a crank on the milling platform that moved the windmill's massive rotor back into the wind. Later versions liberated millers from their labor by using fan tails that mechanically turned the rotor toward the wind. On smaller wind machines, such as the farm windmill, the task is much easier and a simple tail vane will do. The tail vane keeps the rotor pointed into the wind regardless of changes in wind direction.

Both tail vanes and fan tails use forces in the wind itself to orient the rotor upwind of the tower. They passively change the orientation, or *yaw*, of the wind turbine with respect to changes in wind direction without the use of human or electrical power. Without a tail vane or a fan tail, upwind turbines won't automatically stay into the wind. (There are some modern exceptions.) Downwind rotors don't need tail vanes or fan tails. Instead the blades are swept slightly downwind, giving the spinning rotor the shape of a shallow cone with its apex at the tower. This *coning* of the blades causes the rotor to inherently orient itself downwind.

UPWIND AND DOWNWIND

Downwind machines are certainly sleeker than small upwind machines with their tail vanes. Some believe this gives downwind machines a more modern look. They do have one clear advantage. Downwind machines eliminate the cost of tail vanes. But they pay a price, say proponents of upwind turbines. Downwind machines occasionally get caught upwind when winds are light and variable. Some downwind turbines like the Enertech and Storm Master (both no longer manufactured) occasionally *hunt* the wind after a strong gust subsides. Such a turbine may walk completely around the tower as it searches for the wind. Critics of downwind machines add that the tower creates a *shadow* that disrupts the air flow over the blades as they pass behind the tower. This decreases performance, they charge, increases wear, and emits a characteristic sound some people find annoying.

West Texas State University's Vaughn Nelson asserts that upwind machines suffer a similar, but less severe, performance penalty. The wind piles up in front of a tower much like the small zone of turbulence just upstream from a stone in a swiftly flowing brook. The stone creates a much bigger zone of disturbance or wake downstream.

One significant disadvantage of passive downwind machines is yaw control in a high wind. A common method for protecting upwind turbines in high winds is to orient the rotor 90 degrees to the wind. On upwind machines with a tail vane the rotor can be furled (turned) and the rotor will soon move out of the wind. Upwind turbines with active yaw controls mechanically swing the turbine out of the wind. Unless a downwind machine has an active yaw drive, the rotor will always stay downwind of the tower during high winds. Other mechanisms for controlling the rotor in high winds must be used.

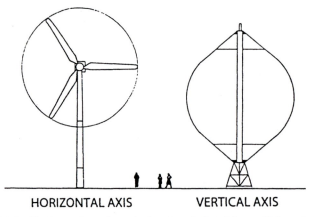

HORIZONTAL AXIS   VERTICAL AXIS

Figure 13-1 Horizontal- and vertical-axis wind turbines. Although the Darrieus or eggbeater turbine on the right (FloWind 19-meter model) spins about a vertical axis, it's equally efficient at harnessing the energy in the wind as the conventional wind turbine on the left (WindMaster 23.5-meter model). Both wind machines are typical of the medium-sized wind turbines used in wind power plants, and each is capable of producing about 200 kilowatts. (Pacific Gas & Electric Co.)

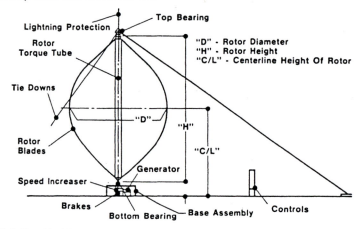

Figure 13-2 Detail of Darrieus rotor with nomenclature.

Figure 13-3 Darrieus configurations. There are several other Darrieus configurations besides the common "eggbeater" design.

Although tail vanes are simple and effective devices for passively controlling yaw, they are limited to wind machines less than 10 meters (33 feet) in diameter. Above this size, the tail vane becomes too unwieldy, and electric motors or fan tails are necessary to mechanically orient the rotor into the wind.

VERTICAL AXIS

The principal advantage of modern vertical-axis wind machines over their conventional counterparts is that VAWTs are omnidirectional—they accept the wind from any direction. This simplifies their design and eliminates the problem imposed by gyroscopic forces on the rotor of conventional machines as the turbines yaw into the wind. The vertical axis of rotation also permits mounting the generator and gear at ground level (see Figure 13-2). This is a feature you'll learn to appreciate if you ever have to service a conventional wind turbine 80 feet above the ground in a howling blizzard.

Vertical-axis turbines, like their conventional brethren, can be divided into two major groups: those that use aerodynamic drag to extract power from the wind (for example, the cup anemometer) and those that use lift from an airfoil. We can further subdivide those VAWTs using airfoils into those with straight blades and those with curved blades. The simplest configuration uses two or more straight blades attached to the ends of a horizontal cross-arm. This gives the rotor the shape of a large H with the blades acting as the uprights of the H. Unfortunately, this configuration permits centrifugal forces to induce severe bending stresses in the blades at their point of attachment.

During the 1920s French inventor D.G.M. Darrieus patented a wind machine that cleverly dealt with this limitation. Instead of using straight blades he attached curved blades to the rotor. When the turbine was operating the curved blades would take the form of a spinning rope held at both ends. This *troposkein* shape directs centrifugal forces through the blade's length toward the points of attachment, thus creating tension in the blades rather than bending. Because materials are stronger in tension than in bending, the blades could be lighter for the same overall strength and operate at higher speeds than straight blades. Although the phi ϕ or *eggbeater* configuration is the most common, Darrieus conceived several other versions including Delta, Diamond, and Y. All have been tried at one time or another (see Figure 13-3).

Darrieus' concept eventually faded into obscurity. Canada's National Research Council reinvented the idea in the mid-1960s, and subsequently Canadian wind development has focused solely on Darrieus turbines. Sandia National Laboratories in the United States has pursued the technology for nearly two decades. Several firms have attempted to commercialize Sandia's work, and 5 percent of the wind turbines in California are of the Darrieus design. However, no one currently manufactures Darrieus turbines, and outside of the programs in Canada and at Sandia, work on the technology has practically ceased.

Darrieus turbines were never reliably self-starting. Their fixed-pitch blades can't drive the rotor up to operating speed from a standstill unless the blades are parked in just the right position relative to the wind. This isn't necessarily a serious limitation. But to provide self-starting capability several researchers in this country and abroad reverted to the H-rotor configuration. By using straight blades they can vary blade pitch as the blades orbit around the rotor's axis. (The blades on Darrieus rotors are attached rigidly to the torque tube or central shaft.) Technocrats identify this kind of wind machine as an articulating, straight-bladed, vertical-axis wind turbine. It's also known as a giromill or cycloturbine (see Figure 13-4).

The H-rotor has one important advantage over the Darrieus design. It captures more wind. The intercept area of an H-rotor is a rectangle. For the same size wind machine—that is, where the height and diameter are the same—the H-rotor will sweep more area than an ellipse does.

LIFT AND DRAG

Regardless of whether a wind machine rotates about a vertical or horizontal axis, it depends on either of two aerodynamic principles to derive power from the wind: drag or lift. Drag devices are simple wind machines that use flat, curved, or cup-shaped blades to turn the rotor. Both cup anemometers and panemones are representative of drag devices. In each the wind merely pushes on the cup or blade, forcing the rotor to spin (see Figure 13-5). Lift devices, in contrast, use airfoils to propel the rotor.

Drag devices characteristically produce high starting torques. Because much of the rotor's swept area is covered with blades, there's a lot of surface for the wind to push against. Drag devices are ideal for pumping water in low volumes. But their inherent drawbacks limit their use for generating electricity. At best only one-third of the power in the wind can be captured by such machines. In comparison, the maximum possible for a lift device is 59 percent (the Betz limit). Drag devices also require more materials than comparable wind machines using lift.

Experimenters have tried numerous approaches to improving the performance of drag devices. Backyard tinkerers often turn their attention first to drag devices because they're easier to understand and construct. The wind pushes on a big wide blade and it moves. What could be simpler? (Lift devices are more complicated. We'll see why in a moment.)

Although the cup anemometer is the most widely used drag device, the farm windmill and the Savonius rotor are the two most successful. Both deliver slightly better aerodynamic performance than true drag devices. Early farm windmills, for example, used flat wooden slats for blades. In 1888 Aermotor introduced its *mathematical* windmill, which substituted sheet-metal blades for those of wood. Aermotor stamped a broad curve into the metal blade to trap more air. It did, and in doing so directed the air to flow over the backside of the following blade. This cascade effect heightened the difference in pressure from one side of the blade to the other, improving Aermotor's performance over that of its rivals. Unfortunately, the "new and improved" farm windmill—all now use Aermotor's technique—still extracts only 15 percent of the power in the wind.

In 1924 Finnish inventor Sigurd Savonius developed an S-shaped vertical-axis wind machine. Principally it's a drag device, but Savonius improved its performance by recirculating some of the air flow between the two halves of the rotor. Air striking one blade is directed through the separation between the two halves of the S and onto the other blade. Researchers have measured conversion efficiencies of almost 30 percent under optimum conditions, considerably more than that extracted by other drag devices. In practice, however, S-rotors, like the farm windmill, extract less than 15 percent of the power in the wind. Because of this limitation Savonius rotors have never been commercially successful. Today they're found only in experimenters' garages.

There are other hybrids as well, wind machines that don't fall neatly into either category. Anton Flettner built several such devices. Using the Magnus effect as a means of propulsion on two upright spinning cylinders, he sailed the Atlantic for New York in 1925. The following year he built a horizontal-axis wind turbine 65 feet in diameter in which he used four spinning cylinders to drive the rotor.

The Magnus effect is the lift or thrust produced when air moves over the surface of a spinning object (see Figure 13-6). It's what produces the curved flight in the curve ball. The pitcher imparts spin to the ball as it leaves his hand. Air rushing over the spinning ball forces the ball off its normal straight-line course. In 1933 J. Madaras constructed a 90-foot cylinder 28 feet in diameter at Burlington, New Jersey, in hopes of using this phenomenon to drive cars around a track. Like similar attempts to harness the Magnus effect, it was abandoned because the spinning cylinders were material-intensive. The same results could be obtained from true airfoils at less expense.

Instead of paddles or cups, lift devices use airfoils like those in the wing of an airplane to power the turbine. The limited number of blades on lift devices contrasts markedly with the multiple blades of drag devices. It seems mysterious that a wind machine with only a few blades can operate more efficiently than one with a large number of blades. But a modern wind turbine, because it uses lift, can capture the same amount of power with a smaller rotor using fewer blades than a multiblade drag device. On the basis of blade surface area, wind turbines using lift can extract 100 times more power from the wind than a drag device. That's why today's wind machines look so different from the farm windmill. Modern wind turbines, those using lift, do much more with less.

Why is this? Why do some wind machines use multiple blades like the farm windmill where others use only a few? Why do some blades taper from the root to the tip where others taper from the tip to the root? To understand the answers to these questions we need to briefly delve further into wind turbine aerodynamics.

AERODYNAMICS

It's intriguing that a sailboat can travel faster than the wind, and even more so when we learn that the boat sails faster across the wind than when the wind is pushing from behind. Mariners discovered this fact intuitively centuries ago. Today we explain the paradox by speaking in terms of lift and drag. The blade of a modern wind turbine is much like the sail of a sailboat—lift propels them both.

To begin, let's look at the factors affecting the lift from an airfoil as found in a wind turbine blade. Air flowing over the blade causes both lift and drag. When you're driving down the highway and you stick your hand outside the window, lift from the air flowing over your hand (a crude airfoil shape) literally lifts your hand toward the roof. Drag pulls your hand toward the rear of the car, dragging it with the wind. The sum of these two forces on a wind turbine blade generates a thrust that pulls the blade on its journey through the air, much like it pulls a sailboat through the water. This thrust is greatest when the blade is slicing through the wind, or the sailboat is sailing across the wind.

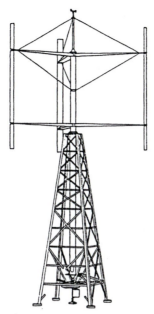

Figure 13-4 Giromill or cycloturbine. Like all vertical-axis wind machines, this turbine could transmit mechanical power to ground level via a long shaft. The wind vane at the top of the rotor orients the blades with respect to the wind.

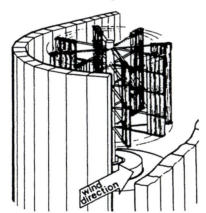

Figure 13-5 Panemone. Simple drag device used in ancient Persia for grinding grain. The vertically mounted blades were made by fastening bundles of reeds onto a wooden frame. The surrounding wall guides the prevailing wind onto the retreating blades. (Sandia)

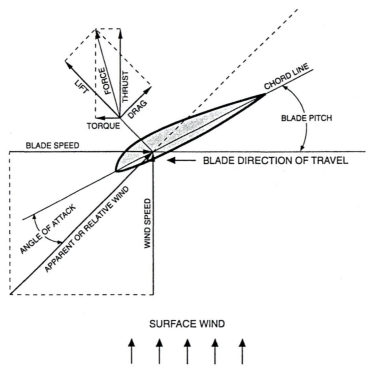

Figure 13-6 A hybrid device that uses the lift created by a spinning cylinder demonstrates the Magnus effect. Spinning cylinders have been used to drive several kinds of wind machines, including a flat car on a track.

Engineers rate airfoil performance by the ratio of lift to drag. Designers want a high lift-to-drag ratio for best performance. The lift-to-drag ratio is determined by the blade's angle of attack—the blade's angle with respect to the *apparent* wind. The lift-to-drag ratio increases with increasing angles of attack until a point is reached where the air flow over the blade becomes turbulent. Lift then deteriorates rapidly, the ratio declines, and the airfoil *stalls*. The angle of attack at which this occurs varies from one airfoil to another.

Stall is a deadly condition in flight. Airplanes literally fall out of the sky when stall occurs, when there's no longer enough lift to support them. It's one of the leading cause of light plane accidents. In a wind machine stall can be put to good use. We'll see why in a moment. But first consider the angle of attack: it's a function of the blade's angle to the plane of rotation—its pitch—and the apparent wind (see Figure 13-7). For now assume the pitch is fixed, which it is on most wind machines.

APPARENT WIND AND THE ANGLE OF ATTACK

The apparent wind is the wind "seen" by the blade. It is a combination of the blade's own motion and the wind across the round. If you recall some of your high school physics you'll note that both the magnitude and direction of the apparent wind depend on the magnitude and direction of its components. For example, if both were equal in speed (say the wind speed was 10 mph and the speed of the blade was also 10 mph) and if they were acting at right angles to each other, the apparent wind would be acting at 10 mph at a 45-degree angle between the two (see Figure 13-7).

If wind speed increases while the blade's speed through the air remains constant, the position of the apparent wind swings toward the wind direction because it has become more influential. As the apparent wind changes position it also changes the angle of attack. Reverse the process and see what happens. Blade speed now becomes stronger and causes the apparent wind to shift toward the direction of the blade's motion, decreasing the angle of attack. Designers must decide how best to deal with this relationship for each airfoil, because there's an optimum angle of attack, a point where the lift-to-drag ratio is optimum and performance reaches a maximum.

For a fixed-pitch blade to maintain an optimum angle of attack, blade speed must increase in proportion to wind speed. As wind speed increases the rotor must spin faster. Another way to say it is that the tip-speed ratio, the relationship between blade speed and wind speed, must remain constant to maximize aerodynamic performance. Most small wind turbines operate this way because it's not only more efficient but also simpler.

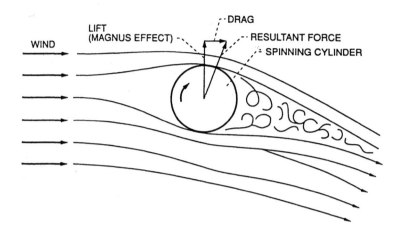

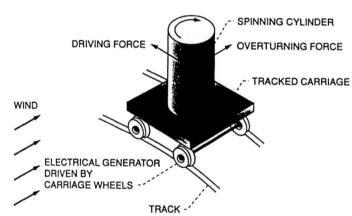

Figure 13-7 Airfoil performance is gauged by the ratio of lift to drag. Lift is determined by the angle of attack. The pitch of the blade, the speed of the blade through the air, and the speed of the wind control the angle of attack and, consequently, lift.

Most medium-sized wind machines, those above 10 meters in diameter, don't maintain the optimum tip-speed ratio because of the type of generator they use and because they take advantage of the airfoil's decreasing performance in high winds. Designers are willing to sacrifice some performance for the simplicity of fixed-pitch rotors driving constant speed generators. As wind speed increases the airfoil begins to stall and performance declines. Stall is desirable because it reduces the rotor's power in high winds, making it easier for designers to build protective controls to keep the rotor from destroying itself.

The amount of thrust driving the rotor is not only a function of the lift-to-drag ratio and the blade's angle of attack, but also the area of the blade and its speed through the air. To increase the load an airplane can lift, you either increase the size of the wings, increase the plane's speed, or do both.

TAPER AND TWIST

For the sake of simplification we've been looking at a blade as if the conditions it sees were constant along its entire length. That may be true for airplanes, but not so for wind turbines. Even when the pitch of the blade is fixed and rotor speed constant, the speed through the air of a point on the blade changes with its distance from the hub. The speed is higher at the tip than near the hub because it has more distance to cover in the same amount of time.

Because blade speed increases with distance from the hub, the apparent wind varies as well. The apparent wind increases in strength, and its position shifts toward the plane of rotation as you move out along the blade toward the tip. If the blade designer wants to maintain the angle of attack (to optimize performance) at the same time blade speed is increasing, the pitch of the blade must decrease toward the tip. As a result, wind turbine blades are twisted from root to tip. The greatest pitch appears at the root and the least at the tip. Glance up at the next wind turbine you see and note that the tip of the blade is almost parallel with its direction of travel for this reason.

SOLIDITY

Wind machine designers long ago learned that blade area (the number of blades as well as their length and width) governs the amount of torque, or turning force, a rotor can produce. The more blades the rotor has for the wind to act on, the more torque it will produce. Greater solidity, the ratio of blade area to the area swept by the rotor, generates greater torque. If you were designing a wind machine for pumping water on the semi-arid Great Plains, you'd want a rotor that provides high torque at low wind speeds. This would assure you that the windmill would be able to lift the pump's piston (and the water with it) during late summer when the need is greatest but the winds are lightest. During the rest of the year you wouldn't really care how well the rotor performed because there would be less demand for water and more than enough wind to pump it.

There's no better example of a high-solidity rotor fitting this description than the American farm windmill. It uses multiple "sails" that taper from the tip to the root so that nearly the whole rotor disc is covered by blades (80 percent solidity). It was designed to deliver high torque at low wind speeds, and it does its job remarkably well.

Southeastern Pennsylvania is renowned for the tidy, prosperous farms of the Pennsylvania Dutch. These descendants of German settlers live a simple life and husband their land. They shun power equipment, farm with horse-drawn teams, and use buggies to get about. Water-pumping windmills are a familiar sight on the Pennsylvania Dutch landscape.

Many in the eastern United States who have seen the Pennsylvania Dutch conclude that the water-pumping windmill must obviously be a good idea if the thrifty Dutch are still using them. These people fail to realize that the Pennsylvania Dutch abhor modern conveniences such as electricity. The farm windmill is their only source of water. Cost is no object. The farm windmill was never designed to deliver water economically. It was designed to deliver water, period. It only had to compete with lifting water by hand. When you're dying of thirst you don't care how much the windmill costs or how much power it produces just so long as it pumps water.

The demands on electricity- or power-generating wind machines are different. We don't need power from wind turbines. Our lives are not dependent on them like those of the Pennsylvania Dutch. For us there are many other sources of power: the utility, photovoltaics, a stand-alone generator. We want power from a source and are willing to pay for it only when it's a better buy—when it's cheaper than from competing sources. To compete with these other sources the wind machine must be designed to extract power from the wind in the most efficient and least costly manner possible. The farm windmill isn't the way to do it.

The multiblade farm windmill looks like it would capture more wind than a modern machine with two or three slender blades. Intuitively, we feel that the rotor should have more blades to capture more wind. If this were true, however, consider what would happen if we carried this belief to its logical extreme. The optimum rotor would cover the entire swept area with blades, in effect producing a solid disc. No air would pass through. The wind would pile up in front of the rotor and flow around rather than through it. The wind speed behind the rotor would be zero. Instead of capturing more wind, we wouldn't capture any. There must be some air moving through the disc and it must retain enough kinetic energy so it can keep moving to make way for the air behind.

We must strike a balance between a rotor that completely stops the wind and one that allows the wind to pass through unimpeded, between the amount of wind striking the rotor and the amount flowing through. Albert Betz demonstrated mathematically that this optimum is reached when the rotor reduces wind speed by one-third.

When the wind flies into the wide vanes of the farm windmill it is deflected slightly as it moves downstream. The combined effect from the wind moving across the blades causes the wind leaving the rotor to spin in a spiral like a corkscrew. To maximize the amount of work the wind can perform (to approach the theoretical limits as near as we can), designers must minimize this deflection and the spiraling of the wind stream in the turbine's wake.

This spiraling effect is greatest, and so is the amount of power lost, in rotors producing high torque. High-solidity rotors such as the farm windmill produce plenty of torque, but they also lose more energy in the wake than do lower solidity rotors delivering less torque. But, you may ask, if we were to lower the rotor's torque wouldn't we be lowering the power it can produce even if it's going to be more efficient at producing it? Yes, if we kept everything else the same. We don't. Power is a product of torque and rotor speed. To deliver the same amount of power we need to increase rotor speed. Decreasing torque while at the same time increasing rotor speed will improve the rotor's efficiency.

Torque is the product of a force acting on a lever. In our case the lever is the blade of a wind turbine. The lever is longest at the tip and shortest near the hub. To reduce the torque produced by the blade, the force acting on it must progressively decrease as the lever arm increases in length or as we proceed along the blade to the tip.

Lift provides the force needed to produce torque. We learned previously that lift is a function of blade area and speed. As we move toward the tip, blade speed increases and so does lift. We now have two factors reinforcing each other: blade speed increases toward the tip, as does the length of the lever through which it will act. Thus, to decrease torque we need to decrease blade area, or solidity, more at the tip than near the hub. The blade, as a result, tapers from the root to the tip. This also explains why so few blades are used. Designers want to keep solidity as low as possible.

Blade speed is a function of rotor diameter and rotor speed. Both are described by a single term, the ratio between the speed of the blade through the air at the tip and the wind speed: the tip-speed ratio. Tip speed increases as either rotor speed increases or the length of the blade increases. Large diameter rotors have higher tip-speed ratios than do smaller rotors spinning at the same speed. A rotor spinning at a faster rate than another of the same size also has a higher tip-speed ratio. For optimum performance, solidity should decrease as tip-speed ratio increases. Drag devices operate at tip speed ratios of one or less compared to lift devices, which operate at tip-speed ratios of five or more.

To summarize, lift devices are capable of extracting more power from the wind with less material than drag devices. For lift devices to perform optimally they must operate at low torque but at a high tip-speed ratio. To achieve high tip-speed ratios and low torque the rotor must have low solidity. This is why modern wind turbines operate at high speeds: the rotor is more efficient. It is not, as has been said by others, because electric generators operate at high speeds. If this were the case you could always use a transmission to increase the speed to the generator.

Wind turbines need only one slender blade to efficiently capture the energy in the wind. The giant German conglomerate Messerschmitt-Bolkow-Blohm built just such a series of one-bladed wind turbines. But there are other, equally important design criteria besides efficiency. Two blades are often used for reasons of static balance. (The one-bladed MBB turbines use a counterweight.) Many modern wind turbines use three blades because they give greater dynamic stability than either two blades or one.

Two-bladed turbines suffer a dynamic imbalance when the wind machine changes direction. When the blades are vertical little force is needed to yaw or to swing the turbine around the tower. But when the blades are horizontal much more force is required because of the rotor's inertia. (The blades like to stay just where they are.) When the rotor is spinning and the wind turbine changes direction, the wind machine and tower are subjected to these oscillating forces twice per revolution: once each time the rotor is horizontal. This causes the rotor to yaw unevenly. On larger machines this effect is dampened with shock absorbers or by allowing the rotor to teeter. Three blades minimize this dynamic problem and are preferred on small machines where yaw dampening or teetering hubs would be too costly.

Low-solidity rotors have one drawback. They may not be self-starting. Remember that the apparent wind flowing over the blade is partly due to the blade's motion. When the rotor is stopped, the lift on the blades from the wind alone may not be enough to start the rotor moving. One solution for rotors using fixed-pitch blades is to spin the rotor up to a speed where it can drive itself. This is a common practice for Darrieus turbines. There are also conventional wind machines that require motoring the rotor up to speed. But most designers are willing to sacrifice a slight amount of performance to gain a self-starting capability.

Bergey Windpower cleverly surmounted this self-starting problem by using a torsionally flexible blade and a pitch weight. This design allows the blades to be set at a high angle of attack for start up conditions. As rotor speed increases, a weight attached to an outboard portion of the blade twists the blade, changing its pitch progressively toward the optimum running position. This pitch weight isn't used to control overspeed but solely to improve the rotor's performance over a full range of wind speeds.

Wind machines that are self-starting begin turning in winds of 8-10 mph (4-5 m/s). Don't be misled by glib talk promoting a "new" wind turbine that runs in low winds. Anybody can design a wind machine to turn in light winds. But why bother? There's no energy in winds at low speeds. The rotor may spin but it won't do much else.

Darrieus turbines are typically not self-starting, though it is now known that Darrieus turbines can self-start under the right wind conditions. These conditions—though infrequent—do occur. When the Darrieus rotor is at a standstill, only the wind across the ground acts on the blade. Because the pitch of the rotor is fixed, the blades stall and nothing happens. Normally, the rotor must be motored up to speed. But on July 6, 1978, all that changed and a new corollary was added to Murphy's Law: "wind turbines that won't self-start, will." Canadian researchers were testing a 230-kW experimental Darrieus rotor on Magdalen Island in the Gulf of St. Lawrence. While repairs were underway the brake was released. Because it was thought the turbine could not start itself, it was left unattended overnight. During the night the wind picked up. By the next morning the rotor was spinning out of control. Eventually the rotor spun off the tower and corkscrewed itself into the ground.

Darrieus rotors have also been plagued by a misperception that they're less efficient than conventional wind machines. This results because one-half of the time the blades are traveling either with the wind or against it. Even so the blades on a Darrieus turbine produce lift for most of their orbit around the turbine's axis. Even when the blades are moving downwind (retreating) they see an apparent wind due to their own motion sufficient to create lift. Only when the blades are parallel to the wind does lift fall to zero.

Sandia Laboratories have found that under ideal conditions Darrieus turbines can extract more than 40 percent of the power in the wind. In other words, their performance is similar to that of conventional wind turbines, not any better but certainly no worse.

Developers of the Musgrove H-rotor have also found that a vertical-axis rotor with fixed-pitch blades can be made to start itself. (The Musgrove design, named after its English inventor Peter Musgrove, uses a novel means of protecting the rotor in high winds....) The designers discovered that decreasing the blade's aspect ratio—its height to its width—by shortening and widening the blades created more lift while the rotor was at rest. The stubbier blades could start the rotor without robbing from performance at operating speeds.

An H-rotor with articulating blades, such as a giromill or cycloturbine, is also self-starting (see Figure 13-4). The pitch of each blade is set according to a predetermined schedule and the position of the blade relative to the wind. The blade's angle of attack is optimized at each position of its orbit around the rotor's axis. Controlling blade pitch with respect to the wind gives the rotor a reliable self-starting capability not found in the Darrieus rotor. It should also deliver better performance because lift can be maximized regardless of whether the blade is advancing into, across, or with the wind. Giromills however, have never lived up to expectations. They're also material-intensive.

BLADES

Blades are one of the most critical, and visible, components of a wind turbine's rotor. Blades can be made from almost any material—and have been. Wood has always been popular. Early farm windmills used wooden slats, and windchargers of the 1930s used wood almost exclusively. Wood is still the material of choice for many small wind machines. It's strong, readily available, easy to work with, relatively inexpensive, and has good fatigue characteristics. "Wood flexes for a living," explains Mick Sagrillo, who runs a small turbine repair shop in Wisconsin. "It works well in high-fatigue applications."

Wood blades are built either from single planks of Sitka spruce or from wood laminates. The blades are then machined into the desired shape and coated with a tough weather-resistant finish. Then the manufacturer covers the leading edge with fiberglass tape to protect the blades from wind erosion and hail damage. This tape is the same as that used on the leading edges of helicopter blades. It's resistant to ultraviolet light and abrasion.

Few new to wind energy appreciate the wind's erosive force. If you need to be convinced of this, pay a visit to the Texas Panhandle or the Tehachapi Pass during the spring wind season. But don't forget to take your goggles. Sand and blowing grit scour anything in their path. This airborne sandpaper has deeply etched the galvanizing on the windward side of towers in the Tehachapi Pass. In areas prone to blowing sand, wooden wind turbine blades have had their leading edges eroded away after only 2 years of use.

Though solid wood planks work well for small machines up to 5 meters in diameter, some manufacturers prefer laminated wood. Designers prefer laminated wood (used in the construction of a butcher's block) in larger machines because they can better control the blade's strength and stiffness, as well as limit shrinkage and warpage. In the laminating process slabs of wood are bonded together with a resin. The resulting block can then be carved into a blade. By varying the types of wood, the direction of their grains, and the resin, a material can be produced that is stronger than any one part alone and stronger than a single plank of the same size. Laminated wood blades have been used on small wind turbines of all sizes.

Thinner slices of wood are also used to produce veneers. Layer upon layer of razor-thin slices are sandwiched together with a resin and molded into the airfoil shape. The process is widely used to build the hulls of sailboats and has been adapted successfully for wind turbine blades both in the United States and Europe. Wood-composite blades fabricated by Michigan's Gougeon Brothers have earned a reputation for strength and reliability in wind turbines up to 43 meters (142 feet) in diameter.

In the late nineteenth century galvanized steel began replacing the wooden blades on the farm windmill, and steel has been used ever since. Steel is strong and well understood. That's why it was chosen by Boeing engineers for the blades on the 300-foot (91 meter) diameter Mod-2, and the 320-foot (98-meter) diameter Mod-5B. It's nothing fancy, just plain structural steel—the same steel used in bridges. Because steel is so heavy, the hub, drive train, and tower must be more massive than on a wind machine with a lighter-weight rotor.

Aluminum is lighter and, for its weight, stronger. It's used extensively in the aircraft industry for this reason. We can fabricate aluminum blades with the same techniques used to build the wings of airplanes: form a rib and then stretch the aluminum skin over it. The blades on

NASA's early Mod-OA were built this way. On smaller machines a simpler method can be used by stamping a curve into the leading edge, folding the sheet metal over the spars, and then riveting it in place.

Aluminum can also be extruded, eliminating all other fabrication steps. It was once thought that blades could be mass-produced this way, extruding blades in the same way we manufacture drain spouts and window moldings by squeezing a hot piece of aluminum through a die. Alcoa and a Canadian company spent considerable money developing extruded aluminum blades for Darrieus turbines. They believed that the Darrieus rotor was well suited for aluminum extrusions because the forces on the blades are in tension.

The blades endure less stress in the Darrieus rotor than they would in a conventional wind machine. They can also use a blade of a constant width such as produced by extrusion. Aluminum, unfortunately, has two weaknesses. It's expensive and it's subject to metal fatigue.

Ever take a piece of wire and break it by flexing it back and forth a few times? That's metal fatigue, and it works the same way in the wing of an airplane or the blades of a wind turbine. Aluminum is a good material when used within its limits. On wind turbines aluminum hasn't been successful. Most of the problems Darrieus turbines in California have encountered are due to metal fatigue. Operators of these Darrieus turbines may eventually replace the aluminum blades with fiberglass. The only successful manufacturer of extruded aluminum blades used them in home light plants during the 1940s when Wincharger switched from wooden blades to extruded aluminum. Some Winchargers can still be found with their blades intact. No major manufacturer builds wind turbines today with metal blades.

Another drawback to metal blades, whether steel or aluminum, is television and radio interference. Metal reflects television signals, and this can cause "ghost" images on nearby TV sets. This has proven to be far less of a problem than first thought, even among the existing wind turbines using metal blades including the 500 Darrieus turbines still operating in California.

Fiberglass (glass-reinforced polyester, or GRP to Europeans) has grown increasingly popular. Like wood, fiberglass is strong, relatively inexpensive, and has good fatigue characteristics. It also lends itself to a variety of designs and manufacturing processes. Fiberglass can be pultruded, for example. Instead of pushing the material through a die, as in extrusion, fiberglass cloth (like the cloth used in fiberglass auto body kits) is pulled through a vat of resin and then through a die. Pultrusion produces the side rails for fiberglass ladders and other consumer products. The pultruded blades on Bergey Windpower's turbines can be easily identified by their constant width and thickness. Pultrusion gives Bergey's single-surface airfoil a strength and torsional flexibility not found in other constructions.

For pleasure boaters fiberglass has become the material of choice. In fact, the techniques used to build fiberglass boats have been successfully adapted by Danish, Dutch, and American companies to build wind turbine blades. These manufacturers place layer after layer of fiberglass cloth in half shell molds of the blades. As they add each additional layer, they coat the cloth with a polyester or epoxy resin. When the shells are complete they literally glue them together to form the complete blade. Nearly all medium-sized European wind turbine blades are made with this technique.

Filament winding is another process where fiberglass strands are pulled through a vat of resin and wound around a mandrel. The mandrel can be a simple shape like a tube, or a more complex shape like that of an airfoil. Originally developed for spinning missile cases, filament winding delivers high strength and flexibility. Though some blades have been made entirely from filament winding, the process is often used only to produce the blade's main structural spar. The blade is then assembled in a mold with a smooth fiberglass shell using the boat-building technique.

HUBS

Like the spokes in a bicycle wheel, the blades become part of the rotor when attached to a hub. The hub holds everything together and transmits the motion of the blades into torque, or turning force. Three aspects of the hub are important: how the blades are attached, whether the pitch is fixed or variable, and whether or not this attachment is flexible.

All conventional wind turbines today use blades cantilevered from the hub, that is, they're supported only at the hub just as the wing of a modern airplane is attached only at the fuselage. During the late 1970s and early 1980s some European designs used struts and stays to brace the blades, following the pattern of the famous Danish wind machine at Gedser. Struts increase the drag on the rotor, but they reduce bending on the root of the blade where it attaches to the hub. Consequently, the spar, the main structural support of the blade, and its attachment to the hub need not be as massive as on a cantilevered blade. Struts and stays work fine on upwind machines as long as the turbine stays upwind. They tend to fail when the turbine inadvertently swings downwind. Early Danish designs were susceptible to this weakness, which led to an industry-wide abandonment of struts and stays for bracing the rotor.

Most hubs are rigid: they don't allow the blades to flap back and forth in gusty winds. The blades may change pitch by turning about their long axis, but they don't change from the plane of rotation. In nearly all wind turbines currently on the market, the blades are bolted directly to a rigid hub. Most don't change pitch. During the late 1980s and early 1990s several manufacturers of medium-sized wind turbines for commercial applications, 25 meters in diameter and larger, reintroduced pitchable blades to control the rotor in high winds.

On some wind machines a rotor made up of two blades may teeter or rock about the hub. The rotor, as a unit, swings in and out of the plane of rotation like a teeter-totter. This teetering action relieves forces on the blade during gusty winds, when the turbine yaws in response to changing wind direction, and when the blade passes through the tower's wake. Though engineers have long stressed its advantages and simplicity, no wind turbines using the technique have proven commercially successful.

Following the hub, the remainder of the drive train consists of the main shaft to which the rotor is attached, the transmission (where used), and the generator.

TRANSMISSIONS

There are three ways to transfer power from the rotor to the generator: direct drive, mechanical transmissions, and hydraulic transmissions. The simplest method is to drive the generator directly with the rotor. This eliminates the need for a transmission and reduces the complexity of the drive train. Direct drive also offers slightly higher conversion efficiencies because no power is lost going through a gearbox. Direct drive, though, requires a specially designed slow-speed generator that may be larger and may demand greater amounts of expensive materials than a conventional generator driven at higher speeds via a transmission. The most successful of the pre-REA windchargers, the Jacobs home light plant, used direct drive. Although the industry flirted with gear-driven machines during the 1970s and early 1980s, most small wind turbines today, especially those featured in this book, use direct drive.

The chief competitor of the old Jacobs generator, Wincharger, took the transmission approach. They used one large helical gear on the main shaft of the rotor to drive a small gear on the generator. During the 1970s Sencenbaugh Wind Electric's Model 1000 used a similar approach. The transmission increased the 350-rpm speed of the wind turbine to 1100 rpm at the generator. Even with this 3:1 gear ratio a low-speed alternator was still necessary. Most generators need 1800 rpm to operate properly; others are designed for 1200 rpm operation.

On small machines such as the Sencenbaugh or old Wincharger it's also possible to use belts and chains instead of gearing. Most home-built machines use belts and pulleys because they're cheap and readily available. Cogged belts, for example, were used by the defunct manufacturer Aeropower. In practice, belts and chains have proven unreliable. Today no one uses either belts or chains as the principal means to transmit power to the generator on commercial wind machines of any size.

As wind turbine models grow in size the need for a transmission becomes more pressing because the speed of the main shaft decreases. For small machines, transmissions with only one or two stages of parallel shafts may suffice. But with medium-sized wind turbines more stages may be necessary, or designers may even opt for planetary or epicyclic gear boxes.

Inventors often suggest using hydraulic transmissions because they can more easily be matched to the torque characteristics of a wind turbine rotor than a mechanical transmission. In principle they should also be simpler. These advantages are offset, however, by greater inefficiencies. The only large-scale test of hydraulic transmissions, the Bendix-Schachle turbine once owned by Southern California Edison, ended in ignominious failure. No wind turbine using a hydraulic transmission has ever been either a technical or a commercial success.

GENERATORS

First and foremost, generators are not perpetual motion machines. They transfer power, not create it. Power must be delivered to a generator before you can get power out of it. (In our case the prime mover, as it's called, is the rotor.) Nor are generators 100 percent efficient at transferring this power. The rotor will deliver more power to the generator than the generator produces as electricity. This leads us to a fundamental principle about the size of wind turbines. The size of a generator indicates only how much power the generator is capable of producing if the wind turbine's rotor is big enough, and if there's enough wind to drive the generator at the right speed. Thus, we once again confront the fact that a wind turbine's size is primarily governed by the size of the rotor.

The generator converts the mechanical power of the spinning wind turbine into electricity. In its simplest form a generator is nothing more than a coil of wire spinning in a magnetic field. Consequently, whether generating direct current (DC) or alternating current (AC), a generator must have:

1. Coils of wire in which the electricity is generated and through which it flows.

2. A magnetic field.

3. Relative motion between the coils of wire and the magnetic field.

By varying each of these conditions you can design a generator of any size for any application.

Power in an electrical circuit is the product of current and voltage. In a generator the armature is the coil of wire where output voltage is generated and through which current flows to the load. The portion of the generator where the magnetic field is produced is the field. Relative motion between the two is obtained by either spinning the armature within the field or spinning the field within the armature. As you would expect, the stationary part of the generator is the stator; the spinning part is the rotor.

The power produced by a generator depends on the size and length of the wires used in the armature, the strength of the magnetic field, and the rate of motion between them. Increase any one, and you increase the potential power of the generator. The size of the wire in the armature determines the maximum current that can be drawn from the generator before it overheats, melts its insulation, shorts out, and otherwise destroys itself. The heavier the wire, the more current it can carry. As long as the wind turbine's rotor continues to provide greater and greater amounts of power as wind speed increases, the generator will continue to produce more current until the generator overheats. To prevent such occurrences, generators have a mechanism for limiting current to a safe maximum.

Generators are rated in terms of the maximum current they can supply at a specified voltage and (for AC generators) at a specific frequency. This rating is given on the name-plate in amps and volts (and frequency where appropriate), as kilowatts and volts, or as kilovolt-amperes (kVA). The generator may be rated for the current it can supply continuously or the current it can supply for only a short period. If generator size is of concern to you, always check which rating is being used. Reputable manufacturers rate their generators for continuous rather than intermittent duty.

Let's turn to voltage, the other half of the power mix. Generated voltage depends on the rate at which magnetic lines of force are crossed by the wire loops in the armature. Designers alter voltage by changing the magnetic field, by changing the rate of motion between them, or both.

The generator's field is provided by magnets. With electromagnets, some power is used to "excite" or "energize" the field around the armature. The strength of this field is a function of the length of wire (the number of coils) in the field windings and the current flowing through them. For example, double the length of wire in the windings and you double the strength of the field, doubling generated voltage.

Many of the windchargers built during the 1930s produced 32 volts. Resistance losses are high when transmitting low-voltage power. Because of this, most reconditioned windchargers were rewound for 110 volts. The old wire was stripped off the generator and replaced with more turns of thinner wire. Less current could be drawn through the smaller wire than before, but the increased length of wire produced a stronger field, increasing the voltage. Generating capability was not affected, power from the generator remained the same, but the balance between the voltage and current changed: voltage increased and current decreased by an equivalent amount.

Permanent magnets can also provide the field. They don't require power for excitation, because they're inherently, that is, permanently, magnetic. The principal means for increasing field strength with permanent magnets is to use magnets with greater magnetic density.

The voltage can also be increased by adding more or larger field coils, by adding more permanent magnets, or by increasing the speed at which the armature windings pass through the field. This can be accomplished by increasing the diameter and length of the generator so there's room for more magnets, or by spinning the rotor faster.

Yes, all this does have some bearing on the design of wind-driven generators. To get a feel for how, let's examine two popular pre-REA wind machines. Both Jacobs and Wincharger used about the same size rotor (14 feet, or 4 meters); thus the power available to the generator and the speed of the rotors were roughly equivalent. Yet Jacobs chose to use a direct-drive generator whereas Wincharger chose a transmission.

To produce the same power and voltage as Wincharger without a transmission, Jacobs had to design a generator that would operate at lower shaft speeds. Jacobs did so by increasing both the diameter and the length of its generator. This allowed the use of more field coils (six to Wincharger's four). The coils were also longer.

The Jacobs generator's greater diameter also increased the speed at the periphery of the armature where it passed the field coils. Doubling the diameter doubles the rate at which the armature cuts through the field. The effect is the same as that from a 2:1 transmission that doubles the speed of the generator.

All in all, the Jacobs generator was considerably larger and used much more copper and iron than did Wincharger's to do the same job. But the Jacobs generator could do that job at a slower speed. Jacobs chose a slow speed generator for long bearing life and simplicity, believing these advantages offset the greater cost.

Barry Commoner's adage, "There's no such thing as a free lunch," puts it succinctly. Whether it's the design of generators or any other wind machine component, there's always a trade-off. You gain something only by giving up something else. You hope that what you gain is more valuable than what you've lost. It's as true today as it was during the 1930s. Small wind turbine designers who stress long life and low maintenance choose lower generator speeds. The price they pay is increased costs.

Manufacturers of small wind turbines intended for remote sites in harsh environments may opt, as Jacobs did, for building slow-speed generators tailored to their wind turbine. That's just what most of today's manufacturers, such as Bergey Windpower, Northern Power Systems, and others, have done. They build specially designed, direct drive, slow-speed alternators.

The trade-offs are also apparent in medium-sized wind turbines. During the early 1980s many American-designed wind turbines that operated at high speeds were installed. These machines were not only noisy, they were also trouble prone. Danish designs operating at much more modest speeds eventually won more than half the California market. Like Jacobs before them, the rugged Danish designs opted for lower speeds to reduce wear and tear. The Danish turbines typically drove a six-pole generator at 1200 rpm, while their American competitors used four-pole generators running at 1800 rpm. Today none of the early U.S. designs are still being built.

ALTERNATORS

Pre-REA windchargers produced DC by spinning the armature within the field. Power was drawn off the rotating armature through brushes. During the 1960s the auto industry began replacing DC generators with alternators. Alternators offer several advantages over DC generators. For a given output, alternators cost less than generators, and an alternator's slip rings last much longer than the brushes in a generator. Slip rings are more durable because they don't carry the alternator's current output as brushes do in a generator.

The battle between alternators and generators is far from over. Some die-hards, such as Mick Sagrillo at Lake Michigan Wind & Sun, believe that DC generators still offer promise. Sagrillo, who rebuilds DC generators, argues that special-purpose generators, such as the Jacobs home light plant, use oversized brushes to ensure long life. These brushes don't wear out as quickly as many imagine, he says. Further, Sagrillo maintains that a generator gives better high-end performance than an alternator. Still, Sagrillo concedes that alternators now dominate the market.

In today's alternator the field, rather than the armature, revolves. Power is drawn off the stator from fixed terminals. Excitation of the alternator's field is provided through slip rings on the rotor, but only enough power passes through the slip rings to excite the field (a small percentage of the alternator's output). There are no brushes and no commutators to wear from the passage of high current. There's no arcing at the brushes. There are no slip rings—no moving contacts—in a permanent-magnet alternator because the field is permanently excited.

In a conventional alternator the field revolves inside the stator. But Bergey Windpower, Marlec Engineering, and SOMA Power all spin the permanent-magnet field outside the stator. They attach the blades of their rotors to the magnet ring that spins around the armature. Power is drawn off from inside the generator. This arrangement, which eliminates the need for slip rings, has become common among small wind turbines.

As the name implies, alternators generate AC. As the rotor spins, current rises and falls like waves on the ocean (electrons in the armature are first jostled in one direction, then alter course and are jostled the other way). The alternator's frequency is the rate at which current rises and falls; it's given in cycles per second or hertz. The speed of the rotor and the number of poles determine the alternator's frequency. Drive the alternator faster and frequency increases; slow the rotor and frequency decreases. This explains why most small wind turbines generate variable-frequency AC. When wind speed rises, the turbine spins faster, increasing frequency (as well as voltage and current). When the wind subsides, frequency decreases.

In a simple alternator the four poles are wired together in series as a single circuit producing single-phase AC. When three groups of poles are arranged symmetrically around the stator, the alternator produces threephase AC, each phase one-third out of sync with the next. Most alternators used in wind systems produce three-phase AC. Three-phase alternators do more with less. The designer can more efficiently pack poles within the generator. Power is determined by the rate at which lines of force are cut by the armature. Thus we can increase power by increasing the number of poles to take up all the available space within the generator.

If you've ever spun the shaft of a toy generator in your hand, you remember how it felt when the rotor would stick slightly as the coils in the armature aligned with the magnets in the field. As the coils passed by the magnets, the shaft would turn more easily. This same effect, cogging, occurs in large generators and motors. Cogging is of interest in wind machines because it can retard the startup of the wind turbine in light winds when the poles are aligned. Increasing the number of poles by arranging them in three phases reduces cogging, enabling the turbine to start more easily in light winds.

VARIABLE- OR CONSTANT-SPEED OPERATION

Wind machines driving electrical generators operate in either of two ways: at variable speed, or at constant speed. In the first case, the speed of the wind turbine varies with the speed of the wind. In the second, the speed of the wind turbine remains relatively constant as wind speed fluctuates.

In all small wind turbines built today, the speed of the rotor varies with wind speed. This simplifies the turbine's controls while improving aerodynamic performance. When such wind machines drive an alternator, both the voltage and frequency vary with wind speed. The electricity they produce isn't compatible with the constant-voltage, constant- frequency AC produced by the utility. If you used the output from these wind turbines directly, your clocks would gain and lose time, and your lights would brighten and dim as wind speeds fluctuated. Eventually you'd burn up every motor in the house. Unless you have a use for this low-grade electricity (heating, pumping water, and so on), the output from these wind machines must be treated or conditioned first, even if it's simply for charging batteries.

Because batteries can't use AC, the alternator's output must be converted to DC. As in your car alternator, diodes—electrical check valves that permit the current to flow in only one direction—rectify the AC output to DC, which is then used for battery charging.

To produce utility-grade electricity, either the alternator's AC or rectified DC can be treated with a synchronous inverter to produce constant voltage 60-cycle AC like that from the utility. Most of these inverters, though not all, are line commutated. They must be interconnected with the utility to operate. The utility's AC provides a signal that triggers electronic switches within the inverter, which transfers the variable quality electricity at just the right time to produce 60-cycle AC at the proper voltage. No utility power is consumed in the process. It's merely used as a signal to coordinate the switching.

Though some manufacturers of medium-sized wind machines are now building variable-speed turbines, most models operate the rotor at or near constant speed. The latter produce utility-compatible power directly. They don't require power conditioning, because they produce electricity synchronized directly with that from the utility. There are two ways to do this.

One method is to drive an alternator at a constant speed so voltage and frequency remain constant. Synchronous alternators are used primarily in the utility industry. Power to the generator is controlled precisely by limiting steam to the turbines. This keeps the generator spinning at just the right speed to maintain synchronization with the utility's other generators. On a wind machine it's much more difficult to control the turbine's speed because the source of power, the wind, constantly varies. Complex and fast reacting mechanisms for changing the pitch of the blades are required to maintain a constant generator speed. To date only a few giant experimental wind machines have been able to justify the cost of synchronous alternators. No commercial wind turbines of any size use this technique today.

INDUCTION GENERATORS

Another approach uses induction generators. These have two advantages over alternators: they're cheap, and they can supply synchronous power without sophisticated controls. Induction generators are simply induction motors (like the motor in your refrigerator) in disguise.

An induction motor becomes a generator when driven above its synchronous speed. Plug an induction motor into an outlet and the motor will turn at 1800 rpm, consuming power. Leave it plugged in, but now drive the motor at 1800 rpm. The motor will no longer consume power from the outlet. You're now supplying it. Spin the rotor just a little faster, say at 1820 rpm, and it won't be consuming electricity, it will be generating it. As you try to spin the motor faster it gets harder to turn. The utility consumes the additional power as you produce it, without rotor speed appreciably increasing.

In a wind turbine which drives an induction generator, when wind speed increases, the load on the generator automatically increases, as more torque (power) is delivered by the rotor. This continues until the generator reaches its limit and either breaks away from the grip of the utility or overheats and catches fire. Technically, induction generators are not true constant-speed or synchronous machines. As the load increases, the generator speed slips by 2-5 percent, or 36-90 rpm on an 1800-rpm generator.

Induction generators have proven extremely popular for wind turbines because they're readily available in a range of sizes, and interconnection with the utility is straightforward. Literally, plug it in and go. Early promotions for the defunct manufacturer Enertech showed its wind machines being plugged into a wall socket. Interconnection is a little more sophisticated today, but the principle remains the same. The wind machine is wired to a dedicated circuit in your service panel or directly with the utility. Utilities are much more comfortable with induction generators than with synchronous inverters because they understand them better. Synchronous inverters, for all their benefits, still remain a mystery to many utilities.

When looking at a wind machine's generator there's no need to be dazzled by the technology employed. Your primary concern is what kind of power it produces. If you want utility-compatible power, then you can't use a wind machine with an alternator that doesn't also include a synchronous inverter.

The inverter shouldn't be something slapped together just for the occasion. Experience with inverters has shown that they must be carefully tailored to the generator. The inverter not only produces 60-cycle AC at the correct voltage but it also performs another important function. It loads and unloads the generator as more or less wind is available. When the inverter and generator are improperly matched, the wind machine will not perform optimally. The rotor may require higher winds than necessary to start, or it may never reach the tip-speed ratio where it performs most efficiently. At the other extreme the inverter may not load the generator sufficiently to extract all the power available.

Likewise, if you want a wind machine for charging batteries at a remote hunting cabin, you won't be able to use an induction generator. They only work when interconnected with the utility.

You will need to look at what's available. Wind machines larger than 10 meters in diameter use induction generators almost exclusively. If you want a slow-speed, permanent-magnet alternator on a wind machine larger than 10 meters (33 feet) in diameter, you're simply out of luck. Mid-sized wind turbines typically are much more complex than their smaller counterparts. Nearly all use transmissions, and many use two generators.

As mentioned elsewhere, don't be swayed by the size of the generator alone. It's only an indication of how much power the generator is capable of producing, not how much it will generate. Ask Danish manufacturers what size generator they have in their machine and they'll look at you quizzically and ask, "Which one?" Danish wind machines often use two induction generators, one for low winds and another, much larger, generator for higher winds.

Induction generators operate inefficiently at partial loads. For a wind machine with a generator designed to reach its rated output in a 25-35 mph (11- 15 m/s) wind the generator would operate at partial load most of the time. Rather than use only one generator, Danish designers bring a smaller one on line first so that it operates at nearly full load in low to moderate winds. As wind speed increases they drop the smaller generator while energizing the larger or main generator. Thus, both generators operate more efficiently than either alone, and overall performance of the wind machine is improved.

The two generators may be in tandem and driven by the same shaft, or they can be side by side with the small generator being driven by belts from the main generator. Usually both generators are spun at the same time and are not brought on line mechanically but by energizing the field electrically. In some designs, the generator is wired in two stages: during light winds the first stage uses only a portion of the generator's capacity, and in higher winds the second stage uses the generator's full potential.

The use of dual generators permits most Danish turbines to operate at two speeds. This enables them to operate the generator and the rotor at a higher efficiency. Though they are not true variable-speed machines and can't take full advantage of the optimum tip-speed ratio, these turbines can bracket the optimum range. This is particularly useful in low winds where efficiency is most crucial.

ROTOR CONTROLS

The rotor is the single most critical element of any wind turbine. It's what confronts the elements and harnesses the wind. Because the blades of the rotor must be relatively large and operate at relatively high speed to capture the energy in the wind, they're the most prone to catastrophic failure. How a wind turbine controls the forces acting on the rotor, particularly in high winds, is of the utmost importance to the long-term, reliable functioning of a wind machine.

The simplest and most foolproof method for controlling the rotor is to decrease the area of the rotor intercepting the wind as wind speeds exceed the turbine's operating range. As frontal area decreases, less wind acts on the blades. This reduces the rotor's torque, power, and speed. The thrust on the blades (the force trying to break the blades off the hub) and the thrust on the tower (the force trying to knock the tower over) are also reduced. This method of rotor control permits the use of lighter-weight and less expensive towers than on wind machines where the rotor remains facing into the wind under all conditions.

Halladay's umbrella mills exemplified the concept. These nineteenth-century water-pumping wind machines automatically opened their segmented rotor into a hollow cylinder in high winds, letting the wind pass through unimpeded. Each segment was composed of several blades mounted on a shaft, allowing the segment to swing into and out of the wind. When the segments are closed, Halladay's windmill looked like any other water-pumping windmill from the period. But in high winds thrust on the segments would force them to flip open. This action was balanced by counterweights so the farmer could adjust the speed at which the windmill would open and close.

HORIZONTAL FURLING

Later developers, such as the Reverend Leonard Wheeler, chose to use the same control concept (changing the area of the rotor intercepting the wind) but in a different manner. Rather than swing segments of the rotor parallel to the wind, Wheeler thought it simpler to swing the entire rotor out of the wind. He couldn't do this with the downwind rotor used by Halladay. Instead, he used a rotor upwind of the tower; a tail vane kept the rotor pointed into the wind.

The tail vane and rotor (wind wheel to old-timers) were hinged to permit the rotor to swing sideways toward the tail. As the rotor furled toward the tail, the rotor disc took the shape of a narrower and narrower ellipse, gradually decreasing the area exposed to the wind. The mechanism for executing this was the pilot vane. The pilot vane extended just beyond and parallel to the rotor disc. Unlike the tail vane, the pilot vane was fixed in position relative to the rotor. Wind striking the pilot vane pushed the rotor toward the tail and out of the wind. In the folded position the rotor and pilot vane were parallel to the wind like the segments of the Halladay rotor. The thrust on the pilot vane was counterbalanced with weights. By adjusting the weights the farmer could determine the wind speed at which the rotor would begin to furl.

As the American farm windmill evolved, the pilot vane went the way of hand cranks on cars. Offsetting the axis of the rotor slightly from the axis about which the wind machine yaws or pivots around the top of the tower produced the same results: self-furling in high winds. When the rotor axis is offset from the yaw axis, the wind's thrust on the rotor creates a force acting on a small moment arm (lever) represented by the distance between the two axes. The wind's thrust turns the rotor out of the wind. The tail vane is hinged, allowing the rotor to furl.

On contemporary farm windmills there are no weights and levers to counteract the furling thrust. Instead they use springs. By adjusting the tension in the spring, the farmer controls the wind speed at which the rotor furls. To see this for yourself, find an operating farm windmill and watch it in high winds. It will constantly fold toward the tail and reopen without any intervention.

Millions of machines using Wheeler's approach to overspeed control have been put into operation around the world. It's what you might call a proven concept. And if it worked reliably for all those machines for all those years, it should still work today. It does.

Nearly all small wind turbines today use furling of one form or another. Bergey Windpower's turbines have operated unattended in wind speeds above 120 mph (54 m/s) as have products by other manufacturers that also use furling.

The Bergey series of small wind turbines carries simplicity even further than the farm windmill. Rather than using springs to control furling, Bergey designs use gravity for returning the rotor to its running position. The hinge pin for the tail vane on the Bergey machines is skewed a few degrees from the vertical. When the rotor furls in high winds it lifts the tail vane slightly. As the wind subsides, the weight of the tail pulls itself down into position, forcing the rotor to swing back into the wind.

Wind machines using this approach, like the water-pumping windmills before them, can be controlled manually by furling the rotor with a winch and cable. The rotor doesn't come to a complete stop when furled. It will continue to spin but at low speeds and power.

VERTICAL FURLING

During the 1930s Parris-Dunn built a windcharger that used a variation on the furling theme. Rather than turning the rotor parallel to the tail vane, they chose to tip the rotor up out of the wind. In high winds the turbine would take on the appearance of a helicopter. As the winds subsided, the rotor would rock back toward the horizontal. Northern Power Systems' High Reliability series, SOMA, and Wind Baron's NEO have all adopted this technology. It's a simple strategy that works well. Northern Power Systems' HR3 model has survived winds in excess of 176 mph (79 m/s) using this approach.

Like the original Parris-Dunn, Northern Power and Wind Baron use a spring to control the wind speed at which the rotor begins to furl. The wind speed at which the rotor begins to pitch back is governed by tension in the spring. The SOMA turbine accomplishes the same effect with a sliding weight. The principal difference among the three manufacturers is the means they use for dampening the action of the rotor and generator as it rocks back and forth. Gusty winds can cause the rotor to tip up, then quickly rock forward, dropping the rotor and generator onto the wind machine's frame, severely jarring the blades and the rotor's main shaft. Both Northern Power and SOMA use a shock absorber that dampens the return of the rotor to the running position. Wind Baron's NEO follows the Parris-Dunn example and simply uses a rubber pad to cushion the blow.

Dr. Peter Musgrove's contribution to wind technology was designing a way to reduce the rotor's intercept area on vertical axis turbines (see Figure 13-8). As mentioned before, the H-rotor configuration offers several advantages over a conventional Darrieus turbine. Its weakness is the tremendous forces trying to bend the blades at the juncture between them and the crossarm. These bending forces can be reduced and the speed of the rotor controlled by hinging the blades. In the Musgrove turbine the blades are hinged to the cross-arm in such a manner that the portion of the blade above the cross-arm is not equal to the portion below. As the rotor spins, centrifugal force throws the heavier portion of the blade away from the vertical, varying the geometry of the rotor. The wind and rotor speed at which this occurs is determined by the weight of the blade and the tension in a spring restraining the blades in the upright position. At high wind speeds the blades approach the horizontal, reducing the intercept area. Though there are some experimental versions in England, no wind turbine using Musgrove's "variable geometry" has been commercially successful.

VARIABLE GEOMETRY VAWT

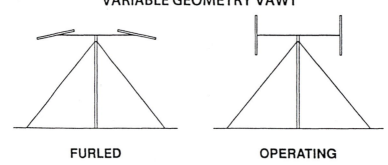

FURLED   **OPERATING**

Figure 13-8 Variable-geometry H-rotor. In this ingenious design developed by Dr. Peter Musgrove of Reading University, the straight blades of the rotor are hinged so that they tilt toward the horizontal at high rotor speeds.

When most people first consider the problem of controlling a rotor in high winds, they think immediately of changing blade pitch. This probably results from our exposure to propeller-driven airplanes. Indeed, a wind turbine rotor can be controlled much like the blades on the propeller of a commuter plane. Like changing intercept area, changing blade pitch affects the power available to the rotor. By increasing or decreasing blade pitch we can control the amount of lift that the blade produces.

There are two directions in which the blades can be pitched: pitching them toward stall, or pitching them toward feather. Blade pitch is usually set a few degrees into the wind. If the blade is nearly parallel with its direction of travel (perpendicular to the wind) it stalls. The blade is feathered, on the other hand, when it is at right angles to its direction of travel (90-degrees pitch), or parallel to the wind. To feather a blade it must be turned farther than when stalling the blade, causing the pitch mechanism to act through a much greater distance.

Stall destroys the blades' lift, limiting the power and speed of the rotor, but it does nothing to reduce the thrust on the rotor or the tower. Though it is simpler to build a mechanism for stalling the blade than it is to build a feathering governor, the technique is less reliable. On upwind machines, thrust on the blades bends them toward the tower. Designs dependent on blade stall as the sole means of overspeed protection have a poor survival record. The blades have a nasty habit of striking the tower. Downwind turbines using stall regulation have had fewer problems because the blades are forced to cone farther downwind and away from the tower. Still, they too have had an overall poor reliability record.

Where changing blade pitch is the primary means of control on an upwind rotor in high winds, the blade should rotate toward full feather. By so doing the drag on the blade is reduced to one-fifth of that on a blade flatwise to the wind.

Governors for pitching the blades appear in a variety of forms. During the 1930s, the Jacobs brothers popularized the flyball governor. Above normal rotor speeds the weights would feather all three blades simultaneously via a mechanical linkage to three weights. (It's important that all blades change pitch at the same rate. If they don't, the rotor will become unbalanced, causing severe vibrations.) This massive 100-pound governor protected the 14-foot rotor reliably when carefully adjusted. On later models, Jacobs also marketed a clever version called the Allied (after a windcharger on which it first appeared) or blade-actuated governor.

Why use weights when you don't have to? The blade-actuated governor uses the weight of the blades themselves to change pitch. Unlike the blades on the flyball governor, the blades not only turn on a shaft in the hub, they also slide along the shaft. Each blade is connected to the hub through a knuckle and springs. The knuckle in turn is attached to a triangular spider. As the rotor spins, the blades are thrown away from the hub, causing them to slide along the blade shaft. When they do, the blades pull on the spider, which rotates the blades toward feather. The springs govern the rotor speed at which this occurs. Like the flyball governor, the blade-actuated governor works reliably when properly adjusted and built to the highest material standards.

In the late 1970s Marcellus Jacobs, the sole surviving founder of the original Jacobs Wind Electric Company, reentered the wind business. (The original firm ceased activity during the 1950s.) Along with his son Paul, Marcellus began manufacturing wind turbines patterned after his earlier models. His company briefly built wind turbines 7-8 meters (21-26 feet) in diameter. Jacobs' redesigned machine didn't depend solely on blade feathering to control rotor speed, since the blade-actuated governor was inadequate for a machine of this size. The new Jacobs turbine was also self-furling. The governor feathered the blades to limit power output to the alternator; overspeed protection was provided by furling the rotor toward the tail.

On small wind turbines mechanical governors, whether or not blade actuated, have proven too costly and unreliable. They are also too maintenance-intensive for the modern wind turbine market. Only the French manufacturer Aerowatt still uses pitch weights to govern the rotor. Aerowatts are used only in France or in French overseas territories. None of the advanced small wind turbines on the market today use this technology.

Despite this trend there are hundreds of small windchargers from the 1930s and from the Jacobs' revival in the 1970s operating in the United States that still rely on mechanical governors. With proper maintenance and a supply of spare parts, these machines will last for several more decades. Owners of these turbines argue that mechanical governors provide better power output in high winds than does furling. In winds above the rated speed, power output drops sharply on machines that furl, while small wind turbines using mechanical governors are able to maintain near constant peak power.

You can change blade pitch without using a mechanical governor. In the bearingless rotor concept the blades are attached to the hub with a torsionally flexible spar. At high speeds the blades twist the spar toward zero pitch, stalling the rotor. Weights attached to the blades are sometimes used to provide the necessary force. There are no moving parts in the hub: no bearings, knuckles, or sliding shafts. Several have attempted to market this technology on medium-sized wind turbines. All have failed because rotor dynamics are far more complex than first envisioned.

Carter Wind Systems' 10-meter turbine best represented this control strategy. The filament-wound, fiberglass spar permitted the blade to twist torsionally. During high winds small weights inside the blades would rotate the blade toward stall in one movement. The flexible spar also permitted the blade to cone progressively downwind of the tower in high winds like the fronds on a palm tree during a hurricane. This design, though elegantly simple, was too unreliable and is no longer manufactured.

Several medium-sized wind turbines currently on the market successfully use pitch control to limit power in high winds. Most of these machines are greater than 25 meters in diameter, so the higher costs and complexity of pitch control can be justified.

AERODYNAMIC STALL

Almost all wind machines without pitch control use aerodynamic stall to some extent for limiting power from the rotor. This is particularly true of medium-sized wind turbines, which use fixed-pitch rotors to drive induction generators. In winds above the rated speed, the tip-speed ratio for these turbines declines because the speed of the rotor remains constant. The angle of attack increases with increasing wind speed for wind turbines operating at constant speed, lowering the performance of the blades below the optimum.

Designers seldom rely on blade stall as the sole means of overspeed protection. Stall is most effective on induction wind machines with fixed-pitch rotors. Induction generators, however, are dependent on the utility for controlling the load. During a power outage the generator immediately loses this load. The rotor, no longer restrained to run at a constant speed, immediately accelerates. Stall now becomes ineffectual for regulating power until a new equilibrium is reached. Unfortunately, this occurs at extremely high rotor speeds.

On an upwind machine with a tail vane the rotor can be prevented from destroying itself by furling the rotor out of the wind. Since tail vanes are limited to small turbines, medium-sized upwind machines and all fixed pitch downwind machines must use a different strategy. Brakes are the most popular.

Once brakes have been selected as the means to limit rotor speed during a loss-of-load emergency, they're also frequently used during normal operation. In a typical fixed-pitch wind machine the brake is applied at the cut-out speed to stop the rotor. Wind turbines using this approach require strong blades should the brake fail and the rotor accelerate to destructive speeds.

Consider the case of a small downwind turbine driving an induction generator that was braked to a halt at the cut-out speed. When the manufacturer, Enertech, first introduced the machine, it stressed that the rotor was stall-regulated and that it could operate safely above the cut-out speed without the brake. The rotor was braked, asserted Enertech's vice president only to minimize wear on the drive train at high wind speeds. The amount of energy in the wind at these higher speeds, he said, did not warrant the cost of capturing it. Mother Nature soon gave Enertech ample opportunities to prove its mettle. The brake failed on several occasions. Rotors went into overspeed, and several Enertechs destroyed themselves. Stall alone wasn't enough to protect the rotor. Enertech later added tip brakes for such emergencies.

MECHANICAL BRAKES

Brakes can be placed on either the main (slow-speed) shaft or on the highspeed shaft. Brakes on the high-speed shaft are the most common because the brakes can be smaller and less expensive for the needed braking torque than those on the main shaft. When on the high-speed shaft, the brakes can be found between the transmission and the generator or on the tail end of the generator. In either arrangement braking torque places heavy loads on the transmission and couplings between the transmission and generator. Moreover, should the transmission or high-speed shaft fail, the brake can no longer stop the rotor.

In general, brakes on fixed-pitch machines should be located on the main shaft where they provide direct control over the rotor. (There's always a greater likelihood of a transmission failure than a failure of the main shaft.) But the lower shaft speeds require more braking pressure and greater braking area. As a result, the brakes are larger and more costly than those on the high-speed shaft.

Brakes can be applied mechanically, electrically, or hydraulically. Most operate in a fail-safe manner. In other words it takes power to release the brake. The brake automatically engages when the wind machine loses power. Springs provide the force in a mechanical brake; batteries, the electricity in an electrical brake; and a reservoir, the pressure in a hydraulic brake.

The problem with brakes of any kind is that they fail—not often, it's true, but once is enough. Brake pads require replacement or adjustment periodically. After extensive use the calipers have to travel farther to reach the disc. If the brakes are spring applied, pressure from the springs decreases and so does braking torque as travel increases. In one 12-meter model built briefly during the late 1970s the brake just didn't supply enough torque to stop the rotor, and there were no backup devices to protect the turbine. Several machines ran to destruction, but some were brought under control when the designer, Terry Mehrkam, climbed the tower, wedged a lever into the brake, and manually forced the pads against the disc. This dangerous practice eventually cost Mehrkam his life.

Experience has taught wind turbine designers that wherever a brake is used to control the rotor, there must be an aerodynamic means to limit rotor speed should the brake fail. There are three common choices for aerodynamic overspeed protection on wind machines without tail vanes and pitch controls: tip brakes, spoilers, and pitchable blade tips. These devices are found frequently on medium-sized wind turbines using fixed-pitch rotors to drive induction generators.

AERODYNAMIC BRAKES

Tip brakes are plates attached to the end of each blade. They're activated by centrifugal force once the rotor reaches excessive speed. When deployed, they slap or drag at the wind. They're simple, effective, and they have saved many a fixed-pitch rotor from destruction. Tip brakes, however, have been likened to keeping your foot on the accelerator at the same time you're stepping on the brake. They keep the rotor from reaching destructive speeds but do nothing to reduce the lift of the blade or the thrust on the wind turbine and tower. Tip brakes are also noisy and reduce the performance of the rotor under operating conditions by increasing drag at the tip where blade speed is greatest.

Most of the power in the wind is captured by the outer third of the rotor. Consequently, it's not necessary to change the pitch of the entire blade to limit the rotor's power and speed. The performance of the blade in this region can be reduced by using spoilers or movable blade tips. In one Danish design if there's a loss of load or the brake fails, centrifugal force activates spoilers along the length of each blade. The spoilers pop out of the blade and change the shape of the airfoil, destroying its effectiveness, reducing power and rotor speed.

Many stall-regulated Danish wind turbines use pitchable blade tips. Medium-sized turbines 15-25 meters in diameter use passive controls to activate the blade tips. At higher than normal rotor speeds the tips are thrown away from the rotor by centrifugal force, causing them to slide along a grooved shaft. As they move along the shaft the tips pitch toward feather. This action decreases lift where it's greatest while dramatically increasing drag. Both spoilers and pitchable blade tips have proven highly successful, though refinements have been necessary. For example, frequently only one or two of the blade tips would activate at the same time, rather than all three.

Both Boeing's 2.5 MW Mod-2 and its 3.2 MW Mod-5B used a similar approach. But instead of using passive controls, Boeing hydraulically drove the tips toward the feathered position. Boeing actively positioned the blade tips to regulate power. Today most fixed-pitch turbines greater than 25 meters (80 feet) in diameter actively regulate the pitch of the blade tips to control power, much like Boeing did.

PUTTING IT ALL TOGETHER

Let's look at two types of wind machines and how their manufacturers put all the pieces together. We'll also look at how they operate under normal and emergency conditions. The first group are the advanced small wind turbines designed specifically for high-reliability, low-maintenance applications. The second group are medium-sized wind turbines like those found in California wind plants and throughout Denmark.

SMALL TURBINES

All small wind turbines today are specially designed for simplicity, ruggedness, and low maintenance. Mike and Karl Bergey quote Antoine de Saint Exupéry to express Bergey Windpower's design philosophy, "Perfection is achieved not when there is nothing more to add but when there is nothing more to take away."

Today's advanced small wind turbines, typically employ an upwind rotor and are passively directed into the wind by tail vanes. All but Northern Power Systems' HR3 drive permanent-magnet alternators directly without the aid of transmissions. All are well suited for stand-alone, battery-charging applications. Through use of a synchronous inverter, some, such as the Bergey Excel, can also be used by homes, farms, and businesses with existing utility service.

These turbines all operate at variable speed. From startup through furling, the rotor rpm increases with increasing wind speed. Similarly, voltage and frequency increase with wind speed. In winds above the rated speed, the blades begin stalling and performance of the rotor decreases. Above the furling speed, the rotor begins to swing toward the tail vane. Power drops dramatically as furling proceeds. (This drop in power is characteristic of self-furling machines. Small, pitch-regulated turbines typically limit peak power.) When high winds subside, the turbine returns to its operating position automatically.

Blade stall and furling are the only means for limiting the rotor's speed and power during both normal and emergency conditions. There are no brakes either to stop the rotor in high winds or to park the rotor for servicing. Nor are there brakes to prevent the wind machine from yawing about the top of the tower in response to changes in wind direction.

The designers of these machines stressed simplicity and ruggedness over greater control. Bergey Windpower, SOMA Power, and Marlec Engineering go one step farther and integrate the hub and rotor housing into one assembly. Because they furl the rotor horizontally toward the tail in their designs, Bergey goes so far as to combine the mainframe and stator assembly into one unit. All are designed for little or no maintenance, with good reason. At windy sites it's not uncommon for a wind machine to be in operation for two-thirds of the time, or about 6000 hours per year. At that rate, a wind machine would operate as many hours in the first 4 months of the year as an automobile driven 100,000 miles at 50 mph. Over a 30-year lifetime a wind machine 3 meters in diameter will accumulate 4 billion revolutions, or the equivalent of a car driven 9 million miles.

In programs where performance has been monitored, wind machines built by both Northern Power Systems and Bergey Windpower have chalked up an impressive record of reliability. Wind turbines built by these manufacturers have been available for operation 98-100 percent of the time they were in service. After a decade of development these designs have proven more dependable in remote power systems than the conventional engine generators they were originally designed to supplement.

Though extremely reliable, the initial cost of turbines using the integrated design philosophy becomes too prohibitive in wind machines above 10 meters in diameter (about 25 kW). At this size and above, a different approach becomes necessary.

MEDIUM-SIZED TURBINES

In contrast to these integrated small machines, the wind turbines found in California and Denmark use off-the-shelf induction generators, transmissions, brakes, yaw drives, electrical sensors, and controls. The numerous components on a medium-sized wind turbine require regular maintenance, a function simplified by clustering the turbines together in one location, as in California wind plants, or within easy reach of the manufacturer, as in Denmark.

This complexity and the resulting need for maintenance thwarted many American manufacturers who attempted to market similar designs for dispersed applications in the United States. These machines, best represented by Enertech's designs, used a fixed-pitch rotor downwind of the tower to drive an induction generator and used a brake to stop the rotor under normal and emergency conditions. If the brake failed, Enertech relied on tip brakes to protect the rotor from self-destruction.

Most of today's medium-sized turbines use fixed-pitch blades bolted rigidly to the hub. Like small wind turbines, most of these machines are self-starting (though some early models, like the Enertech, were motored up to their operating speed). From startup to the cut-in wind speed, the rotor speed varies with wind speed until it reaches the speed at which the generator can be synchronized with the utility.

From cut-in to rated wind speed, the rotor continues turning at the same speed while delivering more and more power. The wind machine may from time to time switch from one generator to another as wind speed varies, changing rotor speed like shifting gears in a car. But overall the turbine operates at constant speed. (The rotor speed does vary slightly, but this is imperceptible to the untrained observer.)

Above the rated speed the blades begin to stall, dumping excess power. Above the turbine's cut-out speed, or with any abnormal occurrence such as excessive vibration, the brake is applied, bringing the rotor to a stop. In the typical Danish design, the turbine then yaws 90 degrees out of the wind to a parked position. When wind speeds fall back below the cut-out speed, the turbine yaws back into the wind and releases its brake. Soon after, the rotor accelerates until it reaches its operating speed.

On American downwind designs, such as Enertech's, there's no yaw control. The rotor stays downwind even when the rotor is parked.

Editor's note: Wind power engineering is highly technical as the reader has seen in this excerpt from Paul Gipe's book. And the technology changes rapidly. So we recommend that the reader refer to the original book for more details and for references for keeping up to date in this realm.

Part Four

ALTERNATIVE MATERIALS AND CONSTRUCTION

Chapter 14

History and Evolution
of Earth Construction

by Paul Graham McHenry, Jr. AIA

From ADOBE AND RAMMED EARTH BUILDINGS
DESIGN AND CONSTRUCTION

The University of Arizona Press, Tucson

The earliest beginnings of deliberately planned and built shelter were much the same in all parts of the world. Then, as now, there were many levels of development at any particular time, the level depending on the social evolution stage. These beginnings go back as far as the earliest archaeological investigations can take us, only the virtually indestructible stone tools remaining.

Humans, at the beginning stage of development, were constantly on the move, following hunting and gathering patterns dictated by the region in which they lived. The migratory nature of their subsistence made impossible the construction of a fixed dwelling place. As hunting and gathering patterns were refined, many of the more desirable locations (caves, cliff sites, with proximity to food and water) were revisited repeatedly. This was the beginning.

The earliest shelters using earth were outgrowths of temporary, seasonal shelters made of brush and small wood members, usually covered with mud for waterproofing. A common term for this type of construction is jacal. Most activities took place out of doors, and shelter was for only the most inclement weather. Some physical details of the building design were for security from animals and hostile neighbors.

The possibility of obtaining and making use of larger structural remembers was dependent on the invention of tools with which to obtain them. Few tools other than sharp stones, a pointed stick, and the builder's hands were available. It was also necessary to have some method for carrying water to the construction site.

As human knowledge of agriculture increased to bring the level of culture from a hunter-gatherer phase to the more intensive cultivation of fixed locations, requirements for shelter increased as well. From a transient existence which afforded little or no opportunity for a fixed dwelling place, humans learned to create surpluses of food and methods to store it. The surpluses created time and a desire for the development of more sophisticated forms of shelter. These first dwellings were partly underground, creating a sort of cave, a form which the builder was familiar with, and were called pit houses.

The pit house was, for the time, the ultimate in environmental design, appropriate technology, and labor economy. It made full use of materials close at hand, required little planning or preparation of the materials to be used. Various techniques of wall building were employed, including puddling of mud, lumps of mud, and a rudimentary type of brick formed in baskets, called turtle construction.

The pit house form used by the Hohokam irrigation farmers of the southwestern United States (100-900 A.D.) was so successful that it remained basically unchanged for more than 600 years. Many of its features and principles are ones that we are rediscovering today, in the form of bermed and partially underground construction, taking refuge from the wind and collecting the sun warmth on protected south slopes.

While civilizations seem to have developed independently in many places on the globe, it progressed at different speeds, making it impossible to establish a firm chronological period for specific stages of development on a global basis. Similar stages of construction technology often occurred centuries or even millenniums apart.

Variations in form and selection of materials was dependent on the local environment. Where stone was most readily available, it was used. Where wood and other organic materials were more abundant, they were used. In both cases, the use of earth was necessary to implement the other material. Where neither stone nor wood were abundant or viable, mud was used alone. All three basic techniques are still being used in developing Third World countries.

Modern industrial countries today make some use of many of the basic techniques, more often in rural locations.

The development of the (adobe) brick, a preformed modular masonry unit of sun-dried mud, occurred with higher civilization levels. Then, as now, the affluence of leisure time of the householder reflected itself in the material selection and architectural form, which in turn led to monumental forms for religious and public buildings. Often crude forms and complex ones existed side by side, as they do today. The use of preformed bricks started with a need for a more efficient, rapid construction technique, as the drying of puddled and shaped mud walls took a long time. Early forms of this are found in the southwestern United States where turtle wall construction occurred. In this form, mud was placed in a basket with a round bottom and either placed on the ground to dry, or laid directly up on the wall where it could dry in place. Other shapes are found worldwide.

Another type of brick common in many areas is cut sod bricks. The Spanish name for this is terrone. These can be procured only in swampy, boggy river bottom lands. They are cut with a shovel from soil having a heavy grass root structure or mat, stood on edge until dry, and then used as bricks to build walls. Tough, durable walls result from these bricks.

The use of bricks in more complex forms also must presume preplanning and some standard of measurement, perhaps the builder's own measuring stick or "rule". Egyptian examples from 2500 B.C. show a high degree of sophistication. Surviving measurement tools and surveying, engineering techniques substantiate this. Wall murals show production techniques of adobe bricks, and biblical references indicate a specialization of tasks, where the Jews were assigned the task of making bricks. The use of straw and responsibility for its supply are noted in Exodus 5:7.

In the Middle East, millenniums of civilization and population pressures created new demands for land and settlements in harsher and environments. Techniques were developed that required no structural members at all, and buildings were built entirely of mud brick. The masonry vaulted forms, presumably developed in the Middle East prior to the Egyptian Dynastic Period, spread to North Africa and then to Roman cities. Later, Moorish invasions of Spain spread the use of these forms there. In turn, they were exported to the Western Hemisphere by Spanish explorers.

In the Spanish Southwest explorers found mud villages in 1540. Settlers from as early as 1590 brought adobe technology from the South, into an area with a long history of earth construction. Their use of adobe brick, not known to the Pueblo Indians except in rudimentary forms, was to set the standard for several centuries. The economic and transportation systems of the time made the use of locally available materials mandatory. The rapid westward expansion of the United States made wide use of this material, not only in the and Southwest, but in nearly all of the western states. Local building suppliers provided "bricks" for sale, along with lumber and quicklime, all produced locally. In general, the settlers followed the local custom and tradition using rocks, logs, and mud, depending on the local conditions.

On the Eastern Seaboard, in many locations including South Carolina, New York, and Washington, D.C., rammed earth was used into the mid-19th century. A treatise was published in

1839 extolling the virtues of rammed earth construction. It is a viable medium in virtually any climate and does not require the curing time without rain necessary for the making of adobe bricks.

With the advent of the railroads pushing West in the 1880s, manufactured materials previously unavailable were in abundant supply. Then, as now, homeowners, builders, and merchants strived to upgrade building materials and emulate the styles of the East. As this pressure increased, the use of adobe bricks gradually declined. In spite of this trend, the use of adobe in rural situations, and for economy in many commercial buildings, still persisted. The great depression of the 1930s brought a rediscovery of the economy of this material, and sparked a short-term interest with some of the oil companies who sponsored research and product development in stabilized (waterproof) adobes. Asphalt emulsion was used as a stabilizing agent. This effort seems to have been abandoned by the oil companies in the later 1940s.

A number of public buildings were built during the 1930s, and at least one school was built of adobe in New Mexico as late as 1940. Some architectural styles were in the traditional southwestern Pueblo or Territorial style, but many were of conventional styles, where the adobe brick was merely another type of common brick that was economical and available.

In the decades since 1940 and World War 11, our devotion to more modern materials led to a decline in the use of earth for building. Most construction in this medium was limited to either residential construction of large luxury homes where the owner could afford to indulge the nostalgia of Spanish Colonial styles, or to the very poor who had no other choice and were limited to what they could produce with their own hands. Thus, a split image was created, that adobe was for either the very rich or for the very poor, with little acceptance in between.

In the relative absence from the scene for a whole generation of architects, engineers, building officials, and builders using earth construction, the expertise became lost.

Changing economic conditions and energy shortages must lead us to a new evaluation of this historic material. Where as recently as 20 years ago adobe construction was dismissed as impractical or undesirable, because of the image of use by the very rich or the very poor, it is now being taken seriously and accepted as a logical building medium. It must again assume its place as an important, energy efficient building material.

NOTES

1. E. Gilman, *The Economical Builder*, J. Gideon, Washington, D.C., 1839.

Chapter 15

Benefits of
Straw Bale Construction

by Athena Swentzell Steen, Bill Steen,
David Bainbridge, with David Eisenberg

From THE STRAW BALE HOUSE
Chelsea Green Publishing Co.

All things considered, straw bales literally stack up as a remarkable building material. They are produced from a waste product that can be sustainably grown in a short period of time, are biodegradable, and can help alleviate multiple environmental problems with their use. They are easy to modify, flexible enough to be used in a variety of ways, solid and substantial, durable over time, and easy to maintain. In addition, they require only inexpensive uncomplicated tools and unspecialized labor, and are easily acquired and affordable in most locations around the world.

Modern building materials, in contrast, tend to be difficult to work with, inflexible, require specialized tools and labor, can be expensive, possess little aesthetic character, are often toxic, and generate significant amounts of pollution and waste as they are produced, maintained, and demolished.

An additional benefit of straw bale buildings not traditionally measured when evaluating building materials is the high level of social interaction and community participation that occurs in this process. People who might otherwise be excluded from the building process become directly and enthusiastically involved.

When straw bales are combined with other materials of similar characteristics, it becomes possible to create buildings that are affordable in all respects, natural in character, and beautiful.

The thickness and subtle curves of straw bale walls have a special character and beauty. Combined with their high insulation value and breathability, these walls create an overall feeling of comfort not found in the thin flat walls often produced from modern materials. Straw bale walls are similar in appearance to old thick stone and adobe walls, reminiscent of European country cottages, Mediterranean villas, and Southwestern adobes. Yet, at the same time, they have an intangible quality all their own.

Sometimes people's personal lives can most easily be read in the walls of their buildings, such as where a deep and softened entryway graciously welcomes one in, where a detailed niche displays precious belongings, where intimate nooks with built-in seats invite quiet repose, or where beautifully beveled window edges frame a treasured view. The thickness of straw bale walls and their ability to be easily modified make it easy to change bale walls according to the needs and creativity of its inhabitants.

The mass and dimensions of straw bale walls can induce physical and psychological feelings of well-being. When combined with a soft adobe or gypsum plaster, the flowing surfaces are not only a pleasure to look at and to touch, but instill a soft sound quality to each room.

When finished with natural plasters and paints, straw bale walls can breathe, resulting in indoor air that feels fresh, invigorating, and clean compared to the low-oxygen, stale, toxic air common to most homes. The high insulation value of bales also helps create a stable environment which is easy to cool and heat and provides far superior living conditions to that of most modern housing.

In the Great Plains, baled homes were preferred because they were extremely quiet and could seal out the howling of the Northerns—winds that can torment a person's mind on the open plains. In the city, bale houses could provide a much needed haven in a noisy and chaotic world. Perhaps it is within these silent, sculpted walls, which impart a sense of timeless peace, that a new and better vision of shelter resides.

EASE OF CONSTRUCTION

Building walls from straw is much less labor intensive than using other materials such as concrete block, brick, adobe, or stone, and requires considerably less skill. Bale building is forgiving, encourages individual creativity, and leads to final structures that are climatically adapted and energy-efficient.

Many people would have a great deal of fear and anxiety about building a home with more conventional materials. The complexity, skill required, time involved, and cost can seem prohibitive and daunting. Building with straw bales relaxes the whole construction process and allows inexperienced and unskilled people the opportunity to become directly involved in creating their own homes.

It has been demonstrated in the United States that the basic methods of straw bale construction can be learned in a two-day workshop. One of the great beauties of this system is that everyone can participate in building a home, including women, children, and others who have been disenfranchised from the building process. This coming together of people to help each other build often generates a great deal of excitement. Group wall-raisings facilitate community-based projects that might not otherwise happen.

After the original Tree of Life Nursery in southern California burned down, the owners received a broad outpouring of community support offering to help them put up a new building. In response to that enthusiasm, owners Mike Evans and Jeff Bohm decided to construct their new building out of straw bales because it would afford community members the greatest opportunity to participate. The event was conducted much in the spirit of an old-time barn raising, and the food, music, and work were so delightful that Mike and Jeff have decided to host an annual wall-raising whether they need a building or not.

ENERGY EFFICIENT

Insulation is rated by R-value, the resistance to heat flow. The R-value of wood is 1 per inch, brick is 0.2, fiberglass batts are 3.0. The higher the R-value the better the insulation. Straw bale buildings are thermally efficient and energy conserving, with R-values significantly better than conventional construction, depending on the type of straw and the wall thickness. Research by Joe McCabe at the University of Arizona found that the R-value for both wheat and rice bales was about R-2.4 per inch with the grain, and R-3 per inch across the grain, which would give a three-string bale laid flat (23 inches wide) an R-value of R-54.7, and laid on edge (16 inches wide) an R-value of R-49.5. For two-string bales laid flat (18 inches wide), the R-value would be R-42.8, and for a two-string bale on edge (14 inches wide), it would be R-32.1. That is two to three times better than the wall system of most well-insulated homes, and often five to ten times better than older houses. Additionally, the mass gained from the plaster of the bale wall can help increase the thermal performance of the wall system.

Straw bale walls can provide greatly improved comfort and dramatic energy savings compared to more expensive conventional building systems, as they allow smaller heating or cooling systems to be installed than in conventional homes because of the increased insulation. Bale building is of special value in severe environments where energy is expensive.

To get the most benefit from the highly efficient walls of a bale building, the building should include a well-insulated attic or roof (straw can be used in many cases), good perimeter foundation insulation, insulated windows and doors, proper sealing to minimize drafts, and optimal ventilation achieved either by plastering and coloring the walls with a breathable finish or by using an air-to-air heat exchanger to efficiently bring in fresh air. The high insulation and mass of bale walls will make it possible to keep the windows open much of the year, providing cleaner air inside.

The traditional designs of many homes optimize solar gain for heating and climate resources for cooling, but are hampered by the lack of insulation. Traditional Chinese rural homes, for example, are oriented with the long axis running east-west and most of the windows on the south side, an ideal configuration for solar heating and natural cooling. Unfortunately, the poor thermal properties of the brick walls reduce many of the advantages of this excellent design. Straw bale building could enable rural home builders to achieve thermal comfort without costly fuel consumption.

The excellent insulation value of straw bales also makes passive cooling systems, such as the cool pool or down draft cooling towers, more practical and efficient for homeowners in very hot, arid areas. It may also make the installation of extra cooling systems unnecessary. In her straw bale house near Huachuca City, Arizona, Mary Diamond installed a cooling tower. It was included in the design of the building because it was calculated that a well-insulated home in the area where she lives would require the extra cooling. The house was built before the cooling tower was completed and moved into during the hot summer months. It was discovered that the straw bale house remained sufficiently cool without any help from the tower, and therefore the cooling tower was never finished. The house's photovoltaic electrical system makes it even more energy efficient.

The savings from reduced utility bills and not having to purchase expensive heating and cooling equipment can help offset the cost of buying more efficient appliances, like a heat exchanger (for severe climates) and a photovoltaic electric system.

ENVIRONMENTAL BENEFITS

Straw bale construction can provide benefits in regions where straw has become an unwanted waste product. The slow rate at which straw deteriorates creates disposal problems for farmers because unlike nitrogen-rich hay, straw cannot be used for animal fodder, and the stems are too long to be thoroughly tilled in. In California, for example, almost a million tons of rice straw are burned each fall, and the fires cast a pall of smoke over the Sacramento Valley for several weeks. Annual straw burning in California produces more carbon monoxide and particulate than all of the electric-power-generating plants in the state combined. This air pollution has prompted the state's Air Resources Board to initiate the process of banning this burning.

Annual Carbon Monoxide Production From
Power Plants and Straw Burning (In Tons)

	TONS BURNED	TONS
Rice straw	1 million	56,000
Wheat straw	97,000	5,000
Power plants		25,000

Source: *California Agricultural Magazine*, Vol. 45, no. 4 (July-August 1991)

A million tons of grass are burned each year in the Willamette Valley of Oregon, creating visual pollution and health hazards. In 1988, a chain-reaction highway accident that was caused by smoke from field burning resulted in seven deaths and thirty-seven injuries. The Oregon Department of Environmental Quality has stated that this smoke is "carcinogenic...containing tiny particles that irritate the lungs." Rice straw may be even worse because of its high silica content and particle size. Here, also, the state government has begun to crack down on burning, and straw disposal is becoming a problem. The Department of Environmental Quality is funding research into alternatives but has yet to come up with an economically viable use for straw.

Large quantities of straw are burned in other areas as well. Close to two hundred million tons of waste straw are produced in the United States every year. Increasing amounts of straw are also burned in Europe and Mexico. The use of straw for domestic fuel has been reduced in eastern China, where extensive reforestation has enabled farmers to begin using wood instead. That could make straw available for bale buildings.

Straw bale construction could be useful in the effort to control global warming and atmospheric deterioration. A large reduction in the amount of straw burned would cut back the production of carbon monoxide and nitrous oxides by many thousands of tons per year. The removal of rice straw from the wet fields for use in bale buildings would substantially reduce methane emissions from microbial decomposition, the second major cause of global warming. Not all straw needs to be disposed of, for if left in alternating swaths or strips on the contour of the land, straw can provide erosion control in fields. Waste straw, however, for which disposal is a problem, could be baled and used in buildings.

There could be a significant decline in the devastation of timber areas if homes were built from straw bales instead of the lumber-consumptive construction methods so prevalent today. In many developing countries, the cutting of firewood for heating is as devastating to forests as woodcutting for the buildings themselves. Energy-efficient bale buildings could lessen this impact as well. The plaster-stucco construction often used with bale buildings could also reduce the need for maintenance and the use of paints and solvents that adversely affect the atmosphere and human health.

According to Matts Myhrman of Out on Bale: "If all the straw left in the United States after the harvest of major grains was baled instead of burned, five million 2,000-square-foot houses could be built every year."

SUSTAINABILITY

In contrast to the timber used for wood framing, straw can be grown in less than a year in a completely sustainable production system. Without developing an elaborate definition, the term sustainable here refers to a system that conceivably could be perpetuated forever. If large crops of straw are removed from a field every year, the use of soil amendments, intercropping, or crop rotations may be required to maintain soil health and fertility. If perennial straw crops are used, the need for such measures will be reduced, as will erosion and runoff.

Straw can be successfully intercropped with other valuable crops, thereby increasing the yield and productivity of the same piece of land. Certain fruit and other useful trees are good candidates. In China, wheat is successfully intercropped with highly valued fruit-producing jujube trees. The sustainable yield of a piece of land is enhanced when each element in the system provides multiple benefits and uses and when the relationship between those elements is beneficial.

The conversion of straw into a sustainable renewable resource to be used as a dominant building material could be especially beneficial in areas like the steppes of Russia and the plains of northern China, where the climate is severe and timber is scarce, but straw is plentiful.

Straw bale construction would also be ideal for many desert areas where winter wheats are grown along riparian belts and river valleys. The soils that make good adobe or earth blocks are often the same soils that are used for cultivation. Using those soils to make bricks, as is happening in Egypt, where agricultural land is at a premium, is clearly not a sustainable practice. Desert areas are also traditionally timber poor.

In timber-poor areas where roof framing materials are needed, assorted poles and bamboo could be quickly and sustainably grown in combination with straw. In areas where straw is not available, it can be grown specifically for buildings. Some economists estimate that half of the land now farmed in Europe will become available as farm subsidies are eliminated. A similar situation may develop in the United States. These lands could be used to grow special building straw while still maintaining the rural vistas that everyone enjoys.

Straw can also be grown on saline or low-quality land. Tall wheat-grass (Aelongatum), for example, is long-stemmed and durable, and productive in soils with high water tables, high salinity, and alkalinity.

The prospect of sustainability for any given product or system is increased if the energy required to manufacture or operate it is kept to a minimum. When straw is evaluated for sustainability as a building material, it rates very high. It bypasses much of the energy and waste needed to produce industrial building materials. For example, the production of one ton of straw requires 112,500 BTUs, in comparison to 5,800,000 BTUs for concrete. According to calculations performed by Richard Hoffmeister at Taliesin West, the Frank Lloyd Wright school of architecture in Scottsdale, Arizona, straw bale walls are at least thirty times less energy intensive than a wood-frame wall with equivalent fiberglass insulation. This reduction can significantly help minimize the environmental and financial impact of construction. Ideally, a sustainable straw-growing operation would seek to grow straw as close as possible to building sites to minimize the energy requirements of transporting it.

Another aspect of straw's sustainability is the material's remarkable durability:

> "My grandfather had a hay bale barn, roughly 40' by 60", that existed until I was an adolescent. That's when it was destroyed and by that time it was about fifty years old. A tornado came through and picked it up and moved it—actually took the building and twisted it roughly ninety degrees and moved it about forty feet. Strangely, it stayed intact, unlike all the wood buildings. The barn had clapboard on the outside and was protected on the inside from the cows by stucco. When it was finally destroyed, the cows were very excited about the straw. They thought that was the best straw they had ever had. They clipped off fences to get to it. That straw was from a sweetgrass that's now extinct."
>
> -ED SANDERS, former Nebraska resident

STRUCTURAL TESTING

In the mid 1980s, the Canada Mortgage and Housing Corporation was the first to sponsor tests of the strength of plastered straw bale construction using a mortared bale-wall system. Even though that wall system is very different from most building methods currently being used, those tests were a significant first step. Walls in those tests had mortar in the joints between the bales as well as plaster on both sides. A 12-foot-long, 8-foot-high wall did not fail when loaded with 18,000 pounds of compressive load and 719 pounds of transverse force. The structural consultants felt the mortared bale-wall system would be adequate for the following loads:

Live loads due to use and occupancy	45 lbs sq. ft.
Snow loads	60 lbs sq. ft.
Wind loads	16 lbs sq. ft.
Dead loads	48 lbs .sq. ft.

Initial tests conducted by Ghailene Bou-Ali at the University of Arizona as part of his master's thesis in civil engineering showed that pinned, unplastered, three-string bale walls were strong and withstood lateral and vertical loads well. The first part of his study measured the compressive strength of unconfined individual bales, producing impressive results when three-string bales were tested laid flat (23 inches wide by 46 inches long). The hydraulic press used for the testing sensed a change in the resistance of the bales at about 72,600 pounds per bale, or

176

10,000 pounds per square foot. That was considered the failure point, although none of the bale strings broke. Deflection of the bales at the point of failure was 50 percent of the original height, and the bales recovered most of their initial height after the load was removed. The ability of a material to perform this way is known as elastic deformation, or simply, the ability to handle a short-term load and recover without permanent deformation. Design strategies to eliminate or distribute point loads, give adequate roof support for snow loads, and accommodate movement are important.

The results from testing three-string bales laid on edge (16 inches wide) were less impressive. The bales demonstrated considerably less strength in this position. Laid on edge, the bales failed at 13,850 pounds, or 2,770 pounds per square foot (with the middle strings breaking). Since the strings in this position go around the bales horizontally, when pressure is applied to the bales they become barrel-shaped, which puts the middle string in tension immediately. Therefore, the testing that was done for bales on edge was really testing the strength of the string. These results seem to indicate that bales used in this position are much better suited as in-fill in non-load-bearing structures and retrofits, or in very small load-bearing structures. Used on edge, bales provide a larger wall area using the same number of bales, while taking up less floor space. They also have a higher net insulation value per inch in that orientation.

The second part of Ghailene's study, conducted on wall panels built of straw bales, also yielded impressive results. Each of three wall panels was loaded with 15,800 pounds, simulating a very large roof load. The panels, 12 feet long and 8 feet high (six courses or rows), were pinned together only with rebar. The bales were bare, with no finish material such as stucco or plaster. The vertical deflection was measured and averaged about 7 inches. That amount of deflection is far greater than that seen in any existing straw bale buildings, leading to speculation about the structural role that stucco or other wall finishes might play in handling high temporary loads, such as snow on the roof. More research and testing are planned in this area. It is worth noting that the many historic load-bearing straw bale buildings in Nebraska do not show evidence of problems from the snow loads they have endured over the years.

In the wall panel tests for out-of-plane lateral loading (a wind load simulation of one hundred miles per hour), the three unplastered panels showed a maximum deflection of 1 inch or less. The six panels used for the lateral tests were the same size as those used for the compression tests, 12 feet long by 8 feet high. They were pinned together with rebar and had two all-thread connections from anchor bolts in the floor to the roof plates on top of the walls.

In-plane lateral loading (pushing on the end of the wall) allowed an average deflection of 4 inches at the top of the wall with a loading of 2,135 pounds applied to the end of the wall. Panels in this test showed a large variation in results, presumably caused by differences in the degrees of compression from the all-thread securing the roof plates. The tightest of the three, which represented a normal condition in a common straw bale wall, showed only a 2 3/8-inch deflection. The addition of any type of wall finish would greatly enhance the performance of the wall panels in this direction.

Additional research and testing are needed to develop a better understanding of bale assemblies for more varied uses—in multistory structures, construction that can withstand heavy snow loads, and appliances linking bales with other materials. There seem to be no serious problems with load-bearing single-story structures (now experimentally approved in Tucson).

During construction of a load-bearing rice-straw building at the Shenoa Retreat Center in northern California in May of 1994, architect Bob Theis had a rice-straw bale wall constructed to test deflection under vertical loading. A significant feature of his test, not included in Ghailene's test, was a series of loadings in succession. That is essentially what happens in areas of heavy snows, when a structure is subjected to loads of falling snow which melt and release the loads, a pattern that repeats itself many times during the winter. Bob's test was conducted as follows.

The wall was built on a concrete foundation and measured 2 feet wide, 12 feet long, and 8 feet (six courses of bales) high. It utilized dense three-string rice-straw bales made expressly as construction material the previous October by Rick Green in Willows, California.

The wall assembly matched the detailing of the wall assembly for Shenoa Cottage, including 1/2-inch diameter threaded rods running up through the center of the wall's width at quarter points along its length. These rods extended through a box beam made of 2-by-8 vertical sides with 3/4-inch plywood top and bottom. Each rod was straddled by two 2-by-8 cross pieces connected to the 2-by-8 sides with beam hangers installed upside-down. This high-strength connection permits the wall to be precompressed via the box beam, by tightening nuts over malleable iron washers on the threaded rods.

After completion of the test wall, the wall height was measured at the corners and the midpoints of the sides. The bolts were then cranked down as tightly as possible with a hand-held wrench, and the heights remeasured. Vertical displacement averaged 3 7/8 inches.

The bolts were relaxed and a test frame constructed over the wall that distributed the weight of five stock tanks approximately 2 by 2 by 6 feet along the length of the wall. The frame suspended two tanks along each side of the wall and one tank on top. The total maximum weight of the test frame and the filled tanks was 7,640 pounds, or 636 pounds per linear foot of wall. This is 1.6 times the design load of four hundred pounds per lineal foot. The wall was loaded by filling the stock tanks with water and the deflection measured. The tanks were drained and the deflection measured again. This cycle was repeated three times until equilibrium was reached, where the deflection and recovery were approximately equal. (At equilibrium, the wall deflected an average of 7/16 inch at a pressure of four hundred pounds per lineal foot; increasing the pressure to six hundred pounds per lineal foot increased the deflection an additional 1/8 inch.) The final height of the wall, loaded at 600 pounds per lineal foot, averaged 31/2 inches below original height after these cycles.

The initial test precompression had depressed the wall an average of 3 7/8 inches, which demonstrated that the threaded rod and box beam assembly could precompress the wall sufficiently to test for differential settlement due to loads up to one-and-a-half-times larger than anticipated.

For the final test, requested by the Building Department, the wall and box beam were covered with mesh and cement plaster approximately 7/8 inch thick. After allowing the stucco to cure, the wall was marked just below the box beam and a transit sighted at this level; the tanks were filled to load the wall and were left full for four days. No deflection was observed at the transit, and no cracking was observed in the stucco.

SEISMIC RESISTANCE

It appears that straw bale building will be of special value in areas where earthquakes are common. Conventional buildings of earth, adobe, or stone (eight out of ten of the world's homes) are extremely hazardous in earthquakes and costly to reinforce. In 1976, during an earthquake in China, 250,000 people were killed, a great many of them from the collapse of unreinforced masonry houses. In Chile in 1985, another earthquake seriously damaged or destroyed 28,000 adobe homes, leaving 150,000 homeless.

In contrast to those buildings, straw bales have a good width-to-height ratio and can be easily and effectively reinforced with wood, bamboo, or metal pins. The nature of the bales, their flexibility and strength, are ideal for seismic design, as long as the connections between the bale wall system and the roof and foundation are adequate. Bale walls may actually absorb much of the shock of an earthquake, instead of transferring it all to the roof as in conventionally built structures. A coating of plaster (reinforced with wire) adds to the strength of these buildings. Additional sheer bracing will help resist lateral loading along with a concrete or wood bond beam for load distribution.

Architect Bob Theis designed the first permitted load-bearing rice straw building in California, which was engineered to withstand seismic forces. The evolution of straw bale buildings in the state of California should help the development of seismic-resistant straw bale design.

AFFORDABILITY

How much does a straw bale building cost? As is the case with a great many things, it all depends. The costs of building vary by region, by climate and site within a region, by the contribution of owner-builder labor, and by codes and permit requirements. In parts of California, permits and fees can cost more than $20,000, more than a small straw bale house might cost.

A good comparison to begin with is the cost of building the same house of two different wall materials. In the words of Ted Varney, a New Mexico contractor, "I can build for someone the identical structure here in Santa Fe out of a 2-by-6 frame with R-19 walls or out of straw bales with R-42 walls for exactly the same price. The difference is that the one built out of straw will be a far superior product in terms of energy efficiency, durability, comfort, and aesthetic character."

Another way of looking at cost is to break down how money is spent in the process of building a house; ideas about this can differ widely. In a 1982 Housing magazine study of the construction costs of a wood-frame house built in Albuquerque, New Mexico, the exterior walls of the house represented 21 percent of the total cost of the house. Other estimates have placed exterior-wall cost as low as 10 to 15 percent. That figure represents 2-by-4 wood-frame construction; the percentage increases rapidly as one begins to consider other materials and methods, such as adobe, rammed earth, double insulated masonry walls, and super-insulated frame construction. According to various estimates, these alternative forms of construction could cost 25 to 50 percent more than baled materials. Builder Burke Denman of Santa Fe estimated that a straw bale home he completed for approximately $95 per square foot would have cost around $130 per square foot built with adobe and two inches of blown-on polystyrene insulation to meet the local energy codes. In his opinion, "For people interested in a thick-wall adobe look with good insulation, straw bale is the least expensive way to go. You can't insulate a wood-frame home to R-40 for the price."

Another variable that influences the cost of straw bale walls is the price paid per bale. Straw grown and baled within the immediate area of the site will decrease the cost of a bale, in some cases as much as 90 percent or more. In areas where straw disposal is a problem, bales could even be free. When bales are purchased from a local farmer rather than the feed stores, the cost is again much lower. The quantity of bales bought at one time also affects the price. Bales can often be delivered directly to the site, which raises the cost per bale (about fifty cents), but is usually well worth it unless you have access to a flatbed truck. A three-string bale bought in bulk from a feed store and delivered to a rural site in southeastern Arizona was $3.50. In New Mexico, two-string bale bought in bulk (three hundred bales) from a local feed store cost $2.75.

Overall costs can be reduced in many ways. Owner-builder sweat equity can help reduce outside labor expenditures. Tony Perry, president of the Straw Bale Association in Santa Fe and chairman of the state technical advisory council on straw bale construction, received a Small Business Innovation Research Grant, part of which will be used in 1994 to construct two proto-type straw bale homes to determine how much sweat equity can be used in building them. He estimates that if the layout and excavation, concrete, electrical, and plumbing are subcontracted and a qualified supervisor is maintained on the job full time, but resident family and friends provide the rest of the labor, a 50 percent savings can be realized over conventional 2-by-6 construction. Other studies suggest that baled houses with significant owner-builder labor (again, not foundations, electrical, etc.) may cost even less than a conventional-type home with similar owner labor when alternative materials and methods are used.

Much of what makes straw bales easily adaptable to the owner-builder is the ease with which a wall can be assembled. By following simple guidelines, a relatively unskilled person can stack a straw wall in a fraction of the time it takes to build a wood-frame wall, not to mention the time involved in building walls with masonry and earthen materials such as adobe or rammed earth.

Additional cost savings can be realized by keeping the building simple, with few floor and roof height changes, extra corners, or special details. A simple rectangular house fits this description, and it might be designed for subsequent additions as requirements change. Using local natural materials such as mud, stone, and timber, which can often be free, can add to the savings. Recycled, salvaged materials and innovative methods such as rubble trench footings can further reduce costs. A home that draws on all these strategies may not resemble a custom high-cost dream house, but it can provide a simple, comfortable, energy- efficient shelter with high levels of owner-builder character, creativity, and beauty.

In an attempt to further define the costs associated with bale building, Richard Hoffmeister of Taliesin West created four cost categories ranging from "very low" to "high." The "very low" category estimated costs at $5 to $20 a square foot, made possible by owner-builder labor, the use of salvaged and scavenged materials, and a pay-as-you-go arrangement. The "low" category lists costs of $20 to $50 a square foot, using the system recommended by Tony Perry, in which one pays market prices for materials, subcontracts part of the construction, and assembles the walls and does the finish work oneself. The "moderate" category defines a home that is totally contractor built for $50 to $80 a square foot, with bales typically used as in-fill and a minimum of custom features. The "high" category refers to $80 or more a square foot, and describes a house that is custom built and has a significant number of details and features.

To make a truly accurate comparison of housing costs, it is necessary to talk about life-cycle cost, or the cost of finance, utilities, and maintenance over the life of the building, which in some cases could be hundreds of years. A simple method of examining life-cycle cost would be to compare four structures with similar maintenance requirements, carrying an 80-percent loan at equivalent interest in cost, finance charges, and energy over thirty years.

See the tables below for the estimated costs and savings for a 1,375-square-foot, three-bedroom, two-bath home in a moderate climate with both heating and cooling demands.

LIFE CYCLE COSTS—30 YEARS

Estimated costs and savings for a 1,375-square-foot, 3-bedroom, 2-bath home in a moderate climate with both heating and cooling demands.

CONVENTIONAL

Construction cost	$ 82,500
Down payment (20 %)	16,500
Finance 118,800	
Energy (heat and cooling)	36,000
Total life-cycle costs	171,300

STRAW BALE — CONTRACTOR- BUILT

Construction cost	$ 82,500
Down payment (20 %)	16,500
Finance	118,800
Energy (heat and cooling)	18,000
Total life-cycle costs	153,300
Savings	18,000

STRAW BALE — PARTIALLY OWNER-BUILT (WALLS, ROOFING, FINISHING) AND WITH SUPER-EFFICIENT APPLIANCES

Construction cost	$ 40,000
Down payment (20 %)	8,000
Finance	57,600
Energy (heat and cooling)	9,000
Total life-cycle costs	74,600
Savings	96,700

STRAW BALE — TOTALLY OWNER-BUILT, USING RECYCLED MATERIALS, AND WITH SUPER-EFFICIENT APPLIANCES

Construction cost (cash)	$ 20,625
Down payment	none
Finance	zero
Energy (heat and cooling)	9,000
Total life-cycle costs	29,625
Savings	141,675

The 30-year savings are important, but a well-built straw bale home should last for more than a hundred years, with very low maintenance costs. The savings become even more impressive—a nice legacy for the family.

LIFE CYCLE COSTS — 100 YEARS

	COST	SAVINGS
Conventional	$ 527,340	——
Straw Bale—contractor- built	467,900	59,440
Straw Bale—partially owner-built	227,780	299,560
Straw Bale—owner- built (as above)	29,625	497,715

More detailed studies are needed with full accounting for life-cycle costs, including utility service and construction costs. A straw bale building would prove even more cost competitive after considering environmental impact and related costs.

Chapter 16

The Building Envelope:
Walls, Roofs, and Foundations

by Adrian Tuluca

From ENERGY-EFFICIENT DESIGN AND
CONSTRUCTION FOR COMMERCIAL BUILDINGS

The McGraw-Hill Companies, Inc.

THE BUILDING ENVELOPE—
INNOVATION THROUGH INTEGRATION

The pursuit of thermally efficient walls, roofs, and foundations has been a catalyst for innovation. Better materials and systems are now available. Better concepts on the role of the building envelope gain ground.

Increasingly, the building envelope is viewed not simply as protection from, but as connection to the environment. This connection is achieved by integration with the lighting, HVAC, and control systems. Within the envelope itself, the concept of integration is often applied to increase construction efficiency while reducing energy use. Envelope subsystems integrate several envelope functions (e.g., thermal protection, structural support, or water and weather protection) into a single, cost-effective component.

This chapter examines the performance of the building insulation system in interaction with the entire envelope, and then describes several innovative applications in detail. A discussion of air leakage and air retarders follows. Finally, two new technologies currently under development are presented: ultra-thin, high R-value panels and insulating structural concretes. A third technology is used in Europe but has not yet been introduced in the United States: a self-drying vapor retarder for roofs.

As part of the design process, architects and engineers create a shape, defined by an envelope, that responds to functional, structural and aesthetic considerations. The envelope encloses distinct spaces and provides controlled access to them. It facilitates and blocks views. It makes aesthetic and symbolic statements. It contributes to the structural integrity of the building and protects it against weather. The last function is of specific interest for this discussion, since in traditional design the envelope is viewed as a cocoon which decouples the building interior from the environment. Mechanical and electrical systems then take over to maintain comfort.

INNOVATION THROUGH INTEGRATION

• An insulating technique for metal roof systems not only increases thermal efficiency, but also reduces condensation potential on interior surfaces.

• Plastic ties between the two faces of concrete panels with core insulation eliminate thermal bridging and moisture condensation.

• Insulating concrete masonry units combine thermal insulation and structural support into a single element. A foundation insulation system combines ground water control and thermal insulation into a single component.

• A membrane system serves as air retarder and weather protection for exterior walls.

• A metal panel under development combines very low weight with high R-value.

• A roof vapor retarder, not yet in use in the US, allows trapped water to vent back into the conditioned space. This keeps the roof dry and allows for early detection of major leaks.

This approach results in buildings that are expensive to operate. If, for instance, all windows in an office building use reflective glass, the solar heat gain will be cut not only in summer but also in winter, increasing the heating load. Further, the amount of daylight will be reduced year-round, foregoing opportunities to dim or turn off the lamps.

A much more attractive approach is to replace the cocoon concept with a membrane concept. An envelope functioning as a membrane is coupled to the environment so that, over the year, the interaction between interior and environment (heat, air, and solar radiation exchanges) results in low-energy use and improved comfort. Returning to the example with reflective windows, north-facing areas could receive only a light tint. If nothing else were done, the slight increase in cooling energy use would be more than offset by a decrease in heating energy use.

However, a good design will take advantage of the opportunity to dim or turn off the lamps during daytime. Lower electricity use for lighting will result in lower cooling loads. Lower cooling loads can result in smaller fans, ducts, and chillers.

This example introduces the concept of integration. The envelope can successfully function as a membrane only if it is integrated with lighting, HVAC, and controls. The means to achieve integration are specific to the function of the building and to the climate. Obviously, a combination of strategies that excel for an office located in the sunny warm Washington, D.C. area will yield disappointing results for a school located in the cloudy, cool Seattle, Washington climate.

The integration concept that brings together the envelope, lighting, HVAC, and controls also applies to the envelope itself, since the envelope is a system. A wall needs structural support, exterior and interior finishes, thermal insulation, and protection of the insulation from moisture and air intrusion. These functions are usually, but not necessarily, accomplished by different components or even by different subsystems. Too often each component is designed independently of the others.

A typical example is the wall detail shown schematically in Fig. 16-1, encountered in schools and dormitories, nursing homes and treatment centers, etc. The floor slab sustains the exterior brick wythe and the concrete masonry unit (CMU) backup wythe. The insulation is located inside the CMU cores. The backup wythe does not receive parging on the exterior surface. The slab edge remains exposed and allows heat to easily flow from the conditioned space to the outside.

When wind blows, the exterior brick wythe bears some of the air pressure. Some pressure is also borne by the concrete blocks. Since the blocks are not parged, they are not likely to pose much higher resistance to the air than the bricks. The pressure differential created across the exterior finish forces the rain into bricks and mortar. During late fall, winter, and early spring this moisture freezes and thaws, engendering spalling. As the finish deteriorates, the water penetrates more easily into the brick wythe accelerating the destructive process.

As air pushes onto one facade, it creates suction on another. Air moves out of the building (exfiltrates) through the leeward wall. Likely entry areas are created by cracks in the mortar joints between blocks and slab. The junction area between wall and windows can also be vulnerable. In its path, the exfiltrating air encounters the exterior shell of the CMU, the slab underside, and brick ties. If the air has significant moisture content (e.g., as in a nursing home with humidification or a kitchen/ cafeteria), that moisture condenses. Condensed moisture reduces the R-value of fill-type insulation, such as perlite and vermiculite. If the core insulation is made of polystyrene inserts, the moisture will probably not affect the R-value, but may accumulate at a higher rate on the exterior shell. In either case, if this shell becomes moist, it deteriorates just like the exterior brick. The ties embedded in mortar rust.

For buildings with winter humidification (be it intentional or as a result of usage), walls with the detail of Fig. 16-1 will tend to have higher repair and maintenance costs over their useful life. Just as important, these walls are not very forgiving to flaws in design or execution. Details that contain significant thermal bridging, or areas where the insulation is left out can result in relatively fast and severe deterioration of the construction. Finally, the energy use of buildings with these walls is higher.

Of course, the air intrusion phenomena described above cannot occur unless there are some pathways of air penetration into the concrete block wythe, such as mortar with cracks. Very good site supervision can result in superior performance, even for the walls of Fig. 16-1. However, from a statistical standpoint, very good supervision is not possible in all projects. Furthermore, even perfect execution cannot confer the intrinsic advantages given by the design described below.

An integrated approach to wall design is presented in Fig. 16-2. The insulation protects the structure and backup wall, which are now at a temperature close to that of the room. Condensation is highly unlikely. A continuous air retarder is placed behind the insulation. The air retarder is effective in stopping most air infiltration and exfiltration. This air retarder bears almost all wind pressure. The brick wythe is intentionally left air-permeable. The wind creates only a small difference in pressure between the exterior and interior surfaces of the brick wythe. As a result, rain is less likely to be pushed into the brick and the probability of spalling is significantly reduced.

This approach works because it integrates all functions of the envelope.

A successful envelope is a membrane, allowing the passage of heat and solar radiation according to season and climate. A successful envelope also integrates its subsystems. Also, a successful envelope preserves the integrity of each subsystem, protecting it from degradation due to air intrusion, moisture intrusion, and thermal short circuiting.

Finally, in a broader context, energy efficiency is part of sustainability. The selection of environmentally-benign materials and systems, with low embodied energy and without adverse effects on indoor air quality is becoming more and more a part of the vocabulary of the modern designer. Space considerations did not permit addressing these important issues in the book. Yet "'green" needs to be merged with energy efficiency just as energy efficiency can only be considered in the context of structure and function.

INSULATION SYSTEMS
THERMAL INTEGRITY AND MULTIFUNCTIONALITY

The primary role of the thermal insulation system is to maintain comfort within occupied spaces. Additionally, thermal insulation protects construction elements (e.g., interior finishes, vapor retarders) from large variations in temperature. The thermal insulation system itself needs to be protected from air and moisture intrusion. To be effective, thermal insulation must also be relatively free of interruptions by construction elements with high conductivity, i.e., thermal bridges. Air intrusion, moisture intrusion, and thermal bridging can degrade the effectiveness of a wall or roof until the energy use becomes excessive and the construction deteriorates.

The energy use is termed excessive given the amount of insulation in the envelope. Assume, for instance, a 6 inch steel stud wall with R-21 fibrous insulation *but without insulating sheathing*. The total R-value of the wall, averaged over its entire surface, could be in the R-10 to R-13 range, depending on stud spacing, types of interior and exterior finishes, etc. This range could be acceptable for code compliance purposes or even for energy use, but is low when considering that R-21 insulation was used to achieve it. Further, if the conditioned space maintains a high humidity level during winter, as is often the case with computer rooms, restaurants, or housing for the elderly, moisture could condense on the steel studs. This example shows that it is quite feasible to specify a wall that is not particularly wasteful of energy but that creates maintenance and repair problems.

Thermal degradation is the primary focus of this chapter. Integration of several functions is the secondary focus. If the insulation system performs functions in addition to thermal protection, it integrates better in the envelope and becomes more cost effective.

For example, a concrete masonry unit made of insulating concrete is a single physical component which serves as both insulation and structural support. Another example is the foundation insulation which also provides protection from ground water.

Protection from thermal degradation and integration of several functions is often achieved simultaneously. in the example of the concrete masonry unit, the insulating concrete not only increases the R-value of the CMU but also reduces the thermal bridging created by the webs.

PRINCIPLES OF THERMAL DEGRADATION

Some of the most effective methods to reduce heat loss through the building envelope involve the *entire* insulation system. These methods protect the performance of insulation materials by reducing or eliminating onsite thermal degradation.

The severity of thermal degradation depends on both system design and construction quality. Research on air intrusion, moisture intrusion, and thermal bridging suggests that the insulation system can lose from less than 5% to more than 60% of its calculated R-value.

PRINCIPLES OF AIR AND MOISTURE INTRUSION

Air circulation in and around the insulation material creates thermal short-circuits which decrease the effective R-value of the system.

This occurs even when the outside air does not cross into the conditioned space, but rather, it simply enters and exits the insulation system. The amount of outside air that does enter the conditioned space (infiltration) is counterbalanced by indoor air which leaves the space (exfiltration). Humid air which exfiltrates from conditioned spaces deposits moisture within the insulation system, damaging both the physical and thermal integrity of the building envelope.

FIBROUS INSULATION

Batts and blankets made of fiberglass and mineral wool can be affected by air circulation both within and around the insulation. Air convection *within* the insulation (Fig. 16-3) occurs only with substantial temperature differential across the assembly, but air convection *around* the insulation occurs readily if the batt or blanket is installed with air gaps on either side. This happens, for instance, when batts intended for wood stud installation are placed in the wider cavity created by steel studs.

To prevent thermal degradation from air convection, all six sides of the insulation material should be in contact with a solid surface to the greatest practical extent.

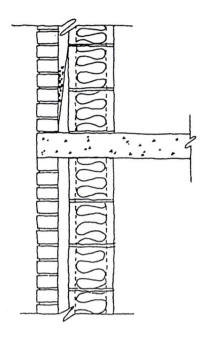

Figure 16-1 Typical wall detail where floor slab directly supports exterior finish.

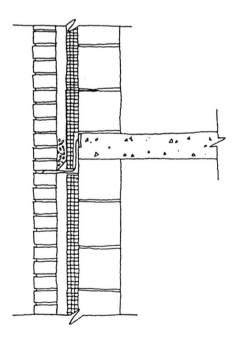

Figure 16-2 Typical wall detail where the slab edge is
covered by insulation and exterior finish

Rigid insulation foam boards are impermeable to air currents and thus not degraded by air convection within the insulation material. However, insulation systems using rigid foam insulation can suffer from air convection *around* the boards. This situation can occur, for example, in cavity walls with concrete masonry backup and brick finish, when the CMU substrate is irregular.

To prevent air convection within rigid foam insulation systems, the boards should be tightly sealed at all four edges. The substrate should be as smooth as possible. The CMU backup wythe, for instance, should be parged. The parging has the additional benefit of sealing discontinuities in the mortar between blocks.

Air diffusion in rigid foam Most types of plastic foam insulation are subject to air diffusion. Currently, most polyurethane, polyisocyanurate, and phenolic foams as well as extruded polystyrene foams are manufactured with HCFCs or HFCs as the blowing/expansion agents. While the ozone-depleting effect of these gases is much less marked than that of previously used CFCs, there are questions, not yet fully resolved, on the adverse effect of HCFC and HFC on the environment. Other alternatives are under development.

The gas in unfaced foam boards made of urethane, polyisocyanurate, and phenolic materials can be replaced by air over time. Air has lower insulating capability. Water can also penetrate into the cell matrix, causing further decrease in R-value, and even destroying the insulation.

Unfaced phenolic insulation boards degrade over several years from about R-8/inch, which is the manufacturer-listed R-value for 6-month-old stock, to about R-4.5/inch. Unfaced polyisocyanurate boards decrease from R-7.2/inch to about R-6.0/inch. Fiberglass-faced products also can age, but to a much lesser extent.

The aging problem can be largely avoided through material selection. Foil-faced boards are only slightly affected by aging, since outgassing can occur only at the edges.

Extruded polystyrene foam has not been shown to significantly decrease its R-value below the nominal R-5/inch through either air or moisture intrusion. Expanded polystyrene is not affected by air intrusion either, although if it has low density it can lose part of its effectiveness by soaking with water (e.g., in a damaged roof with ponding water or in a subsurface installation). However, one advantage of the expanded polystyrene is that it does not contain gas in its cells, and is therefore more benign for the environment than its extruded counterpart.

New foam types A Canadian manufacturer has been producing for several years a version of urethane foam, called polyicynene, which uses CO_2 as the blowing agent and has an R-value of about 4.0/inch. This foam does not outgas and therefore is expected to maintain its R-value over time.

PRINCIPLES OF THERMAL BRIDGING

A thermal bridge is a highly conductive construction element of the building envelope; this element penetrates or bypasses the insulation and acts as a thermal short circuit. See Fig. 16-4 for an example of wall thermal bridging.

In general, thermal bridging can occur in the following situations:
• structural elements which penetrate the insulation system, such as columns, mullions, or balconies
• attachments to and penetrations of the envelope by nonstructural elements, such as piping and railing
• component connections, such as the connection between insulated metal panels
• system connections such as the juncture between wall and roof, wall and floors geometry effects such as exterior angles and corners

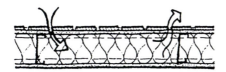

Figure 16-3 Air convection within fibrous insulation.

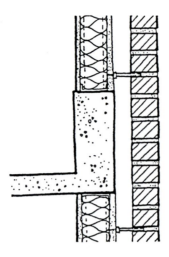

Figure 16-4 Thermal bridging at slab edge.

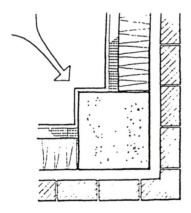

Figure 16-5 Thermal bridging at corner column.

Laboratory tests have shown that the R-value of wall areas with thermal bridging are 10 to 50% lower than the R-value of adjacent areas without thermal bridging.

Computer studies on poor construction practices have indicated a reduction in thermal resistance of over 80%. Most compelling, however, are the results of field investigations of office buildings, which demonstrated 10 to 20% increases in the *overall* envelope heat loss due to thermal bridging. (The areas affected by thermal bridging had their thermal resistance degraded by 25 to 50%.

EFFECTS OF THERMAL BRIDGING

In addition to excessive heat loss through the envelope, thermal bridges cause moisture condensation via two mechanisms:

1. Because thermal bridges lower the temperature of interior surfaces, the condensation potential on and within interior finishes is increased. Excessive condensation can readily occur in spaces with high indoor relative humidity (40% or above).

2. Because most thermal bridges penetrate the envelope, they are often accompanied by air infiltration and exfiltration. Exfiltrating air reaches cold thermal bridge surfaces, and deposits moisture *within* the building envelope.

Consequently, thermal bridging can cause costly maintenance and repair problems. At a minimum, damp and moldy interior spaces lose rental value. in severe cases hidden moisture condensation engenders staining, rusting, rotting, disintegration, and even complete failure of the affected envelope systems.

THERMAL BRIDGES AND VAPOR RETARDERS

Since moisture is more likely to condense on thermal bridges than on other surfaces, it is important to confer protection against such occurrences. In cold climates the vapor retarder should be placed on the winterwarm surface of the insulation, i.e., at the interior surface. For example, a steel stud wall with glass fiber insulation has the vapor retarder placed between the steel studs and the interior gypsum board. in hot and humid climates the vapor retarder, if any, should be placed on the summer-warm surface of the insulation, i.e., at the exterior surface. This distinction is important since in Florida, Texas, and similar locations, moisture tends to migrate from the hot and humid environment into the cool and dry interior space.

Assume a typical CMU construction. If the insulation is placed on the summer-warm surface of the CMU, the concrete blocks will be kept relatively cool by the air-conditioned interior space. The concrete of the CMU is a fairly effective vapor retarder. Water vapor contained in the warm outside air will condense on the exterior surface of the CMU wythe, especially at the shell/web joints, since webs act as thermal bridges, creating cooler lines on the exterior shell. To avoid such problems, the CMU wall should be furred and insulated to the interior. The concrete is now in the summer-warm zone of the wall. Since the CMU is warm, moisture from the outside air can't condense on it.

However, an important point must be made on the furred-in insulation. This insulation should not be foil-faced and the finish should not be vapor-impermeable (e.g., vinyl), to avoid creating a second vapor retarder plane. If such a plane were created, moisture could be trapped inside the wall, between the exterior vapor retarder (the CMU shell) and the interior vapor retarder (the foil facing or the vinyl finish). This moisture generates stains and creates conditions for mold and mildew growth.

RECENT DEVELOPMENTS

The knowledge base on thermal bridges has grown substantially during the past few years and now allows building designers to make thermal improvements within any construction system. Of particular relevance are tests performed by Oak Ridge National Laboratory; National Research Council of Canada; and the American Society of Heating, Refrigerating and Air Conditioning Engineers, Inc. on commercial construction.

The following section presents four specific building systems that are designed to overcome the deleterious effects of thermal bridges.

WALLS AND ROOFS WITH REDUCED THERMAL BRIDGING EXAMPLES

Thermal bridging is usually caused by highly conductive structural components within walls and roofs, such as corner columns, eave beams, and roof supports. Figures 16-5 and 16-6 show examples of thermal bridges. As discussed, thermal bridging not only leads to increased energy consumption, but to greater moisture condensation potential as well.

DATA INTERPRETATION

The following sections present four techniques for reducing thermal bridging in walls and roofs. When developing specific designs, architects might employ materials and methods of construction that are different from those assumed here. Consequently, the *exact* figures on heat loss and moisture condensation will vary. However, the problems created by the four types of thermal bridges will be similar in all cases, and the benefits obtained through energy-efficient alternates will be of the same order of magnitude.

Technical articles from ASHRAE Conference Proceedings provide additional guidance on principles of design without thermal bridges. One source used in this book is the Catalog of Thermal Bridges in Commercial and Multi-Family Residential Construction, developed by Steven Winter Associates, Inc., in collaboration with and under subcontract to Oak Ridge National Laboratory.

STEEL STUD WALLS WITH REDUCED THERMAL BRIDGING

Typical steel stud walls are composed of steel studs, placed at 16 inch or 24 inch on center, with fibrous insulation in-between gypsum board is generally used for exterior sheathing and interior finish. Exterior finishes include brick, glass, metal, vinyl, or wood.

The thermal conductivity of steel is 1000 times higher than that of fibrous insulation. Because of thermal bridging, a wall with 4 inch steel studs at 16 inch on center and R-11 insulation has an overall R-value of only 7.75. This R-value includes the exterior ceramic finish, two layers of 5/8 inch gypsum board, the air films, plus the insulation/stud layer. The R-value of this layer is about 40% below the R-value of the insulation.

The steel studs cause a 60% degradation in the performance of R-19 insulation (Fig. 16-7), reducing the overall R-value of the wall to 12.25.

Insulative sheathing reduces the thermal bridging effect of steel studs (Fig. 16-8). The overall R-value of a 4 inch steel stud wall with R-11 insulation and R-5 sheathing is about R-13.70.

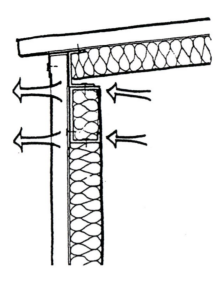

Figure 16-6 Thermal bridging at metal building eave.

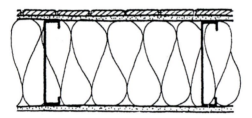

Figure 16-7 Wall with R-19 cavity insulation.

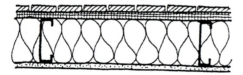

Figure 16-8 Wall with R-11 cavity insulation and R-5 sheathing.

A four-story, 58,000 ft^2 office building has walls with 4 inch steel studs at 16 inch on center and R-11 insulation. The interior finish and exterior sheathing are 5/8 inch gypsum board. The exterior finish is 4 inch face brick positioned 2 inch from the gypsum board sheathing. The tinted glazing is 15% of the gross wall area, has a U-value of 0.49, and a shading coefficient of 0.50. Lighting and office equipment use 3 watts/ft^2, characteristic of many code-complying, but not particularly energy-efficient buildings. Each floor is served by an AHU with inlet vanes, which delivers air via VAV boxes with reheat coils. An air economizer supplies "free" cooling to 62°F Temperatures are maintained at 72°F with 65°F setback during winter, and at 76°F with 90°F setup during summer. The two boilers have 85% AFUE. The chillers are electric-driven with air-cooled condensers.

If an R-11 steel stud wall receives 1 inch of extruded polystyrene sheathing, the thermal bridging, moisture condensation, and energy use are reduced (Fig. 16-8).

Moisture condensation   At 20°F outdoor temperature and 40% indoor relative humidity, each 100 linear ft of the R-11 unsheathed wall creates roughly 260 ft^2 moisture condensation on the interior surface of the wall. The exterior foam sheathing eliminates the condensation potential.

Energy savings   With just R-11 insulation, the annual gas consumption for this building, if located in White Plains, NY, just north of New York City, is 20,435 ccf (hundreds of cubic feet). Adding the R-5 insulative sheathing reduces the annual gas consumption by 10%, to 18,410 ccf.

CONCRETE SLAB EDGE WITH REDUCED THERMAL BRIDGING

Most brick-clad walls have steel stud or concrete masonry backup (Fig. 16-9). The concrete slab edge, if unprotected, may create an area of significant thermal bridging.

The wall system shown in Fig. 16-9 suffer from thermal bridging through the concrete slab edge.

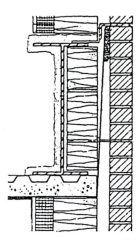

Figure 16-9 Uninsulated slab edge at masonry wall.

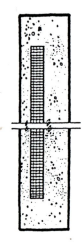

Figure 16-10 Fully encased precast concrete panel.

Adding R-5 rigid foam insulation more than doubles the thermal resistance of the affected area. Although the shelf angle still short circuits the insulation, both heat loss and moisture condensation potential are substantially reduced.

CASE STUDY: LOW-RISE OFFICE BUILDING

A four-story, 58,000 ft² office building has walls with 4 inch steel studs at 16 inch on center and R-11 insulation. The interior finish and exterior sheathing are 5/8 inch gypsum board. The brick cladding is positioned 2 inch from the exterior sheathing. The tinted glazing accounts for 15% of the gross wall area, has a U-value of 0.49, and a shading coefficient of 0.50. Lighting and office equipment use 3 watts/ft².

Each floor is served by an AHU with inlet vanes, which delivers air via VAV boxes with reheat coils. An air economizer supplies "free" cooling up to 62°E Temperatures are maintained at 72°F with 65°F setback during winter, and at 76°F with 90°F setup during summer. The two boilers have 85% AFUE. The chillers are electric-driven with air-cooled condensers.

The steel studs can be sheathed with 1 inch of extruded polystyrene or 1 3/4 inch expanded polystyrene to reduce thermal bridging. If the polystyrene is positioned to cover the slab edge, additional benefits occur.

Moisture condensation   At 20°F outdoor temperature and 40% indoor relative humidity, each 100 lineal ft of uninsulated slab edge can create roughly 66 ft² of condensation area on the steel beam and slab underside. With insulated slab edge, no interior surface is subject to moisture condensation.

Energy savings   With uninsulated slab edge, the annual gas consumption of this building, if located in White Plains, NY just north of New York City, is 20,435 ccf. Addition of R-5 rigid foam sheathing in the wall cavity reduces annual consumption to 15,920 ccf (hundreds of cubic feet), a 22% savings. The insulation at slab edge accounts for 12% savings.

Preinsulated, precast concrete panels are used in offices, hospitals, schools, and shopping malls. Many of these panels have an internal layer of foam insulation fully encased in concrete (Fig. 16-10).

Rigid insulation in precast concrete panels has a conductivity of 0.125 to 0.26. The top and bottom beams are made of concrete with a conductivity of 10 to 15. Because of thermal bridging at the connecting concrete beams, a 5 ft high panel containing R-15 insulation has an overall R-value of only 5.4.

By eliminating the concrete beams and instead using either metal ties or plastic ties to structurally bond the two concrete wythes, the overall R-value of the system increases from 5.4 to 15 and 16.75, respectively.

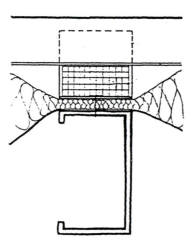

Figure 16-11 Spacer and compressed insulation at metal roof purlin.

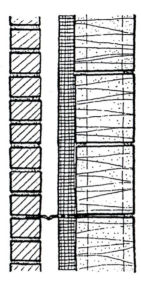

Figure 16-12 Uninsulated slab edge at masonry wall.

Figure 16-13 Exterior foundation insulation.

203

A four-story, 58,000 ft^2 office building has precast concrete panel walls with 3 inch extruded polystyrene insulation (R-5/inch) or 4 inch expanded polystyrene insulation (R-3.75/inch). The tinted glazing (15% of the gross wall area) has a U-value of 0.49 and a shading coefficient of 0.50. Fluorescent lights and office equipment use 3 watts/ft^2. Each floor is served by a separate AHU with inlet vanes, which delivers air via VAV boxes with reheat coils. An air economizer supplies "'free" cooling up to 62°F Temperatures maintained in the office are 72°F with setback to 65°F during the heating season, and 76°F with setup to 90°F during the cooling season. The two boilers have 85% AFUE. The chillers are electric-driven with air-cooled condensers.

If the concrete wall panels are changed from a fully encased configuration (Fig. 16-10) to one with metal connectors, thermal bridging is reduced with beneficial effects for both moisture condensation and energy use.

Moisture condensation At 20ïF outdoor temperature and 40% indoor relative humidity, the fully encased panels could produce roughly 125 ft^2 of moisture condensation or interior finishes for every 100 linear ft of facade. For panels built with either metal or plastic ties , no moisture condenses on interior surfaces.

Energy savings with fully encased precast panels, a building located in White Plains, NY, just north of New York City, will have the annual gas consumption of about 22,960 ccf (hundreds of cubic feet). If replaced with panels built with metal ties, the annual gas consumption drops to 18,950 ccf-a significant reduction of 18%.

METAL ROOFS WITH
REDUCED THERMAL BRIDGING

Conventional insulation techniques for metal roofs use fiberglass or mineral wool batts, which are compressed between purlins and roofing.

When fibrous insulation is compressed at purlin, it loses R-value in the entire zone from the point of maximum compression to the point where it regains full thickness. A roof with R-19 fiberglass insulation has an overall R-value of only 9.9 for the 4-ft-wide strip centered on the purlin.

By inserting a 1/2 inch extruded polystyrene spacer between purlin and roofing (Fig. 16-11), the overall R-value of the 4-ft strip around the purlin is raised from 9.9 to 16.2.

Performance is further enhanced using 2 inch polystyrene inserts plus wire insulation hangers, which allow the insulation to be installed without any compression. The R-value of the 4-ft-wide strip around the purlin now increases to 17.2.

CASE STUDY: WAREHOUSE

This 32,000 ft^2 one-story building has several administrative offices and a large electronics storage area. The construction uses brick faced walls with a U-value of 0.11 for the office area and metal-clad walls with a U-value of 0.12 for the storage area. Clear glass in thermally broken aluminum frames (U = 0.50) accounts for 5% of the gross wall area. The roof uses compressed fiberglass insulation at metal purlins.

Rooftop units (AFUE = 0.80, EER = 7.8) maintain 70°F in the office area during the heating season, with 65°F setback. A constant volume heating and ventilation system maintains 60°F in the storage area during the heating season. The warehouse has a metal roof insulated with R-19 fiberglass, both with and without polystyrene spacers at purlins.

Moisture condensation At 20°F outdoor temperature and 30% indoor relative humidity, the unprotected system could create roughly 40 ft2 of moisture condensation surface per 100 linear ft of purlin. The moist surface area is reduced to practically zero with the polystyrene inserts.

Energy consumption Without polystyrene spacers, the annual gas consumption of this building, located in White Plains, NY, just north of New York City, is 9300 ccf (hundreds of cubic feet). With the addition of 1/2 inch polystyrene spacers the gas consumption drops to 8800 ccf, a 5% reduction.

PRACTICAL CONSIDERATIONS FOR WALLS AND ROOFS
WITH REDUCED THERMAL BRIDGING

Design
• During the schematic design phase, reduce thermal bridging when selecting
wall and roof types. These decisions may affect the aesthetic of the building.

• Plan on small changes during design development. Any attempt to redress major thermal bridging problems could add extra expense to your already established budget.

• Avoid specifying highly conductive materials for those building components which extend across the envelope.

• Focus on the envelope areas with lowest R-value.

• Focus on spaces and buildings that may experience interior relative humidities of 40% and above during winter.

• When thermal bridging is unavoidable, provide a path to eliminate the water formed through moisture condensation.

• Do not attempt to obtain high R-values by increasing the insulation levels between thermal bridge members (e.g., R-30 insulation between steel joists). Such use of resources is ineffective and can actually increase the likelihood of moisture condensation. Instead specify exterior insulating sheathing.

• Provide air retarders for walls with thermal bridges. Moist air that exfiltrates through walls can cause extensive damage through condensation on cold thermal bridges.

Construction

• In construction types with high potential for thermal bridging (e.g., steel stud walls) ensure that all specified exterior insulating sheathing is actually installed.

• Thermal bridging may be created because of construction defects, such as missing insulation. Consider troubleshooting new buildings with *infrared thermography* before occupancy. The test provides a quick and relatively inexpensive method of detecting thermal bridging problems.

• Thermography methods have evolved considerably during the past few years and are no longer restricted to scientific applications.

Operation/Maintenance

• Maintain tight joints in the area of thermal bridges. Air exfiltration can exacerbate moisture condensation problems.

• Maintain low relative humidities in buildings with thermal bridges.

WALLS WITH INSULATING CONCRETE MASONRY UNITS
THE INSULATING CMU

Insulating concrete masonry units can achieve R-values ranging from R-5 to R-15. This range is many times higher than that obtained with conventional, uninsulated CMUs, which typically attain R-values of R-1.0 to R-2.5. Such good thermal performance is obtained with modified geometry, lightweight concrete, and core insulation.

Insulating CMUs are less likely to suffer from thermal degradation than their conventional counterparts. Core insulation reduces not only conduction but also convection, because it obstructs the air spaces. The webs, made of lightweight concrete with density below 105 pcf, are no longer fast conduits for the heat. In normal weight masonry (over 125 pcf), core insulation is easily short circuited by heat flowing through webs. In lightweight masonry the webs have higher R-value and pose similar resistance to the heat flow as the core insulation.

These advances have significantly narrowed the gap in thermal performance between the group formed by *single-wythe and composite walls*, which can now incorporate the high-R CMUs, and *cavity walls*, which were always better insulated and therefore do not benefit as much from the newer technologies. (See Fig. 16-12.)

INSULATING CMU WALL VS. CAVITY WALL

Integrated Functions   By integrating thermal insulation with structural support, insulating CMUs offer a laborsaving alternative to the masonry cavity wall. Insulating CMUs can be used in single wythe or in composite masonry walls. Either insulating CMU configuration decreases construction time by comparison to masonry cavity wall construction, which requires three separate, field-installed functional components-block, exterior rigid insulation, and brick veneer.

Lower Cost Insulating CMU systems tend to cost less than typical cavity masonry walls not only because they reduce the amount of field work, but also because they permit the use of less expensive finishes.

Less Protection to Water Penetration Because the insulating CMU construction lacks the air space of the cavity configuration, wind-driven water can more easily penetrate into the wall. The exterior air retarder, which practically eliminates air and water intrusion, can only be specified for cavity construction. For multistory construction the slab edge is always exposed in the single-wythe wall, but can be covered by insulation in the cavity wall.

For these reasons cavity masonry walls present advantages that are important in climates with significant rain and high wind, especially when freeze/ thaw cycles are present. In many instances, however, the single-wythe system has become competitive in both thermal performance and durability.

Three Levels of Performance Improvement vs. Conventional CMUs From a thermal standpoint, a concrete masonry unit consists of two components-concrete webs and shells, and hollow cores. In a typical normal weight block with two hollow cores, the predominant heat path is through the

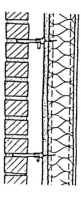

Figure 16-14 Exterior gypsum sheathing as air retarder component.

BUILDINGS WITH REDUCED THERMAL BRIDGING CONSTRUCTED THROUGHOUT THE UNITED STATES

Steel Stud Walls with Insulating Sheathing

• Columbia Presbyterian Hospital, New York, NY

• The Waterside Apartments, New York, NY

• Nehemiah Housing Development, Brooklyn, NY

Insulated Slab Edge in Brick-Clad Walls

• Battery Park City, New York, NY

• Columbia Presbyterian Hospital, New York, NY

• Police Athletic League, New York, NY

• Consolidated Edison Energy Training Center, New York, NY

Preinsulated, Precast Concrete Panels with Plastic Ties

• Mid-rise Condominium, Rochester, MN

• Office Building, Ames, IA

• Factory Building, Columbus, OH

Metal Roofs with Fibrous Insulation and Polystyrene Spacers

• LILCO Cogeneration Plant, Shoreham, NY

• Hofstra University Recreation Center, New York, NY

• Altobello Children's Hospital, Middletown, CT

concrete webs, which act, as thermal bridges around the air spaces. The R-value of a typical 8 inch, hollow-core, normal weight CMU (with concrete density above 125 pcf) is about R-1.

The R-value of a CMU can be increased by modifying the web configuration, by using higher R-value concrete, or by insulating the cores; some enhancements are significantly more effective than others. The following examples demonstrate that high R-value concrete is always essential to obtain a high R-value CMU.

In general, concrete with lower density has higher R-value. There are exceptions. Higher R-value can also be obtained by reducing the amount of sand in the concrete, or by using aggregates with lower conductivity.

1. *Normal weight CMUs with insulated cores—R-2.5 to R-3.5.* A CMU core has an R-value of about 1 due to the airspace it creates. This core can be filled with perlite or vermiculite, can be foamed in place, or can be fitted with rigid insulation inserts. The core R-value can increase to 6 or 7; however, webs of CMUs made with normal weight concrete still have R-values much lower than 1. Heat flows around the insulated cores through the conductive concrete webs, which in effect act as thermal bridges. The overall R-value of normal weight CMUs with insulation in the cores rarely surpasses 3.5.

2. *Lightweight CMUs with insulating fill or rigid foam inserts—R-5 to R-7.* Lightweight concrete (80 pcf to 125 pcf) reduces the heat flow through the webs of the concrete blocks by 50 to 70%. In turn, core insulation becomes more effective, since it is no longer short circuited by highly conductive webs. As a result, the overall R-value of 8 inch lightweight CMUs with core insulation ranges from 5 to 7. Higher R-values can be obtained with even lower density concrete.

3. *Ultra-light, multicore CMUs-R-8 to R-14.* The highest performance of insulating CMUs is achieved by using very light (50 to 70 pcf) low-conductivity aggregate combined with a multicore design which drastically reduces thermal bridging through the webs. The CMUs can reach R-8 without any core insulation, and R-14 when the cores are filled with polystyrene.

The thermal improvements of this design over that in example 2 consists mainly in the multicore configuration. The heat flow path around the cores is significantly lengthened, increasing the R-value of the solid portion of the CMU. The cores, too, have better R-value when empty because they are narrower, impeding air convection.

LIGHTWEIGHT CMUs WITH RIGID FOAM INSERTS

Two-core CMUs can be manufactured with lightweight aggregates such as (a) expanded shale, clay, and slate, (b) slag and scoria, or (c) cinders and fly ash. The density of concrete obtained with these aggregates ranges typically from 80 to 125 pcf. By contrast, normal weight concretes manufactured with gravel have densities of 125 to 140 pcf.

Several configurations of foam insulation for CMUs are available. C-shaped inserts fit into cores of conventionally configured blocks. Another system, uses straight inserts which extend across notched webs; the notches reduce thermal bridging effects.

The core insulation boosts the R-value of the CMU in the 5 to 7 range. C-shaped inserts yield R-values toward the bottom of this range.

Straight inserts reduce thermal bridging at webs; additionally, one manufacturer positions the insert to create two air spaces in each core. This method is more effective. The highest R-value measured to date (R-7) was obtained with straight, foil-faced inserts which create two reflective air spaces.

ULTRALIGHT, MULTICORE CMUs

This innovative CMU uses very low density concrete (50 to 70 pcf) made with polystyrene beads, perlite, vermiculite, or with expanded glass aggregate.

The concrete has an R-value of about 0.5/inch, which is 5 to 10 times higher than that of normal weight concretes.

The block geometry consists of three rows of narrow cores that are arranged in a staggered pattern. This configuration significantly lengthens the heat pathway by comparison to conventional two- or threecore design. As a result, thermal bridging at webs is reduced.

The combination of high R-value concrete and extended heat pathway gives these polystyrene CMUs exceptional thermal performance characteristics. An 8 inch block made of polystyrene concrete has an R-value of about 8. Adding polystyrene foam inserts to the cores raises the R-value to 14. Consequently, a single-wythe wall built with these blocks has a thermal resistance similar to:

- brick/CMU cavity walls with R-10 to R-12 rigid insulation in the cavity
- brick/CMU cavity walls with R-5 to R-7 rigid insulation in the cavity, and R-11
- batt insulation in steel stud furring
- steel stud wall with R-11 batt insulation and R-5 rigid insulation sheathing

Limitations Multicore CMUs cannot be gripped with one hand as can the two-core CMUs, and may therefore increase labor costs to some extent. Also, polystyrene concretes have relatively low structural resistance and cannot be used in load-bearing walls higher than two to three stories. The polystyrene CMU soaks water and must be protected from prolonged exposure to moisture.

Case Study: Low-Rise Office Building A four-story, 56,000 ft^2 office building has a 590 ft perimeter. The building has concrete block walls with furred-in gypsum board interior finish and brick exterior finish. The glazing, which accounts for 15% of the gross wall area, has a U-value of 0.50 and a shading coefficient of 0.50. Fluorescent lights and typical office equipment use 3 watts/ft^2. Each floor is served by a separate air-handling unit with inlet vanes, which delivers air via VAV boxes with reheat coils. An air economizer supplies "free" cooling up to 62°F.

Temperatures maintained in the office are 72°F with setback to 65°F during the heating season, and 76°F with setup to 90°F during the cooling season. The two boilers have 85% AFUE. The chillers are electric driven with air-cooled condensers.

1. Steel studs with R-11 insulation and exterior gypsum sheathing

2. R-6 lightweight CMU with rigid insulation inserts

3. Uninsulated 8 inch polystyrene CMU

The polystyrene CMU results in lower energy use and comparable first cost. Production of these CMUs has been recently discontinued, but the concept proved viable and could be revived in the near future.

PRACTICAL CONSIDERATIONS FOR WALLS WITH INSULATING CMUs

Design

• Polystyrene CMUs (50-70 pcf) have lower compressive strength than CMUs made with typical lightweight concrete (80-105 pcf). For this reason they are not used in load-bearing walls higher than three stories.

• Core insulation is ineffective in CMUs made of normal weight concrete.

• Extruded polystyrene inserts retain R-value over time because they do not outgas and do not absorb water. However, polystyrene is more flammable than polyisocyanurate foams.

• Polyicynene foam is a type of urethane which is C02-based and therefore does not outgas. Because it contains no CFCs or HCFCs, this foam is also more benign to the environment.

• Protect lightweight CMUs against bulk water intrusion with a waterproof finish (e.g., paint, ceramic tiles, brick, normal weight concrete). Lightweight CMUs could absorb more water than normal weight CMUs and could be damaged by freeze/thaw cycles if permanently exposed to weather.

• CMU R-values derived from ASTM tests of full-scale walls are reliable. Two- and three-dimensional computer analyses (e.g., using FRAME, HEATING or CFD2000) also yield accurate results. Calculated CMU R-values are acceptable if obtained with the ASHRAE Parallel Series method, also called the Isothermal Planes method. The ASHRAE Parallel Path method predicts *unrealistically high R-values* for insulating CMUs.

• If the R-value of a wall with insulating CMUs must be increased, it is best to provide insulation on the exterior (winter-cold) of the CMU wythe, such as in an EIFS application. If insulation is located in the interior (winter-warm) surface of the CMU, perform calculations to ensure that water vapor does not condense on the CMU shell.

Construction

• Protect the top of walls built with insulating CMUs against water intrusion even when the walls are erected during the cooling season. The lightweight concrete can absorb water, which can then stain interior and exterior finishes.

• Check for missing rigid insulation inserts. If possible, check for voids using thermography when perlite or vermiculite is used.

• If polyicynene is used as core insulation (on-site foaming), it will probably fill most spaces around mortar deposits, mortar gaps, and misaligned blocks, because it has an expansion factor higher than 60. When expansion is completed, the foam solidifies, developing "skins" at the contact with other materials.

• Give special attention to polystyrene CMUs during shipping, storage, and handling. These CMUs are more easily chipped than the higher density units.

Operation/Maintenance

• Maintain masonry joints in good condition to prevent air penetration in CMU cores.

• Maintain roof/ wall connections in good condition. Water accumulation in CMU cores reduces the R-value of the lower section of the wall and promotes deterioration of concrete.

TYPES OF FOUNDATION INSULATION

Foundation insulation is usually placed on the exterior of a footing or basement wall (Fig. 16-13), under a slab, within a basement wall, or on the interior surface of a basement wall.

Exterior insulation is typically made of extruded polystyrene boards. Integral insulation can be made of rigid inserts, fills (e.g., perlite, vermiculite), or can be foamed in place. Interior insulation is usually fibrous.

LIGHTWEIGHT, INSULATING CMUS ARE USED IN BUILDINGS THROUGHOUT THE NORTHERN UNITED STATES

Lightweight CMUs with Rigid Insulation Inserts
- Sullivan County Health Care Facilities, Monticello, NY
- Middle and Junior High Schools, Albany, NY
- Federal Express Distribution Center, Rochester NY
- Sears Distribution Center, Utica, NY
- Binghamton Regional Maintenance Facility, Bingamton, NY
- Multiplex Cinema, Medford, NY
- Heartland Business Center, Edgewood, NY
- Proctor & Gamble Office/Lab, Norwich, CT
- Municipal Maintenance Building, Niagara Falls, NY
- Fordham University Dormitories, Bronx, NY
- The Brickyard Restaurant, Kingston, NY

Polystrene Multicore CMUs
- Center Islip Congregation of Jehova, Islip, NY
- The Brickyard Restaurant, Kingston, NY
- Shopping Center, Epping, NH
- Stone Machine Co., Chester, NH

Calculation Methods for Ground Heat Loss Foundation heat loss is considerably more complex and more difficult to calculate than heat loss from the above-grade portions of buildings. Foundations lose heat in two directions: upward toward the ground surface and downward toward deep ground zones. Near the surface, soil temperature tracks air temperature closely. The amplitude of soil temperature swings decreases with depth.

Until recently, only mainframe computer programs could accurately model ground thermal dynamics and its effect on building energy use and electric demand. Most designers necessarily relied on the simplified heat loss estimation methods presented in the *ASHRAE Handbook of Fundamentals*.

Recent and near-future developments simplify the task. Oak Ridge National Laboratory has developed guidelines for ground insulation. The schematic design software, ENERGY-10, developed by National Renewable Energy Laboratory, will soon incorporate credible ground heat transfer algorithms.

Cost-Effective Foundation Insulation Using dynamic foundation heat loss calculation techniques, the designer is able to specify foundation insulation and mechanical equipment with increased confidence.

Dynamic computer simulations show that, in moderate and cold climates, foundation insulation is cost-effective when applied to heating dominated buildings. Such buildings usually have a long foundation perimeter and relatively small internal heat gains from lights and equipment.

Moisture Protection The R-value of the foundation insulation system can be compromised if ground water (a) permeates the insulation material, as in insulating fills, or (b) circulates around the insulation board, as in exterior insulation applications. Moisture protection can be achieved by relieving the static pressure of groundwater.

One innovative product, presented below, integrates the insulation and drainage functions.

This product consists of a rigid foam foundation insulation with vertical and horizontal grooves that act as groundwater drainage channels. The grooves are covered with a spun-bonded filter fabric which protects the channels from clogging. The insulated drainage panels have a specified drainage capacity of 5 gpm/linear ft.

By combining both thermal insulation and foundation drainage into one component, this system reduces the amount of site labor and the need for site supervision. Drainage rates are more predictable, and the insulation performance is more reliable. R-values of 6.9 and 10.6 are achieved.

Case Study: Low-Rise Office Building The following analysis examines the advantages of increased foundation insulation in a four-story, 58,000 ft^2 office building located in White Plains, NY, just north of New York City. The calculations were performed using the DOE-2.1 computer program.

Two foundation insulation systems are compared-R-5 perimeter insulation, two foot deep (code required), with gravel drain, and R-6.9 insulation-and-drainage system carried full depth to the footings.

The basecase building, previously described in greater detail— see *Walls and Roofs with Reduced Thermal Bridging*, uses 20,435 ccf gas. The R-6.9 insulation saves 420 ccf of gas annually, but has no effect on cooling electricity consumption. At 45 cents per ccf, the annual savings is about $190. More important, the R-6.9 insulation-and-drainage system will provide a more reliable protection against moisture intrusion.

INSULATION AND DRAINAGE PANELS HAVE ALREADY BEEN USED
FOR SEVERAL COMMERCIAL APPLICATIONS

Commercial Applications
• Lehman College, New York, NY
• Fordham Preparatory School, New York, NY
• Mt. Larretto Nursing Home, Albany, NY
• Bassett Hospital, Cooperstown, NY
• Hartwick College, Oneonta, NY
• Corning Glass, Corning, NY
• Eastern Connecticut State College, Willimantic, CT
• Travelers Insurance Offices, Hartford, CT

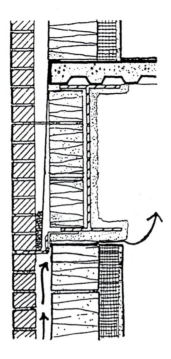

Figure 16-15 Channel airflow at joint in a masonry wall.

Design

> • The insulated drainage panels have standard 2 ft by 8 ft sizes.

> • The cost is about 50% higher than for drainage-only panels. However,
> the insulated drainage panels can achieve cost savings when compared
> with drainage-only panels that are installed in conjunction with separate boards of
> polystyrene.

Construction

> • The rigid insulated drainage panels conform less easily with irregular
> foundation surfaces than aggregate fill or wire core drainage products.

Operation/ Maintenance

> • These panels are less likely to clog than aggregate fill.

> • Because basement walls are kept warm and dry, mold and mildew is unlikely to form.

AIR RETARDERS

Air Retarder Types

An air retarder system (AR) consists of one or more air-impermeable components which are sealed at all seams and penetrations to form a continuous wrap around the building walls.

In some AR systems the function of the airtight component is assumed by an existing construction element. In steel stud walls, for example, the exterior gypsum board sheathing can also serve as the air-impermeable component of the air retarder (Fig. 16-14). In curtain walls, the airtight component may be steel sheet or glass. In either situation, all joints between airtight components must be sealed. In the case of the gypsum board AR, for instance, the joints between boards must be taped and the penetration of the brick ties must be sealed with a bituminous mastic.

However, most AR systems use membranes that serve the specific purpose of impeding air leakage into conditioned spaces. In most large commercial buildings the membranes are liquid-applied bituminous, liquid-applied rubber, sheet bituminous, and sheet plastic. These membranes impede the passage of both air and vapor. In cold climates the membranes must be positioned on the winter-warm side of the insulation to avoid moisture condensation. A typical detail positions the membrane AR on the exterior surface of the CMU wythe. Both membrane and CMU are protected by rigid insulation. The exterior shell of the CMU never reaches the low temperatures at which moisture could condense.

Small commercial buildings with steel or wood stud walls can employ residential-type air retarders. These membranes are not vapor retarders. They prevent air penetration but allow the interior moisture to escape to the outside. For this reason they are typically placed on the winter-cold side of the insulation. Products include spun-bonded polyolefin sheet on wood substrate; thin paperbacked polystyrene delivered in long strips folded in accordion fashion; and pressed wood or paper products with or without punched aluminum foil. (This foil is punched to allow water vapor diffusion.)

Air Leakage Measurements in eight U.S. office buildings found average air leakage rates of 0.1 to 0.5 air changes per hour, which account for an estimated 10 to 25% of the peak heating load.

These air leakage rates are higher than those assumed by most engineers when performing calculations for pressurized buildings. Excessive air leakage has the following effects:

• *Increased energy use* Not only must infiltrating air be heated or cooled, humidified or dehumidified, but air intrusion into the building envelope degrades the effectiveness of the insulation system (see *Insulation Systems*).
• *Discomfort* Localized under-heating and drafts reduce occupant productivity during the winter.
• *Damage* Infiltrating air can carry rain water into exterior finishes and into backup elements, causing brick spalling and other problems. Exfiltrating air carries indoor humidity which may condense in the building envelope, causing rusting and rotting (also, see *Insulation Systems*).

DIFFUSE VERSUS CHANNEL AIRFLOW

Air leakage through a building envelope occurs via two types of airflow. "Diffuse'" airflow is air movement *through* a layer of the envelope, such as wind through loosely woven cloth or through a masonry wall.

"Channel" airflow is air movement *around* a solid retarder, through holes, seams, or joints, as shown in Fig. 16-15. Channel airflow commonly occurs at thermal bridges, where structural components penetrate the building envelope. (See *Principles of Thermal Bridging*.) The long airflow pathways often result in intense cooling of exfiltration air, which, in turn, releases its moisture inside building components.

Both diffuse and channel airflow occur in most wall types. Although diffuse airflow typically accounts for most air leakage, channel airflow creates most problems. Diffuse airflow is controlled by selecting air-impermeable air retarder materials such as bituminous or plastic membranes. Channel airflow is controlled by sealing the air retarder at all seams and joints and by protecting the air retarder system from damage.

RECENT ADVANCES

During the past decade, membrane ARs have experienced the fastest pace of development. Types and applications have diversified and the field experience has increased. With a solid track record in Canada, membrane air retarders are increasingly specified in buildings in the United States. The following section presents two membranes in common use and a new entry in the marketplace.

Membrane Air Retarder Systems Most membrane air retarder systems used today in larger commercial buildings are bituminous or rubber, and are delivered to the building site either in liquid state, for trowel and brush application, or in sheets, which are glued or heat-fused to the walls. One new membrane AR is made of plastic, and is mechanically attached to the substrate.

LIQUID-APPLIED BITUMINOUS MEMBRANE

Liquid-applied membranes consist of compounds which are trowelled or sprayed in place. When cured, they form a flexible, continuous film over the building exterior. The most common compounds are bituminous or rubber-type.

Liquid-applied membranes can be used in any construction type, regardless of geometry, number of penetrations through the envelope, or number of materials. This flexibility has a price. Because liquid membranes are applied on site, they require supervision and quality control.

Specifically, the liquid membranes should not be applied to surfaces that are wet, oily, dusted, or frosted, including surfaces that get moist from internal sources, such as cast-in-place concrete that has been cured for less than two weeks.

Further, although liquid membranes can span hairline cracks, they should be supported by a reinforcing fabric, mesh, or by sheet membrane when they span wider joints.

All these requirements can be easily met by construction teams which have experience in applying bituminous compounds to walls for waterproofing purposes. The training period is brief.

Case Study: Hospital in New York City The new Mount Sinai Hospital, designed by Pei, Cobb, Freed and Partners, was completed in 1989. The building has exterior cavity walls, with the following layers: brick veneer, air space, rigid insulation., concrete masonry units, steel stud furring., and gypsum wall board.

To protect the building against New York's winds and frequent freeze/thaw cycles, the architects wrapped the concrete masonry backup wall in a bituminous air retarder. A trowel-applied membrane was selected because brick tie perforations would have required extensive patching for a bituminous sheet membrane.

Because of the air retarder, the brick cladding does not pose a significant resistance to the wind, and the air pressure inside the wall cavity is not very different from the outside air pressure. Consequently, it is less likely that rain will be entrained into the brick. The air retarder also minimizes air leakage into the building.

BITUMINOUS SHEET MEMBRANE

Bituminous sheet-applied membranes consist of bitumen impregnated fabrics which are either heat-fused or adhered to the wall. All joints are lapped and sealed.

Bituminous sheet membranes are best suited for walls without many perforations. Penetrations and joints must be sealed with liquid-applied membranes. If liquid membrane patching is extensive, the advantage gained through the quick application of the bituminous membrane is lost.

CASE STUDY: LIBRARY

The Wessell Library of the Tufts University was built in 1964, into the south side of "The Hill," a steep slope that marks the historic center of the suburban Boston campus. The original building had 184,000 ft 2 and was clad with limestone panels.

The new addition, designed by Shepley Bulfinch Richardson and Abbott of Boston nearly doubles the size of the building. Energy efficiency and moisture control were among the design goals.

The addition expands the building on two of the three original floor levels and adds a smaller lower level down the slope of the hill on the south and east sides. New construction also partially infills the existing entry courtyard to create a new clerestory lit entry Large windows on the new facades along with clerestories and skylights bring natural light into study and administrative areas. The windows use low-e glazing.

New bookstack areas are kept toward the interior and are efficiently lit with indirect fluorescent fixtures running perpendicular to the shelving.

The original flat-slab concrete structural system is continued in most portions of the addition. Lighter weight steel infill is used where additional weight on the existing structure is constrained by footing sizes.

The steel stud walls are sheathed with gypsum board surfaced with glass fiber. All exterior wall surfaces are then completely covered with a 40 mil membrane made of cross-laminated rubberized asphalt and polyethylene.

This membrane creates an air retarder. By impeding air movement into the building, the air retarder also reduces the moisture transport. For a library, the ability to control the moisture of the air is essential.

The air retarder is covered by 2 1/2 inch of extruded polystyrene board. The exterior finish, composed of granite and limestone masonry veneer, is anchored to either the concrete structure or to the 6 inch metal stud infill walls.

SNAP-ON PVC MEMBRANE

One innovative sheet membrane AR is mechanically attached to the wall. This system consists of a PVC sheet with special PVC profiles, which accommodate the brick ties without compromising the integrity of the air retarder.

The brick ties arrive at the job site already attached to long, extruded PVC profiles. These profiles are' positioned in the horizontal joints of the CMUs. Next, strips of membrane are stretched between and fastened to each row of PVC members. Finally, a second set of PVC profiles snaps over the extrusions already in place, covering the top and bottom of each membrane strip and creating airtight seals.

This mechanically-attached membrane was introduced to the market a few years ago. Should it withstand the test of time, it will provide a compelling alternative to both liquid applied and bituminous membrane ARs for brick and stone-clad facades. Mechanically attached ARs can be quickly applied to the wall .just like bituminous membrane ARs, but require no additional patching.

CASE STUDY-UNIVERSITY OF GUELPH, CANADA

Robbie, Young and Wright Associates designed a large complex at the University of Guelph, in Guelph Ontario. Although all facades are brick clad, some of the backup walls use steel studs and others use CMUs. Both wall types are protected with the PVC snap-on air retarder system.

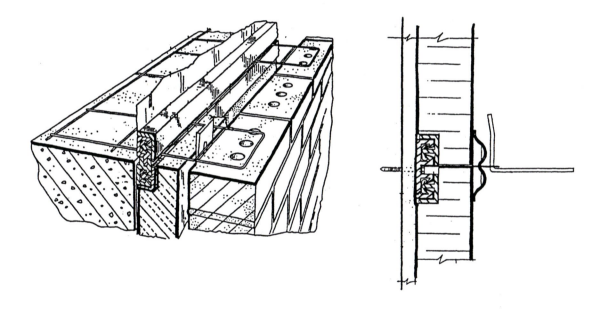

Figure 16-16 Perspective and vertical section through PVC sheet, mechancially-fastened air retarder system. (Kap-Shor Technology, Ltd.)

Design Typically, air retarders for commercial buildings are impermeable to water vapor. In cold climates, to avoid vapor condensation on the inside surface of the membrane, the air retarder should be located on the winter-warm side of the insulation.

Dew point temperature calculations are required to determine how much insulation, if any, can be placed between the vapor-impermeable AR and the conditioned space.

Small buildings may use fibrous insulation in conjunction with air retarders that are permeable to water vapor. These ARs can be made of spun-bonded polyolefin, of thin, paper-backed polystyrene, or of other materials with a perm rating higher than 5. A vapor retarder (e.g., polyethylene sheet) is sometimes installed on the winter-warm side of the insulation if the building is located in a cold climate. Because the ARs are permeable to water vapor, they can be located on the exterior side of the insulation, to protect it from air convection. Bituminous sheet membranes must be patched at penetrations. For this reason, sheet membranes are most effective for applications with few penetrations through the envelope, such as panelized construction. For air-conditioned buildings located in hot, humid climates, if a vapor impermeable AR is specified, it should be placed on the summer-warm side of the insulation. The construction must avoid creating two vapor retarder planes.

Case-by-case analyses should be undertaken for buildings located in climates with both cold and hot, humid periods. Masonry walls have many steel ties that puncture the air retarder membrane. For these construction types bituminous liquid-applied membranes have been generally used.

However, the mechanically-fastened PVC membrane system constitutes an interesting option for walls with brick and stone veneer.

Construction Quality control on site is important to maintain AR system integrity. All penetrations must be sealed.

EXAMPLES OF AIR RETARDER APPLICATIONS

LIQUID MEMBRANE
- Mt. Sinai Hospital, New York, NY
- St. Luke's Hospital, New York, NY
- Mississagua Central Library, Mississagua, Ontario
- University of Toronto, Toronto, Ontario

- Notre Dame High School, Burlington, Ontario

- Resurrection School, Kitchener, Ontario

- Ontario College of Nurses, Toronto, Ontario

- Regional Headquarters for Ottawa Carleton, Ottawa, Ontario

- Museum of Civilization, Hull, Ontario

BITUMINOUS SHEET MEMBRANE

- Rowes Wharf Shops and Housing, Boston, MA

- 1700 West Park Drive, Westboro, MA

- Brampton City Hall, Brampton, Ontario

- Laurentian University, Sudbury, Ontario

- Holocaust Museum, Washington, DC

SNAP-ON SHEET MEMBRANE

- University of Guelph, Guelph, Ontario

- Simcoe & Erie Insurance Office Building, Burlington, Ontario

A pressurization test, performed with a colored gas, can be used to visualize gaps and to implement low cost remedial measures for defects. The method of applying a liquid membrane is very similar to that used to waterproof walls. However, if the contractor has not performed such an installation before, it may be advisable to have a small portion of the wall built first. This portion is pressure-tested. Any installation problems are corrected before the entire building is erected.

OPERATION/MAINTENANCE

- If a membrane sheet air retarder has detached from its substrate, it must be repaired to avoid bypassing by air convection.

- Slashes and holes in the air retarder that may be caused by building renovation must be thoroughly repaired. Discontinuities in the air retarder can have a detrimental effect, especially if they allow "'channel airflow."

This section introduces a U.S. invention ready for commercialization; one promising, but long-term development in a high-tech field; and one energy conservation measure in use in Europe but not yet applied in the U.S.

EVACUATED PANELS

Scientists at the National Renewable Energy Laboratory in Golden, Colorado (formerly called SERI) are developing a process to produce thin evacuated metal panels with impressively high R-values. The panels are made of two layers of sheet steel that are laser-welded and separated by spacers to prevent collapse. Ultimately, researchers hope to achieve an R-value of 10 with a thickness of only 1/10 in.

Two manufacturers have already made prototypes for building panels. The cost of the panels is more than twice the price of rigid insulation, but the expense may be justifiable in applications where space is limited or at a premium. Possible uses include standing seam roofs, pre-engineered metal panel structures, and new or retrofit cladding.

In 1991 the scientists discovered how to switch on and off the R-value of the panels, converting them from insulating to conductive and vice-versa. Practical applications are years away, but might eventually include walls and roofs which allow the building either to cool off or to retain the internal heat needed.

Similar work is being carried at the Oak Ridge National Laboratory on powder-filled evacuated panels. These panels use particles of clay, fly ash, or gypsum and are intended for appliances; should this first application be economically feasible, it will be possible to extend the panels" use to building envelopes.

LIGHTWEIGHT INSULATING STRUCTURAL CONCRETE

In cooperation with a major manufacturing company, engineers at Construction Technology Laboratories in Skokie, Illinois, have developed a low-density, high-compressive strength insulating concrete which uses a synthetic aggregate in place of stone. The R-value of the new material is R-8 / ft, roughly ten times the R-value of conventional 125 pcf concrete.

The new concrete is intended for use in columns, beams, slabs, and balconies of low-rise commercial buildings.

Currently, columns, beams, and slab edges can be insulated to the outside, but no satisfactory method exists to prevent thermal bridging through balconies. Insulation placed above and/or below the floor slab that adjoins a balcony is ineffective; normal weight concrete simply conducts the heat from the next uninsulated floor slab area to the cold balcony slab. The high-R structural concrete offers a practical solution.

Production capabilities for the high R-concrete exist, and demand may be stimulated by building codes which increasingly take into account the detrimental effect of thermal bridging. The high-R concrete is less expensive than normal weight concrete wrapped with insulation.

SELF-DRYING VAPOR RETARDER
FOR LOW-SLOPE ROOFS

Energy efficiency, long-term performance and sustainability of roofs are topics investigated at Oak Ridge National Laboratory (ORNL). The following section draws on work and writings of Desjarlais and Christian of ORNL.

The basic components of a low-slope roof assembly are a membrane for waterproofing, insulation for thermal protection, and a deck for support of the entire system. Additional components may be added for specific reasons. For example an air/vapor retarder may be needed to impede vapor transport into the roof from conditioned spaces.

Moisture in low-slope roof systems has been a long-standing issue for the roofing industry for a number of reasons. Leaks into interior spaces are always unacceptable. Dimensional instability, corrosion, and material disintegration can lead to early failure. Also, wet insulation can lose much of its R-value. A more recent concern relates to the investment in roof insulation made during the past ten to twenty years. The waterproofing membranes on these roofs are aging, leaks are developing, and repair or replacement is required. The choices are to apply a new roofing membrane over the entire old roof, preserve only the undamaged part, of the old roof, or remove and replace both insulation and roofing membrane. Basic questions about reroofing include whether or not recovered wet insulation dries and, if so, how rapidly. (Moisture Effects in Low-Slope Roofs, ORNL/CON-308,1992.)

To control moisture within a flat or low slope roof assembly, two approaches have been used in the United States (excluding IRMA):

1. Provide only a waterproofing membrane above the insulation. No air/vapor retarder is specified on the winter-warm surface of the roof.

2. Provide a waterproofing membrane above the insulation and a vapor retarder membrane on the winterwarm surface of the roof. Typically, this vapor retarder is polyethylene.

In Europe, a third option has been used during the past decade:

3. Provide a self-drying membrane on the surface of the roof that is warm throughout the winter.

The three options are described below.

NO VAPOR RETARDER

This option relies on the integrity of the waterproofing membrane to prevent moisture from entering the insulation. If the integrity of this membrane is breached, moisture accumulates in the insulation. This moisture can be ventilated to some extent by vents below the roofing membrane. However, due to small driving forces, this type of ventilation is often ineffective. Further, a membrane perforated with a field of breather vents may allow external moisture to enter the system through these vents.

If the rate of moisture accumulation is high, water will seep into the structure. Often, this structure is metal decking, or metal decking with concrete on top. The decking collects the water, which could be ponding. This water eventually finds its way into the conditioned space below at joints.

Moist insulation loses much of its R-value. Further, freeze-thaw cycles can actually destroy some insulation types. Either or both phenomena raise energy costs and decrease ceiling temperatures, with the associated effect of higher rate of moisture condensation.

If the space is humidified, moisture may migrate from the space into the roof (since there is no continuous vapor retarder), condensing and entering the cycle described above.

VAPOR RETARDER

A vapor retarder is sometimes installed between the supporting deck and the insulation. This construction significantly reduces the moisture condensation problems, but increases the risk of water entrapment within the roof. Any water leaking through the roofing membrane, or already present during construction, is trapped between the two water impermeable layers. This water reduces the insulation R-value, and can even destroy some types of insulation during freeze-thaw cycles, leading to increased energy use and lower ceiling temperatures. This, in turn, can lead to moisture condensation on the ceiling surface.

SELF-DRYING

According to the self-drying concept, heat energy from spring and summer sun will evaporate winter-accumulated liquid moisture and will drive it downward through a water-permeable deck into the building interior, where it is then evacuated.

A water permeable vapor retarder (WPVR) consists of a synthetic fabric with good capillary suction properties sandwiched between strips of diffusion-tight plastic film. The strips are staggered with an overlap. The size of the overlap and the thickness of the fabric, together with the permeance of the plastic film, determine the permeance of the WPVR. Consequently, the WPVR can be designed as a vapor retarder.

The WPVR membrane stops moisture in the form of water vapor (usually coming from below), but allows passage of moisture in the form of construction water, leaked water, or condensed water. Construction water, leaked water, or condensed water wicks through the WPVR membrane into the space, where it evaporates. In principle, small amounts of water (such as construction water) evaporate unnoticeably. However, if a serious roofing leak were to develop, the moisture will show up almost immediately and near the point of entry. This allows for prompt repair of the roofing damage, before the insulation is irretrievably damaged.

The permeance of the WPVR can be tailored to different climate zones by varying the width of the plastic film strips, the overlapping, and the thickness of the wicking fabric.

APPLICATIONS

The WPVR concept is used in Europe, especially Denmark. Laboratory studies have been performed in the U.S. by Oak Ridge National Laboratory and are also currently under way under the aegis of the American Society of Heating, Refrigerating and Air Conditioning Engineers, Inc. It is probable that the new roof vapor retarder will soon have installations in North America.

Chapter 17

Earth Casting

By Paolo Soleri and Scott M. Davis

From EARTH CASTING:
Silt as a Craft Medium

SILT AND SILT CASTING

Silt casting is basically the use of a very fine type of earth, called silt, to make molds and forms for the casting of various materials. "Casting" means "forming a given material into a particular shape by pouring or pressing into a mold." A mold is a cavity or form that has been made into a particular shape so that a fluid substance can be formed in or on it.

Silt can be formed into almost any shape, so molds can be made in almost any shape. That means that a large variety of shapes and forms can be cast using silt as a molding material. Not only can you form silt into almost any shape, but several different kinds of materials can be cast with silt. These include clay, plaster, wax, and concrete. Each of these are covered in this book.

Silt itself is a type of soil that is very fine in texture. It is an unconsolidated sediment, which means that it has been deposited on stream and riverbeds and banks through a natural process called alluviation. This is the process of erosion and deposition that results in deposits of clay, silt, sand and gravel at places where the stream velocity is decreased. In other words, streams deposit silt in places where the stream current is slowed because of changes in the topography it flows over.

This process tends to deposit clay, silt, sand, and gravel in layers because each of those respective materials is lighter than the next. In this way, silt is related to sand and clay. Gravel is deposited first, since it is the heaviest. Sand tends to settle out on top of the gravel, and silt on top of that. Clay is deposited last, since it is the lightest of the four.

In some places, clay is also found between sedimentary rocks. Usually, silt will be found on top of sand and gravel. In general, silt particles are larger than clay particles and smaller than sand particles. That is, they are between 0.002 and 0.005 millimeters (between 0.0001 and 0.0002 inches) in diameter. The grains are invisible but can be felt. The texture of silt is smooth, not gritty.

The fact that silt is such a fine-grained sediment— in other words, that silt particles are so small— is part of the reason that silt is so useful for art and craft works. Another aspect of silt's usefulness as a craft medium is the fact that when gravel, sand, silt, and clay are deposited, the layers are not completely separate and there is some mixture among them. Some clay is invariably mixed in with silt, and the clay in the silt acts as a binding agent when the silt is packed together. Thus, the right mixture of small silt particles and clay particles makes silt the useful craft medium that it is.

Silt has other qualities that make it useful for different types of craft and construction projects. First, silt is a naturally occurring substance that can be found in almost every geographical area. Second, because of its clay content, silt car be worked and carved either when it's damp or when it's dry. When you want it wet, you can get proper dampness instantly by applying water. Third, silt that has been shaped into a certain form does not crack or shrink. That is, the silt will not develop cracks nor will it shrink because of settling or compaction. Fourth, silt that has been packed together is indeformable. In other words, because silt packs together so firmly, it cannot be accidentally pushed out of shape. Fifth, the silt can be washed away when the casting process is complete. Because of the nature of the material, the force of water sprayed from a hose will remove it once you're finished with it.

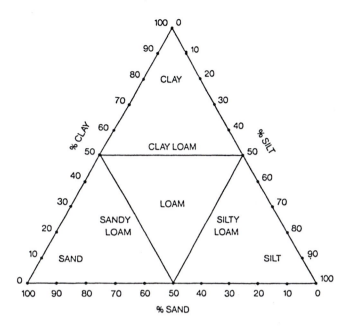

THREE COORDINATE GRAPH SIMPLIFIED FROM
THE SOIL SURVEY MANUAL OF THE U.S. DEPT OF AGRICULTURE

This diagram shows the relationship between sand, silt and clay. As the percentage of sand decreases and the percentage of clay increases, the soil becomes more clay-like. As the percentages of clay and sand decrease soil becomes more silty. A mixture of equal parts sand, silt and clay is called "loam."

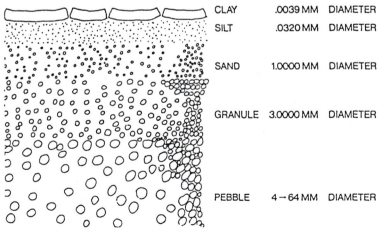

CLAY	.0039 MM	DIAMETER
SILT	.0320 MM	DIAMETER
SAND	1.0000 MM	DIAMETER
GRANULE	3.0000 MM	DIAMETER
PEBBLE	4 → 64 MM	DIAMETER

This diagram shows the layering of clay, silt, sand and gravel in a natural deposit.

233

Soil, sand, and clay can be used in much the same way as silt, but silt has certain advantages over them for craft work.

ADVANTAGES OF USING SILT

Advantages silt has over sand are:

    1. Silt has greater cohesion— that is, it does not fall apart as sand does.

    2. Silt is of finer grain, so it permits more detailing.

    3. Silt does not wash away under a gentle spray of water as sand does.

Advantages silt has over clay are:

    1. It is easy to gently spray it so as to add moisture to the silt body when necessary.

    2. Silt does not shrink as day does.

    3. Silt does not crack as clay does.

    4. Silt is easier to cut and shape in sharp planes and edges.

    5. Silt is structurally more stable.

    6. Silt can be easily hosed away, whereas clay cannot.

    7. Silt can be made ready or reused in a few minutes.

Advantages of silt over soil are:

    1. Silt does not crack or shrink.

    2. Silt is more homogenous and fine.

    3. Silt can be prepared and reused in a few minutes.

    4. Silt is easier to wash away from molds.

The silt-casting technique itself has certain qualities that make it a very versatile craft technique. In other words, silt is a craft medium that can be used for different types of projects in several different ways, using different casting materials. Thus, the silt technique is simple in concept and yet can be used for many different kinds of arts and crafts projects. Silt can be worked with a variety of tools. It can be cut with a knife, trowel, or saw, and patching can be done with a spatula. It can also be filed and sandpapered when it is in a dry condition.

The use of silt allows a directness of expression, especially in sculpture and model making. This allows you to visualize in the third dimension. You can bypass the process of drawing your ideas on paper in two dimensions and then transferring those ideas to three-dimensional materials, and go directly to carving them in three-dimensional form. Also, the use of silt allows you to give a unique brown, "earthy" texture to whatever you're casting that is quite attractive.

The silt technique also varies with the scale of its application. The methods that are used in casting small forms such as clay shells, models, planters, and sculpture can be quite different from the methods used in large-scale concrete casting. Depending on what kind of project you're doing, you can begin with either a positive form or a negative mold.

Silt can be used in casting materials such as ceramics, plaster, wax, and concrete. As we said earlier, silt has a fine texture and so it can be shaped and carved in more detail. Soil can be used for ceramics and concrete casting, and this coarser material produces a rough texture in the final product with less articulation of detail. Other materials, such as "green sand" for metal casting and rocks for concrete, can be used in other variations of the technique.

You may notice that the idea of using soil and silt as a craft medium is very similar to some other types of arts and crafts activities. The silt-casting technique is related simply by its nature to the sand castle "beach sculpture" seen all over the world. The idea of pouring plaster into open molds carved into sand that has been packed into a shallow box is also an obvious method of earth casting. Silt casting is also related to the ancient foundry method of casting metal in sand molds.

Throughout this chapter, the phrase "earth casting" will be used in a general sense to refer to any of the various methods of using different types of soil to make molds for the casting of anything from small clay shells to large concrete structures. The phrase "silt casting" will be used only to refer to techniques that specifically use silt as the molding material. The phrase "sand casting" will be only used in this specific sense also.

LOCATING, PREPARING, AND USING SILT

Here are some general guidelines for locating good sources of silt in different geographical areas:

1. Look around the banks of streams and rivers.

2. Look in shallow places in streams or rivers where you can wade in and collect silt from the bed.

3. Look at the mouths of streams and rivers where they empty into a larger tributary, lake, or bay.

4. Look in flood plains along large streams and rivers.

5. In mountainous areas, silt can be found in places where a stream has come down from the mountains and flows from a gorge onto a plain-a deposit of silt, sand, and gravel at a place like this is called an "alluvial fan."

6. In arid climates and desert areas, washes (natural channels that water flows through during times of rain) and dry riverbeds are good for locating silt. If you don't know of any good places where you can collect silt in your area, consult a soils map in an atlas and then a topographic map of your area to locate any streams where silt can be found.

7. Inquire at sand and gravel companies, since they always have mountains of silt that they want to get rid of.

After you've located a substantial silt deposit, dig into it with your fingers to see how deep it is. Choose a deposit that is not too shallow, so that you won't pick up sand and gravel with the silt.

Collect the silt with a shovel or spade. You can put it into buckets or wheelbarrows for transportation to your workshop or studio. If you are doing very detailed work, almost any silt you find will need to be sifted to remove any organic material such as leaves, sticks, grass, bugs, and so on. Preparing silt for use can be done at your workshop or studio.

A sifter can be easily made from wood and steel-wire mesh or screen. Sift the silt through the wire-mesh sifter, removing occasional sand, gravel, and organic matter.

If you are doing damp silt work, in general the silt should be damp but not wet. To test damp silt for efficient moisture content, squeeze a handful tightly-it should break into clean portions in your hand (not crumble). For some types of silt projects where a silt slurry is useful, you can make a slurry of silt by adding water until the silt is fluid. Different degrees and amounts of moisture can be used for different purposes. Patching of silt forms can be done with one type of slurry while a more fluid mixture can be used for the making of silt forms for the casting of flat concrete panels.

There are some aspects of the silt-casting process which require direct experience in order to fully grasp them. The "feel" of damp silt in your hands, the pile cooling the air around you, the feel of a knife in your hand cutting the silt, "knowing" when the silt is damp enough for a given purpose, cannot be fully described or explained in words. You must experience them for yourself.

1. Look in any general physical geography or geology text for further information about silt, where it comes from, and how it is related to other types of soil.

2. Find the best place in your area to gather silt. You may want to look at a map, and inquire at local parks departments, county agricultural extension services, or sand and gravel companies.

3. Gather some silt, take it to your workshop or studio, and experiment with it. Clean it by sifting it, and try different amounts of water and different degrees of dampness. Just get the "feel" of working with silt and become familiar with it.

CASTING CONCRETE ON SILT AND SOIL

Since the buildings and structures at the Cosanti and Arcosanti sites exist for examination, and their construction has been well documented, we will use them as specific examples to show how to construct concrete structures and buildings using the earth-casting technique.

The projects involving earth and silt-cast concrete that have been executed at the Cosanti and Arcosanti sites provide an example of the versatility of the technique. These projects also demonstrate that structures cast on earth forms can be quite sculptural as well as functional. Casting concrete on earth forms makes it possible for you to pour concrete into shapes that are not possible with more conventional construction methods.

FIVE VARIATIONS

Construction methods that have been used at Cosanti can be broken down into five basic variations of the earth-casting method. The nine structures that were built using these methods will be grouped according to the particular variation of earth casting that was used for their construction, except for the fifth one, which was used to supplement the other four methods. These five basic methods are:

1. The Single-Unit Pile Method

2. Casting In-Place On Scaffolding

3. Casting In Sections On-A-Pile

4. Large Scale, Above-Ground Casting

5. Precasting On Earth Or Silt

The structures covered in this section were built using a variation on the earthcasting technique we will call the Single-Unit Pile method. This is the simplest, quickest and easiest way to cast concrete on earth forms.

TOOLS AND MATERIALS

Soil	Shovels
Silt	Wheelbarrows
Materials for making concrete	Silt working tools (various knives, trowels, floats, etc.)
Reinforcing materials (chicken-wire, reinforcing mesh, reinforcing bar)	Concrete tools Woodworking tools Reinforcing tools

Wood for forms
Wood for scaffolding
Steel scaffolding
Sundry hardware

POSSIBLE PROJECTS USING THESE METHODS

Sculptures
Decorative panels
Canopies
Apses and shells
Dwellings
Other buildings and structures

In general, to use this method, you simply gather a mound of earth, and shape it into the form you desire. Then you pour a thin layer of concrete onto the mold keeping the surface textured, and let it set. The next step is to lay some sort of reinforcing onto the first concrete layer. We recommend that it be done this way so that the reinforcing will be inside the concrete and not poking through the underside of the structure. After the concrete has cured, you excavate the earth out from under the concrete.

There are of course other important aspects to this process, such as making drawings, even very rough ones, of what you plan to build. Measurements must be taken and specifications for the size and dimensions of the structure must be made. Even these can be rough, and some changes can be made as you go along.

We will now describe the construction of some of the structures at Cosanti, so that you can learn from their example.

EARTH HOUSE, BUILT 1956

The Earth House was our first major experiment in casting concrete on earth forms. It is probably the least elaborate of the earth-cast structures at Cosanti and shows how relatively simple this kind of construction can be. I built the Earth House mostly on weekends between 1956 and 1957.

The Earth House consists of an earth-cast concrete roof that sits at ground level. The roof is centered on an earth-cast concrete fireplace and bath. Glass walls at the north and south ends are interrupted by curved concrete windowsills. The roof includes large skylights and is covered with soil.

This structure has a sculptured fireplace at one end and a sculptured shower stall near the center. The earth mold for the roof thus included the fireplace and shower stall. These were dug into the ground and given form as part of the overall process of making the mold.

After doing rough sketches, I surveyed and measured the site where the building would stand. We then outlined the area where the earth mold would be formed.

The earth mold was made by piling soil onto the existing contour. This pile was formed into the shape of the roof with shovels, rakes, hoes, and trowels.

The mold for the shower stall and fireplace was dug into the ground and very carefully shaped and sculptured. Notches and grooves were cut into the mold where lines of structural stress would be. A core was built inside the scooped out hollow of the fireplace, so that a vent would be formed from the fireplace through the roof. Allowance was also made for skylights in the roof of the house. This was done by forming earth in the shape of the skylights and piling it above the level of the top of the roof, so that a skylight would be left in the roof in that area.

After the mold for the casting of this structure had been formed, a first layer of concrete was poured over it. Once again, this was done in order to separate the reinforcing from the mold. Chicken-wire mesh was carefully laid over this thin layer of concrete for reinforcing in the structure. The roof and fireplace were separate castings, but form one continuous shell. The rest of the concrete was poured over the mold and allowed to set and cure.

After the concrete had cured, the volume of earth underneath the roof was excavated out with a Ford tractor and picks, shovels, and wheelbarrows.

The Earth House is 7.6 meters (25 feet) wide and 10.6 meters (35 feet) long. Its floor is 1.8 meters (6 feet) below that of the surrounding desert. The curved and ribbed roof is 7.6 centimeters (3 inches) thick and meets the desert floor on two sides of the house.

CERAMICS STUDIO, BUILT 1958

With the experience in building the Earth House, I began the construction of the Cosanti Ceramics Studio.

The Ceramics Studio consists of a large, earth-cast, sculptured concrete shell that sits a little above ground level. The central area and the east bay of the structure are open to sun and air, and the west bay is enclosed. In the center is a large, circular skylight. Plastic panes in it are separated by earth-cast concrete patterns for a stained-glass effect.

The very large earth mold for this structure was piled and shaped into the form of the planned structure. I then carved V-shaped indentations into the mold that crisscrossed from one side of the mold to the other. These indentations had two purposes. First, they are structural and hold steel reinforcing bars. Secondly, they are really part of an architectural mode. This involves articulating the lines of structural stress in such a way that they appear as aesthetic details.

After the first concrete layer had been poured, steel reinforcing rods were placed into these grooves cut into the earth mold. Then wire mesh was laid on top of the earth mound for more reinforcing. When the structure was finished, the notches that had been cut into the earth appeared as ribs on the underside of the structure.

Variations in color and texture were put in the ceiling of the Studio by placing polyethylene patterns that had been cut into shapes that would fit in between the notches. Wherever these plastic patterns were laid on the earth, the concrete did not contact the earth and so the concrete retained its natural gray color and also was given a smooth texture. After the concrete had set and the earth was dug out from underneath, the plastic patterns were peeled off, leaving a smooth gray surface that contrasts with the rest of the rough, earth-colored concrete.

A small bulldozer was used to excavate under the concrete structure. Remaining earth left clinging to the underside of the structure was washed away with the spray from a garden hose.

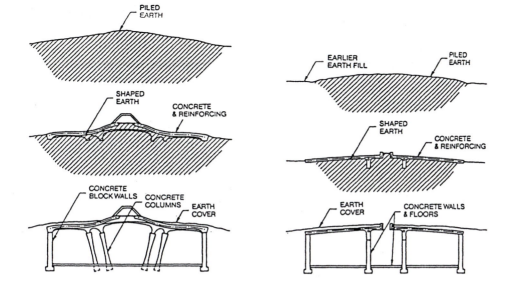

Figure A Casting of the Earth House roof   Figure B Casting the North Studio roof

A low wall was added to the southeast corner of the Studio by precasting it in sections on earth molds and then lifting the sections into position. Worktables and a drying rack for ceramics were added later. The drying rack was earth cast in place.

NORTH STUDIO, BUILT 1961

This structure has characteristics of both the Earth House and the Ceramics Studio. It is like the earth house in that it consists of a roof structure sitting at ground level on concrete block walls. It is like the Ceramics Studio in that it has more of the structural and aesthetic detailing in its ceiling. The shaping and carving of the earth mold for the North Studio was more intricate than for either of the other two.

The soil that was used to form the mold for the casting of this structure was gathered from the area immediately around the site. The mold for the North Studio not only had structural ribs carved into it, but also other details such as light fixtures, posts, and even sections of support beams extending from the ceiling.

Thus, a pattern of structural ribs, light fixtures, flying beams that contain light fixtures, and structural posts were carved in negative into the earth mold, just as similar features were carved into the molds for the Earth House and the Ceramics Studio. The structural posts were dug, in negative, into the earth mold halfway to the planned interior floor level.

241

The precut polyethylene patterns were placed on the mold in appropriate places to produce variations in color and texture in the ceiling.

Once again, steel reinforcing bar was laid into the grooves that had been cut into the mold. Steel mesh was laid onto the mold and a gunite concrete mixture was sprayed on using a gunite machine.

After the concrete had set, a small caterpillar bulldozer was used to excavate the space underneath the roof. Support pillars were then made in the space and emplaced.

METAL STUDIO, BUILT 1964

This earth-casting project was a simpler extension of the work that was done in the construction of the Ceramics Studio and the North Studio. Like most of the other structures at Cosanti, the Metal Studio was constructed with students who participated in Siltpile Workshops here in the 1960s.

The Metal Studio consists of a large, sculptured, earth-cast shell that curves in plan. The shell also is curved in section so that it overhangs the area sheltered by it. It has a number of branching structural ribs cast in the underside that also contain light fixtures and skylights.

The earth mold for this structure was piled against the existing northeast bay of the Ceramics Studio. Wood forms were used at either end of the mold for support. The mold was formed into a curving, arched shape so that the finished structure would be an elongated, curving, hemispherical shell.

After the earth had been piled up and the general shape of the mold was defined, the earth was smoothed down by rubbing it with nailed floats. At the same time, the outlines of the structural ribs were scratched into the surface. The students then began cutting and carving the ribs into the mold. A horizontal trellis-like pattern was also cut, in negative, into the top of the mold. This became a trellis spanning the space between the walls of the outdoor studio. Other details in this casting included light sockets and puckered skylights.

Electrical conduit was included as part of the reinforcing system laid onto the earth mold.

Polyethylene patterns were placed on the mold in between the structural ribs. Concrete was poured onto the main body of the mold and into the negative mold for the trellis span which had been cut into the top of the mold.

The concrete was allowed to cure for about a week, and then the earth was removed from under the concrete.

Part Five

ALTERNATIVE LIVING

Chapter 18

The Case for Reuse

by Nikki & David Goldbeck

From CHOOSE TO REUSE
Ceres Press, New York

What makes reuse a powerful conservation strategy is that, in addition to promoting a healthier environment, it supports a comfortable lifestyle and a productive economy. It is unique in coupling environmental activity with social needs. Many examples illustrate how in relationship to ecological, economic and humanitarian concerns, reuse is more effective—and rewarding—than recycling.

WASTE REDUCTION

Reuse keeps goods and materials from entering the waste stream. Reduced garbage disposal means fewer environmental repercussions such as ground water contamination from leaching landfills and air pollution from incinerators, as well as decreased solid waste management costs (including the cost of recycling), which can ultimately lower the taxpayers' burden. These factors alone are enough to warrant fostering reuse.

• The most exciting inroads in refuse reduction have come from industrial "waste exchanges"—regional and national computerized matchmaking services that link businesses discarding potentially reusable materiel with other businesses that can use it. In 1993 an estimated 15%-25% of the 12 million tons of goods listed were exchanged. (Precise statistics are hard to come by due to insufficient reporting by participants.) Probably more noteworthy is the fact that in 1993 the number of waste exchanges doubled.

Even modest commercial programs can have significant effects:

• The Neighborhood Cleaners Association in New York City estimates that if customers at each of the 1,100-member dry cleaners utilized reusable garment bags, more than 6.6 million plastic bags would be eliminated from the waste stream each year.

• In Los Angeles an arrangement between the major movie studios and Re-Sets Entertainment Commodities brings significant cuts in the city's solid waste, particularly wood. The estimated 250,000 sheets of lauan plywood utilized by the region's entertainment industry each year are now finding a second home among nonprofit theaters and cultural groups, in vocational and wood-shop programs and as the raw material for shipping pallets.

Even one person can make an impact:

• Realizing that tons of used carpeting were going to waste in Minnesota landfills, Peter Hvode developed a business removing these floor coverings from remodeling and renovation projects and reinstalling them in new sites.

• Rosemary and Tom Thornton's reuse business evolved by collecting discarded washers and dryers, reconditioning and selling them. According to the Thorntons every washer they repair is a washer that's kept out of the waste stream.

CONSERVATION OF RESOURCES

By its very nature reuse requires less energy and fewer raw materials than either the production of new items or recycling.

• By reclaiming parts from 11 million vehicles each year, automotive salvage yards in North America save an estimated 85 million barrels of oil that would otherwise be utilized to manufacture new replacement parts.

• Refilling glass bottles that weigh 10.5 ounces 25 times uses 93% less glass than packaging beverages in one-way glass bottles that weigh 5.9 ounces and hold the same volume of liquid. Likewise a refillable bottle that makes 25 trips consumes 93% less energy than extracting raw materials and manufacturing new glass bottles. There are a few long-established companies that continue to refill bottles as they always have and, as recounted in "Beverage Containers," there is an encouraging resurgence of this practice among other bottlers.

• U.S. businesses alone consume an estimated 21 million tons of office paper every year—the equivalent of more than 350 million trees. If offices throughout the country increased the rate of two-sided photocopying from the 1991 figure of 26% to 60%, they could save the equivalent of about 15 million trees.

• Pallet manufacture in the United States consumes an astonishing 40% of the country's annual hardwood timber harvest. According to Big City Forest, a pallet-rescue program in New York City, by reclaiming just half of the pallets discarded annually in the nation's 50 biggest metropolitan areas, 152,000 acres of timberland could be preserved.

• Water is another precious resource that could be conserved through reuse efforts. For example, the ANA Hotel in San Francisco saves 6,000 gallons of water daily by recovering steam condensate from heating and air-conditioning systems and reusing it in the hotel laundry and for car washing.

EMBODIED ENERGY

The energy embodied in an item refers to the amount of energy required to produce it initially. Reuse, unlike recycling, preserves a significant amount of this embodied energy.

• The retreading of a car tire conserves 4.5 gallons of oil compared with the petrochemicals needed to manufacture a similar size new tire. The savings on truck tires is even greater-as much as 15 gallons of oil per tire. As currently implemented in North America, retreading preserves over 400 million gallons of oil every year.

• On average, 30 pounds of construction materials contain the energy equivalent of a gallon of gasoline. Building with salvaged materials perpetuates more than half of this energy investment.

• Remanufacture can save up to 75% of the resources, labor and energy used to produce and distribute new products. Remanufacture is available for automotive parts, copying machines, office furniture, printer cartridges, tools, vacuum cleaners and an assortment of other appliances and equipment. Kodak, for instance, remanufactures about 18,000 copiers for the North American market every year, which is reported to be almost double its production of new copiers, and laser cartridge remanufacture is one of the fastest-growing cottage industries in North America.

POLLUTION

Integral to reuse is that it averts air and water pollution caused by the dumping and burning of waste. The practice of reuse—be it through repair, remanufacture, employing used items or utilizing durable goods in place of disposables—also creates less pollution than either producing a new item or recycling.   A look at paper production and usage is instructive:

• Every year the pulp and paper industry discharges millions of pounds of toxic chemicals into rivers and coastal waters, where they subsequently enter the food chain. Paper mills also emit sulfur dioxide (a contributor to acid rain), acetone, methanol, chlorinated compounds and other fumes, making them a significant source of air pollution. While the manufacture of recycled paper has less of an environmental impact than virgin paper production, the majority of recycled wastepaper must be deinked using a process that creates a sludge that most mills dispose of in landfills. Some companies opt to burn the sludge, creating airborne emissions. On the other hand, products, practices and services that reuse paper or replace it with more durable alternatives can minimize the pollution associated with paper production.

• The manufacture of paper can be reduced by using washable diapers, fabric napkins, cloth handkerchiefs, rags, cloth gift bags, reusable shopping bags, washable air filters and oil filters in vehicles, durable dishes and washable coffee filters and tea infusers rather than their paper-based counterparts.

• Businesses in particular can cut down paper use by duplex copying, billing in two-way envelopes, employing reusable (wipe-clean) paper and fax transmittal sheets, and outfitting rest rooms with cloth hand towels.

• Other paper-reducing reuse strategies include borrowing books from libraries; supporting programs that rejuvenate used greeting cards; turning used paper into envelopes, ornaments and plant pots; and using stationery made from outdated maps.

Of course the impact of pollution isn't limited to the paper industry, and reuse of potentially hazardous wastes also protects soil and ground water:

• The collection and reuse of latex paint keeps numerous gallons of paint out of the waste stream. In upstate New York, the first municipal paint collection day run by Passonno Paint, in April 1994, netted 350 unopened gallons of latex paint (which were passed on to a local nonprofit building renovation program), plus more than 4,000 cans of various amounts, of which 57% contained reusable paint. From this, Passonno was able to produce more than 1,000 gallons of remixed latex paint. In Santa Rosa, a paint giveaway program run by Garbage Reincarnation recirculates about 400 gallons of paint each month, saving the county $76,000 per year—the cost of disposing of this paint in a hazardous-waste landfill. A pilot project run by the city of Seattle computed that by reusing discarded latex paint in municipal programs they could save about $322,000 a year, or 61% of what they spend on hazardous-waste disposal.

• A Canadian-based service that converts waste ink to a reusable product estimates that over a four-year period it saved 55 tractor-trailer loads of waste ink from landfills.

Likewise, using reclaimed oil and antifreeze, rechargeable batteries and long-lasting light bulbs can stem the tide of hazardous chemicals entering the environment.

ECONOMIC GROWTH

Reuse has an enormous potential to create jobs and spur economic activity. A greater interest by the public in keeping things functioning creates employment in the repair sector. Furthermore creative secondary reuse of articles that would otherwise be discarded generates business and employment opportunities.

• Big City Forest, a nonprofit corporation engaged in revitalization of New York City's South Bronx neighborhoods, takes discarded shipping pallets and wooden packaging materials and turns them into new pallets, butcher-block furniture, parquet floor tiles and construction-grade reclaimed lumber. During their 15-month pilot phase in 1992-93, they created 10 new jobs in the community and 27 training opportunities.

• In the Mississippi Delta, the Tutwiler Quilting Project was started in 1988 as a way for women to make money for themselves and their families. Using largely donated textile scraps, about 40 local quilters earn their livelihood sewing blankets, wall hangings, handbags, pot holders, table runners and placemats.

• Numerous creative entrepreneurs all over North America have developed successful businesses by refashioning discards into useful products: clipboards, notebooks, jewelry, clocks and key rings from nonfunctioning computer circuit boards; plant containers using discarded shipping pallets, fence posts, saw mill scraps, old wine vats and used tires; durable handbags, belts and other wearable items out of reclaimed tire tubes; stuffed animals from pre- and postconsumer textile wastes; and much, much more.

• Reuse is so popular that is has even been franchised in stores that buy and sell customers' used clothing, children's furnishings, personal computers, musical instruments and sporting goods. Grow Biz International, a company that manages several of these franchises, expects to have 1,200 Play It Again Sports stores selling used sporting gear by the end of the decade.

• Reuse can also inspire new rental businesses, as demonstrated during the past few years not only by the increased number of general rental outlets but also by the creation of new markets even for bridal gowns and maternity garments.

FINANCIAL SAVINGS

Reuse saves money for individuals, businesses, commercial institutions and nonprofit groups in numerous ways. One way in which savings occur is by decreasing purchasing costs:

• A New York State study estimates that if prisoners isolated for medical, safety or disciplinary reasons were served meals on reusable Lexan plastic trays instead of disposable Styrofoam, the state prison system could save about $800,000 yearly in purchasing costs alone.

• At Mount Sinai Hospital in New York, switching from disposable to reusable pads for only one-third of the hospital's beds saves the facility about $56,000 in purchasing costs and $7,000 in disposal costs.

• Businesses in North America save an estimated $27 million yearly by taking advantage of waste exchanges.

• By purchasing remanufactured parts for state-owned vehicles, Minnesota saves $2,000 on every transmission and 30% on most other parts.

• During the two and a half years that the average baby is in diapers, the use of disposables costs about $1,000 more than home laundering and about $600 more than using a diaper service.

There is also an enormous potential monetary saving as a result of reduced disposal fees:

• A small delicatessen in Massachusetts has cut its weekly disposal bill from $250 to $50 by finding schools and art programs that can utilize its nonfood trash.

• By having the air filters on road maintenance equipment cleaned and then reusing them, Minnesota's Olmstead County Highway Department saves over $650 a year in disposal fees.

• A furniture manufacturer in Virginia shreds the corrugated packing it receives with shipments and uses this instead of polystyrene pellets to ship furniture out. In addition to saving $15,000 in avoided pellet purchases in one year, another $10,000 was saved in waste disposal.

• A retail furniture dealer has found that giving new, unsalable mattresses to a housing program for free instead of discarding them actually saves the store money.

• Reusable shipping containers save one Xerox facility $500,000 annually, and Xerox expects its worldwide effort in this area to reduce yearly disposal costs by $15 million.

TAX BENEFITS

With some limitations goods donated to public schools, public parks and recreation facilities, war veterans' groups, nonprofit hospitals, churches, synagogues, temples, mosques and other nonprofits with a 501(c)(3) tax status (U.S.) or a Registered Charity status (Canada) can be taken as tax-deductible contributions. The amount of the deduction is based on the fair market value of the item at the time the donation is made. This can mean substantial savings to the donor at tax time—and a gratifying chance to help others.

Individuals and businesses take advantage of this tax allowance in many unexpected and inspiring ways:

• ECOMedia, a national organization that provides services to people with severe disabilities, raises money by erasing donated used and surplus computer disks and reselling them at reduced prices to schools and other nonprofit groups. Businesses that donate disks can claim this as a tax-deductible inventory donation.

• Furs no longer being worn can become a tax deduction by donating them to McCrory Bears, a family business that transforms them into teddy bears and returns a portion of the sales to the National Kidney Foundation.

• The Canadian transportation industry has found a new home for many highway trailers by donating them to the Canadian Foundation for World Development, which uses the trailers as libraries, school classrooms, clinics, markets, offices and manufacturing facilities in its overseas projects.

Donation, or charitable reuse, brings needed items to those who might not be able to afford them. It also often brings employment prospects to people who have had trouble finding traditional jobs.

• REMEDY, a pioneering project developed at Yale University Hospital for recovering supplies from operating rooms, sent clinics overseas $454,000 worth of safe medical goods that would otherwise have been discarded. They were able to accomplish this in just the first 19 months of operation, and this reuse effort cost REMEDY less than $500.

• One of the oldest and largest charitable institutions, the Brother's Brother Foundation, established an Education and Book Program in 1980. They have since delivered more than 22 million books, comprised of used books and overstock, to 20 million needy students in over 40,000 schools and universities all over the world.

• In a two-year period, an annual blanket drive in Seattle netted more than 10,000 used blankets and sleeping bags for the city's homeless.

• A project initiated by GQ magazine in 1991 to collect used clothing nationwide has succeeded in redistributing goods and simultaneously assisting the unemployed. The estimated 50 tons of clothing gathered from more than 17,000 publishing and advertising industry employees helps provide wardrobes for unemployed people going out on job interviews and reentering the workforce.

• Skid Row Access, a non-profit enterprise in Los Angeles, provides a place for disadvantaged and homeless citizens in the community to focus their creativity, generate income and become self-sufficient by manufacturing wooden trains, cars, trucks and stick horses from donated scrap lumber.

• Recycle North in Burlington, Vermont, serves as a combination secondhand store and fix-it shop where former prisoners and recently homeless individuals acquire repair skills. In the process, broken VCRs, toaster ovens and other donated household appliances are refurbished and sold.

• By assembling new greeting cards out of used card donations, the kids at St. Jude's Ranch for Children earn money for outings. This enterprise puts more than a million greeting cards back into circulation each year.

ARTISTIC EXPRESSION

Historically, found and discarded items have always been a part of artists' resources. Cultural opportunities in North America that have been fostered by this kind of reuse range from home decor to museum-quality pieces, such as the "junk" sculptures of Nancy Rubins and Leo Sewell. Recognizing that this form of reuse inspires creativity, many schools and children's museums run workshops featuring the use of discards and donated scrap materials.

• Jewelry makers are among the many creative individuals who have succeeded in turning waste into wearable art by producing one-of-a-kind earrings, pins and necklaces from discarded book jackets, old television and computer components, bottle caps and rusted road refuse.

• The Scrap Exchange in Durham, North Carolina, brings out the creative spirit in children by arranging theme birthday parties where kids spend time inventing related decorations, accessories and other take-home artwork using industrial discards.

Mudite Clever, former teacher and founder of ReCreate in Seattle, Washington, sets up activity booths at public events and festivals where children can create silly hats, masks, jewelry or whatever else their imaginations devise from the reclaimed materials she brings with her.

UNLIMITED OPPORTUNITIES

The range of reuse possibilities is enormous, as demonstrated by the more than 200 individual topics and 2,000 resources covered in *Choose to Reuse*. Recycling opportunities, on the other hand, are currently limited to just a few commodities, such as paper, glass, aluminum, certain plastics and the like. Moreover the facilities for making recycled materials into new products are sometimes scarce, as are markets for these items once they're produced. Furthermore products that rely on reuse tend to be less expensive.

PERSONAL PARTICIPATION

Each person can have a direct and profound influence on reuse by choosing long-lived items initially, having things repaired, reselling what they no longer need to a target audience or donating to an appropriate place to guarantee reuse. With recycling the chance for individual impact is much less since, once things reach the recycling center, what happens to them is out of your control.

ENHANCED BUSINESS PROFILE

Environmental friendliness is an influential factor for a growing segment of consumers and businesses when deciding what products and services to buy. In the same way that progressive and smart companies gain a marketing advantage by incorporating recycled materials into the articles they make and sell, attention to reuse can be utilized to promote pertinent products and services.

Chapter 19

Cluster Development

by William H. Whyte

From THE LAST LANDSCAPE
Doubleday & Company, Inc.

We have been considering ways of saving open space. Now let us turn to the question of how to develop it. There is a conflict, to be sure, but you cannot grapple with one problem and not the other. People have to live somewhere, as it is so often said, and if there is to be any hope of having open space in the future, there is going to have to be a more efficient pattern of building. The mathematics is inexorable. The only way to house more people is either to extend the present pattern of sprawl and cover vastly more land, or, alternatively, to use less land and increase the carrying capacity of it. The latter is by far the best approach and at last we are beginning to pursue it. By whatever name it is called—"planned unit development," "open-space development," "cluster development"—it signals a reversal of the land-wasting pattern that had come to seem permanent.

In the great postwar building boom, developers froze on a pattern that used five acres to do the work of one. They had to, or they thought they had to. For one thing, it was a well-known fact that Americans had a deep psychic urge for a free-standing homestead on a large country plot, or as close a replica as possible. The assumption was self-proving, for it was built into the standards of the Federal Housing Administration and the major lending institutions. If a developer wanted mortgage money, he hewed to these standards or he did not get it.

Suburbs were similarly demanding. Most wanted no development at all, not in their area anyway, and they looked to large-lot zoning as their best defense. They reasoned that if they could force developers to provide large lots for each house, there would be fewer houses, and the grounds of those that did go up would conserve the open-space character of the community. Minimum lot sizes varied, but most suburbs pushed them as high as pride and wealth could enforce. The stiffer the minimum, they thought, the more likely the developers would be to leave them alone and go somewhere else.

The developers did go somewhere else, at first, but the respite did not help the suburbs, which soon found that they were not being penetrated so much as enveloped. Later the developers would come back; their first response to the barriers was to leap-frog over them and seek the open country where land was cheaper and the townships had not gotten around to zoning it.

So the best land was ruined first, and when developers got there, they sometimes found the locals had attended to the job already. While the gentry of the rural townships kept a wary eye out for the likes of Levitt, a motley of local builders and contractors would buy up frontage land from farmers and line it with a string of concrete bungalows on overblown lots. Very few people would be housed on a great deal of land, but since the land was along the road, the place would look filled up. The premature development also had the effect of sealing off many hundreds of acres from any kind of effective development pattern, and when the feared invasion did come, the chances for coping with it amenably were gone.

The suburbs farther back were coming under increasing pressure. Developers were filling in the spaces wherever they could and they were pressing relentlessly for variances. Where the minimums were as high as three or four acres, they attacked the ordinances themselves and complained to the courts that such minimums were not for the welfare of the public but to exclude the public that was not rich. Whatever developers' motives in saying so, this was the case, and in some instances the courts struck down ordinances as excessive and discriminatory.

The main problem, however, was not so much the relative size of lots as the uniformity with which they were laid out. With few exceptions, subdivisions homogenized the land with a pattern of curvilinear streets and equal-spaced lots that were everywhere the same, large lot or small, and in the denser areas, the pattern was compressed to the point of caricature. Even though lots were so small that houses would have only a few feet between them, the estate pattern was repeated, producing subdivisions that looked very much like toy villages with the scale out of whack.

These were the little boxes that so outraged people of sensibility and means. Photos of their rooftops and TV aerials, squeezed together—the telephoto lens again—became stock horror shots. But critics drew the wrong conclusions. What was wrong, they thought, was that the houses were too close together, when what was really wrong was that they were not close enough.

For years, planners had been arguing that if lots took up less of the land, subdivisions would be more economical to build and more pleasant to live in. Rather than divide all of a tract up into lots, they suggested, developers could group the houses in clusters, and leave the bulk of the land as open space. It was an ancient idea: It was the principle of the New England village and green, and its appeal had proved timeless. "Garden City" advocates had reapplied it in the planning of several prototype communities; most notably, Radburn, New Jersey, in the late twenties, the green belt towns of the New Deal, Baldwin Hills in Los Angeles during the late thirties.

Some of the utopian expectations with which these experiments were freighted were never fulfilled, but as individual communities, they were, and still
are, quite successful. But they remained outside of the, mainstream. Some of the features found their way into commercial developments, such as the superblock and cul-de-sac streets, but the basic cluster principle of the communities did not. Few developers even went to look at them.

By the early fifties however, the conventional pattern had been pushed close to the breaking point. It not only looked terrible, it was uneconomic, and for everybody concerned. Communities were forcing developers to chew up an enormous amount of land to house a given number of people and to provide an overblown network of roads and facilities to tie the sprawl together. This created havoc with the landscape, and saddled the community with a heavy servicing burden, the costs of which usually outran the tax returns.

For new residents, the open space was turning out to be a chimera. The woods and meadows that so attracted them disappeared as soon as developers got around to building on them, and if the residents wanted to find what other natural features would be next to go, they had only to check the names of the subdivisions being planned. When a developer puts a woods into the name, or a vale, heights, forest, creek, or stream, he is not conserving; he is memorializing. Subdivisions are named for that which they are about to destroy.

The open space of the resident's own lot was not much compensation. It was trouble to maintain but did not provide as much usable space as a small courtyard and nowhere near the privacy. (The open space between the houses strikes a particularly unhappy mean: big enough to mow, too small to use, and a perfect amplifier of sound.) Nor would there be much in the way of neighborhood open spaces. Most communities required developers to dedicate some part of the tract as open space, but it would be a very small space, and quite often a leftover the developer could not use for anything else.

The developers were being hurt more than anybody else. No matter how far and fast they pushed outward to the countryside, land prices kept soaring ahead of them. Contrary to public belief, most developers do not make money on land speculation; they do not have the capital to stockpile land for very long and they have to pay dearly to those who do. Such costs are usually passed on to the home buyers, but by the sixties developers were bumping up against a market ceiling.

The price that builders had to pay for land had risen far more than the price that people would pay for their houses. Between 1951 and 1966 the cost of raw land rose 234 percent. The sale price of the average house and lot, however, rose 87 percent and most of this increase was due to the larger size of the houses; per square foot, house prices rose only 21 percent. Even before tight money hit them, developers were in a bind. They could not mark up their finished product without pricing themselves out of the market, and they had to keep on paying exorbitant prices for their land to stay in the business.

There is one good thing about high land costs. They discipline choice. Since communities would not let developers squeeze more houses onto their tracts, developers had only one way to turn: they could try squeezing the houses they were allowed onto the most buildable parts of the tract and leave the rest alone—that is, cluster, just as planners had been suggesting. The National Association of Home Builders undertook a missionary campaign and began proselytizing builders and communities to try the cluster approach.

Here and there cluster developments began to go up. In several cases developers took the initiative; they retained land planners to prepare an advanced cluster plan and then went to work to sell the community on it. Sometimes it was the other way around, with the community doing the selling. Most typically, however, the genesis would be thoroughly mixed up, marked by plans and counterplans, false starts, and controversy.

To examine the pros and cons of cluster, let us follow such a case.

A medium-size builder has purchased a 112 acre farm in a well-to-do township, on the outer edge of suburbia. The tract is pleasant, gently rolling land with a stream running through the middle and a stand of woods at one end. The site has some defects—a small marsh, for one—but it should make a fine subdivision. Mill Creek Woods, the developer will call it.

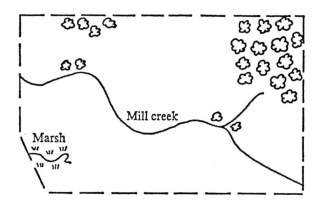

The township has zoned this area for half-acre lots. The developer explores the chances of getting it rezoned for quarter-acre lots, but finds that they are poor so he proceeds to work up a standard plan. This won't take long. He will probably work up the basic plan himself, possibly on the back of an envelope, and then later will turn it over to a civil engineer to be worked up in detail.

The plan almost draws itself. By rule of thumb, the developer knows he will have to subtract about twenty-two acres for roads.

Another six acres he will have to dedicate for playgrounds. This leaves him only eighty-four acres for his half-acre lots and some of the acreage will require extensive land improvement. To squeeze in as many houses as regulations will allow, about 168, he figures to put the creek in a concrete culvert, level the wooded hill and saw down most of the trees. He would like to fill in the small marsh and develop it too, but finds the cost would be too great. He will dedicate the marsh as a park area.

Here is the tentative plan he submits:

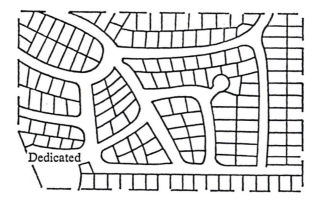

The county planner is very unhappy. He thinks it is a shame to ruin such a fine piece of land with a back layout and he does not think it is necessary. He suggests that the developer start fresh, this time with a cluster approach. The developer is skeptical, but curious. The two go out to the tract and the planner makes a rough sketch of what could be done.

This way, the planner points out, the developer will be able to get up as many houses as before, possibly a few more, and his costs will be considerably less. Under the first plan, he would have had to spend about $4500 a lot for land improvement; under the cluster plan, he will pay about $3000. He will have to lay down only about half as much roadway, his utility runs will be shorter, and he will not have to cover the stream and chop down the wooded hill.

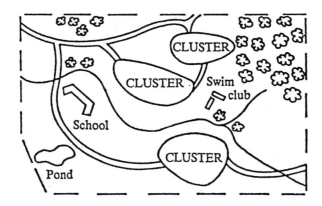

The developer's enthusiasm grows. He wonders, however, about the planning and zoning board, for there is as yet no cluster provision in the local ordinance. The planner thinks that if a really attractive plan is worked up, the zoning boards will go along. At his urging, the developer calls in a professional site planner.

In designing the clusters, there are, a number of possibilities. What both the site planner and the developer would like best is to put the 168 houses into groups of row houses and arrange them around common greens.

Such an economical layout would obviously be the most profitable of all for the developer. But it would also provide a very good buy for the homeowners. Dollar for dollar they would get the most house—whatever the price range—and one easy to maintain. There would be no private open space save the backyard patio, but this would be very usable space, and with the enclosed common green, would make a functional arrangement for families with children. Here is how a cluster would look:

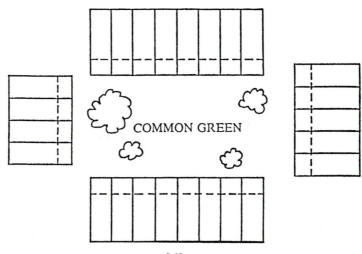

But the people in this particular township wouldn't swallow so dense a pattern, and they would be dead set against row houses. They would seem too much like a garden-apartment project, and there are very few forms of housing that can arouse so much resistance among suburbanites. After taking some more soundings of local opinion, the developer decides to settle on a modified cluster layout, grouping free-standing houses on quarter-acre plots.

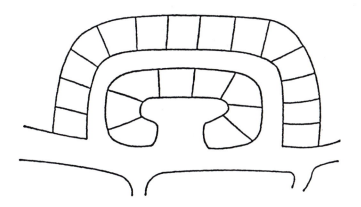

The developer will use stock builders' houses—ranchers and split levels that he has found successful in his other developments. This will sadden the site planner, who may be an architect also and who would like to see clean, advanced designs worthy of his site plan. The developer says he has stuck his neck out far enough as it is. He doesn't think architects know how to cost out a builder's house or design to the market, and he reasons that he is going to have enough trouble selling the cluster idea without saddling it with far-out architecture. (Developers tend to be much too timid on this score, but they do have some reason for their fears. Several of the best of the first cluster proposals were disapproved by local governments, and the deciding factor was not so much the newness of the cluster idea, but of the architecture of the houses.)

The over-all plan, however, remains relatively intact and it is a good one. Of the 112 acres, the house lots take 42, the streets 18, leaving some 52 acres open space to work with. In the center of each cluster there will be a common green and playground. Midway between the clusters there will be a swimming pool, tennis courts, and a clubhouse. The rest of the tract will be treated as countryside with a minimum of landscaping. Paths and bridle trails will be laid along the stream and a few willows planted. The woods will have some of the underbrush thinned out and a small picnic and barbecue area will be fashioned but otherwise it will be left in its natural state and so will the sloping meadows. As for the troublesome marsh, the site planner finds that for the cost of an inexpensive dam it can be turned into a pond. The developer is delighted. He thinks it will be a great merchandising plus and will supply it with a covey of ducks.

The developer will deed some of the open space to the local government. The county planner has suggested that in addition to the gift of a school site, the developer should sweeten up the proposal by also giving a strip along the stream. It would lead to the community park and eventually could be linked with similar spaces in cluster developments that might be built later in the area.

The bulk of the common open space, however, will be deeded to the people who buy the houses. If it were given to the community as a public park, the homeowners would have a legitimate complaint. They are the ones, after all, who will have paid for it. For though the developer will make a big point of his generosity in giving open space, he has already built the cost of it into the purchase price of the homes. The most equitable procedure is to give each person who buys a home an undivided interest in the common open space, and make this part of the basic deed.

To maintain the common areas, a homeowners association will be set up. Each home buyer automatically becomes a member and is obligated to pay his share of the costs of maintaining the open space and operating the recreational facilities. In a cluster development like this, the assessment will probably come to about $100 a year, with the cost rising when and if the homeowners decide to add more elaborate facilities.

Homeowners associations have a good record behind them. A number of them have been working since the twenties and thirties—at Radburn, for example, and the Country Club developments in Kansas City. Some date back much further—Boston's Louisburg Square has been run by a homeowners association since 1840, and New York's Gramercy Park since 1831. Today there are over 350 developments with homeowners associations and with very few exceptions, they are working out well. The key requirements, experience indicates, is that the association be set up at the very beginning and that membership be mandatory.

A question that will inevitably be raised by townspeople is the possibility of a sell-out. Suppose the homeowners later decide to cash in and sell off the common area for additional housing? The record is reassuring. In very few instances have such open spaces ever been converted. One of the green belt communities sold off land when the federal government relinquished ownership, but this happened only because there were no firm stipulations in the original deed. Where there are, it is virtually impossible for homeowners to divide up the common area. The local government, furthermore, can easily remove the temptations entirely. At the time, the developer deeds the title to the homeowners, he can be required to deed an easement to the local government stipulating that the open space remain open.

Since the cluster subdivision will require a change in the local zoning ordinance, a public hearing is scheduled. It will be turbulent. Most of the members of the planning board now favor the cluster proposal, but a number of citizens do not. A vigorous antidevelopment group has been formed ("Citizens for Open Space") and thanks to its agitations and circulars, the hall is packed with nonenthusiasts for cluster. They listen restively while the planner and the developer make presentations with flip-flop charts and slides. Then the questions start. If the developer is so keen on this, what's the catch? If this new type development does not sell, won't we be left holding the bag? Maybe it will sell too well, and then won't every developer for miles be swarming over us? And what kind of home buyers will be coming in? People who have recently moved into the area will be especially zealous on this point. Lower the bars, they will say, and we'll get a new kind of element we've never had before. The meeting breaks up, on a note of acrimony.

But the planning board has been won over and the fact that there has been opposition gives it some extra bargaining power with the developer. It is suggested to him that community resistance might be overcome if he will make a few more concessions in the plan. The developer says absolutely not. He is feeling very put upon by this time and says he is going to chuck the whole thing and sell the land. To a convent perhaps, he adds.

It is not entirely a bluff, but he has sunk too much preliminary money into the project to give up now, and the board knows it. He is persuaded to increase the size of the school tract by two acres and to include the duck pond in the park strip deeded to the township. To lay to rest the fears expressed by the local Garden Club, he also guarantees to preserve a line of sycamores bordering the north part of the tract. The board reciprocates by letting him cut down slightly the width of one of the access roads. A few more items are negotiated, and at length the subdivision is approved.

These first semicluster developments laid the groundwork for what was to, follow. Now there were real-life examples to show skeptical planning boards and citizen groups on cluster tours. Soon a sort of critical mass had built up, and by the mid sixties, cluster communities were going up in most areas. The Federal Housing Administration was now encouraging cluster design and had revised its standards to provide developers with incentives to try it. The leading barracks builder, the Defense Department, was beginning to apply the principle to multifamily housing at military bases.

The big question mark had been the attitude of the consumer and the answer was now at hand. If they had the choice, many people would choose cluster. Conventional, detached-house development still accounted for most new housing, as it still does and will continue to for some years to come. But the test of the marketplace had been met. Most cluster developments were selling as well as conventional developments in the same areas, and in a number of places, spectacularly better.

The best selling were the most compressed. These were the "townhouse" developments, and they caught on so well that the developers themselves were somewhat stunned. In the Los Angeles area one large townhouse development sold out so quickly that developers all over the area junked plans for conventional subdivisions and so swamped the local FHA office with applications for townhouse developments that extra help had to be flown in from Washington to help with the paper work.

Townhouse developments have been such a market success that a standard all purpose layout is emerging. There are some regional variations. In the East, builders do them up as Williamsburg Squares or New England villages. In the West they are more eclectic, mixing colonial, contemporary, oriental, and the gingerbread known in the trade as Hansel and Gretel.

But the basic plans are much the same: groups of two-story row houses, the first floor featuring an open kitchen leading to a living room which in turn opens out through sliding glass doors onto a patio twenty feet square, with a cedar or redwood fence eight feet high, the gate opening onto a common area roughly 100 feet across to the patios of the next row of houses, a play yard at one end with swings, a large concrete turtle, and a sand pit. The area is lit with old-fashioned Baltimore gas street lamps.

The gimmicks are often laid on thick, especially in the lower priced developments, and it is easy to look down one's nose at the whole because of these parts. Several corned-up but significant developments have been dismissed by architects and observers as of no consequence because of their banalities. But overemphasis on facade cuts two ways. For all the laid-on touches, these developments have fastened on a basic plan of commendable simplicity and serviceability. That is why people like them. They buy the houses not because of those gas street lamps, or diamond-shaped panes; they buy because they get more house for their monthly payment than they would elsewhere.

They also get services, and in some developments, a quite encompassing package of them. Townhouse developments not only relieve the homeowner of any mowing, they often take care of the outside of his house, including roof repairs and painting, and some throw in such services as daytime supervision of childrens' areas and corps of baby-sitters. ("The management of Pomeroy West cares for it all. The landscaping, the community center and pool, even your home. Whether it's weeding or watering, repainting or repairs, you have no maintenance worries. Everything is done for you. This gives you time for a weekend at the lake, or a month in the Orient, or just more relaxing moments in your own private gardens. There are no cares of home-ownership here, only the rewards.")

It is quite a package and is especially attractive to older couples who have done their time with a regular suburban homestead. With surprising vehemence, they will talk about the lawns they left behind, and how nice it is to be rid of such tyrannies. Young couples find the service package appealing too. Because they do not have to putter around and paint and fix up, they say, they have more time to be with their children.

Recreational facilities are elaborate, and becoming more so. Almost every cluster development save the very smallest will have tennis courts and a swimming pool, and the way competition is going, Olympic-size swimming pools are becoming standard. Usually there will be a clubhouse or community center and in some instances, a separate building for teenagers.

Some of the larger developments, such as New Seabury on Cape Cod, make recreation their principal motif, and center each cluster around a particular activity—boating on one, for example, riding in another. In most large developments there will be an eighteen-hole golf course, sometimes two, and wherever there is any water, the most will be made of it. Developers will spend a great deal of money to create an artificial lake, as Robert Simon did at Reston, for these not only are good for boating and swimming and scenery—but markedly increase the value of the encircling land. Where there is a waterway, developers will also invest heavily in marinas.

Big developments or small, recreation facilities take a lot of the developers' "front money" for they have found it vital to leave nothing to the imagination of the prospective home buyer. The first thing that most of them build, along with the model houses, is the swimming pool and the clubhouse, which will do double duty as reception center and sales office. Such complexes are often so artfully contrived that once prospects are inside the reception center, there is no way out except by following a labyrinth trail through the models, and back through the sales cubicles.

At this stage, the developments can look oddly like a movie set. The townhouse façades have a two-dimensional quality and one almost feels surprised to find there is something real on the other side of the front door. Activity abounds. Few families may yet have moved into the development, but the swimming pool, snack bar, and cabana club appear to be going full tilt. (In one as yet uninhabited development I visited, a troupe of happy children could be seen cycling around the greens, hour after hour after hour. They dressed up the scene so effectively, I thought they might have been hired as shills. The developer said they certainly were not. But an interesting idea, he said, a very interesting idea.)

The packaging concept has been carried to its ultimate in the retirement communities. For their monthly payment, couples get a small house or apartment unit and a prodigious range of facilities and services—including, among other things, complete medical care, golf courses, minibus transportation, organized recreational and hobby activities, craft shops, social rooms, library, and central clubhouse. Whatever one may think of the concept of such enclaves, physically they have been set up with great skill; the land planning is generally of a very high order and so, often, is the architecture. The Leisure Worlds of entrepreneur Ross Cortese are an outstanding example. Mr. Cortese built so many communities so fast he ran ahead of his market and further building has been stalled for want of financing. The communities that are up, however, furnish some of the best prototypes of cluster design in the country.

Where to now? The cluster approach is opening up some wonderful opportunities, but there are some pitfalls as well. One is that developers will use cluster as a wedge for achieving unreasonably high densities. What appeals most to them is the cluster, not the open space; the doughnut and not the hole. Where they have been allowed to get away with it, some developers have compressed people to the point of claustrophobia, with mean little spaces labeled as commons largely given over to parking.

But compression is not the main problem. In the long run, higher densities are inevitable, whatever kind of layout, and the cluster approach is one of the best ways of meeting the problem with grace. There will be efforts to abuse it, but communities, not developers, lay down the ground rules, and it is up to them to say this many people and no more.

The big danger is standardization. There is a strong possibility that cluster will congeal into a form as rigid and stereotyped as the conventional postwar layout it is replacing. This is already the case with townhouse developments. The basic designs of the first ones have been good, but not so good that they ought to be frozen. They have proved so marketable, however, that developers are copying their externals, gas lamps and all, no matter what the topography or the latitude or the surrounding neighborhood.

Cluster requires a fresh approach to house design. In too few cases do developers have architects design houses for the cluster layout or, indeed, use architects at all. They use stock designs they have been used to. In outlying areas where lot sizes are relatively large, this is not too great a problem; there the conventional detached houses can work fairly well in a cluster arrangement—even the builder's stock ranchers. As lots are compressed, however, the houses and the layout begin to work at cross-purposes. The typical one-story house is designed for a wide suburban lot and throws everything into the façade on the front side, and puts it parallel to the street, which is just the wrong axis for a cluster layout. The windows on the side of the house not only lose their function but become a disadvantage; there is nothing to see except the neighbors' window shades. The vestigial strip of side yard becomes an echo chamber. The better-designed cluster houses solve the problem by doing away with side windows altogether—in the case of townhouses, by necessity.

Exteriors require different handling also. A cluster layout magnifies faults. When detached houses are laid out in conventional fashion, the contrived individuality of the stock models is mercifully separated by enough space to obscure the trumpery; a split-level colonial can be put on the next lot to a rancher without clashing too much, and with enough buffer space and greenery, Hansel and Gretel houses can be assimilated too. Move such houses close together, however, and the result can be a polychromatic mess-an out-of-scale toy village with all the visual defects of a conventional subdivision and no camouflage to hide them.

To go well with a cluster layout, houses should have an underlying unity. This is easiest come by in townhouse developments; even in the most hoked up examples, economic necessity forces the developer to keep the basic structure fairly clean. Variations or no, the houses will be unified by consistent roof lines and set-backs, and the recurrence of certain basic dimensions, as in the height and shape of windows. What makes stereotypes of them is not the uniformity, but the way developers tack them up to disguise the uniformity.

As with the houses, so with the land. There is still too much hack site planning. One of the most difficult things to find out in studying cluster developments is who, if anybody, was responsible for the final site plan. Small developers usually do the basic planning themselves and for professional assistance they tend to favor ex-surveyors or engineers whose principal expertise is an ability to squeeze in the maximum number of lots the rules will allow. The larger and more successful developers do use trained land planners, and often very good ones; whatever the aesthetic, impulses of the developers, they know that they will end up with a more economical layout if they do.

But the lesson comes hard to many developers. often they will bring in a land planner only after it has become apparent that the original hack plan is not going to work very well. Of some sixty developments that I checked, in at least twenty cases the final site plan was drafted as a rescue job. (One of the most encouraging things about studying cluster development is to see the plans that did not get built.)

Site plans are getting better, but the unparalleled opportunities cluster opens up for imaginative treatment of the land are still relatively unexploited. Trees are an example. Since it virtually pays developers to leave as many standing as possible, they do not resort to the practice of sawing down all the trees and starting fresh with saplings. Cluster developments will have more trees around than conventional ones. But that is about it. In a few cases, trees will be used as an element in the architecture of the housing—in some cases, squares have been built around a particularly magnificent old tree, and with striking results. But this is the exception.

The way developers handle earth is similarly uninspired. Wonderful things can be done with the spoil from excavation, especially in prairie or desert areas where there is not a hillock in sight, but efforts are few and they are usually perfunctory. Occasionally a developer will proudly show you a big pile of dirt on which he has planted grass and talk to you about the creative use of overburden. It will look just like a pile of dirt on which grass has been planted—and a convenient justification for not carting the stuff away.

Where there are hills, the potential of cluster design is great but little exploited. As the flat valley floors are being filled up, developers have been turning to the hills, and they have been learning how to do things with rocks and slopes they never did before. They have been doing away with them. They have had to; under conventional zoning and building standards, they have to lay out their subdivisions as though the land were flat and then undertake extraordinary land-grading operations to reduce the topography to fit the subdivision.

The Los Angeles area is a particular case in point. One of the most horrifying sights in the U.S. is that of platoons of giant graders and scrapers chewing into the hills along the San Fernando Valley. Small hills the developers have simply leveled out of existence; the big ones they have chopped up so they look like the side of a pyramid; and on the building "Pads" they have superimposed the same kind of ranchers with which they have covered the valley floor. The result is offensive to the eye, and as periodic slides and inundations have shown, is offensive to nature as well.

The desecration is so unnecessary. By applying the cluster principle developers can work with the slopes instead of obliterating them. This saves money. It also saves the terrain, for developers can concentrate the housing on the knolls and leave the rest undisturbed. The homeowner enjoys more privacy rather than less, and because of the successive changes of elevation, a finer view than he would have in the usual large-lot subdivision.

Where slopes are very steep or rocky, the cluster approach is even more relevant. Much can be done with the cantilever principle, and as Frank Lloyd Wright demonstrated so many years ago with "Falling Water," rocks can be used as structural elements with stunning effect. Unfortunately, this kind of imagination is still restricted to expensive custom homes and "second" homes in vacation areas. It has yet to be applied in any scale to developments.

One reason it has not been is the attitude of municipal engineers. They are a conservative lot, and for hillside plans they demand that developers lay down curbs and gutters and pavements almost as if they were working with a flat piece of land, and they generally insist on streets bigger than necessary. Developers are correct in protesting that the standards are overengineered, but then they have always been saying this about standards; steep slopes or gentle, they have habitually tried to get out of laying down curbs, gutters, and pavements so they can preserve the "character of the site"—and, at $5 a lineal foot, save a lot of money. Understandably, the engineers are skeptical, and many look on the cluster approach as another device of developers to cheat on the regulations. Planners have been arguing the developers' case, and since planners can talk about the public interest with more plausibility than developers, they have had some success in getting hillside standards liberalized. But there are many fights ahead.

Overengineered standards also help explain why streams are treated so insensitively in most developments. Developers are not against streams; they put them in culverts because the regulations force them to, and one reason they like cluster planning is that they can leave the streams. But engineers like concrete. If there is the slightest danger that streams might overflow, they insist that the banks be "stabilized," and they usually mean by this that it be put in a concrete trough. Reston suffered from this: The master plan called for storm sewers in the high-density areas, but the bulk of the drainage was to be handled the way it always was, by the streams. Where banks had to be stabilized, it would be with ferns and trees. The county engineer objected strongly. He wanted concrete. After protracted negotiations, Reston won some of its streams, but it lost some.

The critical problem in cluster planning is the handling of the interior commons and the private spaces. One lesson is abundantly clear. The private space is far and away the most important. The space is usually quite small; in townhouse projects the patios average out to no more than about 20 feet by 20 feet, the dimensions being determined by the width of the houses. But these small spaces are extremely functional. They are fine places for parking infants, for naps in the sun, for the happy hour, and it is a rare one that doesn't have a well-used charcoal grill.

Patios and courtyards also have the great advantage of extending the apparent size of the inside of the house. Since the living room opens onto them through the sliding glass doors, there is a considerable visual sweep from the kitchen in the front of the house to the back of the patio. (In the perspective of developers' brochures, the expanse is so vast the patio is scarcely visible.)

The enclosed court or garden is especially suited to city living and it has been proved many times that people will pay a premium for dwellings that provide them; as a check of real estate ads for New York converted brownstones with south garden will demonstrate, the premiums sometimes reach the fantastic. But this kind of private space has generally been available only in rehabilitated housing. Until recently, designers of city developments were dead set against private spaces. They claimed they were uneconomic, raised maintenance problems, and cluttered up the picture. The projects provided plenty of open space to work with, but the designers preferred to mass the space into common areas and thereby give order and unity to the design.

Much criticism was leveled at these collectives and at length a few projects were put up that included duplex units and gardens. The mating of styles was not always felicitous and to some architects the trend seemed calamitous. I recall visiting a mixed project with one of the architects. We looked down from a tower, which he had designed, to a block of duplex houses with private gardens, which he had not. It was a warm afternoon in fall and the people were busy at one thing or another in their gardens. A pleasant scene, I ventured. A hideous compromise, he said, and with the intense moral indignation that architects can summon up in dismissing designs they do not like, explained that the gardens were an asocial, selfish use of space, and utterly ruinous to the over-all unity.

But the old brutalism has been giving way, albeit slowly. The trend in new urban projects is to have both towers and two- or three story houses and to combine common open spaces with private patios and courts. In comparison to the stark projects of the past, these new ones do tend to look a bit messy, but this defect, if such it is, is apparent only when you are looking down at models. In actuality, the courtyards and gardens tend to enliven the scene for the people in the towers.

The trickiest problem is the relationship between the private spaces and the common ones. In most cases there is a fairly definite separation, with brick walls or high fences enclosing the private space. This method provides the maximum privacy but it does cut down the size of the interior commons and for this reason some architects prefer to treat both kinds of space as one. Save for a low hedge, or line of bricks, there is little, to indicate where the private open space ends and the common space begins. This makes for a cleaner design and a roomier commons.

It also makes for ambiguity, and if architects had to live in their developments they would not do it this way. In almost any development where people live close together there is usually a lot of neighborly contact. Where the houses focus on a commons, the amount of contact is at its greatest. There is more kaffeeklatsching, more visiting back and forth, and while this has its advantages, without fences it becomes mandatory. There is no avoiding it, and a good many people would like to avoid it.

But there is no redoubt, no place to draw the line. Wives complain that if they feel like stretching out on a beach chair to read or just plain rest, their siesta is sure to be interrupted. Then there is the entertaining problem. When couples do their *al fresco* entertaining in full sight of everyone, neighborly relationships can be put to a severe strain. (Will they understand it's an out-of-town couple we haven't seen in years? Shall we ask them to come over and join us just for cocktails? Will they leave before supper?) The poet's point about good fences and good neighbors is true. An in all, experience suggests, private open spaces should be private.

There need be no antithesis between common spaces and private ones. They complement each other; even in very high density developments there should be room for both. When there is a buffer zone of private gardens, interior commons do not have to be very large; the fact they are enclosed by buildings on three or four sides makes them look larger than they actually are.[1]

The usual commons consists of a rectangle of green lawn, some hedges and trees, and a play area at one end. The result is pleasant enough, but if you have seen one you have seen a great many. Occasionally there are fresh touches—an open air pavilion with a huge fireplace, for example—but in most cases the originalities are standard: a piece or so of free form sculpture, perhaps, or a string of those gas street lamps.

As Georgian architects knew so, well, the great advantage of a tight housing layout is the opportunity it affords to design the spaces for the buildings and the buildings for the spaces—at one and the same time, and not seriatim. But few aspects of cluster are so unexploited. If there is to be an interior commons, for example, why not follow through and design the buildings for real enclosure? Open space is at its most inviting when it is approached through a covered passageway, yet this ancient principle has been little applied. Neither has the crescent or the arcade or the circus.

There are many fresh approaches to explore. Do the commons, for example, have to be green? There can be too much and some of the most celebrated garden-city communities suffer from the overemphasis. Without enclosure, or a striking foreground or background, expanses of green can be quite dull, and sometimes they can be downright oppressive. (Radburn, for example, is almost smothered in foliage in summer, and to this observer, looks best in spring.)

Punctuation and contrast are needed, and one of the best ways to provide them is through the paved courtyard or small plaza. It can provide an excellent common area, and tends to heighten the effect of any greenery there is. In few settings does a large tree seem so handsome. The paved court also makes a nice transition between the private open space and the surrounding common areas, all the more so if the housing clusters are surrounded by large expanses of green. They are also the best of settings for a fountain.

The paved court, however, still strikes many people as much too revolutionary for the market. One of the best-looking designs in the country was ditched because of this bias. The site planner had set his clusters in the middle of a golf course. Since there was to be green around them, he planned the common space within each cluster as a paved courtyard. The developer lost his nerve and asked a market consultant to give his judgment. The consultant said it was too radical, and recommended that the spaces be grass and look "pretty and soft."

Such timidity is unwarranted, even by commercial standards. The court has been given a pretty good consumer test for quite a few centuries, and where it has been tried anew it seems to work as well as ever. Charles Goodman's paved courts for the River Park development in southwest Washington are a fine example. Compared to architect Chloethiel Smith's grassy spaces in the neighboring Capitol Park development, Goodman's courts seem severe, but both projects sold well, and in both, the open spaces seem to work quite well—proving, once again, that different approaches can achieve satisfying results.

In rural areas where there is a lot of space to work with, there are many more things that can be done with common areas than have been tried. Grazing, for one thing. If fields and meadows are put to this kind of productive use they look much better than any formally landscaped scene. Sheep, for example, lend just the estate flavor that developers want to promote, and there is no better way to keep the grass cut. Instead of having to pay people to maintain the land, the homeowners can get it done virtually free, and sometimes even make a little. In one Colorado vacation development, the houses are clustered on the slopes, leaving three hundred acres of meadowland as the commons. The homeowners lease it out as pasture land for cattle.

Some people have suggested going so far as to have a complete working farm as the center of a commons; one such scheme has been proposed for the development of a small valley in upstate New York. One can only wish the proponents well, but the experience of subdivisions close to farms suggests that farm activity and its attendant smells is attractive to residents for about one day. After that they raise cain with the farmer for disturbing their peace—starting up his tractors at five A.M., using dangerous sprays, letting their children get into mischief, and such. Another idea that is likely to come a cropper is the equestrian village centered around riding stables. This was proposed in the preliminary plan for Reston but was prudently dropped. There are stables, but they are located well away from any houses. People like to ride horses, developers have found, but they do not want to live near them.

While there are many more things that can be done with the spaces within developments, perhaps the greatest challenge is to find ways to link the spaces. Not much has been done to exploit this potential; by and large, the cluster developments are planned project by project, with little relation one to the other, or to the open spaces of the community. Very large developments, or "new towns," are planned on such a scale that they provide a community open-space system themselves, but while more of these are in the offing, the bulk of future residential growth will be an aggregation of small and medium-size developments.

Yet their open spaces do not have to be a miscellany. With the proper incentives, individual developers can be led to plan their open spaces so that they will eventually fit together in an over-all system. The key is for the local government to anticipate the development that is inevitable and to lay down in advance the skeleton of an open-space network to which each developer will contribute as the area is built up. This presupposes a very vigorous arm twisting of developers but there is a strong indication that if planning commissions were to take this kind of initiative, developers would go along.

Philadelphia has furnished an outstanding demonstration. In the 1950s, there still remained in its far northeast section a five thousand acre expanse of open land. It was mostly farm land, gently rolling and laced with a network of wooded creeks. It was also eminently buildable, and squarely in the path of row-house development. Mulling over the fate of this area, Philadelphia city planner Edmund Bacon, figured that there was no reason why the city should leave the basic land-use pattern for this area up to the speculative builders. The city, he felt, ought to lay down a master subdivision plan. Developers could fill in the details, but the open-space and housing patterns would be so strongly outlined that the end product would be the kind of unity that is usually possible only when one large developer is doing the whole thing.

With a cluster approach, Bacon figured, the total acreage could amenably house some 68,000 people. The area would be divided into a series of neighborhood groupings, and there would be an open space network based on the stream valleys. To obtain plat approval, a builder would have to dedicate these parts of his tract designated as green space to the city. Instead of the usual aggregation of bits and pieces, accordingly, there would be a continuous open-space system that would be highly functional for recreation, and would at once connect and define the neighborhoods. Here is the plan of one section of the area, with the public open spaces indicated by dark hatching.

Builders took to the idea. The master plan did go quite far in telling them what to do, but it provided them excellent densities—about nine units per acre—and considerably less street and land improvement expenses than ordinarily they would have had to bear. The first builder started work in 1959. Since then other builders have joined suit and with few variations from the original plan.

The result is not a showpiece. For so advanced a plan, what one sees on the ground is disappointingly ordinary. The houses, which are in the $11,000-$13,000 range, are basically standard row houses with a few facade variations, and they do not always sit well in the circular groupings laid down by the planners. But the plan works, and one has only to look to the conventional row-house developments a few miles back toward the city to see what a difference it has made. The houses in the cluster neighborhoods have been just as profitable for the builders, no more expensive for the homeowners, yet they are complemented by a magnificent stream-valley network that cost the city nothing and will one day be priceless. They are indeed ordinary neighborhoods, but that is the point. If this kind of amenity can be achieved in middle-income neighborhoods in a city, the potential elsewhere is tremendous.

NOTES

1. An old, but very excellent case in point is Macdougal Gardens in New York's Greenwich Village. This is a block of old houses in which the rear portions of the backyards were combined into a commons. It is an extremely pleasant place and because of the old trees and the adjoining gardens of the houses, the space seems quite large. But it isn't. The width of the commons itself is only thirty-five feet.

Chapter 20

Indoor Air Quality

by Carol Venolia

From HEALING ENVIRONMENTS
Celestial Arts

"The average home today contains more chemicals than were found
in a typical chemistry lab at the turn of the century."

—DEBRA LYNN DADD

Not long ago, when people talked about making their buildings "safe," they were usually referring to security against dangers from outside like burglary or earthquakes. Now, growing numbers of people are concerned about hazards generated from within their homes and workplaces—
airborne gases and particles that undermine their mental and physical health. Recent cases of indoor air pollution in new office buildings and schools have been widely publicized; upon moving
into a shiny new building, occupants complain of nausea, headaches, lethargy, puffy eyes, stuffy
noses, coughing fits, and a long list of other ailments. The phenomenon, known as "Sick
Building Syndrome," is usually attributed to two factors: increased use of volatile synthetic materials, and decreased ventilation rates aimed at energy conservation.

Although the natural atmosphere has always carried bacteria, molds, viruses, pollens,
spores, and dusts, nothing in our makeup prepares us for the onslaught of toxic substances we
now encounter daily. The nature and volume of these poisons is so new that we don't know
what's hit us. Recent studies have shown that indoor air can be two to four times as polluted as
outdoor air. While some contaminants are detectable by smell upon first exposure, many are
odorless and colorless, and thus go unnoticed. Even those with characteristic odors are often ignored; after the initial exposure, our olfactory sensors lose their sensitivity to a given smell. In
many ways, the sleuthing out of indoor irritants is a whole new game.

Sick Building Syndrome has alerted us to some of the hazards and sources of indoor air
pollution, but we are only beginning to recognize the extent of the problem. Dramatic cases in-

volving large numbers of people are relatively easy to notice. But most "environmental illnesses" develop more slowly, and there is often a long lag time between exposure and effect, making assessment difficult. Sensitive people typically suffer for years with symptoms that appear to be viral or psychological in origin before they suspect that they are reacting to something in their environment. Many have forgotten what it's like to feel well, and only recall the real joy of living once the source of their problem has been removed.

Dr. James A. O'Shea, former president of the American Academy of Environmental Medicine, says that roughly four to five million Americans suffer from chemically induced environmental sensitivities, but that only about five percent have been treated for it. "Many people are walking around with environmental illness and don't even know it yet."[1] William J. Rea, M.D., estimates that environmental illness already affects "a good twenty percent of the population, and the number is going to get higher."[2]

It is easy to think that sensitivity to toxic substances in the environment is the problem of the unfortunate few, and that if we're not incapacitated we have no need to be concerned. However, there is a growing belief that highly sensitive people may be early warning signals to us all.

According to natural living consultant Debra Lynn Dadd:

> "Each of us is born with an inherited ability to process substances that enter our bodies, both beneficial and foreign or harmful. Our inherited ability sets a certain built-in limit as to how much exposure to potential toxins we can endure without harm. As long as the amount of toxins coming into our bodies stays under that level and our tolerance threshold is not exceeded, our bodies will adapt and metabolize or excrete the poisons with no ill effects. It is when our bodies become overloaded that symptoms and disease occur. Once that level is reached, even the slightest exposure can produce symptoms."[3]

Dr. Alfred V. Zamm, a physician who treats people with environmental sensitivities, divides the population into three categories:

> 1. People who are sensitive to environmental pollutants, are aware of the problem, and are taking action to improve their situation;

> 2. People who may have environmental sensitivities and don't realize it, but who are "depressed much of the time, tired without good reason, weak and logy and slow-thinking";

> 3. People who appear to be unaffected but who are probably not reaching their potential because they are surrounded by "incipient poisons."[4]

That leaves none of us untouched. Furthermore, people in the "unaffected" category often move suddenly and catastrophically into a "sensitive" category when the effects of the toxic environment reach a point the body can no longer tolerate. The annals of environmental illness are filled with stories of previously productive, happy people who have been crippled by a single sensitizing episode or a cumulative dose of a toxic substance. Their lives often become complicated as sensitivity to one chemical spreads to related substances.

Suzanne Randegger, editor of *Environ* magazine, urges:

> "The more we can avoid the small or unnoticed toxic exposures, the less likely we are to become increasingly sensitized to chemically related substances until we reach the overload stage, where our bodies react indiscriminately."[5]

Since most of us spend 90% of our time indoors, we need to be careful about what we surround ourselves with. The National Academy of Sciences estimates that indoor air pollution already adds from 15 billion to 100 billion dollars to our nation's annual medical bills.[6] Furthermore, indoor pollutants have been found to affect productivity, stress levels, sense of well-being, and absenteeism. In the long run, it is cheaper to make our buildings as pollution-free as possible.

Unfortunately, the magnitude of the problem is not matched by the volume of useful research findings. Though recommended maximum exposure levels exist for various pollutants, no one knows what levels, if any, of indoor pollutants are acceptable over the long term. Little is known about the interactions and synergistic effects of multiple contaminants. For many substances, appropriate measurement techniques are still being developed. And we're only beginning to understand the health effects of indoor air pollutants and ways of controlling them. But the problems are great enough that we can't wait until all the data are in from scientific studies underway or not yet begun. We need to act now, relying on our own rationality and instincts, on the research that has been done, and on our direct experiences and those of others.

The point of this information is not to produce anxiety or paranoia; such a state might be more of a health hazard than indoor air. The point is to help you get a handle on things; awareness and education can lead to positive action. If you are a silent sufferer, you can learn to alter your environment and lifestyle to greatly relieve your mysterious ailments. If you are relatively unaffected, you can take precautionary steps to better assure your continued health and perhaps even improve your present functioning. The goal is to help you create an environment where you can refresh and recharge yourself, unencumbered by insidious assaults.

INDOOR AIR QUALITY HAZARDS

The following summaries of the major indoor air pollutants will acquaint you with their basic characteristics. If you suspect that any of them pose a problem in your environment, refer to the Resources section at the end of this chapter for sources of more detailed information.

FORMALDEHYDE

Considered by some to be the most worrisome indoor pollutant, formaldehyde gas is toxic to most forms of life. Thad Godish, Director of the Indoor Air Quality Research Laboratory at Indiana's Ball State University, says that formaldehyde perils lurk in the vast majority of American homes.[7] Although people's levels of sensitivity to formaldehyde vary widely, repeated exposure can increase one's sensitivity. Many people—especially mobile home dwellers—have had to abandon their homes because of highly irritating formaldehyde levels.

Possible Health Effects. Results of continued or excessive formaldehyde exposure have included irritation of the mucous membranes of the eyes, nose, and upper respiratory tract; skin irritation and rashes; chronic headaches, lethargy, and memory lapses; sleep disturbance; irritability, paranoia, depression, disorientation, and moodiness; chest pains and heart problems; cold or flu-like symptoms including coughing, watery eyes, swelling of the throat, and breathing problems; nosebleeds; nausea; menstrual problems; and possible cancer and other chronic or long-term effects.

Perhaps most serious is the sensitizing effect of formaldehyde. Overexposure, whether occurring suddenly or over time, can result in extreme sensitivity to minute concentrations not only of formaldehyde but of other substances as well.

Sources. The greatest amounts of indoor formaldehyde come from a few products: medium-density fiberboard or particleboard products (such as subflooring, paneling, solid-core doors, and cabinetry), urea-formaldehyde foam insulation (UFFI), and much contemporary furniture (solid wood as well as upholstered), all of which may contain urea-formaldehyde. Lesser emitters that may increase formaldehyde levels are synthetic carpets, carpet glue, drapes, office partitions, oil-based paints and resins, permanent press fabrics, plastics, ceiling tiles, and combustion (tobacco smoke, gas stoves, wood stoves, and kerosene space heaters).

Urea-formaldehyde resin can outgas[8] for the life of the product, but phenol-formaldehyde resin is more stable and therefore less hazardous. For that reason, some experts consider products containing phenol-formaldehyde resin, such as exterior-grade plywood, to be relatively safe.

Remedies. According to Godish, source removal is the only effective way to reduce high concentrations of formaldehyde; all the major sources must be identified and removed. Replace particleboard subflooring with tongue-and-groove boards or exterior grade softwood plywood (except in cases of sensitivity to softwood or to plywood adhesives); choose metal or hardwood cabinets; select solid wood, metal, or old (already outgassed) furniture; replace particleboard or hardwood plywood wall paneling with decorative hardboard, drywall, or plaster.

Alternatively, it is sometimes possible to seal in formaldehyde fumes. A water-based sealer or nitrocellulose-based varnish can be used effectively on particleboard subflooring, hardwood plywood paneling, particleboard shelving, cabinet joints and edges, countertop under surfaces, and unfinished furniture. Such sealants may need to be reapplied every few years. A more durable barrier, though often less attractive, is aluminum foil sealed with foil tape.

If UFFI is outgassing into your home, your best protection is to remove it as completely as possible. After removal, Godish recommends that you treat all cavity wood surfaces with a 3% solution of sodium bisulfite and allow it to dry before installing new insulation. If gypsum wallboard is adjacent to the UFFI, you may need to replace it as well; formaldehyde has been known to seep into wallboard, continuing to contaminate the house. If it is impractical to remove the UFFI, you can caulk or spackle holes and cracks in the insulated walls to reduce passage of formaldehyde. Applying two coats of a vapor-barrier paint or installing canvas-backed mylar or vinyl wallpaper will also help reduce outgassing.

Because heat and moisture accelerate formaldehyde emission, formaldehyde levels can be controlled somewhat by lowering temperature and humidity. Ventilation can also lower formaldehyde levels by dilution. Air filtration may offer additional relief; use specially impregnated charcoals or an activated alumina medium impregnated with potassium permanganate, or both, and replace them as needed.

The level of formaldehyde outgassing from a given source will decrease over time. However, after several years some products still give off enough formaldehyde to cause health problems.

Indoor formaldehyde levels can be determined relatively easily and inexpensively. Some state health departments will perform free tests, or you can purchase a test kit and do the test yourself.

COMBUSTION PRODUCTS

The products of burning common fuels can include carbon monoxide, carbon dioxide, nitric oxide, nitrogen dioxide, and hydrocarbons. In homes, the worst offender is gas; many researchers agree that a healthy house should not even be connected to a gas line. Alfred V. Zamm, M.D., rates gas second only to cigarette smoke as the worst home pollutant. Zamm observes that many women who spend a lot of time in the kitchen become sensitive to gas; they acquire a depression that psychiatry can't cure, but the depression often disappears when their gas range is replaced with an electric one.[9]

Carbon monoxide (CO), an odorless, colorless gas, is the most widely recognized combustion product pollutant. The National Center for Health Statistics estimates that 2% of the U.S. population (over 4.5 million people) is exposed to indoor CO in excess of the EPA's standard for outdoor air.

Possible Health Effects. For many people, headaches, dizziness, and fatigue can result from eight hours around a normal gas stove. Higher concentrations of CO can cause flu-mimicking symptoms, nausea, convulsions, mental confusion, loss of alertness, impaired heart function, and death.

Nitric oxide (NO) and nitrogen dioxide (NO_2) can reduce lung function and increase colds and bronchitis. They have been implicated in long-term respiratory problems, heart disease, and cancer. Hydrocarbons cause cancer in lab animals and can damage the liver, respiratory system, and nerve tissue.

Joseph T. Morgan, M.D., says that gas can have a sensitizing effect similar to that of formaldehyde: "...one of the best ways to induce chemical sensitivity is to be subjected to long-term exposure to natural gas in combusted and/or uncombusted form."[10]

Sources. The main indoor sources of combustion products are tobacco smoke, wood- and coal-burning stoves, fireplaces, gas ranges, self-cleaning electric ovens, automobiles idling in attached garages, water heaters, clothes dryers, and furnaces or heaters that burn charcoal, gas, kerosene, oil, or wood. Combustion products enter indoor air at open flames or via rusted flues, defective pipes, or failed welds. Improperly adjusted or vented heating devices pump out large volumes of CO. In this country, about 200 people die each year from poisoning by space heaters, usually kerosene fueled. But, according to Zamm, even a normal gas oven operating at 350°F for one hour with the vent fan on can cause kitchen air pollution comparable to a heavy Los Angeles smog. Without a fan, CO and NO_2 can zoom to three times those levels or more.[11]

Remedies. The most complete way to eliminate combustion products is to remove all gas-burning appliances and have the gas line capped off at the street. An electric range or a magnetic-induction range can be substituted for a gas range. Homes without gas appliances have significantly lower levels of combustion products than do homes where gas is burned. Debra Lynn Dadd says, "I have seen many clients do everything I recommend except remove the gas from their homes, and their health problems remain. But almost as soon as they turn off the gas appliances, they start feeling better. It's amazing."[12]

Short of removing all gas, you can reduce combustion pollutant levels somewhat. Gas ranges should have hoods vented to the outside, and the fan should be operated any time the range or oven is used. The more powerful the fan and the more enclosing the hood, the better. An open window will also improve air exchange.

When possible, isolate combustion appliances in a room that can be closed or sealed off from the living space. Gas furnaces that are located outside the building—or that use outside combustion air and exhaust it directly to the outdoors—pose minimal health hazards for most people. Maintain your gas appliances for optimum functioning: clean burners and blocked flues, fix cracks and leaks in pipes, and keep appliances adjusted; a poorly adjusted gas stove can give off thirty times more CO than a properly adjusted one.

Woodstove pollution can be minimized indoors by selecting an airtight stove and keeping the flue clean and in good repair. One expert points out that there's no such thing as an airtight flue, and recommends eliminating wood stoves and fireplaces altogether. For most people, however, such an extreme is not necessary.

Radon is as old as the mountains; it is one of the indoor pollutants that we can only partially blame on modern living. It is a colorless, odorless gas that is a byproduct of decaying uranium in rocks and soil. The gas seeps out and decays into radioactive "daughter" products which can then lodge in the lung tissue. Experts disagree about the risks of low to moderate exposures, but it is believed that the combined effect of radon and other indoor pollutants (notably cigarette smoke) may significantly increase hazards. In 1987, The EPA found 20% of the 9,600 homes it surveyed in 10 states to be contaminated with potentially health threatening levels of radon gas.[13]

Possible Health Effects. The EPA considers radon to be the leading cause of lung cancer in non-smokers.[14] EPA statistics suggest that 10% of all lung cancers in the United States are caused by radon; the Consumer Federation of America attributes up to 30,000 lung cancer occurrences per year to radon..[15] And the lung cancer risk from radon may only be the tip of the iceberg of adverse effects. Spending a week—or even a year—in a building with moderate radon contamination probably wouldn't cause cancer. But 20 years in such a house might well increase your risk.[16] Unfortunately, short-term symptoms of radon exposure are yet to be identified.

Sources. The radon content of rocks and soils varies greatly. Soils high in radon have been found in parts of Pennsylvania, Washington, New York, New Jersey, Florida, Texas, Maine, and Vermont. Radon concentrations in rocks range from very low in sandstone to fairly high in granite and even higher in alum shale.

In areas where radon is abundant in the soil, it is sucked directly into the lower levels of the house, especially through cracks in a basement wall or a concrete slab on grade. It can also enter through sump pumps, drains, and fittings around underground utility pipes. Radon-bearing well water can contribute to indoor radon levels as the water splashes from faucets, showerheads, and washing machines. Decorative rock walls around fireplaces, or used as thermal mass in passive solar heated buildings, may introduce radon to the indoors. Concrete, cinder block, or bricks made with radon-bearing materials can also increase radon levels. In Colorado, radon-rich tailings from uranium processing mills were used in the foundations of several schools and more than 4,800 homes.

Remedies. Control methods fall into four categories: ventilation, filtration, removal or sealing, and prevention at the site-selection and building-design stage. For a test of radon levels in your building, contact your state agency that deals with radon, or your regional EPA office.

Increased ventilation can remove radon gas and lessen its concentration indoors. Increasing the air pressure inside a building will discourage the entry of radon (or any other) gas from outside. Whether natural or forced ventilation is used, be careful not to reduce indoor air pressure, thus pulling more radon inside. But even well-designed ventilation won't solve the problems of high radon concentrations.

Filtration is controversial; some say that an electrostatic precipitator will reduce radon levels by removing radon-bearing dust from the air; others say that filtration is useless since radon is a gas.

If radon-bearing soil is a problem, increasing foundation drainage, ventilating crawlspaces or under slabs, or covering earthen basement floors or crawlspaces with non-radon-bearing concrete can reduce infiltration indoors. Sealant applied to the foundation and to interior masonry will limit the release of radon.

For a new structure, careful site selection, material choice, and ventilation design can assure low radon levels from the outset. In Sweden, a piece of land must be tested for radon before a new house can be built. If high radon levels are found, the builder must follow government guidelines to ensure an uncontaminated house.

ASBESTOS

Called "one of the most pernicious indoor pollutants,"[17] asbestos problems have been publicized for years. A fine, fibrous material, asbestos is widespread in walls, ceilings, and elsewhere in many modern buildings. Urban autopsies find asbestos in lung tissues in almost every case.[18]

Possible Health Effects. Asbestos causes malignant tumors in the chest lining or abdominal cavities and increases the risk of cancer of the gastrointestinal tract and the larynx.

Sources. Asbestos has been used inside buildings for fireproofing, decoration, and thermal, electrical, and acoustical insulation. It has been widely used in schools, making school children and school employees especially vulnerable. Asbestos is harmless as long as it stays where it is applied. The hazard arises when fibers are released into the air or water, eventually lodging in the lungs or gastrointestinal tract.

Remedies. In many cases, undamaged asbestos products are best left alone. Some asbestos applications can be sealed to keep fibers from sloughing off into the air. Where asbestos-containing products are crumbling or damaged, repair or removal is recommended; removal must be performed carefully, however, or it can produce even higher levels of asbestos in the air.

HOUSE DUST

House dust is composed of molds, bacteria, mites, pollen, human and animal hair and dandruff, textile fragments, leftover food, and decomposed material. Forty percent of the allergic population reacts to house dust. Of those, one quarter react to the house dust mite.[19]

Possible Health Effects. Since house dust can include particles of almost any allergen, reactions to it cover a full range of allergic responses: runny nose, sneezing, scratchy throat, coughing, fuzzy thinking, and even hives. As a carrier of bacteria and viruses, it can also aid in spreading colds and flu.

Sources. As evidenced by its composition, the sources of house dust are everywhere. Animals, plants, people, fabrics, insects, and anything else that sloughs off fibers or particles can contribute to dust. Though some amount of dust cannot be avoided, it becomes a problem whenever it is stirred up, re-entering the airflow and eventually the lungs. Housecleaning stirs up dust. Neglected furnace filters constantly recharge the air with dust. Sitting on upholstered furniture, moving drapes, and shaking rugs all stir up dust.

Remedies. Ventilation and air filtration will reduce the volume of dust particles in indoor air. Frequent housecleaning is a must, but special care is needed to keep from re-introducing settled dust into the air. Avoid dusters, dry mops, and brooms. Use a damp cloth to clean moldings, sills, light fixtures, shelves, and the tops of door and window jambs. Open the windows when cleaning to blow out any dust you may raise. Vacuum cleaners are tricky; they suck up dust, but the finest particles blow back out through the filter bag. The best solution so far is a central vacuum system that blows the dust outdoors. Second best is a vacuum cleaner that uses water as a filter.

You can avoid providing places for dust to collect by limiting carpets, drapes, wall hangings, window sills, dust-collecting nooks and ledges, and open-front cabinets.

MOLD

Molds exist in the air throughout the year, in varying concentrations. Mold spores are light and easily carried by air currents. Most of us don't realize how many damp, mold-growth-encouraging places there are indoors until we start looking.

Possible Health Effects. In people sensitive to mold, symptoms can include a stuffy, runny nose, sore throat, dry eyes, bronchial troubles, fatigue, and depression. Exposure to large doses of mold may also sensitize people not previously allergic to it.

Sources. A little moisture and darkness is all that molds need to proliferate. Mold grows in damp basements, bathrooms, closets, mattresses, carpets, and old upholstered furniture. In the kitchen, it thrives between the sink and the wall, around the bottom of the cold water pipe, in wooden chopping boards, on the refrigerator door gasket, and in the surplus water tray at the bottom of self defrosting refrigerators. In bathrooms, it grows in tile grout, around the sink, on walls, on the back of the toilet tank, and on the shower doors. Old newspapers, books, or magazines can grow mold, as do flower pots, the surfaces of house plant soil, and any decaying plant material.

Remedies. Get rid of old damp, moldy materials. Clean moldy areas with a borax solution or diluted Zephiran. Ventilate the bathroom and other moisture-producing areas well; hang towels where they can dry. Put a layer of sterile potting soil or crushed stone over houseplant soil surfaces. Install louvered doors on damp closets. If you have a damp basement, air it out and keep it dry. If water gets into the basement via a roof downspout, extend the leader to carry rainwater away and downhill. You may also want to waterproof your basement or install a dehumidifier. If you use a humidifier elsewhere in your home, clean it frequently with water and a stiff vegetable brush. Avoid future mold growth by ventilation, humidity control, sunlight, and regular cleaning of vulnerable areas.

Lead contamination pervades the modern environment. Typical Americans have 100 to 1,000 times the lead in their bodies that their prehistoric ancestors had. No safe level for lead exposure has been demonstrated.

Possible Health Effects. Chronic exposure to low levels of lead produces permanent neuropsychological defects and behavior disorders.

Sources. Inside buildings, the major source of lead is leaded paint. Since lead is now illegal as a paint component, the hazard mostly exists in older buildings. It is particularly dangerous where paint is cracked or peeling, especially where children inadvertently eat it. Some lead may also enter drinking water via old lead pipes or newer copper pipes with lead-containing solder at the joints.

Remedies. Lead paint can be removed, but special precautions should be taken to avoid breathing its dust, letting the dust spread throughout the building, or leaving residue that could enter food or the air. In new plumbing installations, copper pipe can be joined with low-lead solder.

SOFTWOODS

"Natural" isn't always best, especially for people sensitive to softwood vapors. Softwoods (pine, spruce, cedar, redwood, and other conifers) contain volatile resins that outgas for years. Wood paneling, cedar closets, fireplace wood, and Christmas trees can all produce reactions in sensitive people.

AIR IONS

Negative air ions have received a lot of attention as a quick fix for problems ranging from lethargy to arthritis to impotence. But the subject is complex, and scientific research has produced few reliable results to date.

Air ions are atmospheric molecules that have become charged by the loss or gain of an electron. They are constantly being formed and are constantly recombining to neutralize their charges. Air ions are naturally produced by cosmic rays, radioactive soil elements, weather fronts, moving water, and wind. Euphoric feelings around waterfalls or before thunderstorms are attributed to high negative ion concentrations. In open country, under favorable weather conditions, there are typically 1,000 air ions per cubic centimeter of air; in large cities there are approximately 200 ions per cubic centimeter of air.[20]

Researcher Albert P. Krueger, M.D., says that lab experiments support four conclusions:

• Ions are biologically active, affecting living matter from bacteria to human beings.

• Depletion of ions in the air may increase a person's susceptibility to illnesses like respiratory infections.

• An increase in ions and particularly in the ratio of negative to positive ions may be useful in the treatment of burns and respiratory diseases.

• Conditions in urban centers, characterized by air pollution outdoors and artificially controlled climates indoors, lower the total number of small ions in the air and decrease the negative-to-positive ion ratio.[21]

Indoors, air ion concentration is lowered by air moving through metal ducts, cigarette smoke and other air pollution, the static electricity generated by synthetic fibers, and many other human activities. Chronic ion deprivation has been associated with discomfort, lassitude, and loss of mental and physical efficiency.

Sensitivity to air ion concentrations varies widely among people. And although negative ions are often seen as "good for you," and positive ions as harmful, there are reported cases of positive ions having therapeutic effects and of life forms that are harmed by negative ions.

Awareness of air ionization and how it affects you can be valuable. But what to do about it is another matter. If you are living in a polluted city, moving to the rural mountains will probably be good for your health, and air ion concentration will be but one of the reasons why. If you are selecting a heating system, you will be better off with radiant heat than with forced air; again, the ion factor would be one of many.

Negative ion generators have been touted as the solution to air ion depletion or "pos-ion poisoning." With the proper equipment, intelligently used, they may indeed help to improve a bad situation. But irresponsible advertising and detrimental side effects also surround many of them. Potential ionizer hazards include electrical shock, production of ozone and oxides of nitrogen (both highly toxic), outgassing of plastics from warmed ionizer cases, and increased static electricity from improperly grounded units. If you choose to buy a negative ion generator, look for a dealer who has been in business for some time, check for the UL label, make a sniff test for ozone (which has a pungent odor like the fresh air after a lightning storm), and look for an ionizer with a metal case.

Air ionization is one aspect of a complex environmental picture. Krueger himself says that "The effects of ion depletion on people cannot compare with the dramatic respiratory distress caused by toxic air pollutants ...."[22] We need to learn more about how air ions affect our health, and about which human activities improve or undermine a healthy air ion balance. I suspect that if we concentrate on healing environments in general—using appropriate building materials, lighting, heating, fresh air, delight, and so on—we will simultaneously improve the ionic environment.

HOUSEHOLD PRODUCTS

Many products used in and around buildings also contribute to the overall pollution level. Cigarette smoke tops the list, followed by so-called air fresheners, cleaning products, pesticides, laundry aids, floor and furniture waxes, aerosol sprays, paint and varnish removers, hobby materials, soft plastics, foam rubber, dry-cleaned clothes, gasoline, and personal care products such as hair spray, deodorant, nail polish, and nail polish remover.

Pesticides can be particularly troublesome, as some remain chemically active for years. They get indoors by being tracked in, by vapors coming in through open windows, and in the form of mothballs, insecticide strips, and flea collars.

There are less harmful—and often less costly—substitutes for many of these household poisons. You can substitute a liquid or dry form of a product for an aerosol form. You can control odors by cleaning or ventilation, rather than masking them with toxic chemicals sold as air fresheners. You can purchase products designed to have low toxicity (see Resources). You can control pests mechanically (with a fly swatter) or at their source (by unblocking clogged pipes or draining a mud puddle). And you can replace commercial products with homemade ones. If harmful chemicals must be used, they should be used outdoors or in a well ventilated area and stored in a sealed, fireproof compartment, preferably away from inhabited areas.

WATER

We know that our health is affected by water when we drink it, but did you know that bathing or showering in it can also be hazardous? Several recent studies have found that showering in impure water for fifteen minutes can be more dangerous than drinking two liters of the same water.[23] Volatile chemicals in tap water are released into the air at faucets and showerheads, and enter our lungs as we breathe. These chemicals are also absorbed through our skin when we bathe. The skin can carry twice as much of a volatile chemical into the body as do the intestines. Volatile chemicals found in water include chlorine, chloroform, pesticides, radon, PCBs, benzene, and many others.

If you are buying land or a house, have the water supply tested before you buy. If you are not moving, check your existing water. Data on municipal water supplies are usually available from your water company, but you must also consider pollutants that enter the water via the pipes (lead from pipes and joint solder, asbestos from old asbestos-cement pipes). Though it can be expensive, you might choose to have a laboratory test the water as it comes from your faucet; check your telephone directory and get bids from several sources. Once you have a water analysis, you can tailor a filtration system to your needs. Alternatively, you can select a broad-spectrum water purifier that will protect you from a range of possible pollutants—good insurance against fluctuations in water quality.

CLEANING UP YOUR ENVIRONMENT

How is one to respond to this flood of indoor pollution awareness? First, reassure yourself that indoor air quality is manageable. Evaluate your own state of health as an indicator of how quickly or drastically to act. If you've been plagued by mysterious symptoms, and you suspect an environmental cause, a new sense of hope and the eventual symptomatic relief will more than compensate for any time and money you invest in clearing the air.

For most of us, Dr. Zamm has encouraging words:

"If you eat well, avoid worthless or excessive medication, choose the chemicals that you bring into your home carefully, and maintain the house sensibly, your body will probably have enough cellular energy in reserve to fight the alien chemicals and radiation you can't avoid."[24]

If your indoor pollution level or your degree of sensitivity warrant it, you can significantly improve your indoor atmosphere by revamping your ventilation system and changing interior finishes. If you plan to build a new home or other structure, designing and building for healthful indoor ecology will allow you to breathe easily. Whether as a preventive measure, or in response to an existing environmental sensitivity, you can create a milieu in which your system is not assaulted, where your body can process toxic substances it may have assimilated—where you can refresh and recharge yourself.

Builders find that "ecological construction" has much in common with solid, sensible, good-quality building. Many of the materials incorporated were in common use before the advent of synthetic building products. Your choice of materials should reflect your own chemical sensitivities, allergies, and personal tastes, as well as your climate, budget, and other design considerations. No one material or design is universally correct; as with all good design, the key is responsiveness to given conditions.

SITE SELECTION

Many people with environmental sensitivities find that the best solution to their problems is to move to a new location.

Whether you want to create a new home, health center, or place of business, if you take health into consideration when selecting a site, you will be way ahead in providing healthful indoor air.

Evaluating a site includes everything from looking at the soil to assessing the surroundings within a ten-mile radius. Your economic circumstances, health status, and lifestyle will help you pinpoint one or more general areas where you would like to be. The next step is to learn about local weather patterns, including temperature extremes, humidity, and wind directions. Topography may also affect air movement and dissipation of potential airborne hazards. Find out about nearby land uses and pollution sources: agriculture (especially herbicide and pesticide use), forestry, industry, railroads, airports, traffic arteries, refuse disposal sites, power plants, sewage disposal facilities, and toxic waste dumps. Armed with this information, seek out a site on high ground upwind of air pollution sources. Locate your building out of the line of sight of any major power lines and microwave or broadcast towers. Avoid areas with atmospheric inversions. An ideal location is on the shore of a large, clean body of water where onshore breezes provide uncontaminated air.

DESIGN

If you are creating or remodeling a building, the next step is design. Good layout and orientation are as important as material choice in determining the livability and workability of a place. You need to look at your values, lifestyle, activities, and sensitivities, and work with givens such as solar orientation, site slope, and prevailing winds, to arrive at a healthy "fit".

In designing for indoor air quality, a basic principle in the home or the workplace is to isolate and ventilate pollution-producing equipment. A detached garage will keep exhaust fumes away from the indoors. If a furnace is necessary, it can be placed in a vented room accessible only from outdoors. Office equipment, laundry machines, and cleaning and gardening chemical storage can all be confined to spaces sealed to the indoors and vented to the outdoors. Basements are best avoided, as they tend to encourage mold growth.

Building ecologically requires guessing in advance what you want to do in your home. Once you know what you want to do, it is pretty easy to design something that will let you do it—*without adversely affecting your health*.[25]

VENTILATION

As we saw in the summary of the major pollutants, ventilation is a primary line of defense. For relatively low pollutant levels, well-designed ventilation may be the only measure needed. People with environmental sensitivities often find that ventilation at the source of the contaminant allows them to engage in activities that were previously harmful to them.

In tight construction, ventilation may be needed to compensate for the low rate of air exchange with the outdoors. Older buildings receive a complete exchange of fresh outdoor air for indoor air at rates of 1.5 to 3 air changes per hour due to infiltration via cracks around doors, windows, chimneys, and electrical and plumbing passageways. Newer buildings have as few as .2 to .5 air changes per hour. In light of findings about indoor air pollution, 1 to 1.5 air changes per hour are now recommended.

But tight buildings are designed to cut down on fuel bills. Do we have to choose between health and energy conservation? Not with the advent of the heat exchanger, also known as a "heat recovery ventilator" (HRV). In an HRV, thermally conditioned air on its way out of the building passes through thin-walled tubes of metal or paper that interfinger with incoming-air tubes. The desired heat can thus be transferred from the exhaust air to the fresh incoming air, recovering some of the investment made in heating it. The thermal exchange is not total, but HRVs can recover 60% to 85% of the heat from exhaust air,[26] while constantly diluting contaminants in the indoor air. Heat exchangers are most effective where air exchange rates are lowest, gaseous pollutant levels are highest, and the difference between indoor and outdoor temperature is greatest.

An HRV system should be professionally designed and installed to ensure proper equipment selection, sizing, and layout.

Whatever form of ventilation you use, venting a pollutant at its source can reduce the overall ventilation rate required and can make a wider range of activities available to the chemically sensitive. Stove hood vents and fireplace chimneys are typical examples of source ventilation, but indoor health researcher Bruce Small has taken the principle even further. He has designed ways of fully surrounding and venting pollution-causing items in the home, making their use more tolerable. For example, a person who is sensitive to the trace odors of plastic electronic chips and capacitors and burning dust that rise from the back of a television set can enclose that television in a cabinet that has a glass door and a vent or duct to the outside. Hobby and workshop materials, as well as work clothes, can be kept in a vented closet. Cooking appliances can be grouped along one wall for easier venting.

Some basic rules apply to any ventilation system. Be sure that all combustion appliances (furnace, water heater) have their own air supply and exhaust outlet. Locate air intakes carefully to avoid drawing in exhaust air from your own building, other buildings, or passing automobiles. Guard against insulation or other fibrous materials entering a duct system and being combined with indoor air.

FILTRATION

Filtration can increase the effectiveness of any ventilation system. Incoming air can be filtered to remove pollen and other particles. Recirculated air can be cleansed of certain pollutants as it passes through filters. However, if filters are not cleaned or replaced at appropriate intervals, they can harbor bacteria and reintroduce pollutants to the air, creating more problems than they solve.

You might use only one of the variety of filters available, or you might use several in series. Physical or mechanical filtration involves fibrous filters and removes particles such as dust and pollen from the air; the larger particles are most effectively removed. Activated carbon and other chemical filters remove many organic vapors and some inorganic ones, including ozone, carbon monoxide, and nitrogen dioxide; some carbon filters are specially impregnated to remove formaldehyde from the air. Electrostatic filters remove dust, pollen, and smaller particles from the air; "passive" electrostatic filters are preferable to other types, which can generate ozone. Sensitive people should investigate any filter for components that may produce reactions.

Filtration systems should always be designed to handle effectively the types and volume of pollutants that you wish to remove from your indoor air.

BUILDING MATERIALS

Of course, the fewer pollutants you introduce indoors, the less ventilation and filtration you will need. Mary Oetzel, a low-toxic building materials consultant, says that for the general public, "If we can reduce the chemical load in a house by maybe 50% to 60%, we're doing a good job;" for the highly sensitive she recommends reducing the load by 80% or 95%.[27] Whether you are modifying an existing building, constructing a new building, or searching for a building to inhabit, knowledge about non-toxic building materials can help you avoid costly mistakes.

Designer-builder Paul Bierman-Lytle says,

> "We know that natural, healthy products do more than make you feel good, they actually enhance your living and working spaces, improve your productivity, and calm and refresh your spirit."[28]

STRUCTURE

If you are building a new room or a new building, choose structural materials to fit your sensitivities. Many people appear unaffected by standard wood framing, but if you are sensitive to softwood outgassing or mold (which can thrive on wood), you may prefer to investigate other materials. As an inert material, steel framing is the first choice of some sensitive people. Since the steel members arrive coated with petroleum products, they should be washed before being assembled. Concrete and masonry (concrete block, brick, stone) can be "safe" materials if they do not emit radon, if the concrete mix doesn't include toxic additives, and if mold growth is avoided. Other earth materials such as adobe, rammed earth, and clay are well received by many environmentally sensitive people and have a warmer feeling than does concrete.

INSULATION

Fiberglass batts are the most universally acceptable form of insulation. The foil-backed type is generally safe, but the kraft-paper-backed type is not recommended because its asphalt adhesive outgasses and could be harmful to people with petroleum product sensitivity. Batts are available without backing, but a vapor barrier is necessary to avoid mold growth or moisture condensation in the walls. The common type used is polyethylene sheeting; a person sensitive to polyethylene outgassing from behind the wall material might prefer a metal foil vapor barrier.

Blown-in fiberglass or rock wool is often used to insulate existing buildings. Their main drawback is that they introduce particles into the air. Residents are advised to stay out of a building for the day or two while the insulation is being blown in, and then to give special care to ventilation and cleaning to remove particles that settle.

Vermiculite and perlite are only advised for use in masonry cavities that are permanently sealed. Otherwise, breathing their finer particles can cause the lung disease "silicosis."[29]

Rigid polystyrene (styrofoam) and polyurethane release toxic fumes when burned and should therefore only be used on the exterior of masonry walls, if at all.

Blown-in cellulose insulation is made from old newspapers impregnated with fire-retardant chemicals. Anyone allergic to newsprint or ink fumes should avoid it. The dust and chemicals make it undesirable for others. Chronic coughs, headaches, runny noses, and other unpleasant symptoms have been reported by people who use blown-in cellulose insulation.

Urea-formaldehyde foam insulation has already been discussed; avoid it in existing buildings, and don't use it in new ones.

FLOORS

The ideal floor material generates no gasses or airborne particles, needs no wax or other toxic finishes, is easily cleaned of dust, and holds little or no electrical charge.

Concrete provides the most inert floor material—again, if not radon-emitting. It can be colored and textured or patterned while wet to resemble tile or stone. Since concrete is porous, it needs to be sealed. A sealer should be chosen carefully to avoid adding harmful chemicals to the air. Concrete floors and radiant heating tubes make a good team. When using a radiant heated slab, it is best to avoid floor coverings, especially if they are glued down; the heat can volatilize the adhesive and the floor covering, producing fumes for years.

Soil-cement floors have a warmer "feel" than concrete and are not as hard. They, too, can be pressed to simulate tile and can be paired with radiant heating.

Another low-toxic floor material is hardwood nailed to an acceptable subfloor (such as tongue-and-groove pine decking or exterior-grade plywood). Hardwood also requires a finish, which should be selected carefully. Dadd recommends shellac as the most natural wood finish; its main disadvantages are a long drying period and clean-up with alcohol. Polyurethane can be appropriate because it outgasses quickly and doesn't require waxing. It should, however, be applied in warm weather with good ventilation; residents are advised to go on vacation while polyurethane is being applied. Another solution is to buy pre-finished wood flooring if sensitivities allow. (See Resources for sources of other low-toxicity wood finishes).

Nonporous ceramic tile is often recommended for "clean" floors and walls, but some basic principles must be observed to avoid introducing problems. It is best to apply tile on concrete or masonry surfaces. Tile should be set in a thick mortar bed; "thin-set" tile is applied with adhesives that may be harmful. Avoid offensive chemicals in the mortar or grout, such as epoxies, furans, and organic mastics. The grout joints between tiles are notorious for mold growth. This can be discouraged by keeping joints narrow, using larger tiles to make joints less frequent, leaving the grout flush with the surface of the tile rather than concave, and keeping the area as dry as possible. Grout can be sealed with water glass (sodium silicate) or beeswax.

Terrazzo, a material made of stone chips in a cement base and then polished, is preferred by many people. It can either be poured and polished in place or purchased in precast units. It requires sealing and waxing, and so shouldn't be used by people sensitive to such products.

Wall-to-wall carpeting is generally not recommended. It generates dust and vapors, traps house dust which is stirred up by walking on it, harbors mold if damp, is often delivered permeated with insecticides, and can generate a static charge when walked on. When adhesives and/or rubberoid paddings are used in carpet installation, they create additional hazards by outgassing. Area rugs that can be removed for cleaning (without toxic chemicals!)— especially washable cotton throw rugs—are highly preferred.

WALLS

Gypsum plaster is the material of choice for covering interior walls. It can be trowelled over a plaster board lath, and dries to a hard, white, chemically stable surface. It can be the final wall surface as is. If plain white walls are undesirable, tints can be added to the wet plaster before application.

Hardwood paneling (birch, oak, walnut, ash, hickory, maple, beech, cherry, or teak) is not universally recommended, but it can be an excellent wall finish for someone not sensitive to hardwoods. The wood should be nailed, not glued, to the wall.

Brick, tile, stone, and stucco are excellent wall materials for many people. Similar care should be taken when installing brick or stone as when setting tile.

Standard gypsum wallboard is acceptable to many people, but some react to the paper binder on some brands of wallboard. The compound typically used for sealing joints between the boards contains hazardous chemicals, but it can be replaced with trowelled plaster. The biggest drawback to gypsum board is that it needs to be painted or wallpapered.

Paints come in a range of toxicities. Several companies now market "natural" paints. Alkyd-base paints seem to be the best tolerated and are available in an "odorless" version. Casein paints rarely pose a problem in themselves, but their milk base makes them susceptible to mold growth in damp areas. Latex paints are not recommended; their odor persists for many months, and their fumes can perpetuate illnesses. Epoxy paints are durable, but their long drying time makes them inconvenient to use (an epoxy-painted surface should be aged for three to six months). Some paints contain fungicides that may be intolerable to sensitive people.

Before using a particular paint, you can test it for tolerability. One method is to coat a piece of wood with the paint to be tested; when it is thoroughly dry, place it inside your pillowcase, on top of the pillow, where your nostrils will be exposed to it. After a night of sleeping with the paint, you'll know whether you can live with it. Another method is to place a small quantity of paint (or any other substance you wish to test) in a glass jar and leave it in the sunlight for several hours. Then open the jar, sniff the contents, and observe your reactions.

Wallpaper is not recommended. The paper itself outgasses inks and paints and may contribute cellulose particles to the air. Wallpaper paste typically contains harmful chemicals; homemade pastes may encourage mold growth.

Other potentially harmful wall materials are pressed wood panels, cork bound with petrochemicals, and vinyl sheets or tiles. Vinyl is inappropriate both because of its own outgassing and because of the noxious adhesives used in applying it.

THE OASIS

Environmentally sensitive people who live or work with others or in areas that receive mild contamination will benefit from establishing one room as an "oasis" for themselves. At home, it might be a bedroom or study. At work, it could be a private office. Seal off the oasis from other areas, and scrupulously examine and test every item or material installed in the room. Filter incoming air meticulously. The object is to create one place—a haven—where the sensitive person can retreat regularly from the constant irritants outside, allowing the body to relax, process toxic substances, and recharge itself without threats. A person thus recharged is often able to function normally in the "outside" world. In fact, sometimes it is efficient to construct or remodel a single-room oasis, rather than remodel or construct a whole building. An oasis might also be the first step for someone planning a new building; it serves as a testing ground for appropriate materials and appliances.

RESOURCES

GENERAL INDOOR AIR POLLUTION

Indoor Air Quality Handbook for Designers, Builders, and Users of Energy-Efficient Residences, Sandia Report SAND82-1773, September, 1982. Available from: National Technical Information Service, U.S. Department of Commerce, 5285 Port Royal Road, Springfield, VA 22161.

Your Home, Your Health, and Well-Being, by David Rousseau; Ten Speed Press, 1988.

Special Report: Air Filters by Debra Lynn Dadd. Available from: Everything Natural, P. O. Box 390, Inverness, CA 94937.

U.S. Consumer Products Safety Commission (CPSC), (800) 638-2772.

Call your regional Environmental Protection Agency (EPA) office and ask for the Air Toxics Section.

ASBESTOS

Asbestos in the Home, published by the CPSC and EPA, from: Superintendent of Documents, U.S. Government Printing Office, Washington, D.C. 20402; (202) 783-3238.

FORMALDEHYDE

Formaldehyde: Everything You Wanted to Know But Were Afraid to Ask, from Consumer Federation of America, 1424 16th St., NW, Washington, DC 20036 (send SASE).

Indoor Air Quality Notes; No. 1: Formaldehyde—Our Homes and Health; No. 2: Residential Formaldehyde Control, from Indoor Air Quality Research Laboratory, Ball State University, Muncie, IN 47306 (send SASE for each issue).

The Consumer Product Safety Commission, at (800) 638-2772, has a list of labs that will sell you testing kits; some state health departments will test your building at no cost to you.

RADON

A Citizen's Guide to Radon: What it is and What to do About it, and Radon Reduction Methods: A Homeowner's Guide, from your regional EPA office.

"Radon in Water and Air" and "Removing Radon From Water," from the Department of Civil Engineering, University of Maine, Orono, ME 04469.

For a current list of companies qualified to measure radon levels, contact your regional EPA office or state health department.

Air Pollution in Your Home, from your local American Lung Association.

WATER

1987 Buyers' Guide to Water Purification Devices by Debra Lynn Dadd. Available from Everything Natural, P. O. Box 390, Inverness, CA 94937.

"Water," by Michael D. Spence, in *Environ* No. 6.

NOTES

1. Peter Fossel, "Sick-Home Blues," *Harrowsmith*, Sept./Oct., 1987, p. 49.

2. *Ibid.*

3. Debra Lynn Dadd, "Basic Toxicology," *Everything Natural*, January/February, 1987, p. 17.

4. Zamm, *Why Your House May Endanger Your Health*, p. 11.

5. Suzanne Randegger, 'Q & A Dept.," *Environ*, Summer, 1988, p. 23.

6. Suzanne and Ed Randegger, "A Real Rocky Mountain High?" *Environ*, Fall/Winter, 1986-87, p.23.

7. Suzanne and Ed Randegger, "Formaldehyde and Health," *Environ*, Fall-Winter, 1986-87, p. 6.

8. "Outgassing" is the gradual release of gasses from a substance.

9. Zamm, p. 23.

10. Joseph T. Morgan, M.D., letter to the editor, *East West*, July, 1987.

11. Zamm, p. 23.

12. Debra Lynn Dadd, *The Nontoxic Home* (Los Angeles: Jeremy P. Tarcher, Inc., 1986), p. 173.

13. "EPA Finds Radon a Widespread Health Threat," *Chemical & Engineering News,* August 10,1987, p. 18.

14. Lois Ember, "EPA Compiling Data on Extent of Indoor Radon Hazard," *Chemical & Engineering News*, August 17, 1987, p. 22.

15. Lynne Lohmeier, Ph.D., "Indoor Pollution Alert," *East West*, March, 1987, p. 45.

16. LaFavore, Michael, "The Radon Report," *Rodale's New Shelter*, January, 1986, p. 31.

17. California Department of Consumer Affairs, p. ES9.

18. I*bid.*

19. Fanger, p. 196.

20. "Electricity, Conduction of," *Encyclopedia Britannica,* Volume 8 (Chicago: William Benton, Publisher, 1965), p. 202.

21. Albert P. Krueger and Sheelah Sigel, "Ions in the Air," *Human Nature*, July, 1978, pp. 46, 48.

22. Krueger, p. 52.

23. Julian B. Andelman, "Inhalation Exposure in the Home to Volatile Organic Contaminants of Drinking Water," *The Science of the Total Environment* Amsterdam: Elsevier Science Publishers B.V., 1985), pp. 443-460.

24. Zamm, p. 104.

25. Bruce M. Small, "Creating Your Own Safe Environment," *Environ*, Fall, 1985, p. 6.

26. Suzanne and Ed Randegger, "HRVs Help Reduce Home Pollution," *Environ,* Fall/Winter, 1986-87, p. 19.

27. Debra Lynn Dadd, "Less-Toxic Building Materials, An Interview With Mary Oetzel," *Everything Natural,* September/October, 1986, p. 16.

28. Debra Lynn Dadd, "The All-Natural House, An Interview With Paul Bierman-Lytle," *Everything Natural*, September/October, 1986, p. 13.

29. Zamm, p. 149.

Chapter 21

Villages Around the World

From REBUILDING COMMUNITY IN AMERICA:
HOUSING FOR ECOLOGICAL LIVING
PERSONAL EMPOWERMENT, AND THE NEW EXTENDED FAMILY
by Ken Norwood, AICP and Kathleen Smith
Shared Living Resource Center

Throughout most of history, community has been the normal pattern, with people living in large extended families and tribal networks. Even today, much of the world still lives in these kinds of villages. Santorini is just one example. There are countless others—Neve Shalom/Wahat al-Salam, Breuberg, Kamikuri, and the list goes on.

The Village Cluster and other Shared Living Community models are derived from years of investigation into humankind's rich collective history of village and community culture.

Both authors have visited and researched historic and present day villages of cultures throughout the world in order to better understand the relationships between physical environment, social organization, and community. Here we will look at two examples: Ziuma's compound, an extended family village which is part of the larger village of Poa in Burkina Faso, and the historic Native American village of Pueblo Bonito located in what is now northwest New Mexico.

ZIUMA'S COMPOUND

Because of its remote location, Poa is one of the few villages of the Lela people that shows little Western urban influence. Ziuma's extended family compound is one of 10 that make up Zyilliwele, a quarter of Poa.[1] The compounds, each surrounded by cultivated farmland, are 150 to 300 m apart and 30 to 200 m from the main village path. The surrounding farmland, an obscured entrance path, the senior man's shelter, and the solid, undulating walls and heavy wooden gate of the compound all work to create a distinct transition and protective zone between the compound and the larger community.

Once through the compound gate, a visitor enters the main common court or keleu which houses a maze of adobe granaries, a well, several living units, and large open areas. This space serves simultaneously as a circulation, transition, and gathering space. The keleu is encircled by a ring of private living suites inhabited by either an individual or a family group. These private living areas vary in size from three to seven rooms and consist of the kono, a packed earth court; the nachobo, a bathing enclosure; the tutuini, the indoor living area; the zoni and djena or cooking areas; and the djipu, a locked storage area. The kono has one entrance and is the focus of most community life. It is the place where daily chores and rituals are performed, cooking is done, children play, and families talk into the night. The kono, like all spaces except the indoor cooking areas, facilitates a variety of activities depending on the season, the time of day, and the mood of the resident. For example, during the hot season, the kono is also used for sleeping.

Each living unit is private, and is arranged and occupied in a definite order that spatially reflects the social organization and values of the extended family. The senior men and women, for example, are give prominent positions facing the main compound gate. Each unit, including those belonging to the latter, is integrally connected to the others through form and function. From each kono one can see into the keleu, offering all a sense of cohesion and safety. Because some tools such as grinding stones and special cooking pots are shared by adjacent dwellings, a small adobe platform is built that interrupts the surrounding walls and allows access from one private court to the next. In this way, "The architecture reveals at the same time the inhabitants' close dependence and self-sufficiency."[2]

Both men and women take part in building and maintaining the compound. Women carry water and earth which the men knead into clay balls with their feet. The balls are then stacked and molded to form circular walls which intersect with surrounding walls to form a rigid honeycomb structure that effectively dilutes external forces. The women then coat the walls with a locust-bean pod varnish and an adobe-cow dung mixture on which patterns and designs are imprinted. This process serves a dual purpose. It allows individuals to personalize and identify their space, and it waterproofs the dwellings by creating channels in the adobe which break up the flow of rain and allow the adobe to dry more quickly, adding to its strength and durability. This integration of structure, form, and function reflects the intimate unity and interrelationship of the inhabitants to each other and their environment.

Pueblo Bonito, the apparent capital of Chaco Canyon (a region of the Anasazi people), offers another example of how the built environment can both reflect the values of the people and support their social structure and way of life.

Between 1100 and 1300 AD, when their culture was at its height, the Anasazi populated vast areas of what is now northwest New Mexico. Pueblo Bonito is regarded as the "signature masterpiece" of their culture. It is the largest "Great House," a single building which is really more like a city or village, covering nearly three acres and containing 800 rooms, 37 small kivas (circular structures used for gathering), numerous towers, terraces, and a large divided plaza with two great kivas.

The Anasazi seemed to have mysteriously vanished or migrated to some unknown place around 1300 AD. Therefore, we cannot know them from their language, literature, or customs, only from the architecture that remains. We can tell a lot from examining the design, location, and materials used in Pueblo Bonito. We can tell, for example, that they were a resilient and adaptive people with a highly organized community support structure. They must have been to have flourished in such a dry and desolate area if that was actually the climate during their existence The layout of this Great House, as a compact village, along with the complex systems of dams, irrigation canals, roads, and communication relays (fire beacons) that linked the more than 400 sites in the area provide further evidence of the sophistication of their large-scale cooperation and social interaction.

The design of Pueblo Bonito also shows a deep understanding, connection, and celebration of nature and their place in it. The Anasazi used materials native to the area— stone and earth— to create thick walls which soaked up solar heat during the day and radiated it into the rooms at night. The whole complex is oriented to the south, opening to the sun. The high stone wall and cliff to the north provide shelter from the wind and create a solar backdrop during the winter. Abundant roof terraces and plazas, as well as cooking artifacts found there, suggest that they worked communally and socialized outside during the warmer months and inside during the cooler months. The cooler, darker innermost rooms were used for storing and processing corn, squash, and other produce. Complex and varied patterns in the rock and adobe plaster walls suggest both a high level of craftsmanship and a personalization of space.

The circular structures are kivas, which were used for sacred and social occasions. Some believe the kivas represented the existence of a clan form of social organization, with larger kin groups or neighborhoods sharing suites of rooms each with their own kiva or meeting room. The great kivas in the main plaza were thought to be the central gathering places for the whole community.

All we really know about these people is what the architecture tells us— that they were a vibrant people, with a deep understanding of natural cycles, place, order, and community. In Pueblo Bonito, as in Ziuma's compound, the organization of the private dwellings, kivas, and open spaces in an interconnected, hierarchical pattern reflects the inhabitants' desire to balance privacy and community for a supportive and sustainable way of life.

VILLAGE LIFE TODAY

By studying examples from other cultures, we can gain insight into ways of living, interacting, and building that are more socially and environmentally responsible than the methods employed in our society today. We can incorporate into our own society elements from these cultures that seem appropriate to our culture, values, and aspirations. The models of Shared Living Communities presented throughout this book are all variations on the common theme of the village. Very few Americans live in villages today, yet villages still have a powerful pull on our collective imagination regarding "the good life."

What comes to mind when you think of a village? A compelling vision is offered by a visit to Woodstock, New York. A tall, white New England church spire directs you to the triangular-shaped town square, complete with benches, a statue, and a common green that is bustling with activity. The quaint gable-roofed shops and cafes that line both sides of the streets leading away from the village center are filled with local residents, tourists, and city dwellers visiting their country houses. People casually wander from shop to shop, buying groceries, tasting sample treats, and greeting friends and neighbors at every turn. The ambiance is festive. Even store clerks, tellers, and street cleaners find time to watch the children and dogs frolicking in the winter's first snow. Despite the tourist-supported economy and the hordes of cars crowding the streets, Woodstock, like Nevada City, California, Yellow Spring, Ohio, Savannah, Georgia, and other architecturally preserved villages, is as genuine a living village as can be found today in America..

Village communities were once an integral part of our American way of life. Numerous cities throughout the U.S. began as small villages, but as industry and commerce prospered, many were overwhelmed by growth and overrun by the car. Others have simply died out. Remnants of our village community heritage, such as town squares and meeting halls, still persist in some areas, but most of the socioeconomic, cultural, architectural, and environmental character of the original villages has been lost, along with interaction and cooperation between people.

Elsewhere in the world, and hidden away in the U.S., are villages that industrialism and modernization have passed by. In these, the basic elements of a sustainable system of village life continue. In other traditional villages, however, life is not so ideal. We do not want to romanticize all traditional village life. As Robert Gilman explains:

> "While it is true that there is much to be learned from these [traditional] villages,...few people today—including most traditional villagers!—would describe these villages as either full-featured or supportive of healthy development. The work is hard, life expectancy is short, opportunities for personal development and education are few (almost non-existent for women), and the diversity of livelihoods is small..... In addition, the harmony between these villages and the natural environment has often depended on low population densities—a luxury we no longer have."[4]

These problems are not due to the failure of the village way of life, but to overpopulation, oppressive control, and the depletion of natural resources—byproducts of the industrial world, our world.

The Village Acre and the other Shared Living Community models do not represent a return to the past or to arduous methods of production and living. Instead, these new community forms are modern-day villages that draw on the best of the village heritage of cooperation and social, cultural, and resource sustainability. Wood or coal fires for cooking, hand-carried or pumped water, cesspools, uninsulated walls, and other undesirable artifacts of low-tech lifestyles are fortunately gone. Today, we have the environmental design and the social skills and the natural energy technology to create comfortable, attractive, and ecologically sustainable community housing that can combine telecommunications, supportive interrelationships, and self-reliant simple living in one place. We must make the effort to create more of such housing. As Carla Cole, writing in *In Context,* says:

"We all share a common destiny, and traditional villages have much to teach us— from their deeply rooted understanding of community to their tenacity in the face of adversity. By taking the best from what are now called the First and Third Worlds, we have the potential for developing a world in which these sad distinctions no longer apply."[5]

The objective in examining, both historically and conceptually, the extended family village approach to community living is to observe, understand, and improve upon those forms of community organization and habitat design that enable groups of people to cooperatively live in ecologically responsible and socially enriching ways. The new community examples we present serve as valuable educational tools for helping Americans learn how to share long-term responsibilities and resources on a day-to-day level.

These new forms of housing have the potential to instill in people a new sense of what ecological living and personal empowerment can mean. It is useless to criticize single-family houses without providing attractive alternatives. We have to show people how they can satisfy their quality-of-life needs in a co-owned cluster community. The benefits must include an increased sense of privacy, security, belonging, and self-esteem, and cost savings qualities that are needed to attract the fragmented income, ethnic, and cultural groups of our society.

REAL LIFE VILLAGE COMMUNITIES TODAY
— A CULTURAL METAMORPHOSIS

The rising groundswell of interest in participatory community building that has recently re-emerged is telling evidence that many Americans are ready for a new approach to living. The "Village Cluster" model, like CoHousing, seeks to bring the social, ecological, and economic benefits of extended family village life to the largest possible number of people in the United States. The Danish-originated CoHousing model, although new in this country, is rapidly gaining acceptance and leading the way in an extended family "village renaissance." There are already seven completed CoHousing communities in California, Washington, Colorado, and New Mexico, with over 100 more being planned throughout the United States. In Denmark and other Scandinavian countries, 150 or more Village Clusters in addition to other cooperative communities exist today. Underlying this new community, movement are the more than 350 successful and well- established Intentional Communities in this country, and the estimated several thousand housing cooperatives, Urban Cooperative Blocks, group households, nonprofit sponsored Group

Homes, and other resident controlled rental housing— all people-participation based ways of living.

A combination of high housing prices, socioeconomic decline, people willing to experiment with new ideas, and the availability of for-profit developers, nonprofit sponsors, and community facilitation resources are making this form of housing increasingly popular and accessible. Below we review several CoHousing communities that have recently been completed, examining both their form and social composition, as well as their methods of development and management

MUIR COMMONS COHOUSING, DAVIS, CA

Muir Commons was the first CoHousing community to be built entirely new in the United States. Its birth followed the popular reception of the book, *CoHousing,* by McCamant and Durrett. The community members moved in starting in August of 1991. Unlike the buyers of typical developer housing, most of the 45 adults (mostly in their 30's and 40's) and 25 children were not strangers. For almost three years they had been learning about each other and community life at learning core group meetings in which they co-organized and co-designed the community.

The development process began in 1988 with a core group inspired by a slide show given by McCamant and Durrett. Also at this event was Virginia Thigpen, a developer with West Davis Associates who had previously visited several Village Clusters in Denmark. She met with the core group several times and eventually offered them a three acre site in the Aspen housing development she was working on. For Virginia, this was a way to fulfill the City of Davis planning commission's affordable housing requirement and develop a form of housing she felt was needed in our society. For the core group, this meant they had the land, technical resources, and financial backing to turn their dream into reality. The only catch was, they did not have independent control of the project. They nevertheless were able to work successfully with the developer and the developer's architect to design the community. The architect was open to the input and needs of the core group, but because he was not versed in the participatory community design process, there were some conflicts. To ameliorate some of the problems, the core group hired McCamant and Durrett to help them more specifically define what they wanted and needed in the design of the common house and the individual units. Having a clear and unified program, the core group could then better express their needs and negotiate with the developer and architect. After countless hours of meetings, negotiations, and problem solving, the group of single— and two parent families and single adults had a new kind of home—a community.

Muir Commons follows the basic Village Cluster/CoHousing using precepts described later in this chapter. The 26 housing units are smaller in floor area than in typical housing developments. They contain two to three bedrooms, one bathroom (usually), a small living space, and a small kitchen. The common house, a large and beautiful 3,670 sq. ft. structure, is embellished with a well- designed commercial kitchen and food pantry, large dining room, cozy sitting room with a fireplace, laundry room, teen room, children's room, craft room, exercise room, and guest room/study. Outside is a recycling and refuse storage area, a tot lot, a covered patio, and a bicycle parking area.

The common house was intended to be— and is— the heart of the community. Its frequent use has as much to do with the attractive amenities as with the members' commitment to shared evening meals five times per week.

The cooking and cleanup teams operate on a rotating schedule, each working no more than half a day per month. In exchange, they enjoy, without lifting a finger, approximately 20 delicious and nutritious meals per month, each costing approximately $1.50.

From the beginning the group felt it was important to their sense of ownership and community that they, as a group, participate not only in the design, but the building of the community. Due to safety and liability issues, it was not possible for them to work on the construction of the, units. Instead, they took responsibility for all the landscaping work. Because the group volunteered their labor, all of the $50,000 allocated for landscaping went to plants, tools, and other landscaping materials. The site looked rather bare and row-house like in the raw dirt days prior to completion. But now, vegetable gardens and a fruit orchard, flourish and flower gardens, trees, and native plants, along with personalized front porches, sitting courts, and children's play areas, line the intimate pedestrian path that runs east-west through the middle of the clustered units. The feeling is friendly as children play and adults gather to talk and relax. Community members feel proud of their home, because they worked together to create it.

Recently the community has had another opportunity to strengthen their sense of ownership and personal and group empowerment by building a much needed 500 sq. ft. workshop (located on the west end of the north parking lot). The workshop is basically a glorified barn, housing a woodshop, a one-car repair shop, storage space, all the co-owned gardening and building tools, and two covered areas for bikes. The workshop was supposed to be built at the same time as the community. But in the last moments of the final development phase, the developer eliminated it due to financial constraints. In an ordinary single-family house or condo development that would have been the end of the story, but as a co-owned and self-managed community, the members were able to develop a capital fund and obtain a building permit for the workshop. They hired contractors to build the main structure, but did everything else themselves, including painting, wiring, and installing finishes and wallboard.

It is important to remember that what the people of Muir Commons have developed in the way of social bonding, a sense of belonging, cooperative management, support for family and children, and ecological living has not been the result of any dramatic philosophic or ideological fervor. Rather, the core group came together around the simple realization that it was all right to express their need for alternatives to over-priced conventional housing, a rat-race competition for personal and family time, and the lack of meaning in modern life. Now, in their third year, the Muir Commons group has established new meanings for family, community, neighborhood, and sharing. Festive rituals such as monthly birthday parties in the common house are only the beginning.

WINSLOW COHOUSING GROUP, BAINBRIDGE ISLAND, WA

The Winslow CoHousing group was initiated by Chris Hansen who read *CoHousing* in December 1988, started putting up flyers, and organized the first meeting in February 1989. The community is the second entirely new CoHousing project to be completed in the U.S., and the first to be designed and developed by the community members serving as their own developer. The process was intense and exhausting, with over two years of initial planning and designing, eight months of construction, 4,000+ hours of meetings, and about 140 different people involved at some point in the process. But in early 1992, when the first families began moving in, Winslow CoHousing became a reality. Now, 75 people ranging in age from 5 months to 70 years, with most in their late 30's to early 50's (Baby Boomers), live in the 30-unit community.

The community is located on a five-acre wooded site, half of which has been preserved as open space. Three landscaped pedestrian paths lined with living units radiate toward the centrally located common house. The 5,000 sq. ft. common house contains a dining room, commercial quality kitchen, meeting space, childcare and children's activity rooms, a teen space, recreation room, laundry room, and storage space. Outside, there is also a guest house, recycling center, bike shed, gardens, and a fruit tree orchard— the hallmarks of the new village community movement. A multipurpose barn/workshop is being planned.

From the beginning, the group wanted to reduce car trips and car ownership. Therefore, they got a special waiver from the city to build a smaller than code parking lot. They also purposely chose a site on Bainbridge Island within walking distance of the Winslow ferry port for commuters to Seattle, and near neighborhood stores, a post office, library, and schools. Subsequently, some people have sold their cars and now share vehicles with their neighbors.

There are two types of private units: townhouses and flats. The 24 townhouse units range in size from one to four bedrooms. All are self-sufficient with a living room, dining room and kitchen downstairs, and bedrooms upstairs. A large building called the Carriage House contains six additional units— three upstairs, and three downstairs. The three downstairs units are handicapped— accessible to accommodate disabled persons and other members as they age or their abilities change.

Some of the members, who are mostly business and professional people, previously lived in Intentional Communities or other group living situations. For others it is a radical but welcome change in lifestyle, for all members now enjoy the amenities of the community and the sense of empowerment and security that comes from co-owning and managing their own living environment. The community is organized as a market-rate cooperative corporation. Members buy shares in the cooperative and receive a proprietary lease for a specific unit. For many, this provides the financial clout needed to become a homeowner. As Linda Townsend, a single mother in the community, explained, "It was the first time in my life I felt empowered when it came to a financial institution."[6] She qualified for her home loan based not just on her own financial resources, but on those of the whole group.

Opportunities for participation and empowerment continue with ongoing committees that handle the organization of meal preparation and children's activities, among other things. There are dinners in the common house Sunday through Thursday, as well as special meals on holidays.

One of the most exciting features of this community is the daycare center in the common house. The center is supported by six families. For each daycare shift that a parent works they earn two days of care for their children. This is a real benefit for hardworking parents in a society where only half as much childcare is available as is needed.

There is some owner turnover at Winslow, as has been the case in all the new CoHousing communities. Most is due to job relocation and economics, not fundamental problems with the community. This is not to say that problems don't exist, but as Kim Clark, a resident of Winslow explains, "...we have developed a shared sense of what it takes to get along together. We are all willing to be a little softer, to listen to people, and to reconsider what we want in light of what other people want."[7]

NYLAND COHOUSING COMMUNITY, LAFAYETTE, CO.

The first CoHousing community in Colorado, Nyland, is the largest in the U.S., with 42 units on 43 acres. It was founded in 1988 by architect Ron Ricker, who discussed with several friends the possibilities for environmentally responsible communities and shortly thereafter read the book, *CoHousing.* An initial core group was formed which, operating as a partnership, acquired the property, completed a feasibility study, and wrote a land use plan. After 1-1/2 years, they contracted with a developer to take care of the zoning and financing approval, building permits, engineering, and construction of the project, while the growing core, group worked on designing the community and developing an organizational structure. McCamant and Durrett provided community design workshop services to help develop the overall layout and design. A local facilitator was brought in later to help finalize the design and work out specific organizational details.

Families started moving in August of 1992. As of 1994, there are 120 people, including 35 children ranging in age from 18 months to 18 years. The site layout differs somewhat from other CoHousing models, because it has two separate clusters of units, with most of the parking in a common lot. The 6,500 sq. ft. common house is centrally located and contains a large commercial kitchen, dining room, licensed daycare space, and many other amenities. On site there are also a greenhouse, woodworking shop, recycling center, one-acre vegetable garden (in process), and outdoor recreation facilities including a sand volleyball court, basketball court, and soccer field. The group also plans to build a stable and barn. So far, common meals occur four nights a week. Most members hope to increase the frequency of these events, but at present are too busy with landscaping the site and finishing their own units.

The individual units vary in size and layout, reflecting the diversity within the community. There are two large detached custom houses, six houses with their own garages and driveways, and a mixture of duplexes and triplexes. The units have from two to five bedrooms, and some are set up as shared households. One design includes two master bedroom suites, one on each side of a shared kitchen, dining, and living area. All of the houses are market rate, but people from lower and moderate income levels were accommodated, by including some smaller, lower priced units (starting at $80,000) and some rentals, actually suites of rooms in larger houses that the homeowners rent out to individuals or couples who cannot afford to buy. Methods of creative financing have also been arranged by the community to help some people with their down payments.

The community is located six miles outside of Boulder and enjoys stunning views of the Rocky Mountains. Because of its remoteness the community has taken several steps to reduce car trips. First, they pressured for and got local bus service extended past their front entrance and into adjacent communities. Second, they implemented a bus pass program that allows them to ride on any bus in the Denver/Metro area. The program was designed to create affordable transportation alternatives and encourage public transit use. Several car pools have also formed among those who commute to Denver to work. Other members have started a food cooperative to enable them to buy in bulk at a cheaper price, with less packaging waste and less time spent shopping. It is too soon in this young community's life to know if these provisions and the community structure as a whole can significantly reduce the number of car trips the community generates, but they are starting on the right track.

The most unique aspect of this community is the energy efficiency and environmental health program that the house owners participate in. This program is financed by $100,000 in grants from the Colorado State Office of Energy Conservation and the Environmental Protection Agency. Much of the money so far has been spent on energy-efficient insulation and on testing the health safety of various materials. All of the houses were sited on an east-west axis for optimum solar access from the south, and a few have passive solar greenhouses and solar water heating systems. A key goal of the program is to demonstrate that "you don't need a lot of high-tech stuff to be extremely energy efficient." [8]

THE 2-1/2 ACRE PROTOTYPE VILLAGE CLUSTER COMMUNITY

This prototype, 2-1/2 acre Village Cluster community plan combines in one model all the precepts of village housing and community living. It is designed and organized to be ecologically sustainable by making the best use of both human and natural resources.

314

It is designed for an extended family of 16 to 25 people living on a suburban fringe or urban infill site, but could be modified for larger or smaller groups and other locations, urban or rural. We want to stress the importance of carefully considering the location when designing a Village Cluster/ CoHousing community. As we cautioned in Chapter Three, there is a tendency among some core groups to want to locate in urban fringe or rural areas away from the perceived stress and violence of city life. In doing so, they will also be locating far from transit systems, cultural centers, jobs, and stores, thus increasing their car dependency.

The cooperative nature of the Village Cluster makes car pooling and errand sharing feasible, meaning fewer trips, less wear on cars and public roads, less fuel use, and less pollution. Unless a community is highly self-reliant the benefits of cluster housing alone will not outweigh the environmental consequences of increased energy and car usage from living in the country. The ecological alternative is to locate in the city or suburbs near a bus or rail line and create a social and environmental design that includes elements of country living.

Following is an outline of the basic elements which comprise the Village Cluster model, wherever the location is.

The common courtyard has a multipurpose game court, a mini-amphitheater, vegetable and flower gardens, play areas, paths, benches, sitting areas, outdoor eating tables, a stream, a small pond, and other amenities that can be built or added in phases.

Gardens, orchards, and preserved natural areas are located around the edges of the site, and in the common courtyard. The gardens and orchards provide food for the community and may even be a source of income and livelihood for some members.

All buildings are clustered on the site to leave as much land as possible in its natural state and to create areas for gardens and recreation. Meadows, streams, ponds, native trees and wooded areas, and natural contours are preserved to be enjoyed by the members of the Village Cluster and the broader community. Village Clusters in suburban or even urban settings can appear more rural by providing attractive and natural outdoor areas. The goal is to create usable spaces while preserving the integrity and beauty of the natural world.

The passive solar-heated common house is the focus of the community, and is designed for group cooking, shared meals, food processing, social activities, and guest lodging. It has shared amenities such as a sauna, hot tub, library, child care room, work office, computer/telecommunications center and laundry facilities.

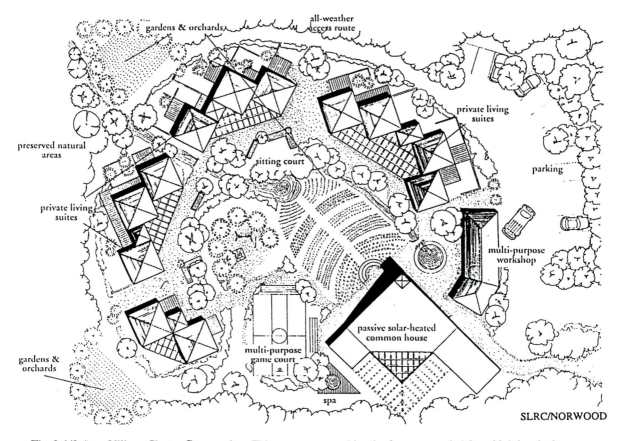

The 2-1/2 Acre Village Cluster Community. This prototype provides the features needed for a high level of self-reliance, natural energy production, low car dependency, a paradise for children, community-based livelihood, and a sense of belonging.

Maximum solar gain is achieved by orienting the building clusters to the south and designing for passive heating and cooling with greenhouses, sun courts, and skylights. Natural ventilation systems, roof overhangs, and vine arbors control the amount of heat gain inside the buildings, while still providing abundant natural light.

Solar water heating and electric power systems are more cost-effective and efficient with a compact cluster of units around the common house.

The infrastructure needs of the community are reduced by clustering the buildings, centralizing energy distribution systems, and restricting parking to an area near the street entrance. This reduces the number of driveways, roads, and power connections.

A multi-purpose workshop with a tool room, art studios, a telecommunications/computer office, a childcare facility, and general storage is adjacent to the common house. This space serves members' home businesses and community-owned enterprises. The building is separate from the common house both for sound insulation and to allow expansion in phases using self-help construction techniques.

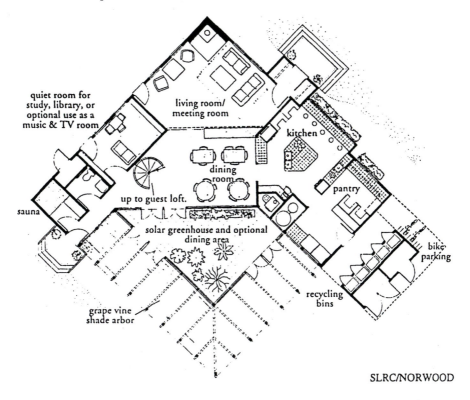

quiet room for
study, library, or
optional use as a
music & TV room

living room/
meeting room

kitchen

dining
room

pantry

up to guest loft.

sauna

solar greenhouse and optional
dining area

bike
parking

recycling
bins

grape vine
shade arbor

SLRC/NORWOOD

Common House for the 2-1/2 Acre Village Cluster. The size of this prototype house is only 2,100 sq. ft., but there are others being built in International Communities from 3,600 to 6,000 sq. ft.

317

Sensitive planting of trees and vegetation reduces the effects of weather extremes. Evergreen trees and dense foliage to the north of the site protect against cold winter winds. Deciduous trees and vine arbors to the south allow solar access during the winter and protect from excessive sun in the summer. Trees and plants also help distinguish spaces, and define pathways, play areas, and gathering spots.

All-weather access routes for delivering supplies to the common house and occasional large items to units are wide enough for trucks. Local codes may mandate, or you may want, emergency access to all the units.

Pathways are ramped and made with a firm but permeable material, such as compacted, decomposed granite instead of asphalt or concrete. This allows easy travel with tote carts, wheeled toys, bicycles, and accessibility for wheelchairs, and allows water to be absorbed and tree roots to breathe. Many a stately oak tree has died from sheltering a paved picnic area or driveway. There are circumstances where impervious surfaces are necessary because of soil conditions or local regulations. Use brick or flat rocks when available.

WHAT MAKES A "VILLAGE CLUSTER" A VILLAGE?

The communities we have just reviewed— Ziuma's compound, Pueblo Bonito, and the various CoHousing developments— provide vivid and compelling images of an alternative way of life. But what is it about these communities that gives them that feeling of intimacy, unity, and calm that we associate with villages? With the 2-1/2 acre Village Cluster prototype, we presented specific elements and design features that define Village Cluster/ CoHousing, but it takes more than these to create a community.

There are several qualities or principles of physical design and social organization that are essential to create and sustain a modern day village community. These principles are universal in nature and can be adapted to serve the needs, values, and ideals of any group. We previously introduced some of the basic principles such as coownership, intergenerational extended family, participatory management, and integration of physical form and social structure. Now, we will examine other related principles necessary to successfully create modern-day, extended family and village communities.

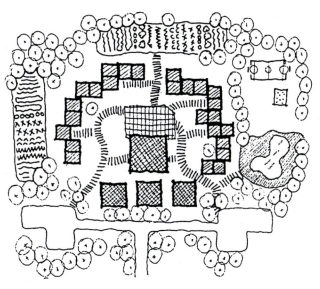

Central Court Plan. This compact layout allows
visual contact among all units.

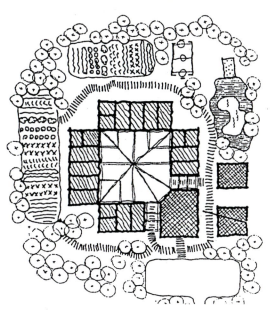

Covered All-Weather Cluster. This can also be
done for a compact village street plan.

SLRC/NORWOOD

Passive Solar Sitting. All buildings face the sun.

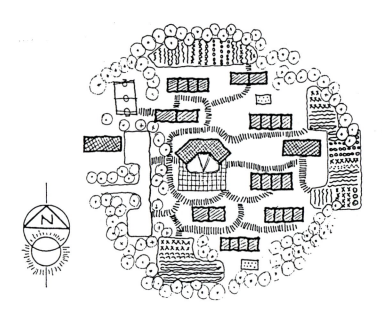

Village Street Plan. This design emphasizes
pedestrian only circulation.

SLRC/NORWOOD

320

A Village Cluster must be small in scale, not so small as to preclude a sense of diversity, space, and freedom, but small enough for all areas to be quickly accessible by foot and visually accessible from a few key areas. The layout should encourage face-to- face interaction, where people are able to know and be known by others in the community, and each person feels that he or she influences the life of the community. Unlike today's cities and suburbs with skyscrapers, seas of parking lots, highways bisecting neighborhoods, and streets with no sidewalks, the Village Cluster is designed for the human, not the car. All components of the village environment— buildings, paths, parks, and vegetation— are scaled to provide visual interest and meaningful experiences for people walking, gathering, or working. Parking on the periphery of the community protects indoor and outdoor living spaces from car noise and visual intrusion. People must walk from their cars through the community to their living unit, instead of driving right into their garage. This encourages personal communication on a daily basis, and reduces the amount of paving, and removes the intrusion of the car.

VILLAGE CLUSTER SITE PLANNING VARIATIONS

These variations of layouts for the Village Cluster model show the diversity of options available to community core groups. Each layout incorporates the basic elements just described, and basic patterns used in traditional villages, while also offering unique characteristics and advantages. Remember, these are just examples.

Each core group can decide for itself which layout works best for them, adapting and embellishing it to meet their group's particular needs and visions. These pedestrian-scale villages can be replicated over and over again with relatively little harm to the environment.

What cannot be replicated ad-infinitum without adverse environmental impact is urban sprawl, and gridiron streets with driveways leading up to every front door.

CONTINUITY, COMPATIBILITY, AND CLOSENESS

Compare the Village Cluster and CoHousing plans to those of Ziuma's compound and Pueblo Bonito, and note the similarity in the overall form and layout. The scale is intimate and pedestrian oriented with a strong sense of closeness and continuity. The designs are compact and well-contained within the site, creating a self-supporting and physically coherent village community with a distinct center, defined boundaries, smaller subcenters of activity, and open areas flowing around the buildings. The line of sight from doorways of living units gives a glimpse of the community.

Clustering buildings is preferred when the goal is to create a social atmosphere that encourages diversity, growth, and sharing. In most housing developments, the houses are spread out with no real connection to one another, alienating residents, especially the young, elderly, and handicapped. In a Village Cluster/CoHousing solution, houses are integrated in a coherent relationship, clustered around pedestrian paths and courts in a manner that provides a sense of enclosure without diminishing the qualities of open space. We have learned from studying historic villages that when the physical environment reflects and supports an interactive cultural and social structure, a sustainable society can be created. We look to the Muir Commons CoHousing in Davis, California as a good model.

Even when a community is built in phases or grows over time, as with some Intentional Communities, a sense of overall continuity is maintained. Similar materials, forms, and building systems are used to tie the dwellings together even if each is personalized by the occupants. In Ziuma's compound, this is done by structurally connecting the units in a honeycomb pattern and then allowing each resident to embellish the walls of their unit with artistic designs. In Muir Commons, the units are designed as row houses with the same roof pitch, outside color, and basic window design, but each unit has front and back areas that the residents can personalize with plants, patios, benches, or artwork. By envisioning the community as a unified entity, people can express themselves, and a sense of security, interdependence, and belonging will likely emerge.

CO-BUILT, CO-OWNED, AND CO-MANAGED

Throughout history, human habitats were not built by outsiders and then sold or rented to the residents. A primary objective in creating Village Cluster communities today is for members to be involved in all phases of development to the greatest extent possible, and for the members to co-own and co-manage the community after it is built.

Even if consultants, architects, lenders, developers, and/or builders are involved in the process, it is the members who are physically, financially, and emotionally invested in and committed to creating a secure and enriching place to live. Being responsible, members feel empowered and in control, leading to a strong sense of belonging and pride. This has been the experience of the Intentional Community, CoHousing, Urban Cooperative Block, and Habitat for Humanity movements.

WORKING WITH WHAT IS GIVEN

Traditional villages rarely use imported labor, materials, or resources to build or operate their community. They work with the materials, resources, and methods of construction that were native to their area and familiar to them and which tend to be more energy efficient, renewable, and ecologically sound, and easier to maintain than those that are imported. Historically, societies that use imported methods and materials tend to be less stable, because they depend on outside knowledge and sources to maintain their environments.

In the U.S. today, it will be difficult to be locally self-sufficient in a consistent manner, but it is imperative that communities be designed and built in a way that minimizes harmful impacts to the land and people, and that encourages the use of safe, locally grown or manufactured materials and native building techniques. In rural, suburban, and urban settings, this is an opportunity to build stronger relationships with surrounding neighbors and suppliers. In this way, each local community gains a sense of place and contributes to the economy and sustainability of the whole region.

COMMON SPACES AND PRIVATE PLACES

A village community provides a distinctive balance between common and private space, offering each person the opportunity to join in the benefits of community living and sharing or to retreat to the solitude and peace of their own private living suite or unit. In Ziuma's compound, the common space is the social and visual core of the community, incorporating cooking and eating functions. The private living spaces are close by, but are intentionally arranged for a high level of privacy. In the Village Cluster, this same balance is accomplished through a hierarchy of spaces— a gradation from private to semi-private to semi-common to common spaces. It is best to think of the common and private areas as a unified whole rather than divided into isolated public versus private realms as is done in conventional housing. Each space in the Village Cluster design helps define the boundaries, size, and functions of the others. A series of transitions such as walls, changes in elevation, materials, and porches help to define each space from the others.

In the Village Cluster approach, the practice is to intentionally design smaller private units, or as in the Village Acre community, individual living suites without kitchens. Because the common house has abundant shared facilities and amenities, nothing is lost by having a smaller house. The common house and the pedestrian street or court become an extension of each house— their living, family, dining, and play rooms— where daily meals, special activities, meetings, and celebrations take place.

A member of Muir Commons, commenting on why they don't like outside groups meeting in their common house, explained, "We think of the common house as our house. So when others meet there it feels strange." Careful thought must be given to the activities, conveniences, and amenities that are most important for common use and to those most important for individual private use. This forethought will translate into lower costs, less energy use, and more space for amenities such as hot tubs or saunas.

COMMITMENT TO SHARING

A commitment to sharing and cooperation is a key precept universal to village communities. In Village Clusters and other Shared Living Communities, members voluntarily share resources, land, energy, and cars, and are co-responsible for the community. This sharing does not mean that each individual loses a sense of self in the group, but rather becomes empowered by the self-esteem that comes from being nurtured and in turn nurturing others.

Some people will view any shared living situation as a threat to their individual families, yet community life often strengthens family life by helping to meet each family's social and daily living needs— which otherwise would be met outside the home and away from family life. The goal for Village Cluster/CoHousing is to create a new definition of "home" to include the closeness, camaraderie, and caring that is shared among an extended family of neighbors, friends, and family. Today's small families will thrive when home is part of a larger community, connected to other people with whom they can share emotional support, joys, hardships and sorrows, responsibilities, and frustrations. Proof of this is found in the testimony of members of existing communities:

> Seif, a 37-year-old owner of a direct-mail advertising company, had concluded [that] traditional single-family housing was all wrong for him: "I was driving down my empty street, past blocks of empty homes, to my empty house," he recalls. "Suddenly the isolation of typical suburban life just hit me...."[9]

> "Finally, we were landowners, and it felt good. We had an identity. It was like getting married. The state and the banks now looked at us as a legitimate being. What would be our community now had a self of its own...."[10]

"I'm savoring the process of building our CoHousing community step by step, observing the alliances that are made, the deep, far reaching sense of unity that is growing...." [11]

"If we didn't have a history of working together and learning to compromise and building trust, we wouldn't be sitting here right now in the common house eating dinner together...." [12]

CONCLUSION

As economic, social, and environmental problems continue, fundamental changes in our homes and lifestyles, our ways of doing business, and our land use and transportation planning become imperative. The Village Cluster approach presents an ecological answer through social interaction that encourages energy savings, resource sharing, and car trip reduction. In the Village Cluster/CoHousing models, physical design and socioeconomic structure are Wed. This integration supports the well-being of the group and its individual members, thereby providing for its own sustainability as a living village.

These thoughts may seem idealistic. And making the transition from single-family house lifestyles to sharing meals in a common house will be a big leap for most mainstream Americans. It will also be a stretch to apply these Village Cluster principles broadly to urban, suburban, and rural locations. Each new community will have its own unique set of problems and processes. However, the socioeconomic and environmental calamities facing us suggest the shift to ecologically sustainable community must be made quickly.

Comprehensive urban planning, such as networks of Eco Villages and Eco Cities linked by high speed and light rail systems could bring about a permanent end to sprawling suburbia. In rural areas, Village Cluster communities can be separated by organic farmlands, thus forming a new rural society within an agricultural Green Belt. In cities, new community housing could take the form of infill, re-use, and mixed-use Urban Cooperative Blocks linked by light rail or bus lines. As density increases around transit stations, urban green strips would form over reclaimed public streets. This is what rebuilding community in America is all about.

1. Jean-Paul Bourdier & Trinh T. Minh-ha, *African Spaces: Designs for Living in Upper Volta,* Africana Publishing Company, New York, 1985, pp. 32-48.

2. Jean-Paul Bourdier, *Op. Cit.,* p. 48.

3. Much of the writing in this section is based on information from the following two sources:
- Peter Nabokov & Robert Easton, *Native American Architecture,* Oxford University Press, New York, 1989, pp. 356-363.
- Jeffrey Cook, *Anasazi Places: The Photographic Vision of William Current,* University of Texas Press, Austin, 1992, pp. 3-24.

4. Robert Gilman, "The Eco-Village Challenge," *In Context: A Quarterly of Humane Sustainable Culture,* No. 29, p.11.

5. Carla Cole, "What About Traditional Villages?," *In Context,* No. 29, p.12.

6. Joan DeClaire, "Come Together," *Pacific Northwest,* August/September 1991, p.15.

7. Various members of Winslow CoHousing, "Winslow CoHousing: A Self-Portrait," *In Context,* No. 35, p.41.

8. Don Lindemann, "Site Development Underway in Colorado," *CoHousing,* Fall 1991, Vol. 4, No. 2, p.6.

9. Claudia Morain, "CoHousing: A '90's Style Return to the Commune," *San Francisco Chronicle,* May 13, 1992, Home Section, p.6.

10. Chris Hansen, "The Winslow Story: A Personal Recollection," *CoHousing*, Fall 1992, Vol. 5, No. 2, p.15.

11. Jon Greer, "Hooked on a New Way of Living," *CoHousing,* Fall 1992, Vol. 5, No. 2, p.15.

12. Ellen Smith, *Op. Cit.,* p.4.

Part Six

ECO
POLITICS

Chapter 22

The Seduction of Planning

by Lynn Scarlett

From FREE MINDS & FREE MARKETS
edited by Robert W. Poole, Jr. & Virginia I. Postrel
Pacific Institute for Public Policy

In January 1989, the township of Mt. Lebanon, Pennsylvania, issued a comprehensive plan "to lead Mt. Lebanon into the twenty-first century." The report intoned: "Goals not stated cannot be achieved."

Nearly 20 years earlier the same community, under the tutelage of a different of policy makers, also prepared a comprehensive plan to ensure that the town's housing, transportation, and other needs were met. In the 1970 plan, a proposed mass-transit sky bus system was called the "brightest ray of hope" for the town's transportation needs. By 1988, there was no mention of the sky bus. It had not been built, nor were any plans to build it described. And improving transportation remained among the planners' priorities.

Across a continent, in sprawling Los Angeles, with a population 400 times greater than Mt. Lebanon's, a distinguished committee appointed by Mayor Tom Bradley issued its report, *Los Angeles 2000*, in November 1988. Under preparation for three years, the report resolved that "we can plan wisely and manage the City's growth...or we can allow it to grow by default."

Urban policy makers— in large metropolises and small towns alike— have planning fever. Few communities have escaped the penchant of policy makers to nudge, prod, and force them along the path to someone's idea of utopia. Even statewide urban management plans are now the rage in Maine, Vermont, Rhode Island, Delaware, Florida, and New Jersey. Details vary, but the thrust is constant: big urban problems require big urban plans.

The idea of urban planning is not new. In the early 1900s, cities began replacing the countryside as the predominant place of employment, and urban populations burgeoned. With growth came problems— crime, pollution, congestion, noise. Today we have vehicle exhaust; in

1900 New York had manure—tons of it. And with these problems has come an understandable urge to mitigate them.

The apparent chaos of cities provided fertile ground for proponents of urban planning. The term itself is seductive, evoking images of order and prospects of perfection. And so, by the '20s, zoning laws— an early planning tool— began to spell out what could be built where. Then came transportation planning and building codes and urban-renewal schemes and redevelopment projects and, most recently, growth-management plans.

Yet urban problems persist. Even the keenest minds with the best intentions can't seem to set the urban landscape aright. How can this be?

With poetic incisiveness, Robert Burn penned in 1785 his often-repeated lines, "The best laid schemes o' mice and men / Gang aft a gley; / An' lea'e us naught but grief and pain, / For promised joy." Planners, or more specifically, public planners, still miss their mark.

This failure is neither surprising nor cause for despair. Much of the chaos that planners fail to mold into order is precisely the dynamism and diversity that drive economic prosperity. "The real problem is not control, but creativity," remarked Jane Jacobs, whose *Death and Life of Great American Cities* upset the discipline of public planning when it appeared in 1961. "Planners' greatest shortcoming…is lack of intellectual curiosity about how cities work. They are taught to see the intricacy of cities as mere disorder. Since most of them believe what they have been taught, they do not inquire about the processes that lie behind the intricacy." To the degree that planners fail to quell this perceived disorder, the vitality of cities fortuitously continues.

Although the apparent chaos may be an asset, not a plague, other problems are real. Vehicles clog highways. Pollutants foul the air. Solid wastes accumulate and outpace landfill capacity. Buildings and infrastructure decay. Housing costs soar. Such city woes deserve attention, but plans— even the current breed of "comprehensive," "imaginative," "regional" public plans— are not the answer (and are sometimes even part of the problem).

Consider a recent megaplan devised by Los Angeles-area legislators. This spring the Southern California Air Quality Management District (AQMD), whose jurisdiction includes all of the greater Los Angeles area, held public hearings on a wide-ranging pollution-abatement plan. The plan includes over 140 sets of regulations, spanning 18 years, that will touch every aspect of life among South Coast residents and businesses. Leaving virtually no stone unturned, the planners would ban trivial sources of pollution— some backyard barbecues, gasoline-powered lawn mowers, and swimming pool heaters. And it would take on more-prominent pollution sources—

vehicle exhaust, oil refinery emissions, and pollution from hundreds of other industrial and commercial processes.

One by one, industry representatives stood before AQMD officials at the March hearings. The proceedings went something like this. A representative of the water-heater manufacturers would stand up, praise the district for its "path-breaking plan to deal with pollution," and then add that, unfortunately, the district had its facts all wrong about water heaters. They don't function the way the plan described. Commercial heaters differ dramatically from residential ones, and so on. Next came the swimming pool representative who also praised the district for its fine work but, alas, lamented that the proposed plan failed utterly to take into account actual swimming pool heating technology. Then followed the barbecue manufacturers, the furniture makers, the oil companies, the butchers, the bakers, and the candlestick makers.

No doubt each business was attempting to protect its interests and mitigate any regulatory costs the new plan might impose— a point that student demonstrators righteously pointed out with signs denouncing all opponents of the plan as greedy businessmen out to destroy Planet Earth. But the self-interested pleas by representatives of various enterprises also illustrated a fundamental problem of planning— the knowledge problem.

As economist Thomas Sowell observed in *Knowledge and Decisions*, "ideas are everywhere, but knowledge is rare." How, Sowell then asks, "does an ignorant world perform intricate functions requiring enormous knowledge?"

Planning is one popular option. In common political parlance, planning refers to the use of centralized, public decision making to define goals and spell out measures to achieve them. As a decision-making process, it is necessarily formal. It is about rule-making and rule enforcement. As a public process, its prescriptions must be specific and leave little discretion to authorities implementing the plan. This inflexibility provides, as Sowell notes, "insurance against the discriminatory use of the vast powers of government. 'Red tape' is an implicit premium paid for this 'insurance.'"

To spell out specific rules, planners need vast amounts of information. To make the AQMD plan work, for example, regulators must accurately predict demographic trends. They must have up-to-the-minute knowledge of the production processes of hundreds of business— and, ideally, be able to foresee what new technology might bring. They must be able to ascertain who is not complying with regulations— whether the violators are families enjoying their backyard barbecues or businesses surreptitiously emitting pollutants.

But public authorities, like the rest of us, are not omniscient. Moreover, the planning process is ill-suited to conveying information. In any centralized and relatively inflexible system, feedback about changing circumstances is slow to enter the decision-making loop. And acquiring knowledge about production processes and diverse community needs is expensive and time-consuming. In short, the process is inefficient— a point amply illustrated by the 20th-century performance of massive planning in the Soviet Union.

For seven decades the Soviet Union has tried to plan its economy. Now, Mikhail Gorbachev acknowledges the inefficiencies, persistent shortages, and corruption that once were reported mainly in underground East Bloc jokes. Even on quality-of-life issues, the Soviet experience is unimpressive: life expectancy has declined, mortality rates are up, pollution grays the horizon. So Soviet leaders have ushered in *perestroika*— a liberalization of the economy that includes more decentralized decision making, some private ownership, more freedom. And the West, with some self-complacence, is cheering on these changes.

But what does the Soviet experience tell us? Forget the big debate—communism versus capitalism— and consider only the issue of planning. The Soviet system is a monumental demonstration of its pitfalls. Complex economic systems require the rapid conveyance of vast bits of information about the ever-changing supply of and demand for different resources.

The very complexity so often cited by city authorities to justify master plans in fact warrants just the opposite— centralized decision making coordinated by the actions of millions of individuals, each privy to information unavailable on a grand scale. Cities are but microcosms of the larger economy. What failed in the Soviet Union for its entire economy is bound to fail also in our cities— and for the same reasons.

Some of the impetus behind planning stems from a very simple fallacy: that only governments plan grandly and only grand plans can bring order. In fact, of course, we all make plans and follow through on them. Many of us even achieve the goals we set out to accomplish. Food gets produced. Buildings get built. Cars get bought. No grand designer spells out a five-year plan for the millions of goods and services we produce and consume. Instead, we rely on that often-neglected process whereby prices reflect the demand for goods in relationship to their supply, informing myriad individual decisions.

Although the overall outcome subscribes to no one individual's particular vision of an ideal community, this is not for lack of planning. And this points up the real function of public plans. They do not establish plans where none exist; they instead replace the plans of individual citizens with those of government officials and the elite that curry their favor.

A telling demonstration of this is found in planners going so far as to instruct builders about the required appearance of their creations. Santa Barbara, California, for example, has decided that only red tile roofs, adobe-colored siding, and earth-colored signage will do for its commercial establishments. Baltimore's planners dictated that its transit facility must have "a cascade of steps," a clock tower, a cafe with umbrella tables, brick walkways, structures of no more than three stories, and so on. Creativity on the part of the developer was, of course, certainly encouraged.

Even as Frank Lloyd Wright was creating his most magnificent buildings, planners had already begun gingerly to impose their visions of grandeur on city development. In New York, one of his buildings had to be constructed behind a wall so that its unconventional concrete-block walls would not mar the view from the street. Today, the structure no doubt couldn't be built at all.

Many planners and citizens deem this issue a spurious one. We cannot concern ourselves with a little loss of freedom of choice when the order and aesthetic appeal of our cities is at stake, they assert. We have to make sacrifices, perhaps even of our freedom, to attain the clean air, pure water, and uncongested roads we all desire.

In fact, however, this loss of freedom will not achieve the intended results. The reasons why are well summarized by Sowell: "The Godlike approach to social policy ignores both the diversity of values and the cost of agreement among human beings." And, he adds, public planning "distorts the communication of knowledge."

Planning involves prescriptions, and prescriptions inevitably raise costs. Developers haggle with city planners to come to some compromise; polluters litigate until they find a technology that will achieve a mandated reduction in emissions; employees demand higher wages in order to keep their employers in compliance with mandated "alternative work schedule" plans. These are all costs of reaching agreements among parties affected by public plans and their accompanying regulations.

Planning also distorts costs by obscuring some costs and increasing others. Banning multi-family dwellings, for example, cuts the supply of housing, and overall housing costs increase. Separating residential from commercial areas drives people into their cars as they commute outside their communities to work. Even as planners may resolve some particular perceived problem, their plans set in motion a series of unintended consequences and unacknowledged costs.

If public planning won't work very well, are we destined to breathe foul air and creep along on congested highways? During the AQMD hearings, its proponents repeatedly charged that a vote against the plan was a vote for pollution. The contention is simplistic in its narrow presentation of the options.

The key to successfully resolving urban problems that seem to require master planning is to understand existing decision processes. Some of the "chaos" that planners and established residents seem so eager to suppress is actually the tangible reflection of diverse preferences among different people. And some, as Jacobs observed, flows from the change that inevitably accompanies a dynamic economy. Efforts to eliminate this chaos cannot be accomplished without suppressing freedom and squelching economic prosperity. Such chaos is the sign of an economy that is working.

But other urban characteristics, like air pollution and traffic congestion, result from decision-making processes in which important knowledge is not being conveyed. People are, for example, choosing to drive to work at rush hour all alone in their automobiles without recognizing that highway space is limited. Or factories are emitting pollutants into the air as if the atmosphere could, without loss of air quality, absorb the emissions in unlimited quantities. Or low-cost housing is not being built. Here the key issue is how best to convey the missing pieces of information so that people alter their behavior.

All decisions, public and private, are shaped by individual preferences combined with external incentives. To change the outcome of decisions, policy makers can either hope to change people's preferences or alter the incentives they face or ignore both preferences and incentives and legislate behavior. The latter course— the planning approach— erodes freedom and entails high information costs. And changing people's preferences is akin to the ill-fated efforts of various Communist regimes to fashion a "new man." Such efforts have failed even when governments resorted to Draconian "re-education."

It is possible, however, to alter the incentives people face in their daily decisions. At the root of many urban problems, especially air pollution and traffic congestion, is the simple fact that air and roads are "free goods" treated as if they are available in unlimited supply. Commuters pay nothing to use the roadways. Polluters pay nothing to dump byproducts into the atmosphere, and most of us capriciously toss out trash as if landfill were limitless. This means that vital information about the relative scarcity of air and roads and landfill is left out of the decision-making process.

Public planning focuses on the ill effects of this imperfect process and imposes regulations designed to achieve some different outcome. The result: In the case of pollution, an AQMD-style compendium of edicts mandating how Los Angeles residents and businesses are to conduct their affairs and to combat the trash problem, we get mandated recycling programs. But such regulations still convey to commuters and polluters no information about the costs of their behavior.

Or, in the case of housing, planners "downzone" urban areas to reduce crowding and congestion. But by ruling out low-cost, high-density housing, they block the ability of the market to respond to people's needs.

Public planning, espoused in the name of harmony and rationality, actually provokes discord. It interrupts the flow of information from consumer to producer and back. And it does nothing to improve the flow of information about scarcities where the marketplace, with its price-coordinated transmission of knowledge, is not working.

Where price signals are absent, as in the use of air and roads, the most effective approach is to introduce price signals rather than presume to plan away the ill effects of their absence. Create institutions— like air rights or toll roads—that get individuals to take into account the costs of their behavior. Faced with higher costs of driving alone down the freeway at rush hour, for example, some people will switch to public transit. Others will carpool. Still others may move closer to work.

And rather than overcoming the "out of sight, out of mind" mentality toward garbage with mandates and city-financed recycling plans, the more effective solution is to introduce pricing that varies depending on how much garbage people produce. City officials in Seattle did just that. Seattle citizens now have choices. They can buy more recyclable goods and produce less garbage to keep their trash bill low. Or they can maintain their old habits, but pay higher costs for the volumes of waste they generate.

Unlike planned solutions to traffic congestion and landfill scarcity, using price signals lets individuals make their own trade-off, their own choices, about how to respond to changing circumstances. As Sowell neatly summarizes, "more options generally mean better results when the larger number of options includes all the smaller number of options." Planning excludes options. As a result, we are all made worse off.

Chapter 23

The Economics of Building Codes and Standards

by Peter F. Colwell & James B. Kau

From RESOLVING THE HOUSING CRISIS:
Government Policy, Decontrol, and the Public Interest
edited by M. Bruce Johnson
Pacific Institute for Public Policy

In the United States, approximately 8,000 jurisdictions are administering some kind of building code. The costs of enforcement and compliance are growing more rapidly than the total costs of government, but for the most part the benefits of the building code system are undocumented. It is widely accepted that there are problems with this system, but little has been done to change the situation. If anything, the system is becoming more entrenched.

Critics of the building code system generally charge that it is too diverse, too prescriptive, and too slow to change. They recommend that code formulation, if not also enforcement, ought to be centralized. It is our position that building codes are not sufficiently diverse and that it is in the anticompetitive nature of codes and standards to be prescriptive and to inhibit innovation. Instead of more centralization, we need to introduce diversity by decentralizing. The system of codes should be abandoned rather than reformed. Market mechanisms can deal fairly and efficiently with issues of building safety, provided that the rules of the game are structured appropriately.

The way in which building standards are written reveals a great deal about the character of the standards and the building codes that ultimately reference the standards. The participants in the standards-writing process and their interests flavor the standards more than do any principles concerning the public health and safety or economic efficiency. This article sets the institutional stage and then develops a model of the choices in levels of building safety. First, the production of building safety and the costs of production are analyzed. Next, the costs of codes are introduced with some elements of these costs being directly integrated into the model. Then the benefits of building safety are brought into the model. The private optimum can be compared with the social optimum and the conditions for divergence can be identified once benefits and costs are considered together. Finally, the inefficiency of building codes is contrasted with the relative efficiency of a system in which the insurance industry writes standards, inspects buildings, and sells insurance, charging premiums in relation to the safety inherent in the particular standard selected.

INSTITUTIONAL ENVIRONMENT
OF CODES AND STANDARDS

A distinction between building codes and building standards is seldom made (see, for example, the California Administrative Code). However, drawing such a distinction is useful in understanding the process by which building codes are created and subverted. Building codes are statutes that pertain to the construction, alteration, or rehabilitation of buildings. Although building standards refer to the same issues, they are merely the recommendations of some group and do not carry the force of law. Codes are mandatory; standards are voluntary. State or local governments impose codes; the groups that create standards are private, governmental, or a mix of private and governmental. Building codes often reference certain written standards. Some of these standards are confusingly called "model codes."

The four most important model code organizations in the United States are the International Conference of Building Officials, with the Uniform Building Code (ICBO/UBC); the Building Officials Conference of America, with the Basic Building Code and Basic Plumbing Code (BOCA/BBC/BPC); the Southern Building Code Conference, with the Southern Standard Building Code and the Southern Standard Plumbing Code (SBCC/SSBC/SSPC); and the National Fire Protection Association, with the National Electric Code (NFPA/NEC). Other organizations that develop model codes are the American Society of Heating, Refrigeration, and Air Conditioning Engineers (ASHRAE); the American Society of Mechanical Engineers, with the National Plumbing Code (ASME/NPC); and the International Association of Plumbing and Mechanical Officials, with the Uniform Plumbing Code (IAPMO/UPC). Most California jurisdictions reference model codes such as UBC, NEC, and UPC.

A number of other organizations are involved in standards development, such as the National Conferences of States on Building Codes and Standards (NCSBCS), an association of state building code officials, and the Center for Building Technology (CBT) of the National

338

Bureau of Standards (NBS). In addition, there is the National Institute of Building Sciences (NIBS), the Occupational Safety and Health Administration (OSHA), the Consumer Product Safety Commission (CPSC), and the Federal Housing Administration (FHA) within the U. S. Department of Housing and Urban Development (HUD).

Most building standards are written by the model code organizations. The members of these organizations are, in the main, code officials. Proposed changes in standards may be submitted to these organizations by any interested party. Generally these proposals are referred to a committee in the relevant area for study and recommendations. The committee is lobbied by special interest groups (for example, trade associations, producers, competitors, and unions). Finally, the committee makes a recommendation to the members of the organization who, in turn, vote on the proposal.

Code officials must be viewed as special-interest groups themselves. Their interests primarily lie in minimizing their own liability and maximizing their own tenure. Local code officials are interested in maintaining the status quo. However, state code officials working through NCSBCS are interested in increasing the technical nature of codes— a change that would shift power away from localities to the state level.

The organizations that lobby the hardest are most directly affected by the standard change. Of course, consumers are affected very little by any single change in the system but are greatly affected by the system as a whole. Thus, consumer groups generally find it unprofitable to lobby on issues of marginal change. Lobbying primarily comes from trade associations such as the Cast Iron Soil Pipe Institute, which has an interest in stopping the use of plastic pipe. Building Code Action, Inc., is funded by a contractors organization in Northern California for the purpose of monitoring the activities of organizations that write standards. The Building Industry Association in California has a small group of lobbyists in the area of codes and standards and the local code officials lobby through an association called the California Building Officials (CALBO).

Although building code enforcement is a government monopoly, the writing of codes via standards is mostly a private enterprise. The organizations that produce standards may be more or less competitive. They are least competitive when they acquire a franchise from the government. For example, a model code or standard called the National Electric Code is sponsored by the National Fire Protection Association, but the U. S. Department of Housing and Urban

Development requires all jurisdictions to adopt this model code in order to qualify for federal funds.

Even without a government franchise, model codes are popular, because they are cheap. A state or local building code can reference a model code (or some portion of it) at no cost. Because of the input of enforcement officials, the model codes can be expected to not expose code officials to substantial liability and to not require a great deal of expertise to interpret. Thus, it is relatively easy to run a building department using a model code. More than three-quarters of local governments with codes do reference model codes. States with codes invariably reference model codes.

After referencing a model code, the local government is likely to modify it. Even though differences among model codes are not great, these modifications can cause marked differences to exist across many local governments. Differences also arise because of the failure of the local jurisdictions to keep current with the latest versions of the model codes.

Differences also exist across jurisdictions in terms of interpreting the same code (that is, codes referencing the same standard) for enforcement purposes. These differences arise because of a lack of clarity in the standard, a desire by code officials to be obtuse because it suits some purpose, or a lack of training among code enforcement officials.

Jurisdictions will often give the code the most rigorous interpretation possible. For example, some California communities using the Uniform Building Code require two separate walls, while others require only a party wall for contiguous townhouses. The two-wall interpretation means one-hour fire rating for each wall or a two rating in total instead of a 1.5-hour rating for a party wall. Even a party wall with a two-hour rating can be produced for several hundred dollars less than the two-wall approach.

The enforcement of building codes is a two-step process. First, plans must be submitted to the building department and approved. Second, on-site inspections must verify that the construction is in accordance with the approved plans. Although there is evidence that sometimes there are large-scale payoffs to code enforcement officials, the payoffs appear to be extortion payments for not harassing builders rather than payments to circumvent code provisions. Enforcement of building codes appears to be rather tight, if varied, in contrast to the generally loose enforcement of housing codes, for example. The tight enforcement suggests a spirit of voluntary compliance that might be explained as an attempt to limit liability.

The system of building codes and standards has been substantially diverted from the goal of protecting the public health and safety to serve the purposes of special interest groups. There is very little chance in this system for questions of economic efficiency to arise and to affect any part of the system.

THE PRODUCTION OF SAFETY

Often a number of different technologies and mixes of technologies are available to reduce the likelihood and severity of a given type of accident or health risk. For example, to reduce the likelihood of collapse due to a snow load, it is possible to use a number of structural solutions, such as a steeper roof or stronger and/or more structural members. Alternatively, one might simply shovel the snow off the roof more frequently. One would not ordinarily mix redundant technologies. That is, it would be wasteful to shovel snow off a roof that is sufficiently strong to carry imaginable snow loads.

In graphic terms, there would be a unique cost curve for each type of solution (that is, a relevant mix of technologies). The lower envelope of those cost curves would indicate the least-cost solution for producing any level of safety (see Figure 23-1). Thus, selecting a particular level of safety to be produced implies a particular technology as well as the level of the technology that should be used. The cost of including redundant technologies would be found by summing vertically the cost curves for the technologies in the manner demand curves are summed for a public good.

COSTS OF CODES AND STANDARDS

There is a substantial controversy concerning the magnitude of the costs imposed on society by building codes. Estimates range from 1 or 2 percent of building costs to 7 percent and higher. Certainly codes cause the building industry to select certain technologies and to reject others. However, the cost differentials of these technologies are in most cases about as uncertain as the relationship between the technologies and the safety produced by them. The costs of codes should relate to the flexibility of the codes, their openness to new products, and their sensitivity to scientific argument rather than intuition and emotional argument.

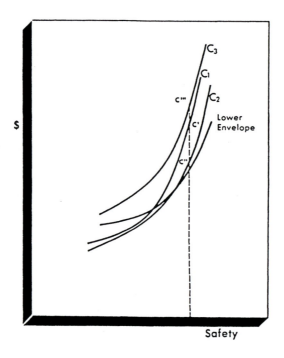

Figure 23-1 The Cost of Safety.

COSTS OF PRESCRIPTIVE VERSUS PERFORMANCE STANDARDS

Criticisms of the building code system generally point out that codes tend to be prescriptive rather than being performance oriented. The terms prescriptive and performance have rather peculiar meanings in this context. A performance standard states a low-order technical objective. For example, the ability of a wall to carry a specific load or resist the spread of fire for a specific length of time are performance standards. In contrast, a prescriptive standard spells out a method for achieving some (generally unspecified) low-order technical objective. For example, two-by-fours 16 inches on center, and a particular thickness of gypsum board, are prescriptive standards. So prescriptive standards relate to inputs, whereas performance standards relate to outputs, albeit of a low order.

In graphic terms, the prescriptive standard refers not only to a particular cost curve in Figure 1 (for example, C2), but also to a particular point on the cost curve (for example, c"). In contrast, the performance standard refers implicitly to a level of safety produced by some range of cost curves. Thus, points c', c ", and c'" may be possibilities under the performance standard. So several prescriptive standards may exhaust the options under the performance standard.

There is certainly no guarantee that the prescriptive standard is the least-cost method of producing the resulting level of safety or even that it embodies a technology that is the least-cost method of producing any level of safety. Similarly, the performance standard may not include the least-cost method. In fact, because building codes only refer to building characteristics and do not include modes of use, operation, and maintenance, it is unlikely that the least-cost method will be included by the code.

There are two reasons why prescriptive standards are so popular. Prescriptive standards minimize the liability of code officials, because they require so little in the way of professional judgment. Similarly, prescriptive standards require very little in the way of professional training for code officials. Those individuals in the enforcement field who advocate the use of performance standards usually understand the liability and enforcement cost advantages of prescriptive standards. Thus, an appeal for performance standards is usually coupled with an appeal for a system of testing laboratories to translate the performance standards into approved prescriptive options.

The preference many analysts have for performance standards is based on the flexibility of performance standards and the increased speed of diffusion of technological innovations imagined under a system of performance standards. We have suggested that the flexibility is within rather narrow bounds. The increased speed of diffusion may also be overestimated. The testing of new products often results in contradictory results. Furthermore, code officials would no doubt still be unwilling to approve a product if it had the slightest aura of decreased safety, regardless of the testing results.

It is interesting to note that neither prescriptive nor performance standards are typically evaluated relative to the ultimate objectives of health and safety produced. Reformers generally call for more rapid and more thorough testing to imbue standards with unimpeachable scientific validity. But it appears that the objective of such testing is to assure the government that basic performance standards are met. The next step is typically not taken. That is, higher-order technical links between performance standards and health and safety are not verified. This limitation leads to the unfortunate tendency to consider the effects of specific standards in isolation.

It is necessary to examine the system of codes and standards as a whole. To do otherwise is to promote redundant features in the codes and standards. That is, one standard might add substantially to safety in isolation, but at the same time, it might add little or nothing to safety when combined with a particular system of standards. In other words, the marginal products of standards often depend on the levels of other standards. For example, requiring smoke detectors might render a number of other standards and technical objectives redundant. The fire ratings of walls might reasonably be reduced if they are to produce safety in a system of standards that includes smoke detectors.

There is a tendency for new standards to be added to the system with no regard for the need to change the entire mix of standards within the system. The cumulative effect is that costs rise substantially with small increments to health and safety. The fact that Muth and Wetzler found that the age of a code is inversely related to buildings costs may provide some evidence of this phenomenon.[1] Yet the potential exists for standards to achieve the same or slightly higher levels of safety with substantial reductions in cost (recall the smoke detector example). Perhaps an avalanche of innovations in the electronic monitoring and control of building systems will bring the need to rethink code systems, but it is more likely that each new device will be added to codes without regard for technical or economic efficiency.

Even if a new product is marginally or inconsequently less safe than currently approved alternatives, there is a tendency to not approve the product. What is worse is that safer products are rejected because there may be an aura of risk that seemingly cannot be dispersed despite overwhelming scientific evidence.

The battle to allow the use of Romex cable in the National Electric Code was protracted, and the result was quite restrictive. The scientific evidence indicates that Romex is superior to the approved alternatives. Yet Romex is restricted to dwellings in buildings of three stories or less. This ruling has been criticized explicitly by HUD and implicitly by NBS research. Still, the ruling stands.

There was a similar battle over the more recent introduction of the flat conductor cable developed by NASA. The approved uses are quite limited now, but the apparent superiority and lower cost of this system suggest that the battle is not yet over. The inertia of the approval mechanism is impressive when faced with strong scientific evidence.

The Uniform Plumbing Code specifies the sizes of vent pipes to protect against siphonage, back pressure, and air circulation. Although reduced-size vents have been proven effective in a California test house and in an NBS study, use of the reduced-size vents is still not approved. There is a tendency to ignore scientific issues and reject new methods and materials even if there is an aura of decreased safety. People cling to the status quo despite the fact that it substantially increases costs. In the case of the plumbing vents, it increases costs by about $200 per dwelling unit.

THE COSTS OF UNSCIENTIFIC RIGOR IN CODES

There is a tendency to ignore scientific questions when a new concept has an aura of increased safety. In such situations, the concept is likely to be added to the standard and referenced in codes. For example, some California communities require compliance with the NFPA standard that calls for sprinkler systems in one- and two-family dwellings. However, there does not appear to be any evidence that sprinklers increase public safety beyond that which is achieved with smoke detectors. The net effect on property damage averted is probably negative (that is, fire damage minus water damage). The additional costs are known to be about $2,000 per dwelling unit.

The total cost of codes includes such elements as the differential cost of building with codes rather than without them, the cost of delays and other problems in dealing with code officials, the cost of enforcement, and the foregone consumer surplus. There has been very little serious empirical work done on providing these magnitudes.

In the only econometric study of the impact of codes on building costs, Muth and Wetzler attempted to estimate the differential cost of single-family housing for model codes over locally drafted or modified codes. They found the differential to be very slight, but the aggregate data they worked with may not have been capable of revealing much about this differential. Unfortunately, their study was not designed to reveal anything about the costs of building with codes as opposed to building without them.[2]

Arthur Young and Company estimated the costs of code enforcement and the costs of excess code requirements for the state of California during the year 1977. At this time, enforcement costs were running $97.5 million and rising faster than the total cost of government in the state and also faster than the value of new construction in the state. The costs of excess building requirements were conservatively estimated to be $74 million.[3]

Energy regulations in the state of California have had a profound effect on the cost of enforcement at the local level. In Los Angeles alone, the enforcement cost for energy regulations in new buildings has been running in excess of $600,000 per year.

BENEFITS OF SAFETY

The owners of buildings receive obvious benefits from increased safety. There is decreased expected mortality, morbidity, and injury to themselves and their families. There is a reduction in expected property damage. Very importantly, there is an expected reduction in the hazards facing other individuals. With building safety, these hazards to others are largely internalized by the building owner. The reason for this is that the building owner is legally liable for the injury to others from accidents that occur on his or her property.

If all the benefits are fully internalized by the owner, there should not be a resource allocation problem from the private determination of the optimal level of safety. There may be an externality problem if the building owner is incapable of compensating others who have sustained damages on his or her property. There may also be resource allocation problems if there are substantial externalities in consumption that are not compensable through the courts. Finally, there may be a problem if consumers of building services are unaware of the risks they face from building hazards.

The fastest way to alienate a general audience from evaluations of the benefits to safety is to mention the value of saving a life. Very little information exists about this issue, and the issue may be entirely avoided by cost-benefit analysis. Some information does, however, exist on the value of marginal changes in the probabilities of accidents. Empirical work can be undertaken to determine the willingness of individuals to spend in order to reduce the probability that their own or another person's death will occur. Data on the voluntary purchase of home fire extinguishers, chain ladders, smoke detectors, gas detectors, and so forth would be very interesting. Because costs have been falling for a number of these gadgets, it might even be possible to get a good estimate of willingness to pay.

A consistent approach would measure the benefit of a project that reduces the probability of a death (or injury) by determining the amount that all concerned individuals would pay or would require in payment to have the project proceed. That is, all those individuals who would gain by the reduction in the probability of Individual A dying (being injured) would be willing to pay an amount to have the safety project proceed.

This analysis of willingness to pay implies that it is consistent with the underlying premise to include externalities in consumption in computing the social benefits of safety. Externalities in consumption result from the welfare of one individual being, in part, a function of the goods and services consumed by another individual. Thus, if Individual B feels better off as a result of Individual A being safer or being better housed or better fed, the benefits that flow to Individual B are termed "externalities in consumption."

Some kinds of death may be viewed by the collective consciousness as more horrible than other kinds. One kind of death may produce more psychic pain for individuals who are not dying (holding suffering of the dying individual constant). Suppose x and y are two types of tragedies, both with the same expected number of deaths per unit of time, but x has low numbers of deaths per incident while y has high numbers of deaths per incident. (Of course, there are fewer y incidents than x incidents.) Holding everything else constant, are y deaths to be avoided more than x, or vice versa? The y incidents will capture more attention in the media and thereby be more prominent in the collective consciousness. If externalities in consumption are included in the cost-benefit analysis, the averting of y incidents will produce more additional benefits than the averting of x incidents.

Some externalities in consumption resulting from a safety project may decrease benefits. There may be individuals who would be made better off by the death (or injury) of Individual A. These individuals will be referred to as Type C. To be perfectly consistent, one should subtract the amount that Type C individuals would accept as compensation to put up with the safety project. This is the same magnitude that Type C people would be willing to pay to stop the safety project.

In graphic terms, the marginal benefits from safety decline as safety increases (see Figure 23-2).[4] The marginal benefits to the building owner are illustrated by the marginal private benefits (MPB) curve, while the marginal social benefits (that is, the vertical sum of the owner's marginal benefits and external marginal benefits) are shown by the MSB curve.

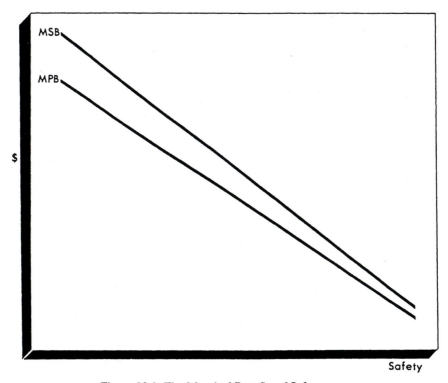

Figure 23-2 The Marginal Benefits of Safety.

The fact that the owner of a building is liable for injury to occupants and passersby is insufficient to cause the divergence between private and social marginal benefits to disappear entirely. Liability is generally limited. For example, the limited partnership form of ownership may be used in conjunction with an asset-poor general partner. Sufficient liability insurance may not be purchased. Thus, without a return to a system of debtors' prisons, liability is insufficient to guarantee that building owners internalize the risks they generate for others.

Even with limited liability, the risks to the users could be internalized by the owner if the users and owners were fully informed of the risks. In this case, one would expect the prices for building services to reflect the risks. But a problem would still exist for the risks faced by passersby and for externalities in consumption.

THE SAFETY DECISION

By integrating the benefits with the costs, it is possible to develop a simple model of safety choice in the absence of codes. Optimal safety according to the efficiency criterion is found where all the marginal benefits of safety equal all the marginal costs, assuming that marginal benefits decrease as marginal costs increase with increasing safety. Marginal benefits are shown in Figure 23-2. The relevant marginal costs are found by taking the derivative of the lower envelope of the cost curves in Figure 23-1. Both marginal benefits and marginal costs are shown in Figure 23-3.

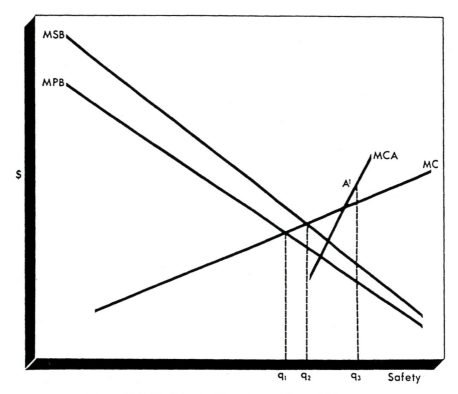

Figure 23-3 The Marginal Benefits and Cost of Safety.

If there is a divergence between the private and social marginal benefits curves, as shown in Figure 23-3, the private and social optimal levels of safety will also diverge. In Figure 23-3, the private optimum is indicated by q_1, while the social optimum is indicated by q_2. This divergence provides the economic rationale for public intervention. Of course, the marginal benefit curves and the marginal cost curves can be expected to shift from situation to situation. Thus, any government intervention must be flexible to be efficient.

DIVERSITY, UNIFORMITY, AND EFFICIENCY IN CODES

Critiques of building codes invariably consider the imposition of uniformity in codes and code administration as important elements in reform of the code system. The argument is that diversity in codes retards the exploitation of potential economies of scale in building production.

In fact, other features of the building code system may be more responsible for the lack of economies of scale than is the diversity of codes and administrations. In addition, there may be some value to this diversity.

The prohibitions against off-site assembly of building components are largely responsible for the higher costs due to weather— including the costs of having a seasonal work force. But the lack of off-site assembly of structural, electrical, and plumbing systems is probably also the most serious impediment to achieving economies of scale.

It is thought that diversity in code enforcement retards the growth of construction firms and the concomitant economies that larger scale would bring. The solution, of course, is said to be higher levels of government enforcing codes. Because Canada is way ahead of the United States in imposing uniformity in codes and centralization in code administration, it would be helpful to have empirical studies of the Canadian experience examine the question of whether increases in scale have occurred. It is also important to discover if any increases in scale have been the sort that have led to economies in production. This is important because there may be scale economies in dealing with centralized bureaucracy that have nothing to do with production.

Finally, there may be some value to diversity in codes. One could construct a hypothesis for regulation (and building regulation specifically) that parallels the conventional arguments concerning diversity in taxes and the level and mix of public expenditures across jurisdictions. It may be that diversity in types and rigor of building codes provides another dimension in which individuals can maximize their satisfaction with their local public sector. They do this not only by voting with their feet but also by having the local building code sensitive to their will as expressed through political participation. Diversity in building codes may be an area in which political externality costs can be held down.

O'Hare has argued that efficiency is lost by imposing constraints on choice such as those imposed by building codes.[5] It is obvious that, if codes require a specific method of safety production as well as a specific minimum level to which the method must be applied, optimal choice of lower levels of safety would be frustrated and welfare loss results (see Figure 23-3). It is less obvious that the optimal choice of higher levels of safety would be frustrated as well. There are two reasons for this. One is that the higher level of safety can only be rationalized by using an unapproved technology. Suppose, for example, that MPB in Figure 23-3 were higher than illustrated but still fell below Point A. If it intersects the MC curve (that is, the derivative of the envelope in Figure 23-1) to the right of q_3, no more than q_3 would be produced if the safety producer is constrained by code to the MCA curve. A second reason for codes constraining safety to no more than the code-mandated level lies in the potential for codes to distort liability. A defense against liability is that the building was built to code specifications and thus the owner (as well as code officials, contractors, and so on) acted in a prudent and reasonable fashion. In this light, a casualty is seen as being caused by an act of God. In graphic terms, the marginal benefits curve would be discontinuous at the code-mandated level of safety if the code specifications are followed. Therefore, building codes can constrain choice from above as well as from below.

A few states have adopted maximum codes. Localities are not allowed to have a code more rigorous than the state code. This approach may solve some problems (for example, exclusionary codes, codes subverted to sell more of some products or use more labor). But whether this approach, in combination with market pressure, is sufficient to deal with overly rigorous and rigid voluntary standards, the source of most codes, is yet to be seen.

Perhaps FTC control of standards writing rules is needed. It has been proposed that the FTC should require standards-writing bodies to justify changes by filing economic impact statements (that is, essentially cost-benefit analysis). This could be viewed as a relief act for economists, but it might be a useful exercise if we are to otherwise maintain the system of codes and standards we now have. It may be a harbinger of coming reform that Building Code Action was recently successful in a suit against the California Energy Commission in which BCA claimed that glazing as well as wall and ceiling insulation regulations were not cost effective. But instead of looking for ways to reform the existing system of codes and standards, it might be useful to consider abandoning this system in favor of private arrangements to ensure that appropriate levels of health and safety are built into buildings.

PRIVATE-SECTOR ALTERNATIVES TO CODES

To what extent can we look to the private sector to ensure building safety? The failure of the private sector to appear interested in the issue of building safety may be more attributable to the crowding out of private initiatives by codes than to the traditional list of the reasons for market failure. Yet other kinds of governmental involvement might be helpful to the functioning of the market in this sphere. For example, it could be helpful to require building owners to carry liability insurance. Tax and subsidy policies might also be useful in some circumstances. But codes are difficult to justify under any circumstances.

Are any health and safety controls needed for single-family, detached housing? It is often argued that "It is unlikely that the home buyer will have the technical knowledge to make an informed decision about the structural integrity of the unit."[6]

A house is a complex product, and it may be difficult for uninformed consumers to determine, in advance, the quality of construction. This problem, however, is not unique to housing. Many products are technologically complex, and it is often difficult for consumers to determine quality of workmanship, Houses differ from other products primarily in the expense involved, not in the nature of the uncertainties. In general, when consumers are unable to determine quality in advance, two types of institutions evolve that provide the information for the consumer. In both cases, the brand name of the supplier becomes important.[7] The manufacturer may make his or her name known to consumers; alternatively, the retailer may use his or her brand name as a guarantee of quality.

With respect to the name of the manufacturer, we may say that, in many markets, firms find it worthwhile to invest substantial resources in name recognition. The firm spends substantial amounts of resources in informing consumers about its products and its efforts to produce quality products. Firms would, of course, have incentives to mislead in this case. However, if a firm produces low-quality products, then consumers can learn of this and avoid these products. Thus, firms that produce low-quality products in fact have incentives not to advertise. The money spent on advertising is in the nature of a signal of quality, because the existence of this expenditure means that firms have more to lose if they produce low-quality products. However, the nature of this result depends on the type of market involved. In particular, a firm can gain a one-time profit from misleading consumers about the quality of its products if it does not depend on repeat sales. In the home-building industry, we might expect repeat sales to be an important portion of total sales (because most builders serve local markets), and therefore we might expect the information conveyed by real estate salespeople about local builders to be significant. Thus it may not be surprising that home builders do invest significant amounts in generating name brand capital.

Even if producers do not find it worthwhile to invest in name brand capital, their reluctance does not preclude this method of guaranteeing quality. In some markets, third parties perform the function of certifying quality when producers are not able to convincingly perform such certification. For example, a department store serves to guarantee consumers a certain level of quality in products offered for sale. The store performs this function partly by agreeing to act as the agent of the consumer in returning defective products to the manufacturer. An equally important part of this function, however, is the testing of products by the store— that is, the employees of the department store presumably are specialists in determining the quality of products offered for sale— and the consumer relies on this expertise. If the store is remiss in its certification of quality, it can expect to lose business. Thus, the brand name capital of the department store serves to guarantee to the consumer the quality of products it offers for sale.

A similar quality-guaranteeing function is performed by firms that use franchising as a distribution method.[8] Here, the national franchisor serves to guarantee the uniformity of quality of product offered by local franchises throughout the market area. The franchisor performs this function by inspecting the quality of local franchisees and by canceling the franchise of any outlets that do not meet acceptable quality standards. The franchisor has an incentive to perform this function because its reputation and hence its profits (from sale of franchise and from its percentage of the profits or revenues of franchised stores) depend on its policing quality. Moreover, franchising is important in markets where there is substantial geographic mobility. In such markets, local residents can learn of the quality of local merchants, but new migrants and transients rely on national franchises for information.

This analysis indicates a plausible method guaranteeing quality in housing markets. Because most sales are very large and because there may not be many repeat sales, due to the local nature of the building market, we may not expect builders to invest substantial amounts in establishing the value of name brand capital. The nature of the market is such that consumers may discount any such attempts on the part of the local builders. Similarly, local real estate firms would have problems in convincing consumers that they (the real estate firms) were doing an acceptable job of certifying quality; that is, consumers would discount any such claims on the part of the real estate firm, because consumers would expect such information to have little value. However, it is plausible to expect a nationally franchised real estate firm to perform such a certifying function. That is, we might expect a firm (or firms) to come into being on a national level and to certify the quality of the houses sold. Because most homeowners move several times during their lives, such a firm, if it effectively policed the quality of the houses it offered for sale, would probably be able to make a profit for itself by its guaranteeing procedures. There have recently come into being national real estate franchises, such as Century 21.

In situations where costly events occur randomly and where it is impossible to determine in advance where such events will occur, insurance is a common remedy. Most consumers are risk averse and therefore are willing to pay a premium to avoid risk. If markets for information about housing quality may be lacking, this may indicate that it is too expensive to determine which houses are likely to suffer from defects. A natural alternative would seem to be insurance. This insurance could be provided by the builder in the form of a warranty, or it would be provided by third-party insurers, as is fire insurance. It is also possible to combine information and insurance. That is, firms would come into being that could inspect houses and guarantee quality; the firm would be liable for any damages that occurred after inspection and certification. This form of insurance against termites is provided by pest control services, and is provided by title insurance companies against title defects. As of now, there do seem to be some firms providing this service for building defects. The Home Owners Warranty (HOW) insurance program is such a plan.

The reason these market remedies have not played a more significant role is that home purchasers are probably overprotected by building codes. No incentives exist to seek market remedies to reduce risk and information cost.

An economic rationale of the need for building codes to control single-family detached housing must be found elsewhere. Perhaps there are externalities in production that affect household members, visitors, passersby, or contiguous properties. But the intrahousehold externalities in consumption should internalize risks for household members, Liability should internalize risk to visitors and passersby. Risks to surrounding properties could easily be handled by private controls. Deed restrictions are frequently used by private subdividers to provide esthetic control. In the absence of building codes, subdividers would find it profitable to introduce economically efficient deed restrictions related to health and safety. The only rationale left is the existence of inter-household externalities in consumption. We are protected from ourselves so that others may be spared the discomfort of seeing the results of our accidents. This appears to be a thin thread from which to hang a public policy that has substantial effects.

The National Commission on Neighborhoods has recommended that a system of private inspection and insurance of all buildings replace the current system of enforcement of codes by government monopoly. This is an interesting concept but may not go far enough. It begs the more interesting issue of what is being enforced. Not much would be gained if codes are still to be imposed by the public sector and if these codes reference standards that are written by the same old process.

It would be possible and desirable to have the insurance industry completely take over the process of building safety regulation. Building liability insurance could be mandatory in the same way that automobile liability insurance is mandatory in some states. Different insurance companies (or the same insurance company) could have different standards associated with different levels of safety and different premia. Thus, diversity could be achieved. If public buildings had the standard to which they were built displayed in a prominent place (for example, "This theater was built in 1985 to an AA standard"), users could make informed judgments of trade-offs between risk and price. Again, if externalities in consumption are a problem, some kind of tax or subsidy policy would be preferred to building codes. A tax might take the form of punitive damages being awarded by courts in the event of injury to people, whereas safety production could be subsidized.

One urban area, the unincorporated section of Harris County, Texas (Houston is located in this county but does have building codes), has no building codes.[9] Before they lend money, private sources such as savings and loan associations require certain specifications to be met. Both the fire insurance companies and the electrical utility have restrictions on the quality of construction before they cover or service the building, respectively. This would indicate that building codes administered by the government are unnecessary.

CONCLUSIONS

The system that produces building standards and ultimately codes is structured so that it does more mischief than good. Innovation is stymied, while codes are made increasingly rigorous and costly.[10] Codes have been subverted by special-interest groups in and out of government to accomplish a number of purposes, from selling more lumber to reducing the liability of code officials. In fact, there is no body of evidence that shows building codes add to health and safety in any way. It has certainly not been demonstrated that the system of building codes is economically efficient or that it produces desirable distributional effects. The system is intellectually and morally bankrupt.

The principal reform mentioned in most critiques of the building code system is uniformity. It is felt that diversity in codes inhibits economies of scale from being exploited. We argue that there are other reasons for small-scale building firms, some of which are related to other aspects of the code system, and that diversity is desirable because of its effects on economic efficiency. By their very nature (by constraining building solutions from both below and above), building codes impose too much uniformity.

A reasonable alternative is to allow the private sector to make the myriad decisions that can provide for diversity consistent with economic efficiency in the production of health and safety.[11] The first step would be for states to require building liability insurance so as to internalize risks to those whose injuries merit compensation by courts. The next step, and all other steps, would be up to the insurance industry and its customers. It might be reasonable to expect that the industry would establish a number of standards of its own. The owner of a building could then select a standard to which his or her building would be built and pay a premium charged by his or her insurance company for the standard selected. The public sector would discharge its responsibility for building safety by establishing the rules within which the market can function efficiently.

NOTES

1. Richard F. Muth and Elliot Wetzler, "The Effect of Constraints on House Costs," *Journal of Urban Economics 3* (1976): 57–67.

2. *Ibid.*

3. Arthur Young and Company, "Testimony Before the Federal Trade Commission on the Proposed Rule for Standards and Certification," (Testimony given before the Standards and Certification Rule Making Proceedings, DKT. 215-61, HX373, Washington, D.C., May 15, 1979). (Unpublished.) This testimony contains an exhaustive bibliography.

4. It should be understood that the construction of marginal benefits curves assumes something about the insurance industry (for example, the insurance industry exists or it does not exist, it involves transaction costs or it does not, and so on).

5. Michael O'Hare, "Structural Inadequacies in Urban Environmental Management," *Regional and Urban Economics 3* (1973): 69–143.

6. Stephen R. Seidel, "The Effect of Building Codes on Housing Costs," *Housing Costs and Government Regulations. Confronting the Regulatory Maze* (New Brunswick, N.J.: Center for Urban Policy Research, Rutgers University, 1980), pp. 71–99.

7. Ellen Jordan and Paul Rubin, "An Economic Analysis of the Law of False Advertising," *Journal of Legal Studies 3* (1979): 527–553.

8. Paul Rubin, "The Theory of the Firm and the Structure of the Franchise Contract," *Journal of Law and Economies 21* (1978): 223–233.

9. Bernard H. Siegan, *Other People's Property* (Lexington, Mass.: Lexington Books, 1976).

10. Many of the issues in this paper regarding specific codes and standards as well as cost estimates come from Andrew Sabhlok, "Testimony before the Federal Trade Commission on Proposed Trade Regulation Rule on Standards and Certification" (Testimony given before the Standards and Certification Rule Making Proceedings, DKT. 215–61, HX33, San Francisco, April 9, 1979). (Unpublished.)

11. The substitution of private sector initiatives for codes has been suggested by John McClaughry, "A New Approach to Building Safety" (Paper presented at NCSBCS/NBS Conference on Building Rehabilitation Research and Technology for the 1980's, San Francisco, December 10, 1979).

Part Seven

WASTE, BIOREMEDIATION, & PERMACULTURE

Chapter 24

Living Machines
New Alchemy: Where It All Began

by Nancy Jack Todd and John Todd

From ECO-CITIES TO LIVING MACHINES
North Atlantic Books

Suppose there were a clever global pollster, assigned to travel the world, questioning people in places as disparate as the far reaches of the Australian outback, or in downtown Detroit, on one of the Greek islands possibly, or in Brazil or on a rural Chinese commune. Suppose the object of the study was to learn what, if anything, is universal to the human experience— what it is that matters to people ultimately. Would there be any commonality of response? Would it be that, after relief from deprivation and suffering, most of us would name love, concern for our children and families, hopefulness, peace of the heart? Or would it more likely be possessions, wealth, power? It seems possible, were we to answer truly, that we would most want those intangibles without which all other achievements eventually prove barren. Yet, as world events attest daily, as a species we behave as though power and material objects alone were worth our striving.

This is a book about ecological design. By this term we mean design for human settlements that incorporates principles inherent in the natural world in order to sustain human populations over a long span of time. This design adapts the wisdom and strategies of the natural world to human problems. Implicit in this study there is a larger question— what is the role of humanity in the greater destiny of the Earth? As scientific research continues to discover, all of us who inhabit this planet share the same kind of genetic material. In terms of biochemical make-up and genetic structures, the similarities between the human being and the bacteria, for example, are greater than the differences. The illusive and pervasive issues of how human beings, as the only self-conscious species, are to live in the world is a logical outgrowth of our new biological knowledge. Even if the present path of industrial society held much promise of survival, which we feel it does not, it is a violent and unhappy world. A reevaluation of the way humans place themselves in the larger world seems timely, if not overdue.

In recent years people everywhere have been experiencing a reawakening of the Earth as a planet, alive and beautiful beyond words. Photographs from space have affirmed its incandescent uniqueness. Scientists, ecologists, and environmentalists are steadily increasing our knowledge of its complexity and vulnerability and are rapidly restructuring our understanding of it. Over much the same period our own research in applied biology and ecotechnology has led to an emerging synthesis of precepts by which the present human community could sustain itself indefinitely without destroying its basis of living support systems. It is a claim, we think, that could not by made for current industrial cultures. Co-evolutionary with a reawakening sensitivity to the life of the planet there has developed a series of insights, methodologies, and technologies that make it possible to create a post- or meta-industrial society without violating fundamental ecological integrity. This ability is as unprecedented as it is timely.

NEW ALCHEMY

Our own work in ecological design began many years ago with the New Alchemy Institute, a research institute in Cape Cod, which we founded with the aquatic biologist and writer William O. McLarney in 1969. In the summer of 1992, its original goals fulfilled, the Institute closed. Although it is not within the province of this book to recount in detail the terrifying and all too probable threats that imperiled the world then, and more so today, the litany of woes, headed by nuclear confrontation and widespread ecological disaster, that prompted us to take some sort of action at that time remains long and familiar. Barring cataclysmic events, we confront daily an unrelenting army of humanly created problems. Regional war, global proliferation of weapons, industrial and agricultural pollution, contamination of air, land, and water, nuclear meltdown, ozone depletion, acid rain, deforestation, desertification, famine, and homelessness are far from ephemeral spectres. They are directly and achingly real to many people in many parts of the world and indirectly affect everyone. Yet it is the same haunting threat of rapid or gradual extinction of much of life on Earth, at least in its larger forms, that has been a catalyst and context for many changes, some of them hopeful, which are beginning to take place. This threat was certainly instrumental to the birth of New Alchemy, and for the thinking and the work that we shall be discussing throughout.

In 1969, compounding the ongoing crises of the Vietnamese War and conflicting social issues of the late sixties, there was an unremitting flow of information about the destruction of the environment. The word ecology, which, like economy, is derived from the Greek *OIKOS*, meaning household or home, was being adapted into the general vocabulary. Unlike the term *environment*, which denotes one's surroundings in an objectified sense, *ecology* by its very inclusiveness implies interconnectedness. This word's incorporation into daily language was some indication of a dawning realization of the complexity of the human interaction with the natural world.

About that same time we were fresh from a more directly experiential event that also had shaken us and given us a realistic sense of our own capabilities. Friends renting a small ranch in the hilly country west of San Diego in California and just north of the Mexican border had asked us for help in studying the ranch so that they could grow toward self-sufficiency in food and energy. Spending time in the dry, sun-drenched hills there, we came to realize that, given the lack of water and almost non-existent soils where only manzanita bushes seemed to flourish in quantity, we had no idea how our friends should proceed. Academic credentials and training in biology were no help in redefining the human place in what had initially seemed a hospitable landscape, at least not within the framework of the ecological ethic. We decided then to undertake an intensive study of the land to examine as many of the aspects of the environment as we were able to. We collected, studied, and catalogued soil samples, soil animals, insects, plants, shrubs, and rocks, and noted trees, birds, animals, and other fauna. Very slowly, some relevant clues began to emerge. Midway up a small gorge we found a plant, the roots of which are known to seek out moisture, indicating the presence of a hidden spring. Below, where the gorge began to flatten out, there was a live oak tree surrounded by an association of plants that included miner's lettuce which we learned required good soil. With this discovery of a source of water and suitable soil, establishing a garden and a move toward food production became a possibility. If the spring were to be tapped as a source for irrigation and fish ponds, then gardens, poultry and other livestock, and eventually orchards could be integrated and an agricultural ecosystem could become an achievable goal. Our hopeful prognosis for the ranch had an abrupt but unhappy end, however, for the rent on the land was raised unexpectedly to well beyond the means of our friends. Shortly afterwards bulldozers appeared on the crest of the hill and began leveling for a colony of weekend cottages.

We emerged from the experience realizing the need for a more secure basis for research. This combined with a desire for the flexibility and freedom to begin to search for relevant knowledge, new and lost, led us outside established academic and scientific institutions to consider an organization of our own. Our initial impulse was to become disseminators of information, thinking, naively, that this would trigger the necessary reform. We became involved in communication with other like-minded people— biologists, naturalists, students, environmentalists, parents, anyone similarly concerned. But even as we decried, privately and publicly, the wastefulness and destructiveness of many of the practices of industrial societies we had little to suggest in the way of other possibilities. We began to ponder the possibilities for ecological analogues to the current, biologically insupportable, industrial methods for sustaining the people of the world. We wondered whether humanity could ever hope to exist again in a mutually supportive and beneficial way within the biosphere. This question, once it had articulated itself, persisted. It gnawed at our minds and expanded to become the underlying intellectual paradigm on which we were to found New Alchemy.

Accepting the likelihood that there were no existing institutes that would allow us the freedom of crossing disciplines, setting different values and priorities as the basis of our work, and looking at biology and agriculture in a larger social and cultural context, we created our own fledgling institute, adopting as we did so a credo that may have appeared pretentious or absurdly quixotic. It was and remains utterly heartfelt. Our logo read:

"The New Alchemy Institute.
To restore the land, protect the seas, and inform the Earth's stewards."

Our approach to so large and amorphous a mandate was to translate it into research which would show how to affect a shift to a more ecological basis for the provision of basic human needs. This was the work we began when we, and soon afterwards Bill McLarney, crossed the country and rented a twelve-acre farm in Massachusetts. New Alchemy settled in on its Cape Cod center in late 1971.

There were only two paid staff members who did the administrative work when we first moved onto the farm. Everyone else then, the half dozen regulars we considered staff, including Bill McLarney and ourselves, had jobs at The Woods Hole Oceanographic Institute or elsewhere. The rest of the work and the maintenance was done by volunteers and friends who gave what time they could. Perhaps by dint of the fact that it was exploring the potential of a new paradigm, New Alchemy, from the beginning, was difficult to fit into existing funding structures. It remained so through the years, as a core staff of about twenty developed a long record as an innovative research and education organization. Although several of the staff commanded large grants when they worked in established academic and research institutions, New Alchemy consistently had to struggle to stay alive financially. Over the years the work was carried on by staff who might see months go by between paychecks, and by apprentices and volunteers.

To investigate a question as large as an alternative means for providing basic human needs, the research was divided into the tangible and more approachable areas of food, energy, and shelter. Starting quite literally from the ground up, we discovered that to work in food production we had first to manufacture topsoil to augment the meager layer already existing on the sandy, glacial terminal morrain which forms Cape Cod. As we did so, we planted the organic vegetable gardens that were the focus of many years of experiments. Subsequently, the agriculture program expanded into research in many other areas including tree crops, a type of farming that is a logical adaptation to the natural state of Cape Cod. Young orchards were started, as well as stands of trees for timber, fuel, manufacture, and food for livestock.

The other major branch of our research in intensive food production was in the field of aqua culture, the culture of fish and aquatic animals. Aware of the growing protein deficiency in the diets of people in so much of the world, we began research into methods of producing protein resources that were both economically accessible and ecologically benign. In investigating possible alternatives to nuclear and fossil fuel energy, our work has been mainly with the renewable sources of the sun and wind. Windmills, looking, as one group put it, "like steeples of a solar age," and small, suntrapping domes dotted the New Alchemy landscape since its first summer. Our efforts proved encouraging in both agriculture and aquaculture within a relatively short time. We began to see a great improvement in the soil and good-to-excellent yields from the gardens and the sun and wind-powered fish ponds. We were emboldened to go on to the issue of shelter—to try to create an integrative form of architecture that would incorporate renewable energies and biological systems in the form of growing areas for plants and fish.

From early on our work found unique direction in this harnessing of wind and solar energy to power biological systems. We built a number of variations of small translucent structures that were both greenhouse and aquaculture facilities. They were microcosms that absorbed and intensified the pulses of natural forces to provide food and an optimal environment for life forms ranging from soil animals, to plants, to fish, to people. As one design improved on another we evolved what was named the bioshelter, the structure at the core of much of the achievement of the Institute during its first decade. Beyond the Institute, it has been a major catalyst in exploring the fruitfulness of a marriage between biology and architecture. It is at the core of most of the design concepts to be described throughout this book— a harbinger for new directions in public buildings, commercial greenhouses, private and aggregate housing, and year-round community gardens.

Whether it was timeliness or Fortune that smiled on us, New Alchemy's work was recognized in a shorter time and on a larger scale than we would have conceived possible in our first seasons. By 1976 we had designed and built two large bioshelters.[1] One was on Prince Edward Island in Canada, established in cooperation with Canadian Federal and Provincial authorities, as a part of conserver society policies. The other was on our farm on the Cape and designed in collaboration with Solsearch Architects. Although bioshelter has become a generic name for such structures, we chose, more poetically, to call them respectively the Prince Edward Island and Cape Cod Arks. As the cell is acknowledged as the basic building block in organic evolution, the bioshelter is likely one day to be seen as a basic building block in ecological design. The Ark in Canada was opened with considerable fanfare, attended by Prime Minister Trudeau and the then Premier of Prince Edward Island, Alex Campbell. The building remains well ahead of its time as an experiment in systemic design and in the incorporation of biological elements into a structure that was greenhouse, aquaculture facility, and residence for the people who worked in it. Seen in retrospect, what we were acknowledging at the opening of the Ark in Canada was a turning point in integrative architecture. After several years of our own research there, monitoring and testing the building, we turned it over to provincial authorities and it is now a commercial trout-raising facility and hatchery.

After 1976, a great deal of research was done in both Arks on interior climate, energy requirements, soil, and vegetable and fish production as well as overall performance. In the Cape Cod Ark an elaborate monitoring system was installed with seventy-six sensors relaying information on the ongoing state of the building to a central computer. Both it and its Prince Edward Island counterpart weathered their first, unusually severe winters, without resorting to other than solar heat except for a wood stove in the living area of the Canadian Ark. Assessing and extrapolating the ongoing performance and productivity of the buildings, we were able to pronounce the Arks viable beyond our early hopes. They were independent of outside energy sources for heating and cooling and yielded well throughout the year, portending an economic base for future replicas.

For almost all of the same period New Alchemy concepts were being researched and tested simultaneously in Costa Rica. In 1973 Bill McLarney founded ANAI (associacion de los nuevos alquimistas). It consists of a small farm located in the Atlantic lowlands, on the Caribbean coast, just north of the Panamanian border. ANAI is an integral part of the Gandoca community there. While maintaining a lifestyle absolutely consistent with that of his neighbors, Bill has been able to bring considerable financial aid and technical innovation into the area. For all that, ANAI remains a Costa Rican organization with in-country directors and local staff and apprentices. Its principal mission has been to integrate locally defined rural development and ecological conservation, which involves work in aquaculture, agricultural crop diversification, and local economic development.[2] Although ANAI is completely independent, there has been considerable exchange between it and New Alchemy, and now Ocean Arks International, in terms of staff, apprentices, and information.

On Cape Cod the Institute expanded so that, with the exception of a small public library and reading rooms, every inch of the farmhouse was crammed with desks and offices. The old dairy barn housed not only a workshop and storage areas, but a lab, a computer facility, and a state of the art super-insulated energy education auditorium which still demonstrates some of the most advanced materials and concepts in conservation. From a starting point behind the house, a series of signs steered ten thousand visitors a year through a self-guided tour of the farm. The education and outreach program offered a number of guided tours as well. Beyond the lawn and the row of experimental bioshelters which dotted the hill overlooking the garden sat an innovative pillow dome (so named because its translucent skin is divided into hundreds of tiny pillows) that was honored at its opening in 1982 by the presence and approval of the late Buckminster Fuller.

Although the bioshelter research, because of its contained nature, lends itself well to description, the agricultural work on the farm also produced encouraging results. Yields of organic vegetables on the steadily improving soil tripled Department of Agriculture averages. Some of the aquaculture in solar driven tanks rivals world production records. Farther back from the gardens, and away from the house, were extensive herb gardens and a growing orchard of young fruit and nut trees continually tested for adaptability to the Cape's climate and soil. The experiment continued behind the barn where many more trees, food-producing and nitrogen-fixing shrubs, and many different species of bamboo, were all patrolled regularly by a vociferous gaggle of weeding geese.

By the end of its first decade, pooling the promising results of New Alchemy's research with that of others in related fields, we began to feel that we had achieved an affirmative answer to our original question. An alternative, ecological human support base was feasible. It was a sound idea to look to biology as a basis of design. We see this as an informed affirmation of the regenerative capabilities of the planet and of the human role as stewards of the Earth. For those of us who accept its validity, it engenders a new and hopeful way of looking at the world. Unlike present industrial practices it is reversible. We can afford mistakes. Failures can be recycled into more useful forms and tried again, leaving open the possibilities for continual choice. The thinking that underlies the ecological paradigm is less a linear Cartesian model but rather of the mode that can better be envisioned through chaos theory or by the hologram, embodying ceaseless mutual causality and interdependence. If information can be defined as a difference that makes a difference, the work done at New Alchemy can be considered to have helped to create a new piece of information, a variable in the overall fund of human knowledge. It represents a new way of knowing. It has reinforced our own conviction that a smoggy guttering out of life is not inevitable, but becomes, through non-action, a choice. This conviction has found strength in the results of countless other like-minded groups around the world in agriculture, ecology, cybernetics, materials science, physics, and humanistic psychology, economics, and politics. Should the ecological paradigm become, as it could, a governing world view and trigger adaptive behavior in significant numbers of people, we would find ourselves with a renewed promise for the future.

NOTES AND REFERENCES

1. For further reading see:

The Book of the New Alchemists (New York: E.P. Dutton, 1977).

The Journals of the New Alchemists, Nos. 4 -7.

John Todd and Nancy Jack Todd, *Tomorrow is Our Permanent Address* (New York: Harper & Row, 1980).

2. ANAI: 1176 Bryson City Rd., Franklin, NC, 28734

3. See reference 1.

Chapter 25

From Bioshelters to Solar Villages to Future Human Settlements

by Nancy Jack Todd and John Todd

From ECO-CITIES TO LIVING MACHINES
North Atlantic Books

The years with New Alchemy, culminating in the design and building of the Arks, laid the foundation for our work in ecological design. It became rounded out for us intellectually as word of our research and its implications for the workability of an ecological paradigm began to spread. New Alchemy's credibility became established. We met a number of people who, through their writings, had been our mentors when we had been establishing the underlying intellectual framework of the Institute. Among them were the economist E.F. Schumacher, author of *Small is Beautiful*, historian and social critic Murray Bookchin, cultural historian William Irwin Thompson, *Whole Earth Catalog* and *Co-Evolution Quarterly* editor Stewart Brand, Buckminster Fuller, anthropologist/ecologist Gregory Bateson, and anthropologist Margaret Mead. From all of them we received approval and encouragement. Gregory Bateson made what was to us the most memorable and heartening statement of reinforcement when he pronounced what New Alchemy stood for "an epistemology with a future."

For several years during this period in the mid-seventies, William Irwin Thompson had been urging people working in futuristic concepts to think in larger terms and to reconsider the nature of human settlement. He advocated a post- or meta-industrial village, which he called the *deme*, as the next unit for design. It was Margaret Mead, however, who was the most immediate catalyst for the next stage in our work. Shortly before her death she sent for us to explain that she thought that the time had come for New Alchemy's work to be applied on a much broader scale. Her message, in essence, was that the creation of the bioshelter had been a good piece of work, useful and relevant, but at the level of the private structure or single family house it was limited. Most of the people in the world would neither be able to afford one nor have access to one. She felt we must begin to envision the same kind of integrative architecture at the level of the block, the neighborhood, or the village.

It was a challenging legacy. We could not, nor would we, have refused. It was a major next step conceptually—the question of how to take the idea of using biology as the model for design, which had proved workable on a small scale in an experimental setting, and begin to apply it on a much broader scale. Our first response was to ask people from a range of disciplines to join us and the New Alchemists to meet together and ponder the question for several days. In April of the year following Dr. Mead's death we convened a conference entitled, *The Village as Solar Ecology: A Generic Design Conference*[1]. We dedicated the conference and the report resulting from it to her memory.

The working hypothesis for the meetings was given in the original proposal which stated:

> "The blending of architecture, solar, wind, biological and electronic technologies with housing, food production, and waste utilization within an ecological and cultural context will be the basis of creating a new design science for the post-petroleum era."

We were not so naive as to expect that we would emerge from the conference complete with a communicable and tangible epistemology for the design of sustainable communities of the future. To have done so would have been beyond the scope of any conference that did not go on for years. At that conference, however, and in subsequent years, a number of design precepts have emerged from our own and other organizations which are fundamental to the planning of existing and new communities. If we are to continue to shelter and feed the people of the world in the coming centuries, we will have to design in a different way than we do now. Gradually, these precepts are being incorporated into existing or planned projects. In 1982 we took a further step toward the application of ecological technology when we created Ocean Arks International. It is a non-profit organization intended to disseminate the ideas and practice of ecotechnology, or ecological engineering, and ecological sustainability throughout the world. Its first project was to design and build a high speed sailing vessel, the Ocean Pickup, for use by fishermen.

That a revisioning of the way we live and think about the planet is crucial was reinforced unexpectedly for us not long after the Village Conference when a young woman from the Wampanoag tribe at Mashpee, Massachusetts visited us at New Alchemy. As always, when the weather is even faintly kind, we were sitting outside on the grass to talk. The general subject of our conversation was the differences in the ways of our respective cultures—hers, the ancestral traditions of the Wampanoags and ours, at least in her eyes, those of an exploitative technological society. What she said to us in essence was, "My people don't understand you or why you do the things you do. We don't understand why you are still trying to take more of our land. Why must you own things. Why must you always have more." Her eyes clouded for a moment as she searched for the right explanation, then she gestured to a nearby flower bed. "A seed, a flower, a tree unfolds according to the instructions it has been given. We have always tried to live by ours. We don't understand yours. How you have been taught to live. What your instructions are."

It is possible that we have forgotten. What are our instructions, as a people, a culture? The observation of our Wampanoag friend was strangely evocative of the words of the poet Annie Dillard, when she says in "Teaching a Stone to Talk," "I want to learn or remember, how to live."[2] At the Solar Village Conference a few years earlier, architect and Royal College of Art Professor in London Keith Critchlow had spoken to us of ancient concepts of design based on a sacred geometry of the Earth itself. The great circle arches, and the mathematical laws that govern the movements of the stars, have found expression in form structures, building and culture. These are the expression of the psyche of a people when the sacred is an underlying energizing force. Carl Gustav Jung spoke of such a time as "a period in which man was still linked by myth with the world of the ancestors and thus with nature truly experienced."[3] It is a world view long gone from us now, but unlike our own governing mythologies of progress and material happiness, it held and satisfied minds and souls for untold ages and generations. As Giorgio de Santillana said in *Hamlet's Mill*, "...it lived on and flowered and let the world live."[4] For longer than we can know, humanity lived in a universe governed by fixed laws at once mysterious and predictable, the visible aspects of which were inhabited by innumerable unseen gods, spirits, and forces. Spirit and matter, humanity and nature were one, an original seamless, undivided dynamic unity that encompassed and enclosed the interplay of all forces.

But then a new cosmology became dominant in the Western world. It has taken place in a brief period, in comparison to the preceding eons. This new cosmology began with some of the philosophers of ancient Greece and evolved over the centuries to maturity in Europe during the Age of Enlightenment. What Louis Mumford has called the mechanical world order[5] came to be increasingly accepted. Reflecting the thinking, among others, of Johannes Kepler who, in 1605, wrote "My aim is to show that the celestial machine be likened not to a 'divine organism' but rather to a clockwork," it became the basis of all scientific exploration. That knowledge which could be measured, quantified, charted, and ultimately objectified was seen as legitimate for study. Basing their thinking on the philosophy of Rènè Descartes, who saw a fundamental division between the separate and independent realms of mind and matter, scientists began to treat matter, including the living world, as lifeless and apart from themselves, leading to both the greatness and the folly of the idea of scientific objectivity. The influence of Cartesian duality was to further lead Western cultures to think of the mind as divided from the body and from the unconscious mind. It remained for Isaac Newton to complete the intellectual domination of the mechanistic world view, by using it as the groundwork foundation for his construction of classical physics. The philosophy and scientific discovery of the Age of Enlightenment produced an explosion in knowledge and provided the basis for the ever-accelerating explorations of science. That science bred the technology that has changed the face of the Earth. Because that technology could not have been implemented without a world view that reflects our fundamental attitudes about life and mechanism, we are at once its benefactors and its victims.

For a long time, certainly into our own childhood, the images of a clockwork universe and of the natural world as functioning mechanistically, machine-like, removed and separate from ourselves held sway. It is still not broadly questioned, but signs of discomfort with it are becoming increasingly common. Feedback from the environment-scarred, denuded hillsides, dying lakes, air murky on the horizon, miles of scrap heaps and automobile graveyards, urban sprawl-has become impossible to ignore. The evidence has gained sufficient proportions that it does not take a philosopher or a specialist of any kind to wonder whether our treatment of the natural world as immune to abuse is the best or even a safe course. Gregory Bateson[6] compared our behavior to the situation in Lewis Carroll's *Alice in Wonderland*[7] where Alice found herself obliged to play croquet with a flamingo for a mallet and a hedgehog for a ball. Neither the flamingo nor the hedgehog behaved in a predictable manner, because they were alive, not lifeless and inert tools with Alice the only living variable involved in the interaction. Dr. Bateson terms it "an inappropriate coupling of biological systems"[8], implying, obviously, that we treat other living systems as inert tools in our mechanical model of the universe. This led him further to question whether information after being processed through the conscious mind is adequate for understanding another biological system, the behavior of which is based on complicated patterning on a non-conscious level.

We have not been inclined to think a great deal about the assumptions implicit to the mechanocentric theory of the universe, the mindset of scientists being no less immune to the pervading climate of thought than that of the rest of us. We have all been nurtured in the unconscious acceptance of the concept of progress and put our trust in linear modes of thought and causality. It is a habit of mind that has become second nature and we are reluctant to trust any other. Alfred North Whitehead observed, "Our science has been founded on simple location and misplaced concreteness," and "science divides the seamless coat—or to change the metaphor into a happier form, it examines the coat, which is superficial, and neglects the body, which is fundamental. The disastrous separation of body and mind which has been fixed on European thought by Descartes is responsible for this blindness of science."

For some time now there have been tremors threatening to undermine the edifice of Descartes and Newton and the acceptance of the strictly causal nature of physical phenomena. Early in this century the general relativity theory of Albert Einstein abolished the concept of absolute space and time, and with it the mechanistic world view. Since that time the cosmology on which we have built our political, economic and social structures has no longer fit the theories being involved on the frontiers of scientific theory and advanced thought. In spite of the daily evidence of our senses and the quantity of information pouring in from the media, books, and scientific journals—deserts expanding, forests dwindling, species vanishing at the rate of one a day, widespread social unrest—we continue to act as though none of this has anything to do with us and our behavior. Reports are published on limits to growth, on the finite carrying capacity of the Earth, on repression and injustice, yet economic and political strategies, both capitalist and communist, continue to be based on assumptions of indefinite exploitation and continued growth. This reflects our world view which was built on now outdated concepts but is no longer cohesive with emerging scientific thought. Gradually, however, as general loss of faith and confidence are becoming evident, this paradigm is fading and another is emerging. As the concept of a mechanistic universe and a schizophrenic attitude to nature are relinquished, we find ourselves on the verge of a cosmology potentially far more cohesive intellectually, more sound intuitively, and more peaceful spiritually.

Such a realization led Murray Bookchin to state in the introduction to *The Ecology of Freedom*, "Such a philosophy has always been more than an outlook or a mere method for dealing with reality. It has also been what philosophers call an ontology—a description of reality conceived not as mere matter but as active, self-organizing substance with a striving toward consciousness."[9] The British physicist David Bohm has further stated that "... inseparable quantum connectedness of the whole universe is the fundamental reality."[10]

It begins to become increasingly apparent then that with the slow dissolving of the mechanistic world view, we are evolving a new or renewed awareness of the universe—one that is internally consistent. No longer must we gloss over the discrepancies between the spiritual and the material, the sacred and the secular. The scientific paradigm points to acceptance of the cosmic dance of Shiva and the dance of quanta—and all of us participate, creatures of light-energy, star matter; all are dancers. The ancients watched the sky and saw with their hearts, Eastern mystics see with the inner eye, and now physicists have looked at the universe with telescope and microscope and all seem to have come to a commonality of understanding. The physicist John Wheeler maintained that the most important aspect of the quantum principle is that it destroyed the concept of the world as "sitting out there." The act of observation in itself makes the observer a participator. Making a measurement, even of an electron, changes the state of the electron to that degree so the universe will never again be quite the same. He concluded, "In some strange sense the universe is a participatory universe." [11]

The idea is an overwhelming one. just as we are beginning to reassume some responsibility for our actions in the context of the Earth, a question of a larger context and consequence arises. Yet no matter how far reaching our ultimate accountability, it seems common sense that it is here, with the Earth and each other, that the healing must begin. And if because we have discarded their myths we can no longer look to the ancient gods for instructions as to how to proceed, science reembedded in the cosmology of a participatory universe and a sense of the sacred may yet prove to be an appropriate guide. Writing in his *Notebooks*, Charles Darwin stated, "The grand question which every naturalist ought to have before him, when dissecting a whale or classifying a mite, a fungus, or an infusorian is 'What are the Laws of Life?'"[12] More than a hundred years later and, by his own admission, not much farther along with so central an issue, Gregory Bateson, in *Mind and Nature*, asked the same question in different words: "What pattern connects the crab to the lobster and the orchid to the primrose and all the four of them to me? And me to you? And all the six of us to the amoeba in one direction and to the backward schizophrenic in another? What is in the pattern," he goes on to ask, "which connects all living creatures? ... the pattern of patterns? ... the metapattern?"[13] And he added that, as of 1978 when he wrote the book, there was no conventional way of even beginning to describe the tangle of the vast network of interrelationships and our ideas about them which would be necessary to grapple with the metapattern. An intuitive recognition of such a metapattern, however rudimentary, was fundamental to evolving the underlying paradigm for New Alchemy and for all the biological design work there.

The chance to participate in a process so much larger than ourselves holds out to us, the heirs of the age of science and technology, the possibility of a new set of instructions—or perhaps the eternal instructions—in a language, that of science, which we understand and accept. The Native American spokesman, Chief Black Elk, once declared that "All life is holy and good to tell" but we chose not to listen.[14] Yet we cannot ignore the rest of life indefinitely. Our understanding must grow to encompass a union of nature and culture in which the sacredness of all life is honored. As long as we saw all other life as outside and apart from ourselves, we treated it carelessly. Embracing the interconnectedness of all life, we can again weave together the rift between sacred and secular, and the totality will be seen as sacred. Perhaps, now, with a synthesis of knowledge of fields as disparate as quantum physics, astronomy, ecology, religion, holography, anthropology, and the contemplation of sacred art, architecture, and geometry, certain harmonies are beginning to be heard, or heard again, and our sense of the world, rather than being cacaphonous and diffuse with the claims of economists and environmentalists, communists and capitalists, the secular and the sacred, begins to make more sense, to ring true. Perhaps a cosmology that is at once beyond memory and still just out of reach of present knowledge, yet somehow alive within us, is unfolding. The stars are still there to remind us that we are both trivial and non-trivial. One way of reaching out toward what we want to bring into being is a careful reassessment of how we are to live; where under the shining sky, in what relation to the sun and the solar winds, and how we are to best care for the living, celestial matter that is the small portion of the Earth on which we find ourselves.

1. *The Village as SolarEcology: Proceedings of the New Alchemy/Threshold Generic Design Conference*, April 16-21, 1979.

2. Annie Dillard, *Teaching a Stone To Talk* (New York: Harper & Row, 1982), p. 15.

3. Carl Gustav Jung, *Memories, Dreams, Reflections*, recorded and edited by Aniela Jaffé (New York and London: Pantheon Books, 1963), pp. 143-144.

4. Giorgio de Santillana and Hertha von Dechend, *Hamlet's Mill: An Essay Investigating the Origins of Human Knowledge and Its Transmission Through Myth* (Boston: David R. Godine, 1977), p. 332.

5. Louis Mumford, *The Pentagon of Power*, Volume II of *The Myth of the   Machine* (New York and London: Harcourt Brace Jovanovich, 1964), p. 86.

6. Mary Catherine Bateson, *Our Own Metaphor: A Personal Account of a Conference on the Effects of Conscious Purpose on Human Adaptation* (New York.Alfred A. Knopf, 1972), p. 15.

7. Lewis Carroll, *Alice's Adventures in Wonderland* (New York: Modern Library).

8. Bateson, *Our Own Metaphor*, op. cit., p. 15.

9. Murray Bookchin, *The Ecology of Freedom: The Emergence and Dissolution of Hierarchy* (Palo Alto: Chesire Books, 1982), p. 14.

10. David Bohm quoted by Fritjof Capra, *The Tao of Physics: An Exploration of the Parallels Between Modern Physics and Eastern Mysticism* (Boulder: Shambhala, 1975), p. 138.

11. John Wheeler quoted by Capra, *The Tao of Physics*, op. cit., p. 141.

12. Charles Darwin quoted by William Irwin Thompson, *The Time Falling Bodies Take To Light* (New York: St. Martins Press), p. 93.

13. Gregory Bateson, *Mind and Nature*: A Necessary Unity (New York: E.P. Dutton, 1979), pp. 8-11.

14. Black Elk, *Black Elk Speaks: Being the Life Story of a Holy Man of the Oglala Sioux* as told through John G. Neihardt (New York: Pocket Books, 1972), p. 1.

Chapter 26

Living Machines and the Years Ahead

by Nancy Jack Todd and John Todd

From ECO-CITIES TO LIVING MACHINES
North Atlantic Books

Reissuing and updating a book in the time frame and global context in which we have worked with this one gives more opportunity for pause than do the average advantages of hindsight. In the interlude between the two editions, the human world has undergone a tectonic shift. No longer bipolarized by the shadow megalomaniac collective identities of the United States and the Soviet Union, the balance of terror has given way to a global structure that is much more diverse and prone to the unexpected.

Since the first edition of the book (ECO-CITIES TO LIVING MACHINES) was published, a time span that would see a child grow from infancy to school age or from adolescence to adulthood, the world has changed radically in ways that then were unforeseen. Looking back eight years, we had yet to witness the rise and fall of Gorbachev, the surge of nationalism in eastern Europe, the crumbling of the Berlin wall, the reunification of Germany, the disintegration of the Soviet Union and the implosion of Communist Party hegemony there, and the conclusion of the Reagan/Bush era here.

We finished the book then fearful that human and environmental problems would not receive the attention they so urgently warranted as long as the world remained a divided armed camp and the arms race, nuclear and otherwise, was seen as the foundation of national security and world stability. Reluctantly, we fell back on the image of the mushroom cloud as that most telling for our time. A change as fundamental as the end of the cold war seemed to fall more in the category of unanswered prayer than that of realistic possibility. But, miraculously, in a few short years, it happened. As a result the power infrastructure of the nations of the world is now wobbling in search of new equilibrium. The United States scrambles for a national identity beyond that of guardian against the Soviet threat, and with a new generation at the helm, may well find an enlightened leadership role. Europe and Japan are seeking expanded roles and countries like Korea, Thailand, and Indonesia are anxious to join the industrialized club. The non-industrialized countries are demanding reformed development policies as the role of transnational corporations as agents of development increasingly is being questioned. And everywhere women are demanding an equal voice in decision making processes at all levels.

With greater frequency one hears a concern for the greatest good of the entire planet and all its peoples being voiced. As a rule, when this occurs, it is within the context of the environmental crisis. But, unlike those years when the world was dominated by the agenda of two nuclear armed camps, there seems to a window of opportunity opening in which we can tackle such problems. The 1992 United Nations Conference on the Environment and Development in Rio de Janeiro may prove to have been a significant early step and catalyst in this direction. Again, unlike the time when the book first saw the light of day, in spite of all the problems, there is a certain yeastiness in the air. The world is more diffuse. If, as mathematician and chaos theorist Ralph Abraham suggests, "with no ongoing chaos, there can be no ongoing creation," then the time is ripe for many of the changes we are advocating.

In the area of education, for example, David Orr, the director of environmental studies at Oberlin has called for a complete restructuring of the educational process and the creation of a curriculum in the ecological design arts that would cultivate the analytical abilities, ecological wisdom, and the practical wherewithal necessary to make human livelihood fit within natural cycles. His curriculum would include restoration of damaged ecosystems, rebuilding the ecological foundations for local and regional economies, and reducing the human impact on nature as well as the development of educational and training programs. Another significant reordering is under discussion as perceptions of national security are redefined. Stewart Brand has advocated harnessing such strong points of the military as discipline, deployment capability, and commitment to the welfare of the country to address environmental and social problems. A genuine conversion of the military to address existing crises could prove an effective force in righting many of the social and environmental wrongs that beset us nationally and globally.

The urgency of the situation demands tackling the problems we have created on as many levels with as many strategies as we can muster. Ultimately, it will further challenge us to change the means by which we sustain ourselves. What is required is nothing less than a fundamental technological revolution that will integrate advanced societies with the natural world to the mutual benefit of both. Because pollution, alteration of the atmosphere, and the loss of soils and of biotic diversity are byproducts of cultures estranged from the great natural systems of the planet, it is essential that we create truly symbiotic relationships with the natural world. Building on the precepts for design discussed throughout the book, we have been working with a number of ideas for affecting such a change. As described in the prologue, our research with living technologies continues to indicate an almost unlimited potential.

THE DESIGN OF LIVING MACHINES

A living machine is a device made up of living organisms of all types and usually housed within a casing or structure made of extremely light-weight materials. Like a conventional machine, it is comprised of interrelated parts that function together in the performance of some type of work. Living machines can be designed to produce food or fuels, treat wastes, purify air, regulate climates, or even to do all of these simultaneously. They are designed along the principles evolved by the natural world in building and regulating its great ecologies of forests, lakes, prairies, and estuaries. Their primary energy source is sunlight. Like the planet, living machines have hydrological and mineral cycles.

Living machines are also, however, totally new, contained environments. To create a living machine, organisms are collected and reassembled in unique ways depending on the purpose of the project. The parts or living components can come from almost any region of the planet and be recombined in any number of ways. Appropriate assembly is based on a knowledge of the niches and the natural history of the organisms that make up the constituent parts as well as a calculated determination of their individual fit into the unique constellation of organisms being assembled by the designer.

In our offices, for example, we have experimented with a living machine that was a pulp and paper digester designed to prevent waste material from impinging on the external environment. Normally, pulp and paper sludge is considered impossible to treat and is disposed of in landfills. We built our small experimental digester from two interconnected, thin-walled, translucent fiberglass cylinders that we filled with water. Light penetrated the top and sides so the internal environment was bathed in sunlight during most of the daylight hours. Inside the cylinders we brought together a complex assemblage of rock minerals, diverse algae species from New

England lakes and ponds, and bacteria, fungi, and protozoans from local environments. To this we added bacteria from Europe and North America, crayfish from North America and fish from Europe, Africa, and South America. Higher plants from every continent except Antarctica were rafted on the surface or integrated within the system. The exotics in the system were either, like goldfish or carp, ubiquitous in this part of the world or were incapable of surviving in the wild in a temperate climate. Examples of the latter include fishes from tropical Africa and South America and floating plants like water hyacinths that cannot survive northern winters in the wild.

Within this ecological digester microbial life attached itself to the pulp wastes, forming a heavy, gooey sludge thereby preconditioned for the animals in the system. The microbes were protected by the gases, especially the oxygen produced by algae and higher plants. Toxic substances were also processed by photosynthetic organisms which, in turn, were sustained by dissolved organic matter made soluble by the bacteria. This living machine required animal filter feeders and detritus eaters to function. They passed the pulp mill sludge back and forth through their guts and intestines, exposing it to digestive enzymes and the complex assemblages of bacteria living there. The original waste material was digested and transformed into a range of byproducts, some useful.

This contained ecosystem was a microcosm comprised of a large number of species. The engineering was global in terms of selection of organisms but specific in design. The functioning system represented an "artificial" state in some senses—in that the original toxins and the array of organisms are the result of human actions—but through care and attentiveness an environment with ecological integrity was established. The quality and characteristics of the pulp mill sludge dictated the organisms and the ratio of each set to the other. Balance was achieved through trial and error initially. Over time, by removing some of the original species and replacing them with others and making other biological and mechanical adjustments the performance and stability of this new environment was optimized. In the course of our investigations with living systems, from the ponds of New Alchemy to the newest living machines to restore degraded waters, several fundamental principles for designing living technologies have emerged (Table 1). These nine principles form the basis of living machine design, and are the synthesis of over twenty years of research into the ways in which the capabilities and powers of nature can be integrated into sustainable living technologies:

TABLE 1

Nine Principles for Designing Living Machines

1. **Microbial Communities** The primary ecological foundations of living machines are predicated upon diverse microbial communities obtained from a wide range of aquatic (marine and freshwater) and terrestrial environments. In addition, organisms from chemically and thermally highly stressed environments are critical. Genetic engineering cannot do what constellations of natural organisms can accomplish when they work in concert.

2. **Photosynthetic Communities** Sunlight-powered photosynthesis is the primary driving force of these systems. Anaerobic phototrophic microbes, cyanobacteria, algae, and higher plants must be linked in a dynamic balance with the heterotrophic microbial communities.

3. **Linked Ecosystems and the Law of the Minimum** At least three distinct types of ecological systems need to be linked together to produce living machines that carry out self design and self repair through time. Such systems have the theoretical ability to span centuries and possibly millenia.

4. **Pulsed Exchanges** Nature works in short term/long term pulses which are both regular and irregular. This pulsing is a critical design force and helps maintain diversity and robustness. Pulses need to be intrinsic to design.

5. **Nutrient and Micronutrient Reservoirs** Carbon/Nitrogen/Phosphorus ratios need to be regulated and maintained. A full complement of macro and trace elements needs to be in the system so that complex food matrices can be established and allowed to "explore" a variety of successional strategies over time. This will support biological diversity.

6. **Geological Diversity and Mineral Complexity** Living machines can simulate a rapid ecological history by having within them minerals from a diversity of strata and ages. The geological materials can be incorporated into the sub-ecosystems relatively quickly by being introduced as ultra fine powders which can be solubilized over short time frames.

7. **Steep Gradients** Steep gradients are required within and between the sub-elements of the system. These include redox, pH, humic materials, and ligand or metal-based gradients. These gradients help develop the high efficiencies that have been predicted for living machines.

8. **Phylogenetic Diversity** In a well engineered ecosystem all phylogenetic levels from bacteria to vertebrates should be included. System regulators and internal designers are often unusual and unpredictable organisms. The development of various phyla has arisen to a large extent from the strategic exploration of the total global system over a vast period of time. This time can be compressed with the consequences of this evolution.

9. **The Microcosm as a Tiny Mirror Image of the Macrocosm** This ancient hermetic law applies to ecological design and engineering. As much as possible, global design should be miniaturized in terms of gas, mineral, and biological cycles. The big system relationships need to be maintained in the living machine.

We have designed and built living machines comparable to the pulp mill digester to grow food, to heat and cool buildings, and to treat sewage, sludge, septage, and boat wastes. It is possible to apply the same kind of biological engineering to the production of fuels like hydrogen gas. Living machines can produce byproducts that can be used in the manufacture of materials ranging from paper products to advanced composite construction materials. They can be linked together to form an engineered ecology, a living technology that can be designed to protect and restore natural environments and support human communities.

Living machines are fundamentally different from both conventional machines and standard biotechnologies, presenting a novel range of qualities which are summarized in Table 2. What they represent, in essence, is the intelligence of a forest or a lake, reapplied to human ends. As with the forest or the lake, their primary source of power is the sun. Like natural ecosystems they engage in a process of self design. They rely on biotic diversity for self repair, protection, and overall system efficiency.

Living machines need not be small nor isolated from larger natural systems. Scale is not an overriding factor, as living technologies, like the natural world, are made up from parts which fuse the genius of evolution. These include such independent attributes of life forms as self repair, replication, and feeding and waste excretion dynamically balanced with interdependent functions like gas, mineral, and nutrient exchanges. The same design principles in nature which extend from the cell to encompass the whole planetary biota, allow living technologies to vary greatly in size. We have designed one living machine to go inside a greenhouse-covered canal twenty-seven miles long intended to purify three hundred million gallons of drinking water daily. We are constructing others for classroom use as part of an environmental education project that would offer programs ranging from kindergarten through college levels.

Looking to the twenty-first century, the potential contribution of living technologies is incalculable. Although fossil fuels are needed for the manufacture of the long lived construction materials, such fuels are not in ongoing use for combustion. Living machines are capable of reintegrating wastes into larger systems and of breaking down toxic materials or, in the case of metals, recycling them or locking them up in centuries-long cycles. Living machines would make it possible to feed large numbers of people, particularly in urban areas, and could be part of a strategy for addressing issues of inequity between peoples and regions. Some of the poorer parts of the planet, especially the semi-arid subtropics could benefit enormously as the tropics are the greatest reservoirs for the necessary spare parts. Living technologies have the further potential to release natural systems from human bondage. By miniaturizing the production of essential human services, they would free nature to evolve in a wild state free from human interference, greatly reducing, in the long term, the human footprint on the ecology of the planet. This is further relevant in that the long term survival of humanity may be predicated on a dramatic increase in the wilderness areas that are the great repositories of biological diversity.

Compared to conventional technologies, living machines have a number of unique qualities. It is their aggregate characteristic, however, that most distinguishes them. People accustomed to the mechanical moving parts, the noise or exhaust of internal combustion engines, or the silent geometry of electronic devices often have difficulty imagining living machines. Complex life forms inside strange, light receptive structures can seem at once familiar and bizarre. They are both garden and machine. They are alive yet contained and framed in vessels built of novel materials, some of which are still in the developmental stages. Living technologies bring people and nature together in fundamentally radical and transformative ways.

Much of the potential of living machines to protect the environment lies in their photosynthetic base. Secondary sources of energy can and often are used for control and light augmentation, yet both the unique adaptiveness and economic viability of living technologies lies in their dependence on photosynthetically-based food chains. They are built with parts that are themselves living populations, often extremely diverse, and comprised of hundreds of species. A key attribute is that components replace themselves as they wear out. The life span of some populations can be as long as centuries if housed within long lived containers. These systems further have abilities to respond and change with variations in inputs. Although the task is set by the designer, when the living machine is left to develop its own immense complexity it may establish biotic relationships not seen in nature and thereby expand its options of diversity. The organisms in the pulp waste digester in our office or in our Providence plant have never experienced the exact constellation of relationships they do as parts of living machines. When they adapt to new, contained environmental conditions they have the potential to evolve unprecedented relationships.

An important aspect of living technologies, and of natural systems in the wild, is that they are pulse driven. Daily, seasonal, and sporadic variations stamp themselves deeply on their internal ecology. The background of pulse creates the resilience, agility, and vigor for the systems to recover from external shocks, a response impossible for conventional machines. Occasionally a living machine may be overwhelmed by overloading or light deprivation and lose critical organisms, affecting its ability to carry out its task efficiently. Yet even under severe stress, some internal circuits will continue to function, perhaps requiring reseeding in order to bring the system back to its original task.

Control species within these contained ecosystems orchestrate the overall ecology. We are as yet uncertain as to whether there are control hierarchies, or whether a threshold number of living parts is the basis of control. Occasionally organisms can upset control functions, disrupting the functioning of the overall system. In the pulp sludge digester, for example, the activity of one very vigorous species of fish kept the pulp particles in suspension, making material unavailable for the detritus feeding organisms. Removing the fish solved the problem.

The building blocks of ecological design are the life histories of the organisms. It is essential to graft the evolution of living technologies onto a foundation of a wide ranging knowledge of natural history. For example, once many years ago while traveling with Bill McLarney in Costa Rica, in several small upland streams we found large fish of the genus Brycon. The streams gave little evidence of food for the fish inhabiting them yet the fish were a good size. We subsequently discovered that Brycon could not only catch but digest the hard, seemingly inedible fruits that fell into the stream from overhanging trees. Closer investigation of the anatomy of the fish revealed terrifying looking teeth for shredding very hard materials and a long, serpentine-shaped intestine capable of digesting them. Again we were reminded that the world is a vast repository of unknown biological strategies that could have immense relevance should we develop a science of integrating the stories embedded in nature into the systems we design to sustain us. Conservationists and preservationists rightly honor nature and struggle to protect the pristine natural places that remain but the survival of civilization equally may require another fundamental step. It may be essential for us to find ways of decoding the natural world and of using its teachings to reshape and redefine our tools and technologies. Good farmers and gardeners have long had this kind of relationship with nature. With the unfolding and application of ecology it is possible to extend this relationship into new dimensions.

The development of living technologies had to await the advent of ecology. It had also to wait for the materials sciences to evolve to the point at which energy efficient and environmentally responsive materials could be manufactured cost effectively. Generally, the containment vessels for living machines need to be fabricated from light, high light-transmitting, flexible materials that can be bonded and waterproofed. Such materials must be capable of handling a variety of stresses, including high pressure and ultraviolet radiation.

Economically and energetically, living machines make enormous sense. They are cost competitive in some areas of food growing and in purifying concentrated wastes. In that living machines avoid hazardous chemicals[1] and are pollution free in operation, they appeal to environmentalists. The greatest hindrance to the widespread adoption of living technologies arises, ironically, from the very phenomenon they are intended to solve; the estrangement of modern cultures from the natural world. Nature remains invisible to so many people. We anticipate that the aesthetic and emotional qualities of living machines in addition to their functional and economic soundness will hasten their acceptance. They can be designed to be beautiful—evocative of the deep harmony found in nature. New economies that are an outgrowth of the wisdom of the natural world would create a new and hopeful dimension for the future.

With the nineties we face the years to come paradoxically armed with the dual realities of greater urgency and greater promise than was the case when we concluded the first edition of this book. Then we sadly concluded that the predominant image of the age was that of a burgeoning mushroom cloud. That horror is far from banished but another possibility is emerging, stronger now than it was before. Should a greater ecological awareness begin to shape our thinking, new symbols would arise that could bind the scientific and the spiritual and would reinfuse all life with the essence of the sacred. We would be increasingly capable of envisioning the 'blue, true dream' that is the living Earth luminous in the darkness of the surrounding sky. On the planet's surface we would begin to see landscapes that are wild and landscapes that support ongoing generations of human and non-human communities, villages, and cities that mirror intense concentrations of activity and culture, great wind powered sailing ships on the seas and smaller ones plying coastal and inland waters. Such a world is unlikely to be idyllically Utopian. It still would be inevitably scrappy and difficult. But it could be the matrix for the continuing coevolution and unfolding potential of the natural and human worlds.

It has been our intent with this book to paint, for our readers, word pictures of the possible—doing so in the frankly partisan hope that they will be persuaded of the validity of the concepts. It is an attempt on our part to say, as Robert Frost did, if less poetically, "You come too."[2] It will be a shared mutual venture into the unknown, offering for the present nothing more nor less than hope, in the ongoing search for those instructions that, if we begin to think and believe and act appropriately, may yet help us go on living on our shining, blue-green, home planet.

Table 2

A Comparison of Living Machines with Conventional Technologies

ENERGY	LIVING MACHINES	CONVENTIONAL TECHNOLOGIES
Primary Sources	The Sun	Fossil fuels, nuclear power
Secondary Sources	Radiant energy	Internal biogenesis of gases Combustion and electricity
Control	Electricity, wind, and solar electric	Electrical, chemical, and mechanical
Capture of External Energy	Intrinsic to design	Rare
Internal Storage	Heat, nutrients, and gases	Batteries
Efficiency	Low biological transfer efficiency in subsystems, high overall aggregate efficiency	High in best technologies, low, when total infrastructure is calculated
Flexibility	Inflexible with regards to sunlight, flexible with adjunct energy sources	Inflexible
Pulses	Tolerant and adapted	Usually intolerant, tolerant in specific instances

Design

LIVING MACHINES	CONVENTIONAL TECHNOLOGY
Parts are living populations	Hardware based
Structurally simple	Structurally complex
Complex living circuits	Circuit complexity often reduces
Passive, few moving parts	Multiple moving parts
Dependent entirely upon environmental energy and internal storage systems	Energy intensive
Long life spans ... centuries	Short life spans ... decades
Materials replacement	Total replacement
Internal recycling intrinsic	Recycling usually not present Pollution control devices used
Ecology is scientific basis for design	Genetics is scientific basis for Biotechnology Chemistry is basis for process engineering Physics for mechanical engineering

Table 2 *(continued)*

Materials

LIVING MACHINES	CONVENTIONAL TECHNOLOGIES
Transparent climatic envelopes	Steel and concrete
Flexible lightweight containment materials	Reliance on motors
Electrical and wind powered air compressors/pumps	Structurally massive

Biotic Design

LIVING MACHINES	CONVENTIONAL TECHNOLOGIES
Photosynthetically based ecosystems	Independent of sunlight
Linked sub-ecosystems	Unconnected to other life forms
Components living populations	Only biotechnologies use biotic design
Self design	No self design
Multiple seedings to establish	
Internal structures	
Pulse driven	
Directed food chains: end points are products including fuels, food, waste purification, living materials, climate regulation	

Control

LIVING MACHINES	CONVENTIONAL TECHNOLOGIES
Primarily internal throughout complex living circuits	Electrical, chemical, and mechanical controls applied to system
Threshold number of organisms for sustained control	External orchestration and internal regulation
All phylogenetic levels from bacteria to vertebrates act as control organisms	
Disease is controlled internally through competition, predation, and antibiotic production	Through application of medicines
Feedstock both internal and external	Feedstocks external
Modest use of electrical and gaseous control inputs orchestrated with environmental sensors and computer controls	Sophisticated control engineering

Table 2 *(continued)*

Pollution

LIVING MACHINES	CONVENTIONAL TECHNOLOGIES
Pollution, if occurs, is an indication of incomplete design	Pollution intrinsically a byproduct Capture technologies need to be added
Positive environmental impact	Negative or neutral environmental impact

Management and Repair

LIVING MACHINES	CONVENTIONAL TECHNOLOGIES
Training in biology and chemistry essential	Specialists needed to maintain systems
Empathy with systems may be a critical factor	Empathy less essential

Costs

LIVING MACHINES	CONVENTIONAL TECHNOLOGIES
Capital costs competitive with conventional systems	The standard
Fuel & energy costs	High fuel and energy costs
Labor costs probably analogous—still to be determined	The standard
Lower pollution control costs	The standard
Operation costs lower because of reduced chemical and energy input	The standard
Potential reduction of social costs, in part because of potential transferability to less industrialized regions and countries	Social costs can be high

1. Björn Guterstam and John Todd, "Ecological Engineering for Wastewater Treatment and its Application in New England and Sweden," in *AMBIO: A journal of the Human Environment* (Royal Swedish Academy of Sciences), Vol. 19, No. 3, May 1990, p. 173-5.

2. Robert Frost, "The Pasture," in *Poetry and Prose* (New York, Chicago, San Francisco: Holt, Rinehart, and Winston, 1972), p. 16.

*   *   *

(The text is the second edition, published eight years after the first. Changes in the world and developments in the authors' own work were significant. Likewise the authors' extensively refer to their previous edition, making light of changes in circumstances and knowledge both personally and globally.)

Part Eight

ARCHITECTS AND THEIR WORK

Chapter 27

The House That Max Built

by Eugenia Bone

From METROPOLIS MAGAZINE
December 1996

On the outskirts of Austin, designers and researchers are rethinking the way we build houses. The nonprofit center, known affectionately as Max's Pot, is an 18-acre ecolab where founder Pliny Fisk III and his wife, codirector Gail Vittori, concoct environmentally sound and sustainable building technologies. So far it's the birthplace of more than 20 products, most of which, like the Solar-Tube (a solar water heater) and Calcrete (a mixture of caliche earth and concrete that makes super-brick), are designed from renewable or widely available resources with the environmental impact of their entire existence in mind. This means consideration was given to raw materials, manufacturing processes, the extent to which resources are used to transport the products, and how they're recycled once their usefulness has ended.

THE GREEN BUILDER PROGRAM

Fisk, who holds master's degrees in both architecture and landscape architecture, and Vittori, the former head of Austin's Solid Waste Advisory Commission, work with a battalion of students, interns, and volunteers, as well as with a roster of designers, engineers, and technicians. A number of projects are simmering: policy initiatives (like the Green Builder Program developed in conjunction with the city of Austin), ecological land planning, product design and fabrication, laboratory analysis of indigenous building materials, research programs (like one on bioregionalism that seeks to hook up areas with similar climactic features, flora, and fauna), workshops, lectures, publications, and finally, several sustainable design and demonstration projects.

The Advanced Green Builder demonstration house combines many of the center's innovations, mostly prominently GreenForms - an open-ended, post-and-beam system that is the basis of the building's framework. These columns, struts, and roof and floor joists support a variety of other elements that together create a distinct overall design. GreenForms come to life only when a site is chosen and regional materials and personal taste are factored in.

The house that Max built is not just definitively green--it's definitively Austin. Area industry and farming concerns and the materials they produce have greatly influenced the design. This is no mere celebration of regional style, where rounded rocks from the Rio Grande make their way into a couple of chimney stacks, but a comprehensive study in local climate and culture. The house would not look the same in Vermont, for example, where different flora, geology, climate, and industries prevail, not to mention different design influences and lifestyle needs.

Were it built near a forest, the skeleton of the demonstration house would be of wood. But in Austin, it's made of rebar, a material very much at hand in post-boom Texas and one of the highest recycled-metal-content products on the market. "I'd have to have a sustainable forest within 200 miles of my house in order to compete with rebar," says Fisk, who gleefully adds that crushed cars account for 98 percent of the material. In that sense, GreenForms is ultimately two things: it is a building methodology where the user employs regional resources, and it is a new engineering technology for rebar (although other materials can also be used). In classic Erector-set fashion, GreenForms' parts can be unbolted and reused and new segments can be bolted on when additions are desired.

INDIGENOUS MATERIALS

The demonstration house is perhaps most demonstrative, though, in its bounty of wall systems (with a total of nine different materials to choose from). Earthen walls account for most of them: there's adobe, rammed earth (walls made by compressing sandy loam under intense pressure), stabilized earth (earth mixed with any ingredient that enables it to withstand weather, in this case, an enzyme that is in effect a natural glue), and caliche (a material indigenous to the Southwest that's high in calcium carbonate, which when mixed with concrete made from coal fly ash, a by-product from coal-burning utilities, creates Calcrete). "They all look earthy", Fisk says, "And they're all beautiful." Traditionally, earthen walls are covered with some sort of sealant -- the Mexican tradition is to bind adobe walls with vivid paints and plasters. But for those who can't see themselves living in a turquoise room, one of several clear sealants -- like a linseed oil and wax cocktail - will do the job and bring out the natural earth tones.

When earth needs to be combined with other materials, Fisk looks to local industrial by-products. "When we started 10 years ago it was impossible to get fly ash," he says. "But now we consider it another indigenous material." And because accessing regional industrial by-product materials is also about accessing people, a vital component to sustainable design is creating a network of local jobs and manufacturers that keep commerce in the area. In fact, the center sees healthy regional economies as part of the overall goal of the "Green Formsification" of America. For example, another wall system featured in the demonstration house is made of panels that incorporate expanded polystyrene ("Styrofoam") -- not a product you'd immediately think of as green. However, the panels come from a Fort Worth manufacturer that recycles 30 to 50 percent of its Styro waste in making them. Additionally, the gas released by the foaming of Styro is harnessed as energy and used to help power the plant. As far as Fisk is concerned using these "Styrofoam" walls in the Austin area makes both economic and green sense.

Three different types of straw walls are also employed in the house. In one, wool from local sheep (mohair to be exact) is sandwiched between straw to form four-foot by eight-foot panels. (Fisk imagines the use of mohair in building technologies as having a positive secondary economic spin-off: "Maybe if there were another market for mohair, it wouldn't have to be subsidized," he says.) Another finds its roots in the small nearby towns of Fredericksburg and New Braunfels, which were settled by German immigrants in the 1850's. Chopped straw is mixed with water until it is the consistency of pancake batter, and then it's poured into wood frames. Called *fachwerk,* or half-timber, it recalls the classic Swiss chalet or Stratford-on Avon-style house: its charming precedent stands to pacify those who may be put off by Fisk's upstart innovations. A third technique features bales of straw wound with wire and stabilized with some kind of pinning, like bamboo. All three straw walls are plastered with caliche and fly ash composite.

The straw used in Max's Pot house comes from oat or wheat fields within a 10-mile radius of the site. "It's a great way to support regional farmers," remarks Fisk. Straw bales have met strict fire safety standards in New Mexico, and other states are in line to approve the material as well, including Texas.

Sustainable forests are rare around Austin, and although somewhat plentiful, mesquite trees are too twisted to make decent plank. But Max's Pot has found a wood fiber product that can be used for the Dutch-style window doors, as well as a number of other applications, like fencing, decking and wooden frames. It is manufactured about 85 miles away, by a company located next door to a factory that extracts cedar oil from juniper trees, a process that wastes a lot of wood fiber. Mixing the leftover fiber with liquefied postconsumer PET plastic (from soda bottles), the company produces a sturdy wood substitute called AERT.

Materials made from renewable resources are only part of the picture. Sensible water use is essential to the ecological sustainability, and in this arid area of Texas, it's particularly vital. Besides cutting down on consumption we need to rethink waste water, according to Fisk. "We have to see that the water we are dirtying is actually being nutrified and reused," he says. "My waste water, from a money flow standpoint, could assist in the growth of my herbs, could be used to green my landscape."

"GREEN" WASTE TREATMENT

At the demonstration house, waste water is treated in wetland pools that line the entrance walk. "The solid human wastes don't go directly into the beds," Vittori points out. "We have a hybrid system that includes a composting toilet -- a fairly standard commode that holds one pint of water versus standard low flush, which is 1.6 gallons -- and wetlands. The wastes compost and the gray water goes into the wetlands." Local plants, like water lilies, carrizo reed, and cattails, are chosen for their efficiency in uptaking the nutrients. Another, dwarf Virginia creeper, which is also known as American ivy, is also a drought-tolerant native species: it shades the western side of the building from the sun's harsh rays.

Some areas of Austin are sprawling faster than city planners had anticipated, and this has pushed them to begin considering individual waste water systems as an alternative to laying new collection pipes. Maureen McReynolds, environmental and regulatory manager of the City Water and Waste Water Department in Austin, is among those who are intrigued by what's going on at Max's Pot. "We are really excited about the different things [Fisk and Vittori] are looking at," she says. "Dr. Fisk is very creative and he really does have a lot of innovative ideas in terms of both building materials and waste water and in a rapidly growing area, these are issues that speak to the city."

Alternative energy also comes into play. Taking full advantage of the strong Texas sun, the house is roofed with photo voltaic panels that produce almost all of the energy needed by the average American household. Radiant heating devices are laid into caliche or poured concrete floors, and a gas-fired hot water heater doubles as the heat source. In addition, wood-burning stoves are employed. Meanwhile, butane and propane (not ozone-depleting CFCs) are the fluids used in the air-conditioning system. And, just as it's positioned to utilize the sunshine, the house is also oriented to catch gentle hilltop winds, and features a central breezeway. Known as a dogtrot, it is a classic ranch feature.

The Texan lifestyle determines many aspects of the house's design. "At least three-quarters of all Texan households barbecue outside," Fisk says, "so we asked ourselves, 'Can we provide a more user-friendly kitchen?' The reason for this is, the first thing people do when they move into a new home is tear out the old kitchen and start fresh. Kitchens are highly personal spaces that should respond to people in a flexible manner. That's why Max's Pot created the plug-in-kitchen-on-wheels, which can be scooted around to serve the needs of different cooks.

Because of the considerable research involved, the price of the house -- about $250,000 -- isn't substantially less than your average wood-frame-two-bedroom home. The goal, though, is to build for $20 to $40 per square foot. And, of course, the cost to unbuild is minimal. "At the end of the building's life," Fisk says, "you can unscrew the rebars and take them elsewhere, and plough the rest of the structure into the soil."

The aesthetic of the demonstration house is undeniably Austin-based: the materials - organic and otherwise - the energy and water-use systems, and the siting have all been dictated by what the locality provides. But there's also an inherent philosophical regard for truth in building. Fisk and Vittori decided early on not to hide any of the functional aspects of the house. "Part of what this structure is trying to do is to show how a building works," Vittori says. "It's an aesthetic of revealing versus disguising. By revealing the operational elements, it becomes an educational resource."

Fisk hopes that "everyone in America will become Max Potters in 10 to 15 years." For that to happen, he and Vittori realize that they must prevent GreenForms from becoming funny-looking Buckminster Fuller type eccentricity embraced by a few utopians in the Southwest. "Green Forms is an armature through which you can connect to your region and personal design aesthetic."

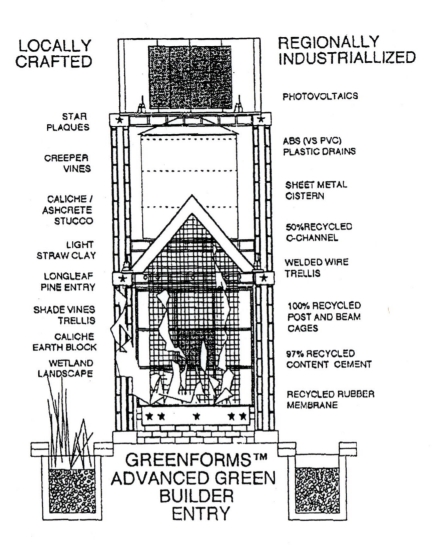

LOCALLY CRAFTED

REGIONALLY INDUSTRIALLIZED

STAR PLAQUES

CREEPER VINES

CALICHE / ASHCRETE STUCCO

LIGHT STRAW CLAY

LONGLEAF PINE ENTRY

SHADE VINES TRELLIS

CALICHE EARTH BLOCK

WETLAND LANDSCAPE

PHOTOVOLTAICS

ABS (VS PVC) PLASTIC DRAINS

SHEET METAL CISTERN

50% RECYCLED C-CHANNEL

WELDED WIRE TRELLIS

100% RECYCLED POST AND BEAM CAGES

97% RECYCLED CONTENT CEMENT

RECYCLED RUBBER MEMBRANE

GREENFORMS™ ADVANCED GREEN BUILDER ENTRY

SOUTH ELEVATION
SCALE   1/16" = 1'-0"

Chapter 28

ENVIRONMENTAL SHOWPLACE HOUSE

Arizona Public Services Co.

Edward Jones, Architect
The Jones Studio Phoenix, Arizona

Phoenix Architect Edward Jones says extremes are the one constant in the desert and buildings must respond to them all if they are to survive. The desert is not a rich source of construction materials and many things are often brought from far away. Yet, Jones believes durability and local production are the most effective means to global sustainability, resource efficiency and environmental responsibility in buildings, leaving desert architecture doubly challenged to make what they build better for the environment.

According to Jones, this "Environmental Showcase Home" is intended to illustrate some of the possible responses to that challenge. The home was "planned as a four bedroom, three bath, three car garage home," he says. "The 2,640 square-foot residence provides significant energy, water and construction materials savings . . . even beyond the prototypical 'energy efficient home.'" It is intended as a showcase of ideas, the messages of this one residence are aimed at the broader realm of production home building, in hopes of greatly reducing the impact of residential construction on the environment.

> "Unlike similar projects, and production building as a whole, (we) open-mindedly explored many criteria including climate, site, material efficiency, water savings and indoor air pollution reduction, without falling back on a predetermined 'style' or image. (This building) seeks to ask what every line in the drawings and every component of the finished project is doing to make it more responsible and more efficient."

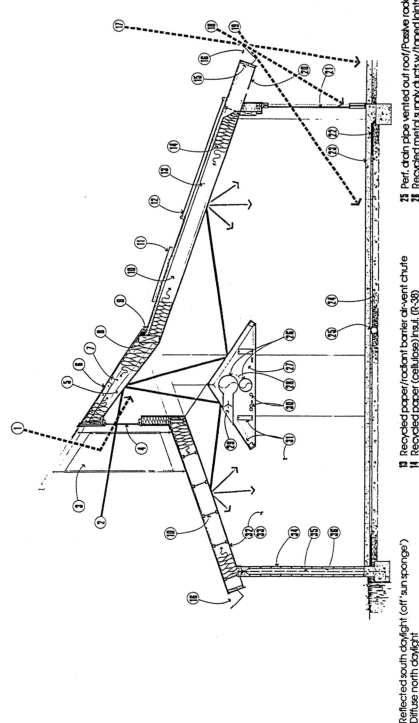

1 Reflected south daylight (off 'sun sponge')
2 Diffuse north daylight
3 'Sun sponge' fabric shade/reflector
4 Clear, highly insulated clerestory (R-8)
5 Finger-jointed lumber in a few areas
6 Recycled/Recyclable metal roofing
7 Oriented Strand Board (OSB) roof sheath'g
8 Parallel Strand Lumber (PSL) wood beam
9 Vent for roof air-vent chutes
10 Engineered wood roof I-Joist (LVL & OSB)
11 Photovoltaic panel array
12 Unglazed solar pool heat collector array

13 Recycled paper/radiant barrier air-vent chute
14 Recycled paper (cellulose) insul. (R-38)
15 Laminated Strand Lumber wood subfascia
16 Recycled/recyclable oversized gutters
17 High summer solstice midday sun angle
18 Spring/Fall equinox midday sun angle
19 Low winter solstice midday sun angle
20 Recycled/recyclable plastic/wood comp. lumber
21 Green, heat-absorbing, highly-insulated glass (R-9)
22 Recycled polystyrene perimeter insulation (R-11)
23 Integral color, polished con. floor w/recycled flyash
24 Plastic vapor barrier/radon barrier

25 Perf. drain pipe vented out roof/Passive radon control
26 Recycled metal supply ducts w/taped joints
27 Return air plenum (inside triangular chase)
28 Variable Air Volume (VAV) control box beyond
29 Supply air diffuser/butterfly damper
30 Plumbing/electrical/home automation control runs
31 Recycled/recyclable metal framing (interior walls)
32 Recycled paper face sheet gypsum wall board
33 No-VOC interior paint (white)
34 Sandblasted, insulated CMU walls w/flyash (R-24)
35 CMU wall system post-tension rod (no 're-bar' in wall)
36 Non-CFC blown polyurethane insulation (R 6.5 per inch)

402

Chapter 29

A Home for Everyone

by Donald MacDonald

From DEMOCRATIC ARCHITECTURE
Practical Solutions to Today's Housing Crisis
Whitney Library of Design

FAILURES IN PLANNING

Until the late 1970s the usual approach to providing low-income, and even some middle-income, housing was to build large institution-like projects, crowding in as many units as possible. The majority were concrete and steel boxes, benefiting little if at all, from architectural amenities. Psychologist Robert Sommer described the mentality behind them:

> "In mental hospitals of the early 1950s [when many of the projects were built], the line was, 'If you give the patients anything nice, they won't take care of it.' For public housing tenants it went, 'If you provide good architecture, they won't appreciate it.' There is the same denigrating we/they dichotomy in all these assessments of people's response to their surroundings. We know what's best for them and they don't. Even if we provide what they say they'd like, they won't take care of it and will probably destroy it."[1]

Some projects, however, were designed by distinguished architects, among them Pruit-Igoe in St. Louis by Minoru Yamasaki and Twin Parks Northeast in New York by Richard Meier and Partners. Pruitt-Igoe, drawing on the Swiss architect Le Corbusier's ideas for urban design, consisted of forty-three eleven-story buildings in a park like setting. It won a national design award.

The high-rise Twin Parks Northeast was also acclaimed, in this case for the way it was integrated into a neighborhood of low-rise buildings. Today's supporters of contextualism would find the claim farfetched. The project's integration depended on its blending into the city street grid pattern by way of the modular spacing of the high-rise solids and voids.

Neither project won any praise from its tenants, however. People refused to live in Pruitt-Igoe because of vandalism and serious crime, and in 1972, just fifteen years after it was completed, the city of St. Louis dynamited the project.

Twin Parks Northeast also failed miserably. Within a few years after it opened in 1973, many of its 523 apartments had been vacated, indeed some were burned out. A report about what went wrong cited specific design and construction deficiencies, vandalism, and inadequate maintenance -- which was precisely what could be said about most of the low-income projects built after World War II. But the underlying problem at virtually all of them, whether architecturally graced or not, was the pervasive paternalism of the people who developed the projects: We know what is best for the tenants and they do not.

As it turned out, the government agencies, planners, and designers did not know what was best or even passably good. What did Le Corbusier's ideas about urban design and Meier's about contextualism have to do with the daily lives of the people for whom the projects were built?

What did the other impersonal, often ugly, steel- and-concrete slabs have to do with the wishes or desires of the people who lived in them? No wonder the projects were vandalized and crime-ridden. Their "scale, scope, and impermeability," as Sommer put it, were "oppressive to the human spirit."[2] Treat people inhumanely, and they are apt to respond in kind. The deterioration of projects nationwide became so serious that many cities followed the example of St. Louis and tore a number of the projects down.

Because of the calamitous fate of such housing projects, there has been a revival of interest among planners and government agencies in the mass-produced Levittown houses built for middle- income families after World War II. However, the informing mentality behind Levittown differed little from that of the projects. The developer Levitt and Sons built the first Levittown (as the communities were named) in 1947; it consisted of 17,000 identical Cape Cod-style single-family houses side by side row after row on a 1400-acre site in a suburb of New York City. The concept was to minimize costs by placing "the machine in the service of the hearth." Virtually every component of the house, from the lumber to the nails, was standardized and manufactured in large quantities to the developer's exact specifications. Trucks delivered bundles of materials to each site, and the construction workers and machinery moved from site to site performing exactly the same operations. It was the assembly line applied to housing construction. For its second development, this one in Bucks County, Pennsylvania, the firm intended to elaborate the concept into a planned community of neighborhoods replete with parks, playgrounds, and schools. Things did not quite work out that way because of political problems, but they did work in the third Levittown, which was built in New Jersey in the 1960s.

Similar planned communities were built in the 1950s and 1960 by other large developers outside major cities throughout the country. In northern California, the usual type of house was the "stucco box," so called because the stucco walls were left flat and blank, with no architectural detailing other than pastel colored paint. It was a chintzy version of the International Style. Some of the communities were less rigidly designed than the Levittowns: curved streets instead of the strict grid pattern, some differences in size, and a little variety in the basic Cape Cod, ranch, or other style of the homes. (In fact, the New Jersey Levittown also varied the designs and street layouts.)

Nevertheless, every community was homogeneous. Essentially, they were horizontal versions of middle-income housing projects. And not only the architecture was homogeneous. All the residents of a community earned more or less the same income, shared similar values, and (until enactment of the civil rights laws of the 1960s) were white and in some instances of the same ethnic background. The historian Daniel J. Boorstin pointed out the paternalistic nature of the communities:

> "In large developments where the developer had a plan, and even in the smaller developments, there was a new kind of paternalism: not the quasi-feudal paternalism of the company town, nor the paternalism of the utopian ideologue. This new kind of paternalism was fostered by the American genius for organization, by the rising twentieth-century American standard of living, and by the American genius for mass production. It was the paternalism of the marketplace. The suburban developer, unlike the small-town booster, seldom intended to live in the community he was building. For him community was a commodity, a product to be sold at a profit. And the suburban homeowner often moved into a whole town which had been shaped in advance by a shrewd developer's sense of the market."[3]

It can be said for the developers that at least they got relatively inexpensive houses built at a time when people were desperate to buy them, and since the early 1980s their example has been the basis for a new approach to the housing shortage in urban areas. Emphasis has been placed on small dwellings priced to enable people with modest incomes to buy them.

One such development began in 1982 with the Nehiamiah Houses in Brooklyn, which consisted of street after street of two story row houses. Eighteen story row houses. Eighteen feet wide and fifty-five feet deep with brick facades, the houses were- in the words of the architectural historian Richard Plunz "reminiscent of nineteenth-century mill housing. The only significant difference is the setback from the street, which serves as parking for the family automobile...The relationship between Nehiamiah Houses and the nineteenth-century goes beyond appearance. The houses hearken back to Gilded Age private philanthropy for the 'deserving poor'... upwardly mobile families whose advanced status is rewarded with superior housing at reduced cost." While much of the site had already been cleared for urban renewal, a number of buildings in good condition were razed for the project on the dubious grounds of cost efficiency. One of the people who would be displaced remarked angrily:

> "Now they're talking about building a one-family house out of inferior materials and putting my family in there, putting two families in a one-family house. The Nehiamiah plan started off by saying, we want to build on empty lots. Now they went from building on empty lots to now taking this man's furniture store, acquiring our grocery store. Where will we have the shops? Where will we go? Where will my father go? He has finished paying for the house, now they want him to pay for another mortgage."

Another project, the Charlotte Gardens, begun at the same time as the Nehiamiah Houses but located in the Bronx in the shadow of some burned-out apartment buildings, consisted of prefabricated houses with a house-trailer type of construction. Plunz compares it with the early Levittown. Commenting on the development, he says, " Charlotte Gardens is another variant on the philanthropy of the Gilded Age. It is not housing for the poor in the same sense that public housing programs were, with their legally enforced policy of open admissions for any family that needed housing, regardless of economic circumstance or social problems. Like Nehiamiah, Charlotte Gardens represents an opportunity only for the 'deserving poor' which is to say the lower middle class, with the economic and social wherewithal for assimilation into the myths and privileges of cottage ownership."[4]

Although the Nehiamiah and Charlotte Gardens developments have one positive aspect-they offer separate houses and ownership for people who want them-they exemplify the disdain and authoritarian imposition of conformity that have generally characterized housing for all but the well-to-do or fortunate. The houses are more containers than homes. A true home has three qualities: It must afford the occupants as much individual privacy as possible, it must offer a reasonable sense of security, and above all, the dwelling must be congenial, agreeable to one's outlook on life.

Of privacy, the environmental psychologist Robert Gifford has said that it is "an important part of the individual's sense of self or identity." He goes on to discuss in privacy:

> "A residence is already a relatively private space. In the developed world, the walls and doors provided by our houses are probably the commonest mechanisms we actually use to manage privacy, even though some surveys report that many individuals associate residential privacy with exterior factors, such as lot size and distance from neighbors ... within the house, different levels of privacy are needed for different family members. Of course, if a house is very large, privacy is not a problem unless it is so large that family members become isolated and alienated from one another. More often, unfortunately, the problem is insufficient space or poor arrangement of the available space.... Outside the residence itself, privacy may vary as a function of design in multiunit housing projects. [D.P.] McCarthy and [S.] Saegert studied privacy in the lobbies, elevators, and other public areas within low-rise and high-rise buildings. Naturally, such areas offer less privacy than a person's own apartment, but McCarthy and Saegert found that public areas in low-rise design were judged by residents to offer more privacy than public areas in the high-rise design.... Clearly, there is no universal design for residential privacy. Each family or client's needs must be carefully considered if the designer is to provide a cost-efficient yet private dwelling. However, some groups are sufficiently similar that some design considerations may apply to most buildings serving them."[5]

The second requisite attribute is security. Because of the growing crime rate, sociologists, psychologists, and, of course, criminologists have studied the problem of security intensively. What they have generally found is that strong locks and barred windows do not assure safety. More important is what architect and urban designer Oscar Newman calls "defensible space design" of the housing environment "by grouping dwelling units to reinforce associations of mutual benefit; by delineating paths of movement; by defining areas of activity for particular users through their juxtaposition with internal living areas; and by providing for natural opportunities for visual surveillance."[6] Newman was referring to multiunit buildings, particularly housing projects, but the principle also applies to private houses.

Privacy and security are not enough to make a dwelling democratic, however. In addition to meeting physical needs, housing must suit a person's or family's cultural outlook, social relationships, habits, and idiosyncrasies as much as possible. The attribute of congeniality is the crux of democratic architecture. It means respect for individuality, for the right of self-expression and self-determination.

While the ideal would be to build each home in accordance with the specific needs of the people who will live in it, the fact is that we rarely know beforehand who that will be and, of course, there are also economic constraints. Consequently, the basic designs have to meet categories of needs within a range of budgets. Middle-income couples with children, low-income single-parent families, the infirmed elderly, alcoholic vagrants, adventurous wanderers, the self-employed working at home, upper-income executives, craftsmen who want their workshops in their homes, and so on require different designs, which might have to be modified to accommodate ethnic preferences. The first step in the design process therefore is to conduct interviews and study whatever one can find to determine what the people who fit the category want — a procedure that would be anathema to the "create beautiful buildings" architects and too much trouble for many others. Interviewing can be difficult. Finding the people concerned and getting appointments is time-consuming. Some people are inarticulate. Others are wary of anyone who appears to represent authority or is condescending, which architects tend to be. In addition, a lot of explanation might be required. People often know very little, if anything, about codes, construction methods, and budgets, not to mention basic architecture. The whole process involves mutual education, and for the architect it can be an invaluable source of inspiration.

A design concept that meets a group's fundamental needs does not necessarily satisfy the individual members of the group. To individualize a building, the design should enable people to make adjustments themselves. Frank Lloyd Wright developed one way in his "build-it-yourself" Usonian Automatic Houses. The basic structural element of the house was a homemade concrete block. Anybody with rudimentary skill and a great deal of patience could make a mold out of sheet metal or wood, pour in concrete to form the blocks, then fit them together with light metal rods to build the walls, upper floors, and roof. Other basic elements consisted of a simple concrete slab for a combined foundation and floor, and bathrooms and kitchens easily assembled from mass-produced products. As Wright said, "Here then, within moderate means for the free man of our democracy, with some intelligence and by his own energy, comes a ... house that may be put to work in our society [to] give us an architecture for 'housing' which is becoming to a free society because, though standardized fully, it yet establishes the democratic ideal of variety — the sovereignty of the individual.[7]

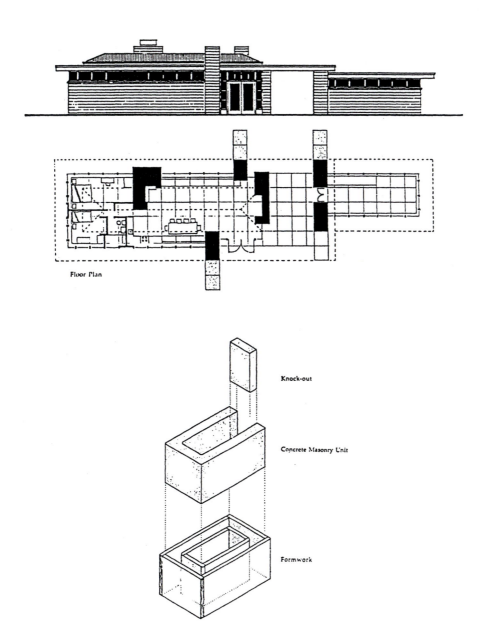

Floor Plan

Knock-out

Concrete Masonry Unit

Formwork

Frank Lloyd Wright Usonian "Automatic" concrete block, build-it-yourself home of the 1940's.

While the build-it-yourself concept is attractive in many respects, it is impractical for people who have to work eight hours a day, and in any event the concrete blocks proved very difficult for amateurs to handle. However, the idea of a more or less standardized unit with the capability of "do-it-yourself" changes, or having someone else do them for you, is practical. Many houses are built with unfinished attics or basements to permit the creation of new rooms. But there are other ways, too, even in apartments, to allow for modifications, and the capability should be a fundamental design element. Privately owned houses should also permit simple external modification to suit the owners' taste and, if site conditions allow, expansion to meet changing needs.

ENVIRONMENTAL IMPACT

Almost as important as the design of housing is the question of where it will be built. We can no longer ignore the environmental damage caused by expansion into undeveloped suburban areas. Jane Jacobs' solution was to halt the flight to suburbia by developing our cities and making them attractive and stimulating places to live.

A study by the Real Estate Research Corporation on the economic and environmental impact of new residential development provides strong support for her conclusion. Results of the study indicate that high-density housing of the type found in urban areas is considerably less expensive from both an economic and environmental point of view than suburban sprawl, traditionally characterized by block after block of single-family homes lined up in the conventional grid pattern. The purpose of the study was "to help the mayor, the city manager, the planning board, and other concerned local officials" answer such questions as whether the added tax base provided by residential growth would offset the costs to the community and what were the effects of development on air and water pollution, wildlife, open space, energy and water consumption, and the lives of the new residents and their neighbors.[8] To every question the answer was that high density is better. For example:

• Costs for roads and utilities are about fifty-five percent lower. Therefore, local governments save money to the extent that they bear financial responsibility for the installation of infrastructure. Operating and maintenance costs are also lowered.

• Only about half as much land is required. So the potential for preserving open space, with the trees still standing and the grass still growing, is much higher.

In addition, there is less need for public transportation.

- Air pollution from heating and automobiles is about half, with most of the reduction coming from the fact that residents do not have to drive as far.
- Pollution from storm water and sediment is less, because the total paved area is smaller.
- Energy consumption is less because of the reduced use of autos and public transportation.
- Fewer traffic accidents occur.

The answer to continued sprawl is to confine new construction as much as possible to developed urban and suburban areas. In most communities there is plenty of space available vacant lots too small for the usual housing or commercial building but quite suitable for one or more cottage-type homes; border areas between commercial and residential zones that are excellent for mixed-use development (as are many other areas); air rights over developed property, roads, and utilities; and even backyards that can accommodate small houses.

But infill can, and very often does, provoke furious resistance, particularly in the more prosperous neighborhoods, where the thought of introducing low-income or even middle-income homes or stores raises the specters of plunging property values and an undesirable mix of different ethnic groups and classes. Very often the specters are just that-phantoms born of irrational fears. Whether they are or not, true democracy involves an intermingling of people without regard for their class or color or work, and I venture to say that if there were more such mingling many of the fears and social problems would disappear.

AFFORDABILITY

The central issue, of course, is how to reduce the cost of housing, and that requires a thorough reexamination of long-cherished ideas about housing standards. The first requisite change is in the traditional concept of livable space. Over the years, the notion has developed that a certain amount of space has to be allotted for each person and for each activity. In the United States, it has been generally accepted as gospel that there must be an eight foot high bedroom for every two people (because precut lumber studs are eight feet long). A middle-class mythology of space has emerged. The assumption is that what people would like to have is what they have to have, whether or not they can afford it. As a result, a great many people have no space at all.

The cost of housing can be substantially reduced if that way of thinking is reversed. A design of affordable housing should not start with the question of how to build least expensively to meet certain space requirements, but what is the maximum amount of space that can be provided for someone who can pay a certain rent or mortgage. If it means lowering the ceiling and reducing the size of the bedroom to meet the budget, that has to be done. A 7-foot, or even 6.5-foot, ceiling is ample as long as there is adequate ventilation. A sixty-four-foot-square bedroom will easily accommodate a double bed and a dresser.

In fact, bedrooms in the traditional sense can be eliminated entirely, or the number reduced, if we get away from the idea that space has to be assigned a function. As everyone who has lived in a studio apartment knows, a living room can be turned into a bedroom easily enough. Extend the concept to what would ordinarily be a multiroom unit occupied by a family with children. With a series of partitions, a single room can be used as living space during the day and divided into bedrooms at night or divided whenever needed for the sake of privacy. The same principle can be applied to a small house or one floor of a two-story house. For a family it provides considerable flexibility, an instant guest room, additional bedrooms as the family grows, rooms of different sizes for children of different ages, or an area that can be a so-called family room during the day and bedrooms at night.

In addition, order and common sense have to be brought to the labyrinth of codes that make it very difficult, if not impossible, to build low-cost housing. On the surface, and viewed individually, many of the code provisions appear to be justified. Who would argue that we should not conserve energy, prevent fire damage, reduce health hazards, and ensure the structural safety of buildings under a wide range of loads? But when we balance risks and costs, when we consider ideals of security in terms of the urgent need for housing, what are the priorities?

For example, do we always have to have double walls with insulation and double-glazed windows to save energy, even in a moderate climate like California's? Under what conditions are fire sprinklers and one-hour fire-resistant walls necessary even though they greatly increase the cost of construction? Which is more important to health: a hallway between the bathroom and the kitchen or not having a bathroom or kitchen at all? Must all stairways be designed in the expectation that they will be climbed by people with heart conditions, despite the fact that to do so costs more because of the required space? What are reasonable fiber-stress requirements in wood construction, based on sound engineering for realistic loads, not on what the lumber interests say? Moreover, for every code there is a different regulatory agency, for every agency there are different procedures, for each procedure there are stipulations and modifications, and on top of all this there are planning departments and review boards and special interest groups.

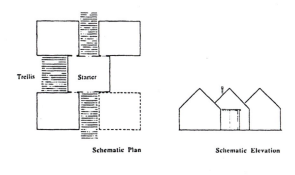

Trellis   Starter

Schematic Plan

Schematic Elevation

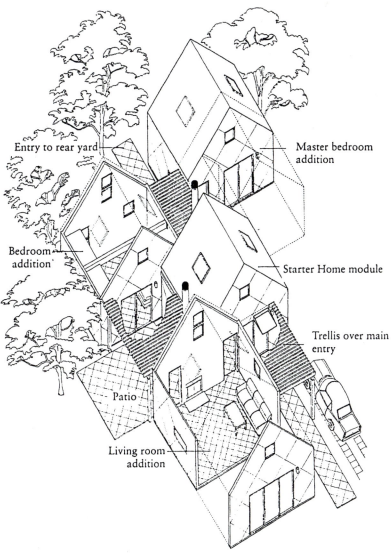

Entry to rear yard

Master bedroom
addition

Bedroom
addition

Starter Home module

Trellis over main
entry

Patio

Living room
addition

Axonometric showing the spatial expansion of the original Starter Home. All four corners of the house allow exterior boxes to be added, which can contain some of the functions that are condensed in the original Starter Home. For instance, one box could be a master bedroom addition with its own bathroom. Another box added to the front could serve as a garage and workshop. A box could also be used to make a new living room, leaving the original house with a kitchen and a comfortable family room for dining and lounging. Off each of these masses are exterior patios, which further enhance the livability of the home.

Axonometric viewing the front elevation, showing the cottage construction system and layout of the interior spaces.

Window

Operable skylights

Roof: 2 x 10 joists with R-30 batt insulation

Construction: Members joined with joist hangers, corner clips, and tie downs

Roof slope: 45°; minimum to allow loft space without second story

Bathroom door: Mirrored sliding type

Loft: Carpeted; 1-1/8-inch structural plywood floor reduces height

Storage

Hot water heater: Minimum size (20-gallon); one on each side for fuel efficiency

Closet

Square footage: 238 sq. ft. living area; 62 sq. ft. loft

Furniture

Square floor plan: Most economic and stable for wood frame construction

Windows: Aluminum frame; double glazing

Exterior design: Adaptable to owner's preferences

Sliding glass entry door: More economical than hung door

Canopy: Prefab. steel frame and glass; bolt-on attachment

Exterior wall: 2 x 4 wood studs sheathed in plywood

Plywood siding: Paint least expensive finish material

Expansion: living/dining module addition at front

Foundation: Insulated slab on grade covered with underpad and carpet

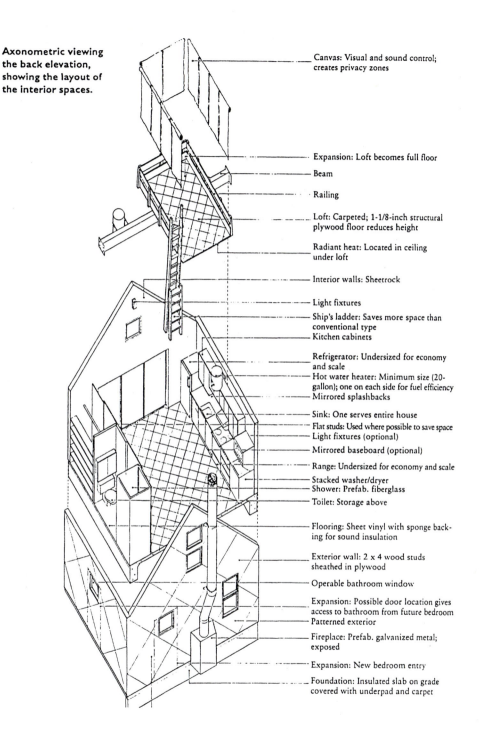

Axonometric viewing the back elevation, showing the layout of the interior spaces.

Canvas: Visual and sound control; creates privacy zones

Expansion: Loft becomes full floor

Beam

Railing

Loft: Carpeted; 1-1/8-inch structural plywood floor reduces height

Radiant heat: Located in ceiling under loft

Interior walls: Sheetrock

Light fixtures

Ship's ladder: Saves more space than conventional type

Kitchen cabinets

Refrigerator: Undersized for economy and scale

Hot water heater: Minimum size (20-gallon); one on each side for fuel efficiency

Mirrored splashbacks

Sink: One serves entire house

Flat studs: Used where possible to save space

Light fixtures (optional)

Mirrored baseboard (optional)

Range: Undersized for economy and scale

Stacked washer/dryer

Shower: Prefab. fiberglass

Toilet: Storage above

Flooring: Sheet vinyl with sponge backing for sound insulation

Exterior wall: 2 x 4 wood studs sheathed in plywood

Operable bathroom window

Expansion: Possible door location gives access to bathroom from future bedroom

Patterned exterior

Fireplace: Prefab. galvanized metal; exposed

Expansion: New bedroom entry

Foundation: Insulated slab on grade covered with underpad and carpet

The objection often raised to code modifications is that in paring the codes the poor receive inferior housing, that they are deprived of the comfort and safety enjoyed by the wealthy, and that injustice is being perpetuated. But is that really the point of view of the people who are homeless, or of families who are forced to share apartments with relatives, or of young couples who cannot afford to buy a house? Safety and space are measured by needs, not by abstract theories. Legitimate concerns about fire, structural integrity, and health are one thing, but standards developed essentially for upper-middle -income homes require serious reevaluation.

AESTHETICS

Questions are also inevitably raised about the aesthetics of buildings designed to respond to individual needs and to reduce costs. Won't that mean a hodgepodge of shapes, colors, and ornamentation, as well as some ugly boxes? Regarding the hodgepodge, the answer is hopefully yes; about boxes, the answer is no, provided architects respond creatively to human needs and stop boxing themselves in by ideologies and mannerisms. If one design characteristic can be said to be most expressive of democracy, it is fragmentation. In a true democracy, the diversity of people and goals, economic individualism, social and physical mobility, and variety of organizational structures defy the orderliness and consistency that have been the traditional objectives of architectural design. More appropriate objectives are disharmony, contradiction, flux, and disparity. They can be represented among buildings and within buildings by the introduction of a variety of forms, spatial relationships, and materials to achieve purposeful chaos within the order imposed by functional, economic, and environmental constraints. For the architect, acceptance of fragmentation as an objective of design can be an exalting creative experience. It liberates, allowing a natural flow of ideas, particularly in the vital initial stages of design. But the approach takes courage and strength. The architect has to reject easy, tried solutions to problems. He has to take chances and be prepared to fall.

Fragmentation, however, does not mean disorder and originality for their own sake. Its purpose is to satisfy the functional and aesthetic needs of the people who inhabit buildings, not to be a realization of the architect's subjective impulses. Although a creative architect undoubtedly commences the design process by unleashing his imagination, his ultimate success will depend on how well he harnesses his freewheeling thoughts to the requirements of the people he is serving. I want to emphasize the word *serving* here, because that is what we architects do and always have done. We place our artistry at the disposal of clients. Historically, we have served monarchs, priests, oligarchs, and more recently-tycoons.

NOTES

1. Robert Sommer, *Tight Spaces: Hard Architecture and How to Humanize It* (Englewood Cliffs, N.J.: Prentice-Hall, Inc., 1974), p.2.

2. Ibid., p.v.

3. Daniel J. Boorstin, *The Americans: The Democratic Experience* (New York: Random House, 1973), p. 290.

4. Richard Plunz, *A History of Housing in New York City* (New York: Columbia University Press, 1990), pp. 330-334.

5. Robert Gifford, *Environmental Psychology: Principles and Practice* (Boston: Allyn Bacon, Inc., 1987), pp. 210, 219-220.

6. Oscar Newman, *Defensible Space* (New York: Collier Books, 1973), p. 4.

7. Quoted in Bruce Brooks Pfeiffer and Gerald Nordland (eds.), *Frank Lloyd Wright in the Realm of Ideas* (Carbondale and Edwardsville: Southern Illinois University Press), p. 72.

8. Real Estate Research Corporation, *The Costs of Sprawl* (Washington, D.C.: U.S. Government Printing Office, April 1974), Executive Summary, p. 1. The report was prepared for Council of Environmental Quality, Department of Housing and Urban Development, and the Environmental Protection Agency. For the purposes of the study, prototypes were developed of different communities, each consisting of 10,000 dwelling units on 6000 acres of land. *Low-density sprawl* was defined as an entire community "made up of single family homes, seventy-five percent sited in a traditional grid pattern and the rest clustered. Neighborhoods are sited in a 'leapfrog' pattern with little contiguity. This represents the typical pattern of suburban development." *High density* was defined as a planned ("meaning general compactness of development") community in which "housing is composed of forty percent high rise apartments, thirty percent walkup apartments, twenty percent townhouses, and ten percent clustered single family homes. All of the dwelling units are clustered together in contiguous neighborhoods, much in a pattern of a high density 'new community'" (Executive Summary, p., 2). Prototypes of four other communities were also studied.

Chapter 30

Mickey Muennig --
A Natural Architecture

"A house should live and breathe as much as possible . . . not in nature, but as a part of nature."

-MICKEY MUENNIG, Architect

Mickey Muennig arrived in Big Sur, California in 1971. He fell in love with the dynamic natural setting of this rugged California coast, and stayed on to become part of Big Sur's nature-oriented way of life. In the process, he became the community's preeminent architect.

Muennig's approach to ecological design is relaxed and "soft-spoken." He blends his buildings with their sites by echoing the natural contours of the land. His buildings' curves and angles are a composite reflection of the land, the ocean, clouds, view orientations and the south-western solar arc.

The land slopes, views, and solar orientation of Big Sur face the same general west and southwest direction, so there's a pre-existing continuity of environment. This makes some aspects of design easy, as nature and the architect are working in partnership with one another. On the other hand, most architects don't have to deal with the California coast's extremes of wind, rain, fire danger and soil movement.

These challenges of site and climate have made Mickey a technologist as well as an ecol-ogist. He learned the secrets of waterproofing and microclimate manipulation the hard way, and his know-how is second to none. Thus he can provide a sealed roof to support a richly planted sod roof, protective rain- and wind-facing fenestration, and passive solar systems that are so subtle and simple, you hardly know they're there. They're just natural to his architecture as his buildings are just natural extensions of their landscapes.

F.S.

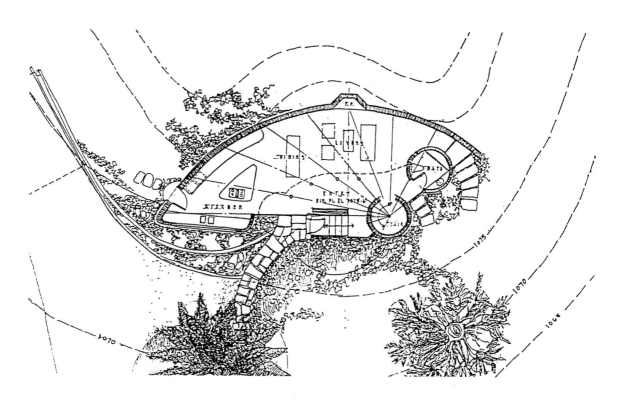

Plan and elevation of the Felicia Bright residence by Mickey Muennig. Big Sur.

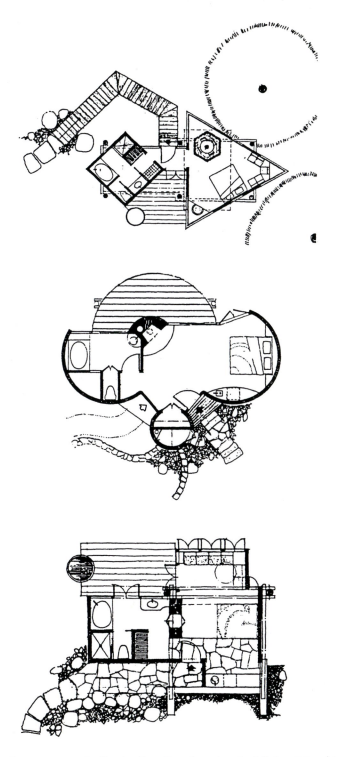

Plans of apartment units for the Post Ranch project by Mickey Muennig. Big Sur.

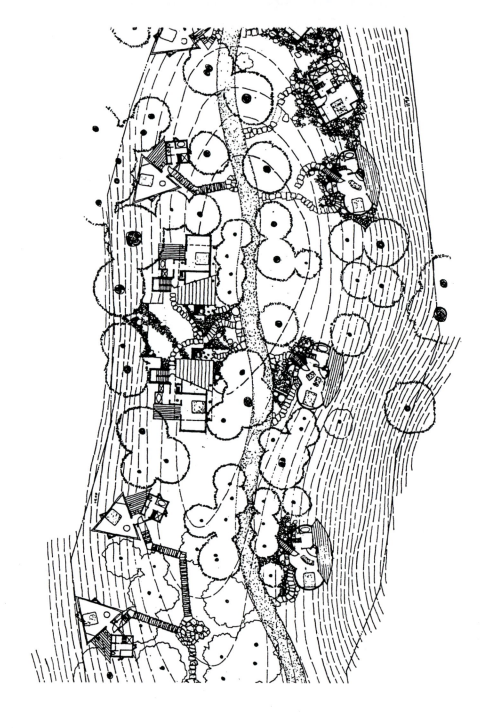

Partial site plan of the Post Ranch project by Mickey Muennig. Big Sur, California.
Some units are well above ground within the lower branch levels of pine trees, others are semi-underground
and/or with bermed walls and planted sod roofs on the cliff overlooking the ocean.

Chapter 31

Bart Prince's Passive Solar Home and Studio

Bart Prince became dedicated to architecture since his teens. While studying at the University of Arizona, he met Bruce Goff who became his mentor. Since then he has pushed a radically unconventional design career and has built many of the most striking and innovative buildings to be found in the Southwest and California. His own home is an excellent example of his integrated, site-sensitive, approach to design.

Prince built his Albuquerque home to make best use of an long, narrow suburban lot. To create a vista over the rooftops of his neighbors, he raised the living portion of the home to three stories. At the same time, he assured personal privacy through room orientation and judicious rationing of fenestration at the lower levels.

Prince exploited a long southern exposure with shaded glazing and clerestories, to capture low sunlight that heats transparent water-filled storage cylinders on both the lower and upper floor levels. The transparent tubes are integral parts of the design, which is a modular composition of small to large circular elements. When the outside temperature cools, the water cylinders release their ambient heat, to maintain climate balance inside the building.

The water-filled transparent cylinders are not only a functional, integral part of the building's operating system, they're an elegant design feature in themselves. While the overall building form is not restrained by convention, the thinking behind it is totally systematic -- a blend of freedom and structure characteristic of the organic tradition.

The orientation of all the building's primary spaces and major design features, such as sun screens, berm walls for insulation, privacy walls, and highly controlled fenestration, are all direct responses to the problem of solar orientation. The realities of the site and sun were as much a part of the program and thinking behind this design as the life and work patterns of the owner.

F.S.

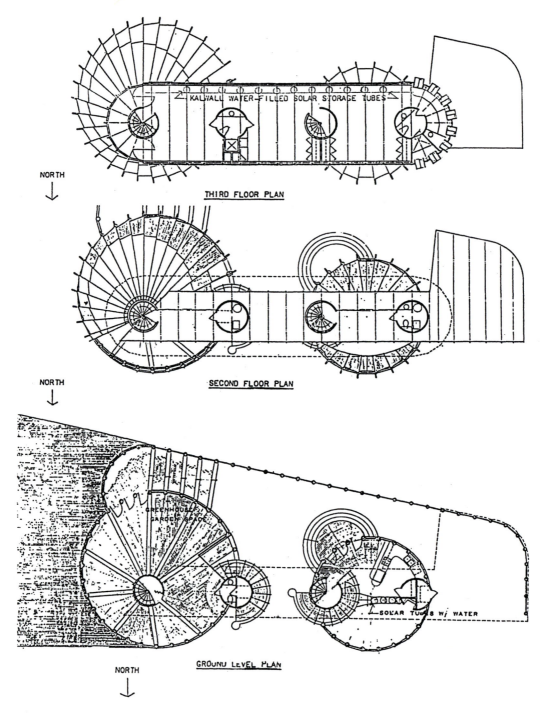

Plans of three levels of the Bart Prince home and studio.

Site orientation, judicious use of solar screening
and solar storage tubes provide a consistent, year-round comfortable interior climate.

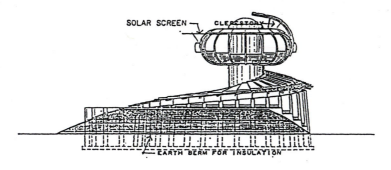

EAST ELEVATION

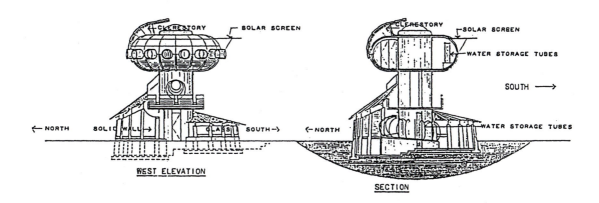

WEST ELEVATION

SECTION

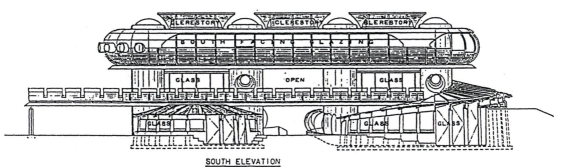

SOUTH ELEVATION

Exterior elevations of the Bart Prince home and studio.

All climate control elements are fully expressed as visual design features.

Chapter 32

Ken Yeang:
A Marriage of Ecology,
Technology, and Design

"External walls should act like a filter that has variable parts to control good cross ventilation, provide solar protection, regulate wind-swept rain, and discharge heavy rain."

-KEN YEANG, ARCHITECT

Ken Yeang developed a sensitivity to technological design values as a student at the Architectural Association in London and honed ecological sensitivity through study with Profession Ian McHarg at the University of Pennsylvania.

Since 1975 he has practiced in Malaysia and has created some of the world's most exciting buildings in the eco-design realm -- an architecture he calls "bio-climatic." With projects through Kauala Lumpur, China, Vietnam, and Japan, he has set an enviable standard for site-sensitive design on a grand scale.

Yeang brings a much deeper theoretical approach to his work than most of his peers, as evidenced in this observation:

"We can conclude that in order to fully appreciate the ecological implications of any design the designer will need to analyze the built environment in terms of its flow of energy and materials throughout its life cycle from their source of origin to their sink. Following from this analysis, the designer must simultaneously anticipate at the design stage all the desirable impacts on the ecosystems along this route. This analysis can be conveniently conceived using the concept of an open system, i.e., in terms of inputs to the system, functions within the system, outputs from the system, and the relationship of the environment to the system."

Designing With Nature, the Ecological Basis
for Architectural Design. Ken Yeang. McGraw-Hill, 1995.

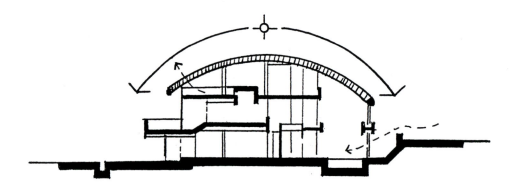

The "Roof-Roof" house. It's cooler in the shade, so it's a natural idea
to put a shade roof over the main roof in a hot climate.
The building design augments natural air flow.

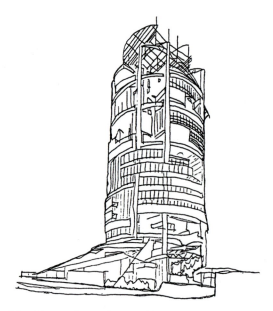

The Menara Mesiniaga Building, Kaula Lumpur, 1989.
Skycourts, passive solar heating, vertical landscaping, natural ventilation, energy-saving automatic HVAC
controls, and generous access to sunlight.

Chapter 33

Eugene Tsui:
Evolutionary Architecture

In describing the meaning of "Evolutionary Architecture," Dr. Eugene Tsui says:

"Our man-made environment permeates and affects every aspect of our daily lives. It is therefore imperative that we build a world with imagination and intelligence. We can no longer ignore the natural laws of economy, structural and spatial efficiency, energy conservation, and the unity of form and purpose. Let us create an architecture that graces the landscape and utilizes the natural elements of wind, sun, water, and earth, and does not destroy or disrupt the living environment. Our lives, thus engaged, would be imbued with a Nature-understanding appropriate to human intelligence."

Tsui's aesthetic and technical innovations are inspired by the inner structures and geometries of natural objects. Few, if any, architects have looked as deeply within nature structure as has Tsui, and even fewer have expressed the unrestrained variety of form that nature inspires.

Besides uninhibited nature pattern and the unique forms suggested by experimental new materials, Tsui also dramatizes the formal and aesthetic possibilities of eco design elements. Ecological tools become expressive architectural displays of solar photo-voltaic panels, water remediation, wind farming, geodesic structure, and passive solar radiant heat systems. His designs are a synthesis of internal forces determined by human needs and external physical responses to natural forces.

Eugene Tsui holds post-graduate degrees in architecture and city planning, and holds a doctorate in architectural education from the University of California, Berkeley. He was a protégé of Bruce Goff for seven years and studied in Germany with Dr. Frei Otto. Tsui has taught at San Francisco State University and is currently with the San Francisco Institute of Architecture.

F.S.

"Aquaterra," a project for a display home using a foundation isolation system for seismic control, recycled wastewater system, and experimental construction materials. Recycling systems, wind and solar power generators, and a water flow pollution-removal system are all emphasized as visual design features.

"Solarrius," a passive solar Arctic alternative energy research center designed for the Arctic Gas Pipeline Corporation near Fairbanks, Alaska. Aerodynamic orientation to minimize wind impact, tap root foundation, and parabolic solar collector, are all site-specific design elements for creating a self-sufficient environment within a harsh environment

Chapter 34

Glen Small -- Land in the Sky

From THE FUTURIST
June 1977

"Space, use, structure, and decoration are run together in one continuum of experience."

-GLEN SMALL

"Biological architect" Glen Small offers a vision of a city so in tune with both nature and technology that it can house 11 million people without damaging the land on which it is built.

The word "megastructure" has come to suggest a harsh, concrete-block environment, primarily because of such well-known examples as *Habitat* at the 1967 World's Fair in Montreal. But a megastructure can also mean a combination of many objects and systems in ways that complement each other and create a diversified but harmonious whole. Nature offers breath-taking examples of huge ecological megastructures that combine mountains, valleys, forests, streams and animals.

Our problem as human beings is to interact with these natural systems in ways that will cause a minimum of disruption. Too often in the past we have behaved like uninvited and unwelcome guests, looting and trashing our surroundings.

Having come to recognize that nature generally knows best, there is now a movement among architects to grow buildings from living plants, or to induce the suspended minerals in the sea to form structures suitable for human use. I support these efforts but find that my own interests lie somewhere between totally artificial and totally natural construction processes. Nature is the ultimate machine, and I believe that as human technology increasingly learns to apply the principles of nature, the two will merge to become technological nature.

This union of nature and technology is what I am trying to achieve in my work. People say that the structures I draw look "alive." They are alive, not in the sense that nature produced them independently of human control, but because they carry out all the different functions of living systems, respond to their environment, and grow. Certainly they are not "dead" as are many of today's buildings which were constructed without regard for their surroundings or their effect on any form of life other than human beings.

The point of designing visionary architecture such as the BiomorphicBiosphere Megastructure is that it allows us to think seriously about what we truly *want* to do, instead of limiting our thinking to present-day building practices. Rather than devoting all our efforts to dealing with the problems of the present, as serious as these undoubtedly are, we need to fashion an ideal, a positive goal toward which to strive. Otherwise, we risk adopting patch-up methods that may only compound our previous mistakes. Just as the causes and implications of problems like pollution, overcrowding, poverty, and starvation are interconnected, the solutions to these problems can only be found if we achieve a comprehensive vision.

Nature had a smoothly functioning system of balances long before man began seeking ways to combat disease and protect himself from predators. His success in doing so has resulted in a human population that is now too large to survive in primitive agricultural communities surrounded by wilderness, or to live off naturally occurring foodstuffs. Instead, we must reshape our existing cities to harmonize with nature and yet still provide all the technological and natural resources needed to sustain a large human population.

THE SELF-SUSTAINING CITY

The Biomorphic Biosphere Megastructure (BBM) is designed to house all the facilities provided by today's communities for shelter, social contact, industry, transportation, food production, recreation, energy generation, etc., and yet be entirely self-sustaining. Although only the physical appearance of the BBM can be described in any detail here, the structure has important implications for social organization as well.

Structurally, the BBM somewhat resembles a tent. Central core members rise from the ground at intervals like tent poles. From these supporting members are suspended a net-like skin of flexible material whose open mesh provides the framework into which self-contained units can be fitted as needed. The BBM can expand both horizontally and vertically by activating computer-guided building machines located at strategic points throughout the structure. Hence, the building can begin small and expand over time. Ultimately, the megastructure might cover many miles and reach as high as 8,000 feet. The optimum population density for such a BBM, assuming an average height of around 5,000 feet, would be 250,000 people per linear mile.

I believe that BBMs should be built in existing urban centers because these areas represent the greatest blight that needs to be rebuilt. Also, cities have the manpower and support facilities required to initiate and sustain the building process through its early stages. Starting at a central location within an existing city, the first elements of a BBM can be built to span over existing structures, touching the ground only at a few points. The material to build the BBM can come initially from the city it is replacing. Such materials a steel and plastic can be recycled from the demolition of old buildings. Additional materials should come from renewable natural sources. (Soybeans now can be turned into plastic, and in the future many construction materials may come from agricultural products.)

Eventually the entire city might be recycled, leaving only a few buildings of historic or architectural interest as protected monuments. People and industries would move up into the BBM and the now vacant land could either be used for recreation, agriculture, or allowed to revert to wilderness.

THE GREEN MACHINE

One of the values of visionary thinking is that it reveals possibilities that might otherwise come to mind. For example, a low-cost housing project utilizing space frame and Airstream trailer technology for Venice, California. Economical, enjoyable, and 100% self contained.

The Green Machine would produce 75% - 100% of electrical needs from concentrating tracking collectors, 100% heating from the greenhouse and flat plate collectors, 100% of the drinking water from the rain, 100% subsurface irrigation at ground level from recycled sewage, 100% of garbage recycled, and 100% of fruit and vegetable needs from the gardens, greenhouses, and fruit bearing trees.

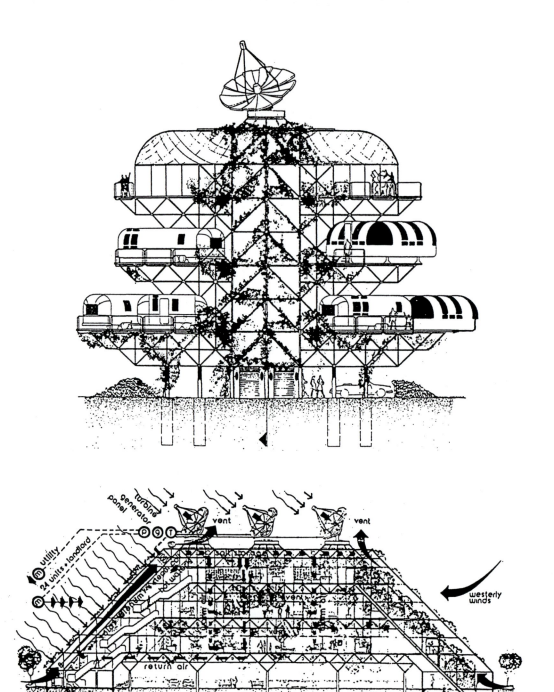

Green Machine cross sections.

An experimental urban multilevel low income housing project for the city of Los Angeles. The design addresses ecological self-sufficiency, moveable, comfortable compact living units, large communal spaces, preservation of the land and aesthetic pleasure.

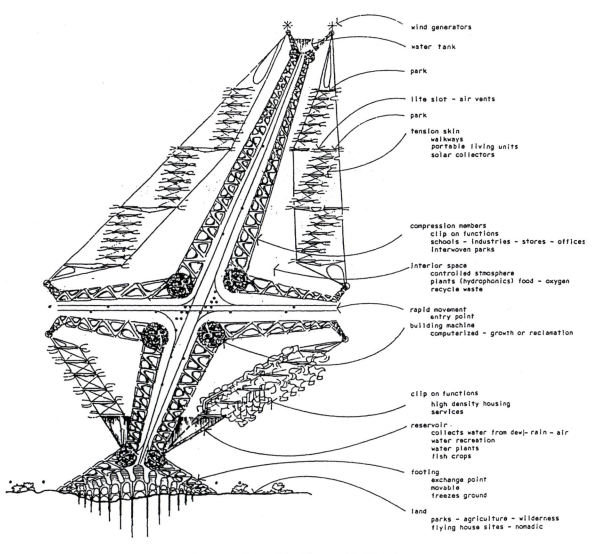

wind generators

water tank

park

lite slot – air vents

park

tension skin
    walkways
    portable living units
    solar collectors

compression members
    clip on functions
    schools – industries – stores – offices
    interwoven parks

interior space
    controlled atmosphere
    plants (hydrophonics) food – oxygen
    recycle waste

rapid movement
    entry point
building machine
    computerized – growth or reclamation

clip on functions
    high density housing
    services

reservoir
    collects water from dew – rain – air
    water recreation
    water plants
    fish crops

footing
    exchange point
    movable
    freezes ground

land
    parks – agriculture – wilderness
    flying house sites – nomadic

Cross section of the Biomorphic Biosphere.

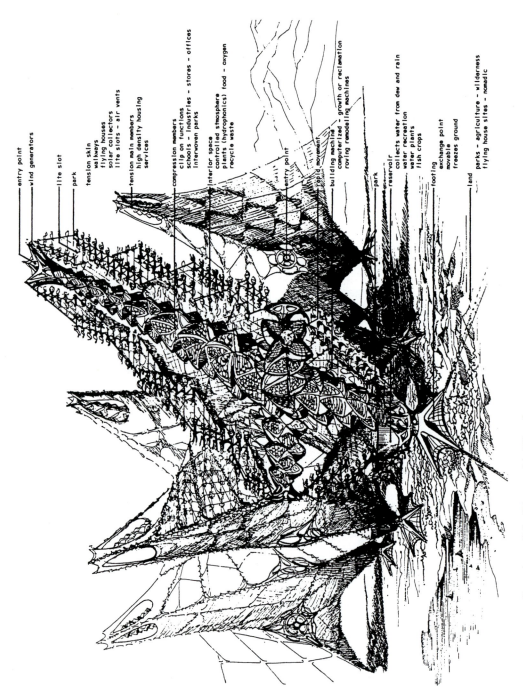

entry point
wind generators

lite slot

park

tension skin
walkways
flying houses
solar collectors
lite slots – air vents

tension main members
high density housing
services

compression members
clip on functions
schools – industries – stores – offices
interwoven parks

interior space
controlled atmosphere
plants (hydrophonics) food – oxygen
recycle waste

entry point

rapid movement

building machine
computerized – growth or reclamation
roving remodeling machines

park

reservoir
collects water from dew and rain
water recreation
water plants
fish crops

footing

exchange point
movable
freezes ground

land

parks – agriculture – wilderness
flying house sites – nomadic

Overview of the Biomorphic Biosphere megastructure.

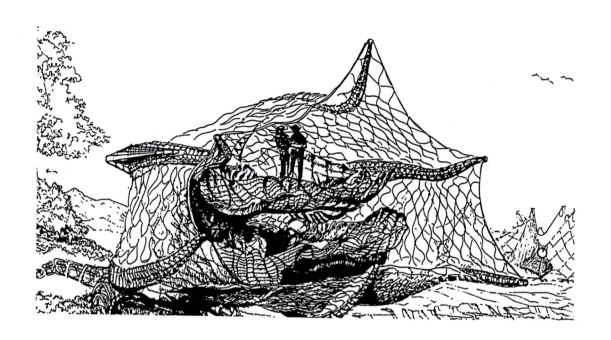

Biomorphic Biosphere family living unit.

Chapter 35

Daniel B-H Liebermann Eco-Village Project

"Organic architecture is both the rational and the international architecture of the future . . . "

-DANIEL B-H LIEBERMANN

Daniel B-H Libermann practices in Berkeley, California and at his Point Reyes studio in Marin County. He received Master of Land Planning and Architecture degrees from Harvard University, and studied for two years with Frank Lloyd Wright at the Taliesin Fellowship. He has taught at the College of Environmental Design at UC Berkeley, Polytechnical University of Turin, Italy, and the NTH Norwegian Technological University, and is a lecturer at the San Francisco Institute of Architecture.

Daniel Liebermann has made a number of remarkable discoveries in his work. One is that a curvilinear environment is experienced visually and physically as noticeably larger than a rectilinear one. This allows a small home of 900 sq. ft. to comfortably hold a hundred or more people for a social function. And the main living space of that same home is typically perceived as being several hundred square feet larger than it actually is.

He has also pioneered in giving aesthetic expression to some remarkably prosaic materials and alternative construction methods, as illustrated in this chapter, including tires, recycled paving, earth construction, and other hybrid combinations of low-cost or recycled materials.

He describes the Zendik project (an agricultural and ecological study center in Texas shown on the next few pages) as: "An intentional community of youth, disenfranchised by the status quo, thirsts for an opportunity to experiment in shared living, in an environment which encourages the expression and development of their talents and emotions."

F.S.

/ cedar pole radial roof
/ salvaged truss

topology
... terraces ... logarithmic lines
... retaining walls
wind
... cooling high roofs ... weather vanes
... louvered pyramidal skylights
wind & water
... dripping water veils at eaves
... drip irrigated sod roof
wind force
... aerodynamic roof shape for
downward thrust ... structural strength
& weight to resist lift ... connection to
ground ... horizontal, vertical, and
torsional resistance
wind as energy
... generators, airspeed vanes,
windometers on roof
sun
... thermal induction in winter through
skylights, glass walls, absorption
into massive retaining wall,
flooring & sod roof
... insulation in summer through
reflective roof surface , cellular
insulation , drip irrigated sod roof,
insulated glass , overhanging
eaves & overhanging trees

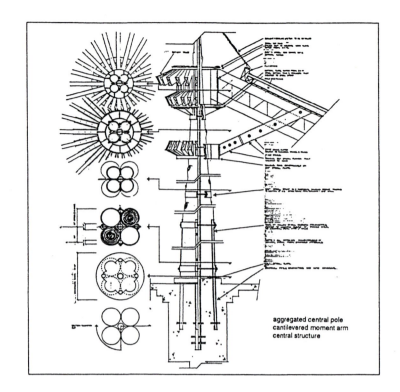

aggregated central pole
cantilevered moment arm
central structure

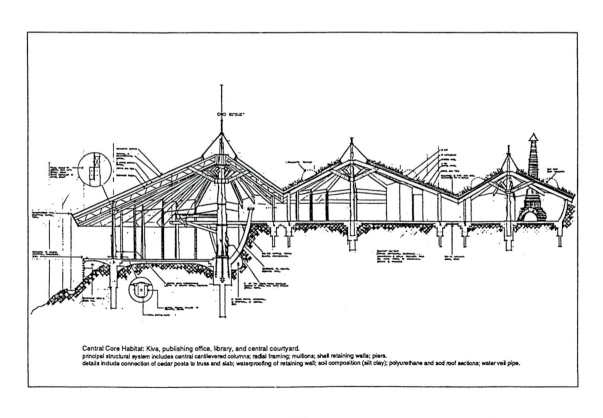

Central Core Habitat: Kiva, publishing office, library, and central courtyard.
principal structural system includes central cantilevered columns; radial framing; mullions; shell retaining walls; piers.
details include connection of cedar posts to truss and slab; waterproofing of retaining wall; soil composition (silt clay); polyurethane and sod roof sections; water veil pipe.

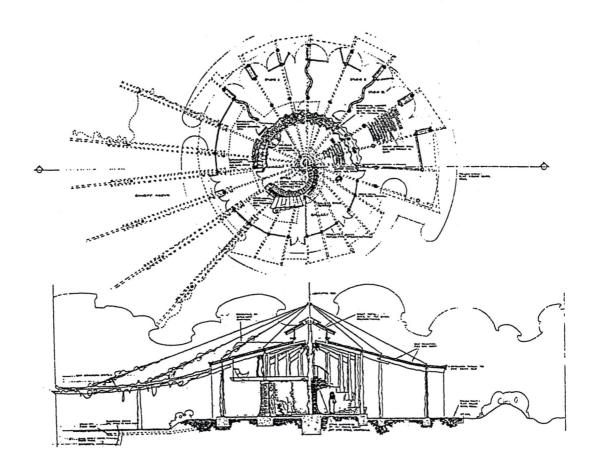

Plan and cross section, spiral plan habitat.

A rammed earth technique using used tires and rebar allows irregular curved walls to be built with the possibility of vertical curves. Rammed earth walls are durable, strong when loaded vertically, and have excellent insulation properties. In hot climates, they absorb the sun's energy during the day and then release it at night, creating a relatively stable internal temperature.

The curve of the walls makes them inherently more stable than straight walls; they can therefore have greater and more varied openings without being de-stabilized.

plan view of construction method for a circular plan building

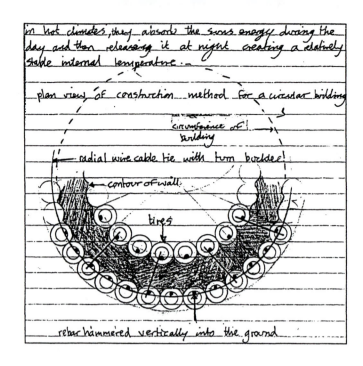

in hot climates, they absorb the suns energy during the day and then releasing it at night creating a relatively stable internal temperature.

plan view of construction method for a circular building

circumference of building

radial wire cable tie with turn buckle

contour of wall

tires

rebar hammered vertically into the ground

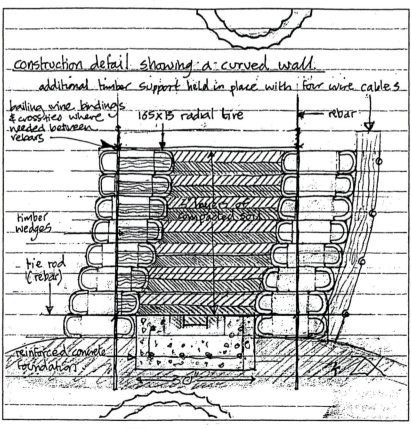

construction detail showing a curved wall.

additional timber support held in place with four wire cables

bailing wire bindings & crossties where needed between rebars

165x13 radial tire

rebar

timber wedges

tie rod (rebar)

reinforced concrete foundation

444

Concrete domes can be formed over earth as well as air. Using a horse or tractor-compacted earth mound as the form, highly complex shell-like structures can be built. After the concrete has cured, the earth is removed, leaving an elaborate space underneath.

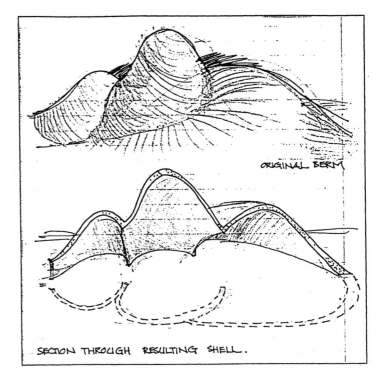

ORIGINAL BERM

section through dome

SECTION THROUGH RESULTING SHELL.

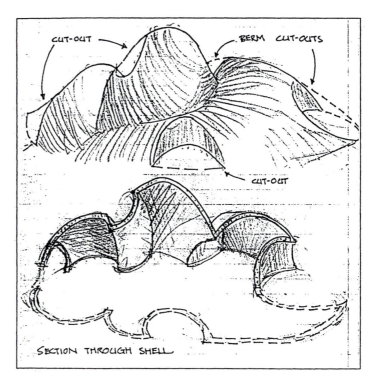

CUT-OUT   BERM CUT-OUTS

CUT-OUT

SECTION THROUGH SHELL

445

Rammed earth walls using oil drums and wire cable as forms allow for the same irregular, curved walls to be built.

plan view for a circular building & cross-section through wall

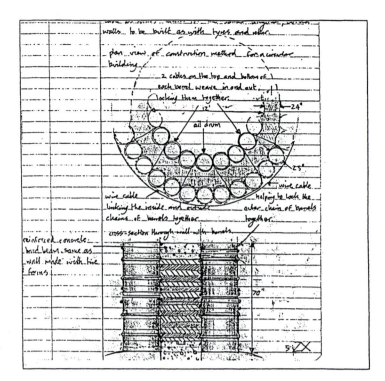

Rammed earth berm with cut-outs: Compacted layers of soil are built up using a tractor and hand tools. A reinforced concrete edge beam is poured; once this is in place the cut-outs are carved out of the berm to create secondary spaces.

plan and section of berm

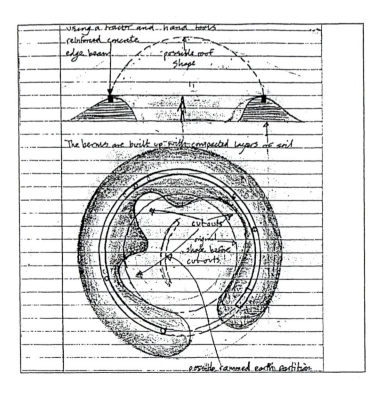

446

Chapter 36

Phil "TC" Hawes
Eco Design Activist

"One of the goals of organic architecture is to create living spaces that satisfy, thrill, and excitee . . . "

-Phil Hawes, PhD

Phil ("Thundercloud") Hawes is best known for conceiving and designing the Biosphere 2 project near Tucson Arizona. That was a notable achievement to be sure, but just one of a long string of ecological projects over an immensely productive lifetime.

The idea of the Biosphere 2 was to make a running start to find out the problems that will come up in totally self-contained environments such as exploratory stations on Mars. Aside from our earlthy environment ("Biosphere 1"), this hadn't yet been done on a large scale such as will be required for interplanetary exploration. Some scientists argued for a go slow, piece-by-piece approach; others supported the idea of going full blast and sorting out the problems in full scale. And that is what happened with Biosphere 2. The fact that there were environmental problems in their first experiments was not a problem. The goal of the experiment was to find such problems. There were, however, management disagreements which later led to change in stewardship from the originators of the project to Columbia University. Biosphere 2 will continue to be used as an advanced ecological research laboratory and educational institution.

Phil Hawes pioneered some of the earliest straw-bale buildings in the Southwest, designed and built adobe housing developments, and created habitats and sustainable architecture and planning projects around the world, from Portugal and Southern France to Katmandu. He also built a ferro-cement ship that has been around the world numerous times, walked 600 miles through the Australian outback, and, in terms of ecological architecture, has more or less been everywhere and done everything. He teaches for many educational institutions, including the San Francisco Institute of Architecture.

F.S.

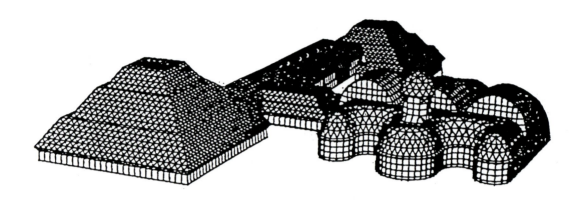

Biosphere 2, a self contained ecological laboratory constructed near Tucson, Arizona.

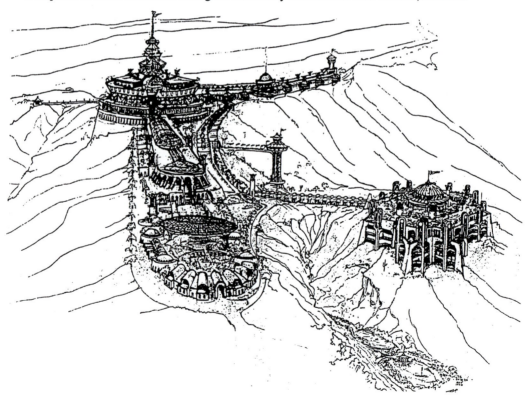

Perspective sketch of a support village and Marian atmospheric simiarlation chanber research laboratory.

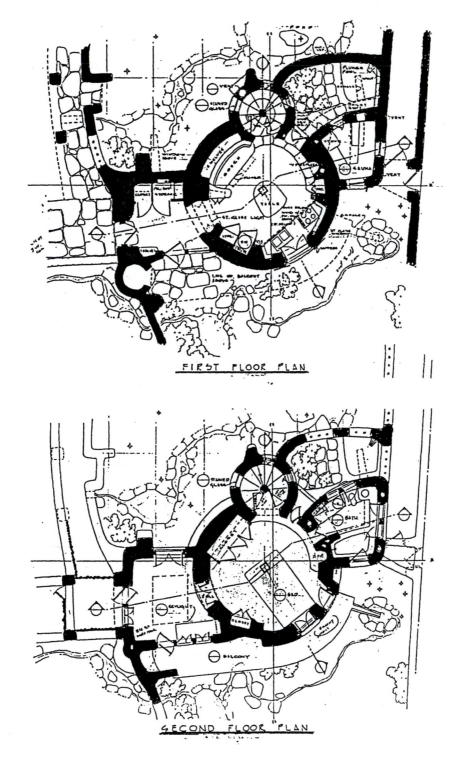

FIRST FLOOR PLAN

SECOND FLOOR PLAN

Plans, multi-story adobe residence.

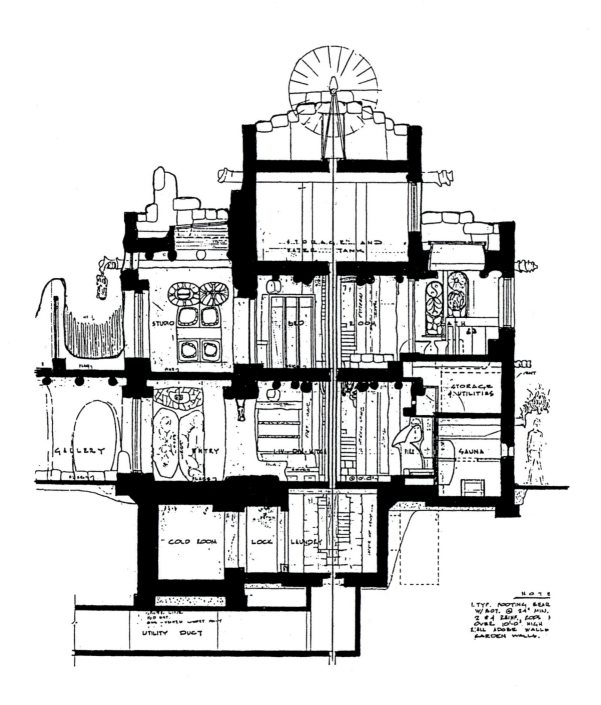

Cross section, multi-story adobe residence.

Chapter 37

Steve Badanes and The Jersey Devil

"Designers are going into the more trendy stuff and social responsibility is not one of them. Building is not one of them. Originality doesn't seem to be one of them."

-STEVE BADANES

The original Jersey Devil is a mythological imp who likes to scare people. A young team of designer-builders who built their first house, the "Snail House" in a New Jersey suburb, took on the name and emblem. Their approach to architecture -- on-site design, ecological senstitivity, and hands-on creation rather than paper design, has inspired young architects ever since.

Jersey Devil co-founder Steve Badanes, has left a trail of buildings across the U.S. -- all thoughtfully designed, all built with great personal dedication and care, all true to Badane's primary environmentalist values.

The "Snail House" contained object lessons in ecological design that would be expressed in every project to follow. Its curved upper window strip matches the solar arc from east to west, its central thermal mass chimney (built from sewer pipes) stores daytime heat and facilitates natural ventilation, and its shape reduces internal spatial volume from a traditional building of the same size floor plan by 40%.

The "Silo House" that followed was built from prefabricated grain silos converted to residential functions. This was Badane's first effort at an active solar collector system, admitedly crude by today's standards, but a breakthrough at the time.

The Jersey Devil, as a group effort, is gone. But a new generation of architect-builders -- some trained by Steve Badanes at the University of Washington -- is emerging. They're expanding on the principles and ideas that guided a team of idealistic Princeton graduates in the 70's. And they'll be the ones to carry and expand the tradition throughout our new century.

F.S.

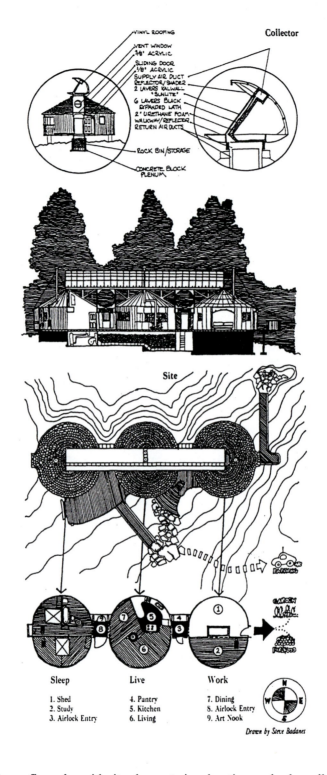

VINYL ROOFING
VENT WINDOW
3/8" ACRYLIC
SLIDING DOOR
1/8" ACRYLIC
SUPPLY AIR DUCT
REFLECTOR/SHADE 2
2 LAYERS KALWALL
"SUNLITE"
6 LAYERS BLACK
EXPANDED LATH
2" URETHANE FOAM
WALKWAY/REFLECTOR
RETURN AIR DUCTS

ROCK BIN/STORAGE

CONCRETE BLOCK
PLENUM

Site

Sleep

1. Shed
2. Study
3. Airlock Entry

Live

4. Pantry
5. Kitchen
6. Living

Work

7. Dining
8. Airlock Entry
9. Art Nook

Drawn by Steve Badanes

The "Silo" House, floor plan with site plan, exterior elevation, and solar collector system.

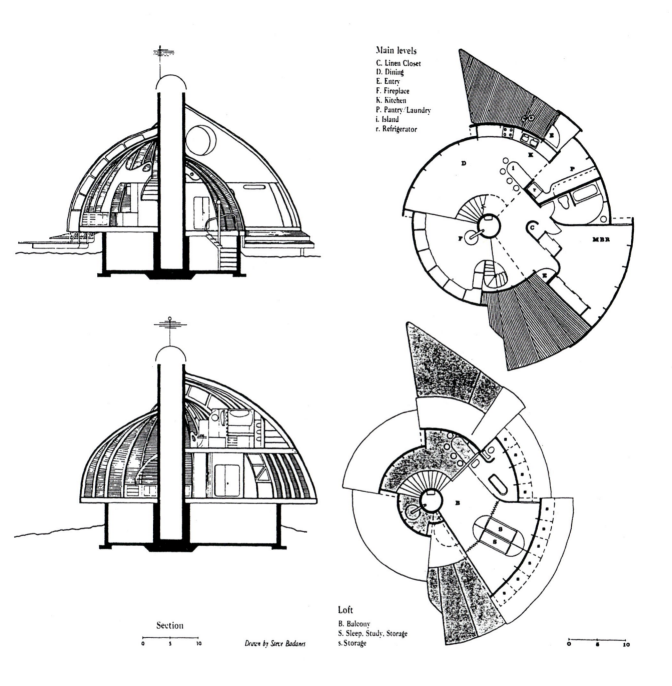

Main levels

C. Linen Closet
D. Dining
E. Entry
F. Fireplace
K. Kitchen
P. Pantry/Laundry
i. Island
r. Refrigerator

Section

0   5   10

Drawn by Steve Badanes

Loft

B. Balcony
S. Sleep, Study, Storage
s. Storage

0   5   10

The "Snail" House, plans and cross sections.

Chapter 38

Biohaus: An Advanced 21st Century Home

by Charles L. Sholten

M. ARCH: San Francisco Institute of Architecture
Taliesin Fellowship
Xnohipe Design

Editor's note: This and the project featured in the next chapter was a school design studio assignment -- a home/laboratory for the architect of the Bisophere 2, Dr. Phil Hawes. The projects demonstrate the variety of creative solutions that are possible for an identical site, client, and ecological design program.

The Biohaus is designed for Dr. Phil (T.C.) Hawes and a desert site near Oracle, Arizona, overlooking Biosphere 2. The residence incorporates a bioremediation facility where Phil and his team will conduct biological and ecological research. The design program required that the complex would integrate organic and ecological design principles and utilize the site and climate to best advantage.

Rocks and soil from the site form the desert masonry superstructure. Boulders on the site remain undisturbed and are integrated into the central core of the home. Energy-efficient glass maintains a comfortable interior climate while maximizing views. Native flowering plants provide added shade and pleasant scents on south and west facing façades. Water misters are used as needed to give moisture to native gardens and add humidity to the desert air.

The main living area incorporates a large rock outcropping at the center of the dwelling. The cooking area of the kitchen-workspace ties into the hearth for ventilation and heat retention. The living and dining space have an open plan which also includes a large outdoor terrace to view sunsets and Biosphere 2. The terrace is cantilevered above the desert floor for minimal site disturbance and to provide for a shaded area below. A floral covered pergola and ramp leading from the carport gradually slopes down to meet the sunset terrace for universal acces-sibility.

The guest studio is located just beyond the main living quarters. The guest bath is across the hall and features an open roof above a natural pond near the core of the home. The rock outcropping here will provide total privacy and a serene desert atmosphere. A Japanese style soaking tub is built into the rocks for relaxation and bathing. A radiant heated floor adds warmth and comfort.

Beyond the studio and guest bath is the master suite. An outdoor entry provides added privacy from the main residence. Thick adobe walls retain needed winter heat and allow for recessed window seating. Centered in the ceiling above the master suite is an operable aperture skylight for nightly views of the heavens. Two large hemispherical window ports offer horizontal views outside the suite. Towards the rear of the suite lies a tiered meditation space which gradually leads to a skylit niche for a favorite art piece. Through a large walk-in closet one reaches the master bath and a private outdoor garden.

Above the Biohaus roof, centered above the hearth is an observatory. The chimney stack doubles as a mast to hold a translucent canopy. The flat carport roof adapts to a roof-top Zen garden with light colored pebbles and rock outcropping from below. An elevator from ground level transports users to the sky deck and lower level maintenance and storage areas below. A tunnel from the lower level leads to underground facilities below the bioremediation center.

The bioremediation lab will clean the Biohaus waste water and serve as a laboratory to study plant life and "Living Machine" bioremediation systems. All waste water would be completely recycled throughout this desert complex. Fourteen five-hundred gallon tanks store water along the north side of the structure for minimal evaporation and minimal visual intrusion. An office flanks the laboratory to the east and an artist's studio flanks it to the west. A helical staircase is the focal point of the lab which connects the two levels.

The Biohaus is to function independently from traditional energy sources. All electricity is produced from photovoltaic panels integrated into the roof and structure. Solid waste is naturally treated in composts and bioremediation techniques. Food is grown on site in the greenhouse laboratory and surrounding gardens. This complex can remain self-sustaining and super-energy efficient for hundreds of years with proper care and maintenance.

Finally, the Biohaus includes an integrated landscape of ancient art and ceremony. Large vertically placed rocks called 'steles' will mark the spring and fall equinoxes as well as the summer and winter solstices. A stone kiva placed south of the complex maintains an ancient legacy for nighttime story telling and cosmic connectivity.

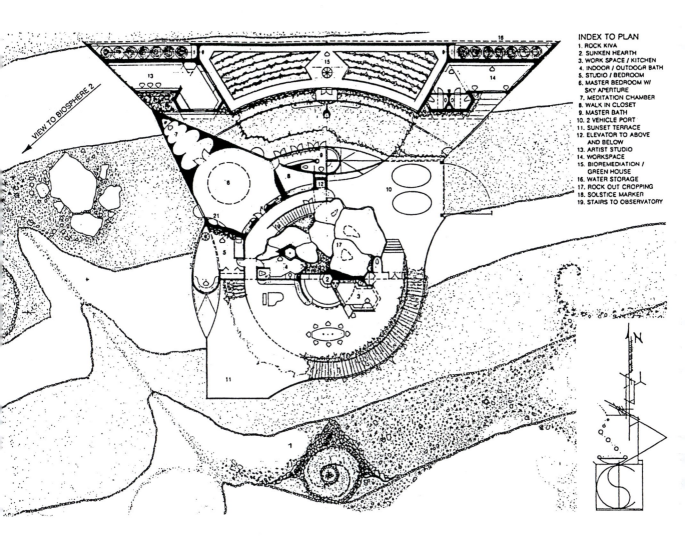

INDEX TO PLAN
1. ROCK KIVA
2. SUNKEN HEARTH
3. WORK SPACE / KITCHEN
4. INDOOR / OUTDOOR BATH
5. STUDIO / BEDROOM
6. MASTER BEDROOM W/
   SKY APERTURE
7. MEDITATION CHAMBER
8. WALK IN CLOSET
9. MASTER BATH
10. 2 VEHICLE PORT
11. SUNSET TERRACE
12. ELEVATOR TO ABOVE
    AND BELOW
13. ARTIST STUDIO
14. WORKSPACE
15. BIOREMEDIATION /
    GREEN HOUSE
16. WATER STORAGE
17. ROCK OUT CROPPING
18. SOLSTICE MARKER
19. STAIRS TO OBSERVATORY

Main floor plan. (Biohaus project by C. L. Sholten.)

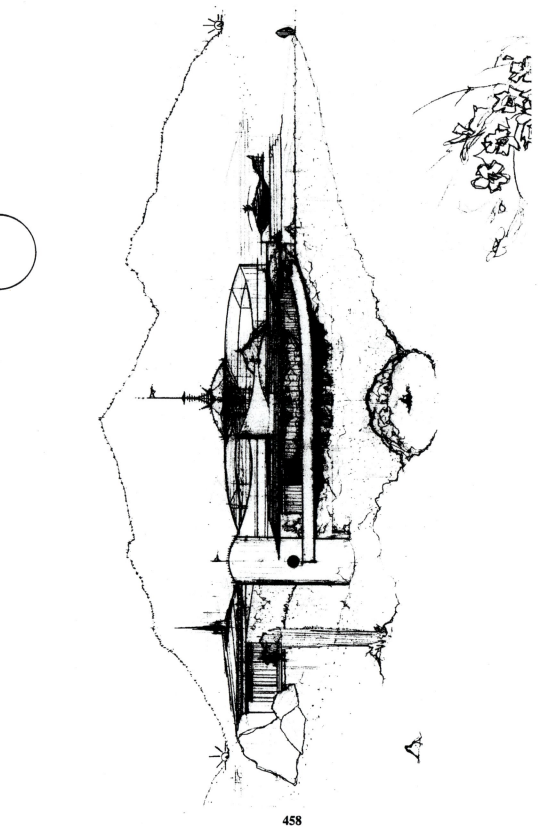

South facing perspective. (Biohaus project by C. L. Sholten.)

Chapter 39

Biohaus --
Another Interpretation

by Suren Gunasekara. M.ARCH
San Francisco Institute of Architecture

*"Wind -- the unseen sculptor of the landscape. The fuel of an
ecological traveler. A house that is a homage
to Phil Hawes, the sailor and ecologist."*

-SUREN GUNASEKARA

Editors note: Like the project in the preceding chapter, this is a design of a desert home for ecological design pioneer, Dr. Phil Hawes, architect of the Biosphere 2. Both projects illustrate the range of design options that open up when designing according to client-sensitive, site-sensitive, and eco-sensitive principles.

The client, Dr. Phil Hawes, has built extensively around the world in his 35+ years of dedication to the principles of ecology and ecological design. This home is to be a refuge in between his travels, a place to contemplate his dream-child, the Biosphere 2, and a living laboratory in which to conduct ongoing bio-eco-architectural studies. Adopting the idea that others could possibly express his needs even better than he could, students were assigned to interpret his needs and design his new home, the "Biohaus."

The site, in the Sonoran desert, is a place of extreme conditions. It has an abundance of sunlight and heat during the day and cold, windy nights. The climate is hot and dry, with occasional flash flood conditions.

The house plan shown here is generated through sight-lines. The view to the south is that of the biosphere. The view has been somewhat constricted to reduce solar gain, and as a symbol of the view to Phil's past. The house opens up to the hills in the north, it is the future; an area that remains ecologically undamaged. The house is stepped to closely follow land contours.

Since there'll be many visitors, public and private spaces are carefully separated, the most private, located in the upper levels are reached by a hidden spiral staircase.

The site and climate conditions inspired the roof forms which are like sails -- convex and concave. The convex forms face south, so as to deflect heat and light away from living spaces within. The concave forms tend to open up to the north, to allow for the entrance of breezes and northern light, and to allow for surrounding views.

The interior spaces located on the south are curved so as to radiate warmth and light back into the space, thus reducing the need for artificial lighting.

The roof forms are designed to channel rainwater into cisterns/lenses that are located beneath the first floor level. This water is then geo-thermally cooled or heated to be used in the radiant floor heating system.

The 40-foot cooling tower helps maintain the indoor air temperature during its hot days. This tower is designed applying Hassan Fathys' ideas as a precedent. The spaces are further cooled by a series of water troughs or ponds, that cool the interior by evaporation as the wind passes over them.

In the winter, the rock outcropping, (which has been integrated into the design) will function as a heat sink, due to its thermal mass, as do the adobe/ cob walls. These walls/vertical planes are constructed using a hybrid of adobe and cob construction. Glazing is used in conjunction with this hybrid wall construction. These materials are a synthesis of modern and traditional materials, combined with ecological intent.

The horizontal surfaces will be constructed out of ferro concrete. Each roof will be a double shell, forming an air pocket in between, so far as to reduce the heat transfer and keep the inner shell cool.

The open plan lends itself to a flow of space, as well as minimizing construction materials. The verticality of the design and the minimization of its footprint, helps to protect and preserve as much as possible, the fragile microbial mat that surrounds the site.

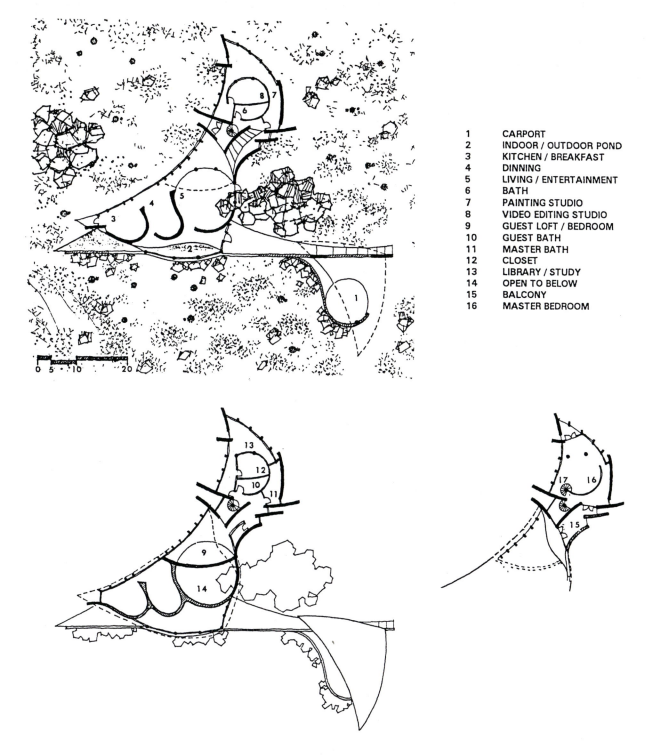

1	CARPORT
2	INDOOR / OUTDOOR POND
3	KITCHEN / BREAKFAST
4	DINNING
5	LIVING / ENTERTAINMENT
6	BATH
7	PAINTING STUDIO
8	VIDEO EDITING STUDIO
9	GUEST LOFT / BEDROOM
10	GUEST BATH
11	MASTER BATH
12	CLOSET
13	LIBRARY / STUDY
14	OPEN TO BELOW
15	BALCONY
16	MASTER BEDROOM

Three-level floor plan of Suren Gunaseskara's design for the Phil Hawes BioHaus.

461

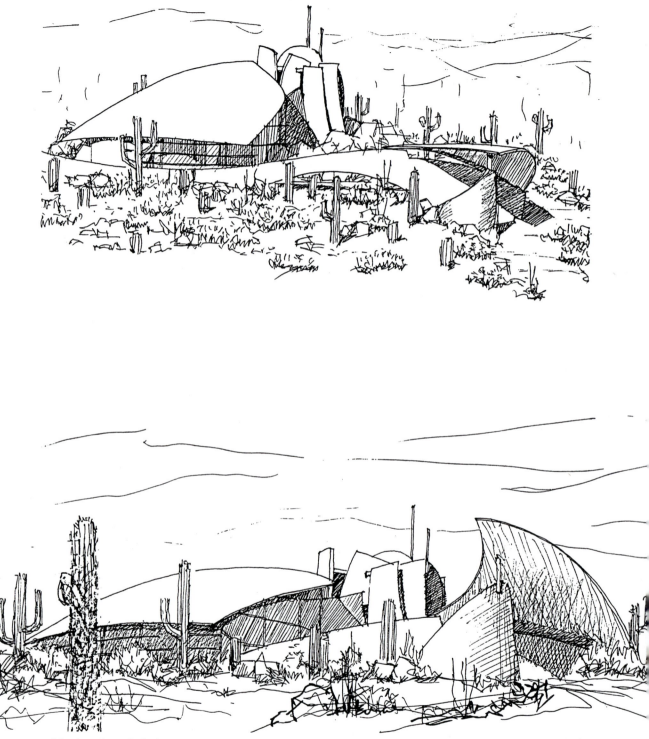

North and south-facing perspective views of Suren Gunaseskara's design for the Phil Hawes BioHaus.

Chapter 40

Organic Architecture

by Kendrick Bangs Kellogg

From THE MAKING OF AN ORGANIC ARCHITECT

Walking down the hall of the University of Colorado's department of architecture in 1955, I came upon a picture of Frank Lloyd Wright's "Falling Water". I was a second-year student there and had attended three schools of architecture - but up to that time I had no idea how beautiful architecture could be, or that there was a way of thinking about architecture that was complimentary with nature, and at the same time, expressive of our time.

Why hadn't the schools shown me this direction earlier? Why were schools not encouraging young hungry minds to quest for the opportunity of creative thinking? It was a common problem then, and from what I have heard from many students, is remains so today.

During spring vacation that year, a group of us made a pilgrimage to visit Frank Lloyd Wright's Taliesin West in Scottsdale, Arizona. While touring the complex, I broke away from the group on the main terrace and entered Wright's drafting room where I saw him peering out towards the terrace muttering to the half a dozen apprentices in the room, "I wonder if there is anyone out there that I know." I realized that Wright, then in his 80s, was losing his contemporaries. (Shortly thereafter, I was introduced to Wright as a potential apprentice and asked to come back the next day to talk with him - but that is another story.)

Later the same day, we all gathered in a semi-underground concrete shelter with bench seating for about 40 people with a stage up front where Wright began to talk. Looking out over the assembled members of the AIA, he essentially told them that they were responsible for raping mother earth - and they knew what this made their offspring. After it was all over, they all stood up and applauded.

Where did "organic architecture" come from? The idea organic architecture was not originated by Frank Lloyd Wright. As early as the 18th century architects were beginning to protest against conformity and non-functionality in architecture and planning. He merely carried it to a new level.

As far back as 1737, Francis Blonde seriously acted on the idea that true style should reveal the individual character of each structure and the demand for individualism was closely related to the newly arising requirement of each character.

The subsequent history of architecture in Europe is sprinkled with the names of men who expressed a similar revolutionary vision.

Revolutionary, founding father, architect and President Thomas Jefferson inspired a new approach to a more functional architecture on this side of the Atlantic. He was followed by Henry Hobson Richardson (1838-1886) known as the father of "living architecture", who helped create a distinctly American idiom. He, in turn, inspired such greats of American architecture as Louis Henry Sullivan, and then Wright. Like Jefferson, who drafted the Bill of Rights, Mr. Wright believed in individual rights, specifically in allowing a new style of architecture for every individual.

Why is organic architecture important? Organic architecture is a metaphor for living architecture rather than dead architecture.

The purpose of organic architecture is to advance the value of diversity in a compatible relationship with our natural environment. It should emphasize the potential and environmental fulfillment of individual experience and expression as an intrinsic necessity of our survival. It is the ultimate site-specific human architectural environment.

I think, in a capsule, if you can understand that "there is nothing beautiful which is not practical," you've got it.

I am convinced that the so-called "context", as it pertains to the "compatible community," is ruining the natural landscape. Committees of discretionary review and stylistic regulations are not the way, because the very nature of a committee of discretion and conforming regulations necessitates perpetuation of conformity only of another kind of mediocrity. I think we could treat each community as an individual and define each geographically as small as possible, and within that, encourage even more diversity.

On the side of a hill in the high desert of southern California amongst immense boulders, a composition of clustered wing-like concrete "umbrellas."

There are no walls in the ordinary sense. Interior spaces are separated by large boulders. The 26 curving roof forms are separately by glass for natural light all around. It is a living-working environment for the artist owners.

Towards the back of the large central interior working space is a large pod. It rises up to be a 20 foot circular bedroom area with a 360 degree view of the desert and the large central space below. The bath is in the back, served by a ramp from the sleeping area, against a waterfall spilling over a massive boulder behind the bathing pool. Outside the bath is a swimming pool of mosaic natural washed stones with a 10 foot wide spilling sheet waterfall plunging down some 12 feet into a crevasse, as seen looking up from the main approach on the west.

The shelter for vehicles is underground 200 feet away near the entrance at the bottom of the hill.

The thermal mass of stone and concrete makes the operation of the use of The building includes highly efficient evaporative coolers and water-radiant floor systems but they're rarely needed. The thermal mass of stone and concrete creates a comfortable natural climate, well suited to the high dry desert life which has extreme changes in temperature.

Materials: washed concrete aggregate, native rock, glass, existing natural boulders.

Aerial perspective.

"Although the utilitarian functions are the same, this should not be classified as a 'house', as it suggests a common connotation, which obviously this is not. It is a sculpture with the added benefits of being able to live in as a 'house' and an 'art studio'." Kendrick Kellogg.

Afterword

Although this book was created to be a comprehensive overview of every major facet of contemporary ecological design, there is no way we could include all of the many ecologists, builders, educators, architects, land planners, etc., who are making it all happen.

So to those many worthy souls who were not included: Please forgive our lapse, and don't feel slighted.

We are creating a "catalog" of ecological design professionals, builders, companies, and institutions. That list will be available at no cost to anyone who contacts us at SFIA@aol.com. Or write or call the San Francisco Institute of Architecture Information office, Box 749, Orinda, CA 94563. 1-800-634-7779.

Fred A. Stitt, Architect
Editor, *Ecological Design Handbook*
Director, San Francisco Institute of Architecture
and the Ecological Design Consortium.